Contents

SMP Further Mathematics Series

Mechanics and Vectors

TERRY HEARD

CAMBRIDGE
UNIVERSITY PRESS

Published by the Press Syndicate of the University of Cambridge
The Pitt Building, Trumpington Street, Cambridge CB2 1RP
40 West 20th Street, New York, NY 10011–4211, USA
10 Stamford Road, Oakleigh, Melbourne 3166, Australia

First published 1986
Reprinted 1994

Printed in Great Britain by
Athenaeum Press Ltd, Newcastle upon Tyne.

British Library cataloguing in publication data

School Mathematics Project
Further mathematics: mechanics and vectors
1 . Mechanics, Analytic – Examinations, questions, etc.
I. Title
531'.01'51   QA809
ISBN 0 521 33940 5

Preface

The course of mechanics presented in this book builds on the elementary kinematics and particle dynamics contained in most single subject A-level mathematics syllabuses. While it is specifically designed to cater for the SMP Further Mathematics section on mechanics and vectors it should also be found useful for other A-level further mathematics courses, and in some parts of higher education.

The work develops two main themes. The first is the motion of a particle in two dimensions (Chapters 1–7); this is described vectorially in terms of cartesian, polar and intrinsic coordinates, including parameters and the radial-transverse and tangential-normal components of velocity and acceleration. Following a necessary chapter on conics there is a full treatment of motion under a central force with natural emphasis on inverse square law orbits. The second strand (Chapters 8–16) concerns rigid bodies, starting with elementary statics. Moments in three dimensions lead to the definition of the vector product, which is used for further statics, geometrical applications, and the kinematics of a rigid body in three dimensions. A chapter on systems of particles is the basis for the final discussion on the dynamics of a rigid body moving in two dimensions.

Each chapter is divided into sections which contain exposition, worked examples and questions in the text (numbered consecutively Q.1, Q.2, ... throughout a chapter); these questions are an essential part of the course, so full solutions of them all are given. Following each section is a graded exercise, for which answers and some hints are given. A few of the results in the exercises are needed subsequently; these are shown by an asterisk (*). At the ends of Chapters 3, 6, 12 and 16 are project exercises where a sequence of questions develops a more substantial piece of mathematics. There are also two miscellaneous exercises of past School Mathematics Project (SMP) or Mathematics in Education and Industry Project (MEI) A-level questions; thanks are due to the Oxford and Cambridge Schools Examinations Board for permission to reproduce these.

It is recognised that some students will be working on this course in parallel with their single subject A-level studies. Therefore in sections 1.1, 1.2 and Chapters 2, 6 and 8 the technical demands have been kept as light as possible, so that students can make an early start here; in particular, no calculus is needed in Chapter 8. When results from a single subject course are quoted a Note gives a reference, usually to the SMP *Revised Advanced Mathematics* (*RAM*) series (published in three volumes by the Cambridge University Press), though there are of course many other sources.

It is a pleasure to acknowledge the help I have received from many quarters. The original draft SMP Vectors and Mechanics book stimulated my thoughts, though it seemed best to start the writing afresh. Mr John Hersee has been unfailingly encouraging (and patient), and his staff at the SMP Office have coped cheerfully with typing and distributing trial versions and collecting reactions. The students and teachers who cooperated in these trials have made many helpful suggestions. Above all I am grateful to the advisory team of Dr Jack Abramsky, Mr David Knighton, Mr Ian Warburton and Dr Alan Weir; their astute, expert and unstinting guidance has contributed greatly to the final form of this book.

TJH

1

Particle dynamics

1.1 BASIC KINEMATICS

In mechanics we apply mathematics to analyse the motion of objects and the forces which cause this, including the important special case when there is no movement. The study of motion itself is called *kinematics*, while the investigation of the connections between motion, force and mass is called *kinetics*.

We start by summarising the basic kinematics of a particle moving in a plane (Note 1.1). The position P of the particle at time t is given by means of its *position vector* $\mathbf{r}(=\mathbf{OP})$ relative to an origin O fixed in the plane. As t changes, $\mathbf{r}$ varies (unless the particle is stationary), and P moves along the path of the particle (Fig. 1).

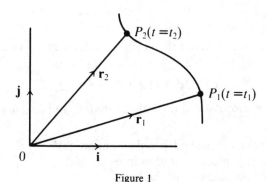

Figure 1

It is often convenient to write

$$\mathbf{r} = x\mathbf{i} + y\mathbf{j},$$

where $\mathbf{i}$ and $\mathbf{j}$ are perpendicular unit vectors fixed in the plane. We shall also write this in column vector notation,

$$\mathbf{r} = \begin{bmatrix} x \\ y \end{bmatrix}.$$

During the period of time in question, each value of t gives a unique position vector $\mathbf{r}$, which in its turn has unique components $x\mathbf{i}$ and $y\mathbf{j}$. Therefore the relations linking t to $\mathbf{r}$, x, and y are all functions. A variable t which is used to specify the position of a point in this way is called a *parameter*, and if $x = f(t)$ and $y = g(t)$ then f and g are *parametric functions*.

1

The *velocity* **v** is the rate of change of **r**, so that

$$\mathbf{v} = \frac{d\mathbf{r}}{dt} = \frac{dx}{dt}\mathbf{i} + \frac{dy}{dt}\mathbf{j} = f'(t)\mathbf{i} + g'(t)\mathbf{j}.$$

Newton's dot notation gives a briefer way of showing differentiation with respect to t

$$\mathbf{v} = \dot{\mathbf{r}} = \dot{x}\mathbf{i} + \dot{y}\mathbf{j} = \begin{bmatrix} \dot{x} \\ \dot{y} \end{bmatrix}.$$

Velocity is a vector quantity, with magnitude and direction. The magnitude of the velocity is called the *speed*,

$$|\mathbf{v}| = \sqrt{(\dot{x}^2 + \dot{y}^2)}.$$

The rate of change of velocity is another vector quantity, called the *acceleration* **a**. Thus

$$\mathbf{a} = \frac{d\mathbf{v}}{dt} = \frac{d^2\mathbf{r}}{dt^2} = \frac{d^2x}{dt^2}\mathbf{i} + \frac{d^2y}{dt^2}\mathbf{j} = f''(t)\mathbf{i} + g''(t)\mathbf{j},$$

or alternatively $\mathbf{a} = \dot{\mathbf{v}} = \ddot{\mathbf{r}} = \ddot{x}\mathbf{i} + \ddot{y}\mathbf{j} = \begin{bmatrix} \ddot{x} \\ \ddot{y} \end{bmatrix}.$

Example 1

With the origin at ground level the position vector **r** of a tennis ball t seconds after it is hit is given by

$$\mathbf{r} = 12t\mathbf{i} + (1.2 + 5t - 4.9t^2)\mathbf{j},$$

where **i** and **j** are horizontal and vertical unit vectors and distance is measured in metres.

(a) How high above the ground was the ball initially?
(b) Find the velocity and acceleration in terms of t.
(c) What was the initial speed of the ball?
(d) Find the greatest height reached by the ball.
(e) Find how far the ball travels horizontally before hitting the ground.

Solution

(a) $t = 0 \Rightarrow \mathbf{r} = 1.2\mathbf{j}$, so the ball was initially 1.2 m above the ground.
(b) $\mathbf{v} = \dot{\mathbf{r}} = 12\mathbf{i} + (5 - 9.8t)\mathbf{j}$
   $\mathbf{a} = \dot{\mathbf{v}} = -9.8\mathbf{j}.$
(c) When $t = 0$, $\mathbf{v} = 12\mathbf{i} + 5\mathbf{j}$ and $|\mathbf{v}| = \sqrt{(12^2 + 5^2)} = 13$, so the initial speed was 13 ms^{-1}.
(d) The ball is at its greatest height when it is moving horizontally, i.e. when the **j**-component of **v** is zero. This occurs when $5 - 9.8t = 0$

$$\Leftrightarrow t = 5/9.8 \approx 0.51.$$

When $t = 0.51$, $\mathbf{r} \approx 6.1\mathbf{i} + 2.5\mathbf{j}$,

so the greatest height is 2.5 m (to 2 s.f.).

(e) The ball hits the ground when the **j**-component of **r** is zero, i.e. when
$1.2 + 5t - 4.9t^2 = 0$

$$\Leftrightarrow t = \frac{5 \pm \sqrt{(25 + 4 \times 4.9 \times 1.2)}}{9.8} \quad \text{(using the quadratic equation formula)}$$

$$\approx 1.2 \quad \text{or} \quad -0.2.$$

The negative root is irrelevant here, so the ball hits the ground after 1.2 s. Using the **i**-component of **r** we find that after 1.2 s the ball has travelled $12 \times 1.2 \approx 14$ m horizontally. ☐

Q.1 The expression for **r** given in Example 1 defines a simplified model of the motion of the tennis ball. List some of the factors which have been ignored or simplified in forming this model.

Example 2
The position vector of one tip of a figure skater's skate at time t is

$$\mathbf{r} = (\cos t + 2 \cos 2t)\mathbf{i} + (\sin t + 2 \sin 2t)\mathbf{j},$$

where time is measured in seconds and distance in metres.

(a) Sketch the path.
(b) Find the velocity and acceleration when $t = 1$.
(c) Find the greatest and least speeds during the motion.

Solution
The following table gives **r** for values of t from 0 to π at intervals of $\frac{1}{10}\pi$.

t	0	$\frac{1}{10}\pi$	$\frac{1}{5}\pi$	$\frac{3}{10}\pi$	$\frac{2}{5}\pi$	$\frac{1}{2}\pi$
r	$\begin{bmatrix} 3.00 \\ 0.00 \end{bmatrix}$	$\begin{bmatrix} 2.57 \\ 1.48 \end{bmatrix}$	$\begin{bmatrix} 1.43 \\ 2.49 \end{bmatrix}$	$\begin{bmatrix} -0.03 \\ 2.71 \end{bmatrix}$	$\begin{bmatrix} -1.31 \\ 2.13 \end{bmatrix}$	$\begin{bmatrix} -2.00 \\ 1.00 \end{bmatrix}$

t	$\frac{3}{5}\pi$	$\frac{7}{10}\pi$	$\frac{4}{5}\pi$	$\frac{9}{10}\pi$	π
r	$\begin{bmatrix} -1.92 \\ -0.22 \end{bmatrix}$	$\begin{bmatrix} -1.21 \\ -1.09 \end{bmatrix}$	$\begin{bmatrix} -0.19 \\ -1.31 \end{bmatrix}$	$\begin{bmatrix} 0.67 \\ -0.87 \end{bmatrix}$	$\begin{bmatrix} 1.00 \\ 0.00 \end{bmatrix}$

(a) Plotting these positions and the others for times between π and 2π gives the path as shown in Fig. 2.
(b) The components of velocity and acceleration are given by

$$\dot{x} = -\sin t - 4 \sin 2t, \quad \dot{y} = \cos t + 4 \cos 2t;$$
$$\ddot{x} = -\cos t - 8 \cos 2t, \quad \ddot{y} = -\sin t - 8 \sin 2t.$$

When $t = 1$, $\mathbf{r} = \begin{bmatrix} -0.29 \\ 2.66 \end{bmatrix}$, $\mathbf{v} = \begin{bmatrix} -4.48 \\ -1.12 \end{bmatrix}$, $\mathbf{a} = \begin{bmatrix} 2.78 \\ -8.12 \end{bmatrix}$.

The velocity and acceleration are shown on the diagram at a scale of $\frac{1}{4}$ with respect to distance.

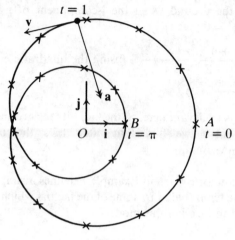

Figure 2

(c) The speed is $|\mathbf{v}| = \sqrt{(\dot{x}^2 + \dot{y}^2)}$.

Now $\dot{x}^2 + \dot{y}^2 = (-\sin t - 4 \sin 2t)^2 + (\cos t + 4 \cos 2t)^2$

$$= \sin^2 t + 8 \sin t \sin 2t + 16 \sin^2 2t + \cos^2 t + 8 \cos t \cos 2t + 16 \cos^2 2t$$

$$= 17 + 8(\cos 2t \cos t + \sin 2t \sin t),$$
$$\text{since } \sin^2 t + \cos^2 t = \sin^2 2t + \cos^2 2t = 1$$

$$= 17 + 8 \cos t, \qquad \text{using the expansion of } \cos(2t - t).$$

The greatest and least values of $17 + 8 \cos t$ are 25 (when $t = 0$) and 9 (when $t = \pi$). So the greatest and least speeds are 5 m s^{-1} and 3 m s^{-1}, at A and B respectively. ☐

Exercise 1A

Throughout this exercise the units of distance and time are the metre and second respectively.

1 The position vector $\mathbf{r}$ of a point is given by $\mathbf{r} = t^2\mathbf{i} + 2t\mathbf{j}$. Draw a graph of the path for $0 \leqslant t \leqslant 5$. Calculate $\mathbf{r}$, $\mathbf{v}$ and $\mathbf{a}$ when $t = 3$ and show your results on your graph.

2 A stone is thrown from the point with position vector $2\mathbf{i} + \mathbf{j}$, where $\mathbf{i}$ and $\mathbf{j}$ are horizontal and vertical unit vectors. The stone's initial velocity is $10\mathbf{i} + 17\mathbf{j}$, and it has constant acceleration $-9.8\mathbf{j}$. Giving answers to 2 s.f., find

(a) its velocity $\dot{\mathbf{r}}$ and position vector $\mathbf{r}$ after t seconds,
(b) its speed after 1 second,
(c) its straight line distance from the origin after 2 seconds,
(d) the direction in which it is travelling after 3 seconds.

3 Given that $\mathbf{r} = \begin{bmatrix} 6t^2 - t^3 \\ 18t - 3t^2 \end{bmatrix}$, find $\mathbf{r}$ when $t = -1, 0, 1, \ldots, 7$, and sketch the path for $-1 \leqslant t \leqslant 7$.

Find **v** and **a** in terms of t. Find the velocities at the two instants when the particle is at the origin. Prove that the magnitude of acceleration is always at least 6 m s^{-2}. Where is the particle when its acceleration has magnitude 6 m s^{-2}?

4 Given that $\mathbf{r} = 5 \cos \omega t\mathbf{i} + 5(1 + \sin \omega t)\mathbf{j}$, where ω is constant, describe the motion and show that the acceleration is constant in magnitude. What can you say about the direction of the acceleration? If the motion is in a vertical plane with $\mathbf{j}$ vertical, show that the object is travelling horizontally when $t = \pi/2\omega$.

5 Given that $\mathbf{r} = 4 \cos (0.1\pi t)\mathbf{i} + 3 \sin (0.1\pi t)\mathbf{j}$, describe the motion and find the direction of motion when $t = 12$. What is the greatest speed and when does it occur? When is the acceleration parallel to $\mathbf{i}$?

6 Show that the motion of a particle for which

$$\mathbf{r} = \begin{bmatrix} 3 + 4 \sin^2 t \\ 1 + 2 \cos^2 t \end{bmatrix}$$

is an oscillation along part of a straight line. Draw a sketch to illustrate this, and give the equation of the line. What is the period of the oscillation? Where is the particle and what is its speed when the acceleration is zero?

7 By differentiating $\mathbf{v} \cdot \mathbf{v}$ with respect to t, show that if a particle has constant speed then its acceleration is perpendicular to its velocity.

1.2 OTHER PARAMETERS

In Example 2 we found that the curve with parametric equations

$$x = \cos t + 2 \cos 2t, \qquad y = \sin t + 2 \sin 2t$$

has a double loop, and crosses itself at $(-2, 0)$. It is possible to eliminate t and obtain a relation between x and y, but the result is complicated and not very helpful (Note 1.2). It is certainly not possible to find a *function* which maps x to y, since as many as four values of y may correspond to a single value of x; similarly there is no function which maps y to x. This is one of the many curves that are best dealt with by using parametric equations.

The variable used as the parameter need not represent time. It may be more convenient to express $\mathbf{r}$ in terms of a varying angle θ or distance s or gradient m, or in terms of a variable p which has no specific geometrical or physical meaning.

Example 3
When a wheel rolls without slipping along horizontal ground the path of a point P on its rim is called a *cycloid*. Find parametric equations for a cycloid.

Solution
Let the wheel have radius a and centre C. Suppose that P is initially at the origin O on the horizontal ground (the x-axis), and that since then the wheel has turned through θ radians, so that

$$\mathbf{CP} = \begin{bmatrix} -a \sin \theta \\ -a \cos \theta \end{bmatrix}.$$

If the point of contact between the wheel and the ground is N then, since there is no slipping,

$$ON = \text{arc } PN = a\theta$$

and $\mathbf{OC} = \begin{bmatrix} a\theta \\ a \end{bmatrix}$ (Fig. 3).

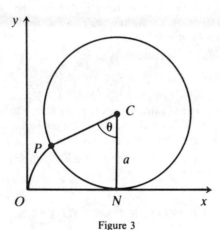

Figure 3

Therefore $\mathbf{r} = \mathbf{OP} = \mathbf{OC} + \mathbf{CP} = \begin{bmatrix} a\theta - a\sin\theta \\ a - a\cos\theta \end{bmatrix}.$

The parametric equations are $x = a(\theta - \sin\theta)$
$$y = a(1 - \cos\theta).$$ $\square$

Q.2   Sketch the cycloid.

From the parametric equations $x = f(p)$, $y = g(p)$ we can find the gradient at a point on the curve by using the chain rule $dy/dx = dy/dp \times dp/dx$ and the fact that $dp/dx = 1 \div dx/dp$ (Note 1.3).

These give $$\frac{dy}{dx} = \frac{dy}{dp} \bigg/ \frac{dx}{dp}.$$

Values of p for which $dy/dp = 0$ and $dx/dp \neq 0$ give points where the tangent is parallel to the x-axis, with $dy/dx = 0$. Values of p for which $dx/dp = 0$ give points at which dy/dx is undefined; if $dy/dp \neq 0$ at such a point then dx/dy is zero, showing that the tangent is parallel to the y-axis. But if both $dx/dp = 0$ and $dy/dp = 0$ then dy/dx and dx/dy both take the indeterminate form $0/0$, and there may be no tangent (Note 1.4). A point at which dx/dp and dy/dp are both zero and where the direction of the curve changes sharply is called a *cusp*. For example, for the cycloid

$$x = a(\theta - \sin \theta) \Rightarrow \frac{dx}{d\theta} = a(1 - \cos \theta)$$

$$y = a(1 - \cos \theta) \Rightarrow \frac{dy}{d\theta} = a \sin \theta,$$

so that $\qquad \dfrac{dy}{dx} = \dfrac{\sin \theta}{1 - \cos \theta}.$

If $\theta = 0, 2\pi, 4\pi, \ldots$ then $\dfrac{dx}{d\theta} = \dfrac{dy}{d\theta} = 0$; the cycloid has a set of cusps for these values of θ, at the points where P meets the ground (Fig. 4).

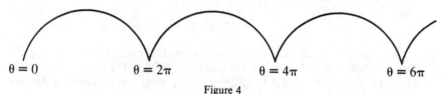

$\theta = 0 \qquad\qquad \theta = 2\pi \qquad\qquad \theta = 4\pi \qquad\qquad \theta = 6\pi$

Figure 4

Exercise 1B

1   Sketch the curves with the following parametric equations; a and b are positive constants.
  (i) $x = 3p + 2, y = 5p - 1$;
  (ii) $x = 5p - 1, y = 20p - 1$;
  (iii) $\mathbf{r} = \begin{bmatrix} p + 1 \\ p^3 - 3p^2 \end{bmatrix}$;
  (iv) $\mathbf{r} = \begin{bmatrix} 3 \cos p \\ 3 \sin p \end{bmatrix}$;
  (v) $\mathbf{r} = (2 + 4 \cos p)\mathbf{i} + (5 + 4 \sin p)\mathbf{j}$;
  (vi) $\mathbf{r} = (2 + 4 \cos p)\mathbf{i} + (5 + 4 \cos p)\mathbf{j}$;
  (vii) the *parabola* $x = ap^2, y = 2ap$;
  (viii) the *hyperbola* $\mathbf{r} = \begin{bmatrix} a \sec p \\ b \tan p \end{bmatrix}$.

2   Find, by eliminating p, the equations connecting x and y in question 1. In which cases is there a function mapping x to y?

3   For each curve of question 1 find the position vectors of all points where the tangent is parallel either to $\mathbf{i}$ or to $\mathbf{j}$.

4   The one-way stretch with matrix $\begin{bmatrix} 1 & 0 \\ 0 & k \end{bmatrix}$ transforms the circle $x^2 + y^2 = a^2$ into an *ellipse*.
  (i) Show on a single diagram the circle and the ellipses obtained for $k = 2, \frac{3}{4}, \frac{1}{2}$.
  (ii) Prove that the image of the point $(a \cos \theta, a \sin \theta)$ on the circle is the point $(a \cos \theta, b \sin \theta)$ on the ellipse, where $b = ak$. Hence show that the equation of the ellipse is $\dfrac{x^2}{a^2} + \dfrac{y^2}{b^2} = 1$.

(iii) Find the matrix of the transformation which maps the ellipse on to the circle $x^2 + y^2 = b^2$.

5 Fig. 5 shows a straight rod with pegs at X, Y and a pencil at P, where $PX = b$, $PY = a$. The pegs run in perpendicular grooves OX, OY, which are taken as x- and y-axes. By using the angle θ shown, prove that the locus of P is an ellipse. This device is called an *elliptic trammel*.

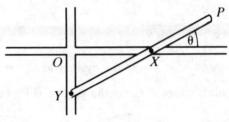

Figure 5

6 A man stands on a ladder which slips down, in a vertical plane, with its top Y against a vertical wall and its base X on the horizontal ground. The man's feet are at P, where $YP = a$ and $PX = b$ (Fig. 6). By using the angle θ as a parameter, find the locus of P. What is the locus of the man's head if he remains vertical?

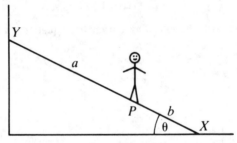

Figure 6

7 Sketch the *astroid* $\mathbf{r} = \begin{bmatrix} a\cos^3 p \\ a\sin^3 p \end{bmatrix}$ and find its equation in terms of x, y, a. Find $d\mathbf{r}/dp$, and locate the cusps.

If the tangent at the point P on the curve meets the x- and y-axes at X and Y, prove that $XY = a$ for all positions of P. Thus a line of fixed length a sliding between perpendicular lines (like the ladder in question 6) will always touch the astroid. By drawing many positions of such a line, produce the astroid as an envelope.

8 A rod OA of length a rotates in a plane about a fixed point O. Another rod AP of length b rotates about A in the plane in such a way that the angle between AP and OA produced equals the angle θ between OA and a fixed line Ox (Fig. 7).

(a) Write down the vectors **OA** and **AP**, and deduce that
$$\mathbf{OP} = \begin{bmatrix} a\cos\theta + b\cos 2\theta \\ a\sin\theta + b\sin 2\theta \end{bmatrix}.$$
(b) Show that if $a = 1$, $b = 2$ then the path of P is the curve of Example 2.
(c) Sketch the path of P:
(i) if $a = b = 1$ (a *trisectrix*); (ii) if $a = 2$, $b = 1$ (a *cardioid*).

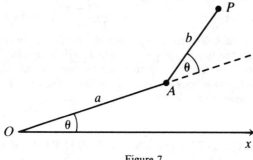

Figure 7

9 For the cycloid of Example 3 find the vectors $d\mathbf{r}/d\theta$ and **PN**. Show that $d\mathbf{r}/d\theta$ may be obtained by turning **PN** through a right-angle. Deduce that the direction of motion of P is perpendicular to PN. Give a mechanical explanation for this.

10 A wheel has centre C and radius $2a$; L is a fixed point on the wheel and M is a fixed point on the flange of the wheel, so that $CL = a$, $CM = 3a$, and CLM is a straight line. Initially CLM is vertically down and the wheel touches a horizontal rail (the x-axis) at O; the vertical through O is the y-axis. The wheel then rolls without slipping along the rail; when CLM has turned through the angle θ the wheel touches the rail at N (Fig. 8).

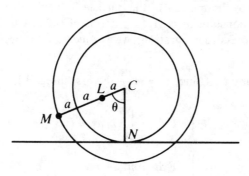

Figure 8

Write down the vectors **OC**, **CL**, **CM** and hence find parametric equations for the paths of L and M. Sketch these paths (called *trochoids*).

11 By finding where the line $y = mx$ meets the curve $y^2 = x^3$, obtain parametric equations for x and y in terms of m. Sketch the curve. What value of m gives the cusp? This curve is called a *semi-cubical parabola*; how is it related to the curve $y = x^{3/2}$?

12 (a) By finding where the line $y = mx$ meets the curve $x^3 + y^3 = 3axy$ (where a is a positive constant) obtain the parametric equations $x = \dfrac{3am}{1 + m^3}$, $y = \dfrac{3am^2}{1 + m^3}$ for the curve. What value of m must be excluded from these equations?

(b) Show that if m is small $x \approx 3am$, $y \approx 3am^2$, and hence that $x^2 \approx 3ay$. Show in a similar way that if m is large $y^2 \approx 3ax$. Sketch these approximations to two parts of the curve.

(c) Show that, for $m \neq -1$, $x + y + a = \dfrac{a(1 + m)^2}{1 - m + m^2}$. Deduce that the whole of the curve lies in the half-plane $x + y + a > 0$, and that as m approaches -1 the curve approaches the line $x + y + a = 0$, which is its *asymptote*.

(d) Sketch the complete curve with its asymptote. Indicate on your sketch the way in which the curve is traced as m increases from $-\infty$ to ∞. (This curve is called the *folium of Descartes*.)

1.3 FORCE DEPENDING ON DISPLACEMENT

The fundamental equation governing the motion of a particle is Newton's second law:

$$\mathbf{F} = m\mathbf{a}$$

resultant force = mass × acceleration.

When we know the force we can form differential equations using the calculus relations

$$\mathbf{a} = \frac{d\mathbf{v}}{dt} = \frac{d^2\mathbf{r}}{dt^2}, \qquad \mathbf{v} = \frac{d\mathbf{r}}{dt}$$

and then determine the motion of the particle by solving these equations. In particular, if $\mathbf{F}$ is constant or is given in terms of t then $\mathbf{v}$ and $\mathbf{r}$ can be found directly by two successive integrations; we assume that this procedure is familiar (Note 1.5).

It is worth noting that since $\mathbf{F} = m\dfrac{d\mathbf{v}}{dt}$ the first integral is

$$\int_{t_1}^{t_2} \mathbf{F}\, dt = \int_{\mathbf{v}_1}^{\mathbf{v}_2} m\, d\mathbf{v} = [m\mathbf{v}]_{\mathbf{v}_1}^{\mathbf{v}_2}$$

$$\Rightarrow \int_{t_1}^{t_2} \mathbf{F}\, dt = m\mathbf{v}_2 - m\mathbf{v}_1,$$

which is the impulse–momentum equation for a variable force $\mathbf{F}$ (Note 1.6).

Sometimes the force acting on a particle depends only on the position of the particle. One very important example of this is the gravitational attraction which governs the motion of planets and satellites; Chapters 4 and 5 deal with this in detail. The rest of this section is concerned with the motion of a particle along a straight line. The position of the particle on the line is then specified by a single coordinate, x say, and we may use the scalar equivalents of the relations given above:

$$F = ma \quad \text{and} \quad a = \frac{dv}{dt} = \frac{d^2x}{dt^2}, \qquad v = \frac{dx}{dt}.$$

There is now a useful alternative expression for the acceleration (not available when working with vectors):

by the chain rule
$$\frac{dv}{dt} = \frac{dv}{dx} \times \frac{dx}{dt} = \frac{dv}{dx} \times v,$$

so that
$$a = v\frac{dv}{dx}.$$

When the force F is given in terms of x it is natural to use this expression for the acceleration, so that the equation of motion is

$$F = mv\frac{dv}{dx}.$$

Integrating this gives

$$\int_{x_1}^{x_2} F\,dx = \int_{v_1}^{v_2} mv\,dv = [\tfrac{1}{2}mv^2]_{v_1}^{v_2}$$

$$\Rightarrow \int_{x_1}^{x_2} F\,dx = \tfrac{1}{2}mv_2^2 - \tfrac{1}{2}mv_1^2,$$

which is the work–energy equation for a variable force F (Note 1.7). From this v can be found in terms of x and the initial conditions, giving $v = f(x)$ say. Then since $v = \dfrac{dx}{dt}$ we have $t = \displaystyle\int \frac{dx}{f(x)}$.

In principle this gives a formula for t in terms of x, which we may be able to rearrange to give x in terms of t, but in practice approximate methods may be needed to deal with the integration.

Example 4
A particle of mass $\tfrac{1}{8}$ kg moves along a straight line under the action of a force of magnitude $2/x^3$ N directed along the line away from the origin O, where x m is the distance of the particle from O at time t s. Initially the particle is at rest at $x = 1$. Find x in terms of t.

Solution
The equation of motion is

$$\frac{2}{x^3} = \tfrac{1}{8}v\frac{dv}{dx}$$

$$\Rightarrow \int v\,dv = \int \frac{16}{x^3}\,dx$$

$$\Rightarrow \quad \tfrac{1}{2}v^2 = -\frac{8}{x^2} + C.$$

When $\qquad\qquad x = 1, v = 0,$ so $C = 8.$

Therefore $\qquad\qquad v^2 = 16(1 - 1/x^2)$

and $\qquad\qquad v = 4\sqrt{(1 - 1/x^2)},$

taking the positive root since the force and hence the velocity are in the positive sense.

Since
$$v = \frac{dx}{dt},$$

$$\int \frac{dx}{\sqrt{(1 - 1/x^2)}} = \int 4 \, dt.$$

But $\dfrac{1}{\sqrt{(1 - 1/x^2)}} = \dfrac{x}{\sqrt{(x^2 - 1)}}$, and $\displaystyle\int \frac{x}{\sqrt{(x^2 - 1)}} \, dx = \sqrt{(x^2 - 1)} + C'$.

Therefore
$$\sqrt{(x^2 - 1)} + C' = 4t.$$

When
$$t = 0, \, x = 1, \quad \text{so} \quad C' = 0.$$

Hence
$$x^2 - 1 = 16 \, t^2$$

and
$$x = \sqrt{(16t^2 + 1)},$$

taking the positive root since $x > 0$ always. $\qquad\qquad\square$

Exercise 1C

Questions 1–5 refer to the motion of a particle along a straight line; x m is the displacement from a fixed point on the line, and v m s^{-1} is the velocity.

1 Given that $v = 4\sqrt{x}$, show that the acceleration is constant, and find its value.

2 Prove that if v is proportional to x then so is the acceleration.

3 A force $9x^{-1/2}$ N is applied to a particle of mass 3 kg which is initially at rest at $x = 4$. Find the velocity when $x = 25$.

4 Fig. 9 shows the velocity–displacement graph, with equal scales on the x- and v-axes. The normal at P meets the x-axis at N. Show that the acceleration is represented by QN.

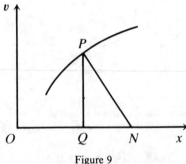

Figure 9

5 If a particle moves from rest with a positive acceleration show that its velocity–displacement graph must start parallel to the v-axis.

6 A particle of mass m is projected along the x-axis from the origin with velocity u, and is then subject to the force $-a \sin bx$. Prove that it moves to infinity if $u^2 > 4a/mb$.

7 A particle is projected vertically upward from a point on the earth's surface with initial velocity U. The force on the particle due to the earth's gravitational attraction is inversely proportional to x^2, where x is the distance from the centre of the earth. If all other forces are neglected, show that

$$v^2 = \frac{h}{x} + k,$$

where h and k are constants.

By considering the acceleration due to gravity at the earth's surface, g, show that $h = 2gR^2$ and $k = U^2 - 2gR$, where R is the earth's radius.

Deduce that the particle will never return to earth if U exceeds $\sqrt{(2gR)}$ (the *escape velocity*). Taking $R = 6370$ km and $g = 9.81$ m s^{-2}, calculate the escape velocity.

8 A plug of mass m and a piston are separated by a distance a in a hollow cylindrical tube of cross-sectional area A. The air trapped between the piston and the plug and the air beyond the plug are at atmospheric pressure P_0. Both the piston and the plug are airtight but each can move freely inside the tube.

The piston starts to move with constant acceleration f towards the plug and compresses the air between the two according to pressure × volume = constant. The air beyond the plug remains at pressure P_0 and so the plug begins to move.

Find a differential equation for the distance between the piston and the plug and hence find (but do not attempt to evaluate) an integral for the time elapsed in terms of this distance. [MEI]

1.4 SIMPLE HARMONIC MOTION

In many situations the forces acting on a particle moving along a straight line reduce to a single force directed towards a fixed point of the line and proportional to the distance of the particle from this point. In these cases the particle is said to move with *Simple Harmonic Motion* (SHM).

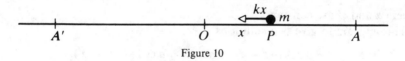

Figure 10

Let the fixed point be the origin O and let the force on the particle be $-kx$, where k is a positive constant; thus when x is positive the force is in the negative direction, and vice versa, so the force is always directed towards O.

The equation of motion is

$$-kx = m\ddot{x}$$

or

$$\ddot{x} + \omega^2 x = 0,$$

writing ω^2 for the positive constant k/m. This is the standard equation for SHM.

As before, we start solving this by using $v\dfrac{dv}{dx}$ for the acceleration:

$$v\frac{dv}{dx} = -\omega^2 x$$

$$\Rightarrow \quad \tfrac{1}{2}v^2 = -\tfrac{1}{2}\omega^2 x^2 + C,$$

where C is constant. From this

$$2C = v^2 + \omega^2 x^2,$$

which, being the sum of two squares, is never negative, and is zero only in the trivial case when the particle is permanently at rest at O. Therefore C is positive, and we may write $2C = a^2\omega^2$, where a is a positive constant. Then

$$v^2 = \omega^2(a^2 - x^2), \qquad (1)$$

an important result connecting the speed and the displacement. Since $v^2 \geqslant 0$, x must lie between a and $-a$, so that the particle must always lie on the line segment AA', where $x = a$ at A and $x = -a$ at A' (Fig. 10).

For each value of x between $-a$ and a we can find θ such that

$$x = a \cos \theta,$$

where θ varies continuously with t as the particle moves.

Then $$v = \dot{x} = -a \sin \theta \dot{\theta}$$

by the chain rule.

Substituting in (1) gives

$$a^2(\sin^2 \theta) \, \dot{\theta}^2 = \omega^2 a^2(1 - \cos^2 \theta) = \omega^2 a^2 \sin^2 \theta$$

$$\Leftrightarrow \qquad \dot{\theta}^2 = \omega^2$$

$$\Leftrightarrow \qquad \dot{\theta} = \pm\omega$$

$$\Leftrightarrow \qquad \theta = \omega t + \alpha$$

$$\text{or} \quad \theta = -\omega t + \alpha',$$

where α and α' are constants.

This appears to give two solutions,

$$x = a \cos(\omega t + \alpha) \quad \text{and} \quad x = a \cos(-\omega t + \alpha').$$

But since either choice of sign must give the correct values of x and v when $t = 0$, we have

$$a \cos \alpha = a \cos \alpha' \quad \text{and} \quad -a\omega \sin \alpha = a\omega \sin \alpha',$$

i.e. $$\cos \alpha' = \cos \alpha \quad \text{and} \quad \sin \alpha' = -\sin \alpha,$$

from which $$\alpha' = -\alpha + 2n\pi.$$

The second solution is thus

$$x = a \cos(-\omega t - \alpha + 2n\pi)$$

$$= a \cos(-\omega t - \alpha)$$

$$= a \cos(\omega t + \alpha)$$

since the cosine function is even.

The complete solution is therefore

$$x = a \cos (\omega t + \alpha).\tag{2}$$

As $\cos (\omega t + \alpha) = \cos \omega t \cos \alpha - \sin \omega t \sin \alpha$, putting $A = a \cos \alpha$, $B = -a \sin \alpha$ gives the following alternative form, which is sometimes easier to use,

$$x = A \cos \omega t + B \sin \omega t.$$

Q.3 Find A and B in terms of the initial displacement, x_0, and the initial velocity, v_0.

Equation (2) shows that OP is the **i**-component of the vector **OQ** of length a which rotates with constant angular velocity ω. As Q moves uniformly around the circle with centre O and radius a its projection P on the x-axis oscillates between A and A' with SHM (Fig. 11).

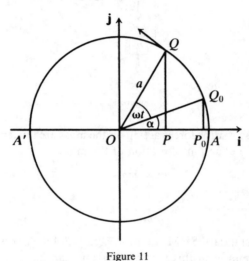

Figure 11

The time for one complete oscillation (there and back) is the time Q takes to go once around the circle, which is $2\pi/\omega$; this is called the *period*. Its reciprocal $\omega/2\pi$ is the *frequency*, which is the number of complete oscillations in unit time. The greatest displacement a is called the *amplitude*, and the constant α which determines the initial position P_0 is called the *phase angle*.

Q.4 What is the acceleration of Q? Check that the **i**-component of acceleration is proportional to x.

Example 5
A light spring has stiffness k, i.e. when the spring is extended by length x its tension is kx. The spring hangs vertically with a mass m attached to its lower end. This mass is pulled down so that the spring's extension is x_0, and is then released from rest. Find the period and amplitude of the subsequent oscillations.

What difference does it make if the spring is replaced by an elastic string of the same length and stiffness?

Solution

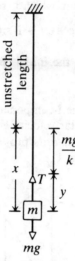

Figure 12

When the extension is x the forces acting on the mass are the tension $T = kx$ and the weight mg. The equation of motion of the mass is

$$m\ddot{x} = mg - kx,$$

i.e.

$$\ddot{x} + \frac{k}{m}x - g = 0.$$

This is not the standard SHM equation because of the constant g term. This snag, which is common in this sort of question, can be resolved by a simple substitution: we write

$$\ddot{x} + \frac{k}{m}\left(x - \frac{mg}{k}\right) = 0,$$

and then let $y = x - \dfrac{mg}{k}$ (so that $\ddot{y} = \ddot{x}$), giving

$$\ddot{y} + \frac{k}{m}y = 0.$$

This shows that the mass moves with SHM centred on $y = 0$, i.e. $x = mg/k$, which is of course the equilibrium position when the mass hangs at rest. Since $\omega^2 = k/m$ the period is $2\pi\sqrt{(m/k)}$. The distance from the centre ($x = mg/k$) to a point where the particle is at rest ($x = x_0$) gives the amplitude $x_0 - mg/k$.

The mechanical difference between a spring and an elastic string is that a spring can exert a thrust when compressed (i.e. $T = kx$ even when $x < 0$, a negative tension meaning a thrust), whereas a string becomes slack (i.e. $T = 0$ when $x < 0$).

Now the least value of x is at the top of the oscillation, where

$$x = \frac{mg}{k} - \left(x_0 - \frac{mg}{k}\right) = \frac{2mg}{k} - x_0.$$

If $x_0 \leqslant 2mg/k$ then $x \geqslant 0$ throughout the motion, so having a string makes no difference. But if $x_0 > 2mg/k$ the previous solution applies only until $x = 0$. At this point the string becomes slack and the mass rises and falls as a free projectile until the string tautens; then the SHM equation becomes valid again.

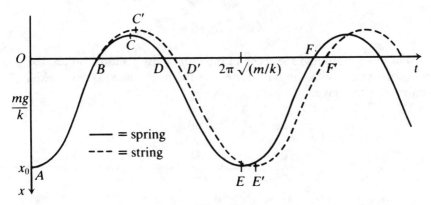

Figure 13

This is illustrated in Fig. 13. The solid curve $ABCDEF$ is the displacement–time graph (a cosine wave) when there is a spring. For a string the curve AB is the same, then $BC'D'$ is the parabolic graph of a free projectile. (Why does the mass rise higher and take longer to return to O in this case?) The curve $D'E'F'$ is the same shape as DEF, but shifted along the time axis. Both motions are periodic, the period with the string exceeding $2\pi\sqrt{(m/k)}$ by the time DD'. ☐

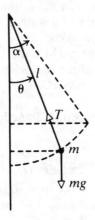

Figure 14

A *simple pendulum* consists of a particle (called the *bob*) suspended from a fixed point by a light inextensible string or rod and swinging freely in a vertical plane. Suppose that the bob, of mass m, is released from rest when the string, of length l, makes an angle α with the vertical, and that after time t the angle between the string and vertical is θ (Fig. 14). The forces on the bob are its weight and the tension is the string. The tension does no work since it is always at right angles to the direction of motion of the bob. Therefore the gain in kinetic energy of the bob equals the work done by the weight. The bob has vertical displacement $l(\cos\theta - \cos\alpha)$ while gaining speed $l\dot\theta$, so

$$\tfrac{1}{2}m(l\dot\theta)^2 = mgl(\cos\theta - \cos\alpha)$$

$$\Rightarrow \quad \tfrac{1}{2}\dot\theta^2 = \frac{g}{l}(\cos\theta - \cos\alpha). \tag{3}$$

From this we can find the speed of the bob at any position; notice that this and subsequent results are independent of the bob's mass. Differentiating (3) with respect to θ gives

$$\dot\theta\,\frac{d\dot\theta}{d\theta} = -\frac{g}{l}\sin\theta.$$

But

$$\dot\theta\,\frac{d\dot\theta}{d\theta} = \ddot\theta \quad \left(\text{like } v\,\frac{dv}{dx} = a\right),$$

so

$$\ddot\theta = -\frac{g}{l}\sin\theta.$$

This differential equation cannot be solved in terms of the simple functions we have available, but if θ remains small then $\sin\theta \approx \theta$, so instead of the exact equation we can use

$$\ddot\theta = -\frac{g}{l}\theta.$$

This is the equation of angular SHM with $\omega^2 = g/l$, and therefore the period of a complete small oscillation is $2\pi\sqrt{(l/g)}$. (See Exercise 1D question 12 for further discussion of the accuracy of this small angle approximation.)

A 'seconds pendulum' has complete period 2 seconds ('tick, tock'), so its length is g/π^2 (≈ 0.9941 m at Greenwich). Other periodic motions are sometimes described by giving the length of the *equivalent simple pendulum*, which is the simple pendulum with the same period.

Q.5   Show that for SHM with period T the length of the equivalent simple pendulum is $gT^2/4\pi^2$ ($=g/\omega^2$).

Exercise 1D

1   A particle of mass $\tfrac{1}{2}$ kg executes SHM. When it is 0.4 m from the centre of its path its speed is 1.5 m s^{-1} and the force acting on it towards the centre is 5 N. Find the period and the amplitude.

2 For SHM with amplitude 5 m and period 8 s, find the shortest time taken to move from 4 m on one side of the centre to 2 m on the other side.

3 A particle performs 3 complete SHM oscillations per second, during which its greatest speed is $2\,\mathrm{m\,s^{-1}}$. Find the amplitude, the greatest acceleration, and the length of the equivalent simple pendulum.

4 Seamen use the following 'twelfths rule' to estimate the depth of tidal water from the depth of low water: in a 6-hour rise, the rise in each hour is 1, 2, 3, 3, 2, 1 twelfths of the total rise. Show that this agrees well with taking the variation of depth to be simple harmonic with period 12 hours.

5 On a certain day high water for a harbour occurs at 4.30 a.m. and low water at 10.50 a.m. The depths at high and low water are 6 m and 2 m. If the tidal motion is assumed to be simple harmonic, find, to the nearest minute, the latest time before noon that a ship drawing 5 m can enter the harbour.

6 A cook causes a non-stick frying pan to perform vertical SHM with period T and amplitude a. In the frying pan is a pancake; prove that this remains in contact with the pan provided that $T \geqslant 2\pi\sqrt{(a/g)}$.

7 Suppose that, in Example 5, $m = 1\,\mathrm{kg}$, $k = 14\,\mathrm{N\,m^{-1}}$ and $x_0 = 2\,\mathrm{m}$. Find the least value of x (i.e. at the highest point reached) and the period (a) for motion with a spring, (b) for motion with an elastic string.

8 A particle on the end of an elastic string oscillates vertically. While the string is stretched the particle has SHM with centre O, amplitude a and maximum speed $\sqrt{(nga)}$. When the particle is at height h above O and moving upwards the string becomes slack. Find the height above O that the particle reaches, and show that this is greatest when $h = a/n$.

9 The string of a simple pendulum of length l initially makes a small angle α with the vertical. At a distance $3l/4$ below the point of suspension is a small fixed peg which obstructs the string as the pendulum swings (Fig. 15). Find the distance travelled by the bob in one complete swing, and the length of the equivalent simple pendulum.

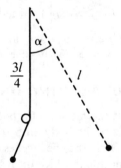

Figure 15

10 Two elastic strings of natural lengths a and b and stiffnesses h and k respectively each have one end fixed to a mass m. The remaining ends are fixed at two points on a frictionless horizontal table at a distance $2(a + b)$ apart. Find the extension of the string of natural length a at equilibrium. If the mass is moved slightly towards one of the fixed points on the table and then released, what is the period of the oscillation?

11   A particle P of unit mass moves in a plane under the action of a force $\mathbf{F}$ which is directed towards the origin O and has magnitude proportional to OP, i.e. $\mathbf{F} = -\omega^2 \mathbf{r}$, where $\mathbf{r} = \mathbf{OP}$ and ω is constant. Show that at time t the position vector of P is

$$\mathbf{r} = \mathbf{r}_0 \cos \omega t + \frac{1}{\omega} \mathbf{v}_0 \sin \omega t,$$

where $\mathbf{r}_0$ is the initial position vector and $\mathbf{v}_0$ is the initial velocity.

Plot the path of P in the case $\omega = 2$, $\mathbf{r}_0 = \begin{bmatrix} 5 \\ 0 \end{bmatrix}$, $\mathbf{v}_0 = \begin{bmatrix} 2 \\ 4 \end{bmatrix}$.

12   The greatest angle the string of a simple pendulum makes with the vertical is α.
(a) Starting from equation (3) of §1.4 show that

$$\dot{\theta}^2 = \frac{4g}{l} \left(\sin^2 \frac{\alpha}{2} - \sin^2 \frac{\theta}{2} \right)$$

and hence that the period T is given by

$$T = 2\sqrt{(l/g)} \int_0^\alpha \frac{d\theta}{\left(\sin^2 \dfrac{\alpha}{2} - \sin^2 \dfrac{\theta}{2} \right)^{1/2}} .$$

(b) Use the substitution $\sin \phi = \sin \dfrac{\theta}{2} \Big/ \sin \dfrac{\alpha}{2}$ to deduce that

$$T = 4\sqrt{(l/g)} \int_0^{\pi/2} \frac{d\phi}{\left(1 - \sin^2 \dfrac{\alpha}{2} \sin^2 \phi \right)^{1/2}} .$$

(c) This is called an elliptic integral; it cannot be evaluated in terms of simple functions, but we can obtain an approximation by using the binomial approximation for $\left(1 - \sin^2 \dfrac{\alpha}{2} \sin^2 \phi \right)^{-1/2}$ and then integrating. Show that if $\sin^4 \dfrac{\alpha}{2}$ and higher powers are neglected this gives

$$T = 2\pi \sqrt{(l/g)} \left[1 + \tfrac{1}{4} \sin^2 \frac{\alpha}{2} \right].$$

(d) Hence show that the error in T due to the small angle approximation $\sin \theta \approx \theta$ is about 4% when $\alpha = 45°$. What value of α gives an error of 1%?

1.5 FORCE DEPENDING ON VELOCITY

It is common experience that the motion of a body is often affected by forces which depend on the velocity of the body. For example the air resistance to a cyclist increases with speed, while the effectiveness of pedalling decreases. This section therefore deals with motion in which the resultant force changes with the velocity.

Example 6
The engine of a lorry of mass 8000 kg produces constant power of 60 kW. Find the time taken and distance travelled while the lorry accelerates from 5 m s^{-1} to 10 m s^{-1} (a) when the resistance to motion is neglected, (b) when there is constant resistance of 4000 N.

Solution
If the tractive force produced by the engine is P N when the speed is v m s^{-1}
then the power is Pv W (Note 1.8), so $Pv = 60\,000$ and $P = 60\,000/v$.
  (a) The equation of motion is

$$\frac{60\,000}{v} = 8000\,a \quad \Rightarrow \quad a = \frac{15}{2v}.$$

To find the time T we use $a = \dfrac{dv}{dt}$:

$$\frac{dv}{dt} = \frac{15}{2v}$$

$$\Rightarrow \quad \int_5^{10} \frac{2v}{15}\,dv = \int_0^T dt$$

$$\Rightarrow T = \left[\frac{v^2}{15}\right]_5^{10} = \frac{1}{15}[100 - 25] = 5.$$

To find the distance travelled X we use $a = v\dfrac{dv}{dx}$:

$$v\frac{dv}{dx} = \frac{15}{2v}$$

$$\Rightarrow \quad \int_5^{10} \frac{2v^2}{15}\,dv = \int_0^X dx$$

$$\Rightarrow X = \left[\frac{2v^3}{45}\right]_5^{10} = \frac{2}{45}[1000 - 125] = 38.8.$$

So the lorry takes 5 s to accelerate, and travels about 39 m in that time.
  (b) The equation of motion is now

$$\frac{60\,000}{v} - 4000 = 8000\,a$$

$$\Rightarrow \quad a = \frac{15}{2v} - \frac{1}{2} = \frac{15 - v}{2v}.$$

To find T,

$$\frac{dv}{dt} = \frac{15 - v}{2v}$$

$$\Rightarrow \quad \int_5^{10} \frac{2v}{15 - v}\,dv = \int_0^T dt.$$

Now

$$\frac{2v}{15 - v} = \frac{30}{15 - v} - 2,$$

so

$$T = \int_5^{10} \left(\frac{30}{15 - v} - 2\right) dv = [-30\ln(15 - v) - 2v]_5^{10} \approx 10.8.$$

To find X,
$$v\frac{dv}{dx} = \frac{15 - v}{2v}$$

$$\Rightarrow \int_5^{10} \frac{2v^2}{15 - v}\, dv = \int_0^X dx.$$

Now
$$\frac{2v^2}{15 - v} = \frac{450}{15 - v} - 30 - 2v,$$

so

$$X = \int_5^{10} \left(\frac{450}{15 - v} - 30 - 2v\right) dv = [-450 \ln(15 - v) - 30v - v^2]_5^{10} \approx 86.9.$$

So the lorry now takes about 11 s to accelerate, and travels about 87 m in that time.   □

Notice that in (*b*) the maximum speed of the lorry in these circumstances is 15 m s^{-1}, when the tractive force equals the resistance. This is called the *terminal speed*, but it is not reached in a finite time, as can be seen by putting 15 as the upper limit in the integral used to find T.

When a particle moves through a resisting medium (such as air or a liquid) its motion is opposed by a resistance force R which increases from zero with the speed v in such a way that $R \to \infty$ as $v \to \infty$. There is therefore a speed at which R equals the weight of the particle; this is the terminal speed. If the particle falls from rest its speed will never exceed the terminal speed.

The exact way in which R depends on v in any particular case is difficult to determine, but there are two simple models which have proved useful. In the first, which applies at small speeds, the resistance is taken to be proportional to the speed, i.e. $R = k_1 v$. For large speeds it is better to use the second model, in which the resistance is proportional to the square of the speed, i.e. $R = k_2 v^2$. The values of k_1 and k_2, and what is meant by 'small' or 'large' speeds, depend on many factors. For example, for a sphere of diameter 1 cm moving through air with 50% relative humidity at 10 °C and pressure 1 atmosphere, experiments show that $R = k_1 v$ with $k_1 \approx 1.6 \times 10^{-6} \text{ kg s}^{-1}$ for speeds up to 20 cm s^{-1}, and $R = k_2 v^2$ with $k_2 \approx 2 \times 10^{-5} \text{ kg m}^{-1}$ for speeds above 100 cm s^{-1}. There is no simple formula connecting resistance and speed for speeds between 20 cm s^{-1} and 100 cm s^{-1} (Note 1.9).

Example 7
A particle of mass m is projected vertically upwards with initial velocity u. The air resistance is kv when the velocity is v. Investigate the motion.

Solution
With the upward direction taken as positive the two forces acting on the particle are its weight $-mg$ and the air resistance $-kv$. The equation of motion is

$$m\frac{dv}{dt} = -mg - kv$$

$$\Rightarrow \int \frac{m \, dv}{mg + kv} = \int -dt$$

$$\Rightarrow \frac{m}{k} \ln (mg + kv) = -t + c.$$

Since the initial velocity is u,

$$\frac{m}{k} \ln (mg + ku) = c.$$

Therefore
$$t = \frac{m}{k} \ln (mg + ku) - \frac{m}{k} \ln (mg + kv),$$

i.e.
$$t = \frac{m}{k} \ln \left(\frac{mg + ku}{mg + kv} \right). \tag{1}$$

The particle is at its highest position ($v = 0$) when

$$t = \frac{m}{k} \ln \left(1 + \frac{ku}{mg} \right).$$

After this the particle falls, so v is negative and $-kv$ is positive, indicating correctly that the air resistance is now upward. Therefore the same equation of motion applies when the particle is falling.

From (1)
$$\frac{mg + ku}{mg + kv} = e^{kt/m}$$

$$\Rightarrow \quad \frac{mg + kv}{mg + ku} = e^{-kt/m}$$

$$\Rightarrow v = \left(\frac{mg}{k} + u \right) e^{-kt/m} - \frac{mg}{k}. \tag{2}$$

As a check, notice that $t = 0 \Rightarrow v = u$ and that, as $t \to \infty$, $v \to -mg/k$, the terminal velocity (at which the air resistance equals the weight).

The upward displacement y can be found directly by integrating (2):

$$y = -\frac{m}{k} \left(\frac{mg}{k} + u \right) e^{-kt/m} - \frac{mgt}{k} + c',$$

where
$$0 = -\frac{m}{k} \left(\frac{mg}{k} + u \right) + c'$$

so that
$$y = \frac{m}{k} \left(\frac{mg}{k} + u \right)(1 - e^{-kt/m}) - \frac{mgt}{k}. \qquad \square$$

Q.6 Show that the greatest height reached by the particle is

$$\frac{mu}{k} - \frac{m^2 g}{k^2} \ln \left(1 + \frac{ku}{mg} \right).$$

Q.7 If the air resistance in Example 7 is kv^2 show that the equation of motion is

$$m\frac{dv}{dt} = mg - kv^2 \quad \text{for} \quad v > 0.$$

but

$$m\frac{dv}{dt} = mg + kv^2 \quad \text{for} \quad v < 0.$$

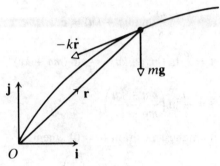

Figure 16

Similar methods can be used to find the two-dimensional trajectory of a projectile when the resistance to motion is proportional to the velocity. For then the forces are the weight $m\mathbf{g}$ and the resistance $-k\mathbf{v} = -k\dot{\mathbf{r}}$ (Fig. 16), and the equation of motion is

$$m\ddot{\mathbf{r}} = m\mathbf{g} - k\dot{\mathbf{r}}. \tag{3}$$

The $\mathbf{i}$ and $\mathbf{j}$ components of this give

$$m\ddot{x} = -k\dot{x} \quad \text{and} \quad m\ddot{y} = -mg - k\dot{y};$$

the second of these equations has already been solved in Example 7.

Q.8 Solve the equation $m\ddot{x} = -k\dot{x}$ to find $\dot{x}$ and x in terms of t, with $\dot{x} = u$ and $x = 0$ when $t = 0$.

Q.9 Suppose that the particle is projected from the top of a high cliff (so that it takes a long time to hit the ground below). What happens to x as $t \to \infty$? What does this imply about the shape of the trajectory?

Alternatively we can solve the original vector equation (3) as follows.

$$m\ddot{\mathbf{r}} = m\mathbf{g} - k\dot{\mathbf{r}}$$

$$\Leftrightarrow \qquad \ddot{\mathbf{r}} + \frac{k}{m}\dot{\mathbf{r}} = \mathbf{g}, \tag{4}$$

which can be integrated to give

$$\dot{\mathbf{r}} + \frac{k}{m}\mathbf{r} = t\mathbf{g} + \mathbf{u}, \tag{5}$$

since $\mathbf{r} = \mathbf{0}$ and $\dot{\mathbf{r}} = \mathbf{u}$ when $t = 0$.

If we multiply throughout (4) by $e^{kt/m}$ we notice that the left-hand side is the derivative of the product $e^{kt/m} \dot{\mathbf{r}}$:

$$e^{kt/m} \ddot{\mathbf{r}} + \frac{k}{m} e^{kt/m} \dot{\mathbf{r}} = e^{kt/m} \mathbf{g}$$

$$\Leftrightarrow \qquad \frac{d}{dt} (e^{kt/m} \dot{\mathbf{r}}) = e^{kt/m} \mathbf{g}.$$

Integrating this gives

$$e^{kt/m} \dot{\mathbf{r}} = \frac{m}{k} e^{kt/m} \mathbf{g} + \mathbf{c}.$$

Since $\dot{\mathbf{r}} = \mathbf{u}$ when $t = 0$, $\mathbf{u} = \frac{m}{k} \mathbf{g} + \mathbf{c}$ and so $\mathbf{c} = \mathbf{u} - \frac{m}{k} \mathbf{g}$. Therefore

$$e^{kt/m} \dot{\mathbf{r}} = \frac{m}{k} (e^{kt/m} - 1)\mathbf{g} + \mathbf{u}$$

and

$$\dot{\mathbf{r}} = \frac{m}{k} (1 - e^{-kt/m})\mathbf{g} + e^{-kt/m}\mathbf{u}.$$

Substituting this in (5) and rearranging (check the details!) gives

$$\mathbf{r} = \frac{m}{k^2} (kt - m + me^{-kt/m})\mathbf{g} + \frac{m}{k} (1 - e^{-kt/m})\mathbf{u}.$$

For other laws of resistance it is not usually possible to find the trajectory exactly, so approximate methods have to be used to solve the differential equations of motion.

Exercise 1E

1   A ball-bearing of mass 5 g falls from rest through a viscous fluid. The resistance to motion is $0.02v$ N, where v m s^{-1} is the velocity. Find the terminal velocity V. How long is it before the ball-bearing's velocity is $0.9 V$, and how far has it fallen in that time?

2   The force of resistance to the motion of a car is proportional to its velocity, and the car has maximum speed V. In tests the car is driven in two ways: (a) so that its engine produces constant power, and (b) so that the engine produces constant propulsive force. Show that method (b) takes nearly three times as long as method (a) to increase the speed from $\frac{1}{4}V$ to $\frac{3}{4}V$.

3   On aircraft carriers, aircraft are brought to rest after touchdown by means of an arrester hook underneath the aircraft engaging with an arrester cable mounted between a pair of supports on the carrier deck distance $2a$ apart. The cable lies at right angles to the path of an aircraft. Each end of the cable passes below deck and is connected to a system of hydraulic pistons so that, as cable is pulled out by an aircraft, a restraining tension is exerted which is a constant D times the rate at which it is pulled out at each end.

Derive a differential equation governing the distance travelled by an aircraft after engaging with the arrester cable and hence find an expression for D in terms of the mass m of an aircraft, its speed V at touchdown and a, if it is to be brought to rest in a distance a. Assume that the hook engages at the centre of the cable and that the cable is inextensible.   [MEI]

4   A vehicle of mass m moves in a straight line subject to a resistance $P + Qv^2$, where v is the speed and P, Q are constants. Form an equation of motion, using the expression $v(dv/dx)$ for the acceleration. Hence show

   (a) that if $P = 0$ the distance required to slow down from speed $\frac{3}{2}U$ to speed U is $(m/Q) \ln (\frac{3}{2})$.

   (b) that if $P > 0$ the distance D required to stop from speed U is given by $D = \lambda \ln (1 + \mu U^2)$ where λ, μ are constants. Express these constants in terms of the data.

   Use the above results to estimate the landing run of an aircraft of mass 10^5 kg assuming that the speed falls from 90 m s^{-1} to 60 m s^{-1} under air-resistance only, given by $125 \, v^2$ N, and that subsequently the air-resistance is supplemented by a constant braking force of 7.5×10^5 N.   [MEI]

5   A particle is projected vertically upwards with speed u. Show that if the air resistance at speed v is kv^2 per unit mass then the particle's greatest height is $\dfrac{1}{2k} \ln \left(1 + \dfrac{ku^2}{g} \right)$ which it reaches in time $\dfrac{1}{\sqrt{(gk)}} \tan^{-1} \left(\dfrac{u\sqrt{k}}{\sqrt{g}} \right)$. Check that if k is small these are approximately $u^2/2g$ and u/g respectively.

6   A parachutist is free-falling vertically at 50 m s^{-1}. At an altitude of 500 m he deploys his parachute. The parachute is assumed to open instantaneously and the total upward force then exerted on the parachutist is proportional to the square of his speed. Under these conditions his speed tends towards a terminal value of 10 m s^{-1}. Find how long he takes to reach the ground after deploying his parachute. [MEI]

7   A body is subjected to gravity, an upward thrust of $10g$ per unit mass and a resistive force of $av + bv^2$ per unit mass where a and b are constants and v is the speed of the body. The resistance is such that $av = bv^2$ when $v = 100$ m s^{-1} and the terminal upward speed is 500 m s^{-1}.

   Find an expression for the speed as a function of time and find how long the body takes to reach half its terminal upward speed if it starts from rest.   [MEI]

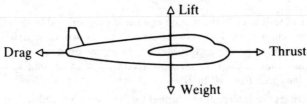

Figure 17

8   When an aircraft of mass m is in steady level flight with speed u the four forces shown in Fig. 17 are in equilibrium. Suppose that the aircraft is slightly disturbed from steady flight, so that when its height above the original line of flight is x its speed is v.

   (a) Assuming that energy is conserved, show that $v^2 = u^2 - 2gx$.

(b) Assuming that the lift varies as the square of the speed, show that

$$\text{Lift} = mgv^2/u^2.$$

(c) Deduce that the aircraft oscillates vertically with SHM of period $\pi u \sqrt{2/g}$. (This is called the *phugoid oscillation*.)

9 By differentiating equation (3) of §1.5 show that for a projectile moving with resistance proportional to velocity the acceleration is in a fixed direction and has magnitude proportional to $e^{-kt/m}$.

10 For a particle of mass m projected with velocity $\mathbf{u}$ from the origin and moving with resistance $-k\mathbf{v}$, where k is small, show that the position vector at time t is approximately

$$\mathbf{r}^* - \frac{k}{m}(\tfrac{1}{6}t^3\mathbf{g} + \tfrac{1}{2}t^2\mathbf{u}),$$

where $\mathbf{r}^*$ is the position vector it would have in the absence of resistance.

11 A projectile of mass m is fired with speed U at an angle α above the horizontal in a vertical gravitational field g. The projectile is subject to a resistive force, with a magnitude proportional to its speed, which opposes its motion. The resistive force is such that in free fall the projectile would reach a terminal speed of V.

Find the horizontal and vertical displacements of the projectile at time t after firing and hence find the equation of its trajectory.

If the resistance is weak, show that an approximation to the range of the projectile is

$$\frac{U^2}{g}\sin 2\alpha \left(1 - \frac{4}{3}\frac{U}{V}\sin \alpha\right).$$

2

Kinematics using polar coordinates

2.1 POLAR COORDINATES

The common method of describing the position of an object by means of its distance and bearing from a known fixed point is the basis for a useful system of coordinates introduced by Newton in 1671.

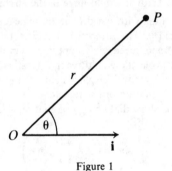

Figure 1

In this system the position vector **OP** of a point P in a plane is specified by its length $r\,(=|\mathbf{OP}|)$ and the angle θ which **OP** makes with the fixed unit vector **i**. As usual, the angle θ is taken to be positive if the sense of rotation from **i** to **OP** is anticlockwise. The ordered pair of numbers (r, θ) are then the *polar coordinates* of P; in this context the origin O is called the *pole*.

One slight drawback with polar coordinates is that, for a given point P, the angle θ is not uniquely defined, since for any integer k the angle $\theta + 2k\pi$ would do just as well. We shall normally use the value of θ for which $0 \leqslant \theta < 2\pi$. For the pole itself, $r = 0$ and θ is undefined.

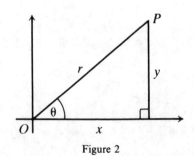

Figure 2

There are simple connections between the polar coordinates (r, θ) and the Cartesian coordinates (x, y) of the same point. From Fig. 2 we have

$$x = r \cos \theta, \qquad\qquad y = r \sin \theta,$$

$$r = \sqrt{(x^2 + y^2)}, \qquad \tan \theta = \frac{y}{x} \quad (x \neq 0).$$

Care must be taken to choose θ in the correct quadrant when converting from Cartesian coordinates to polars. For example, the points P and Q with Cartesian coordinates $(2, 2)$ and $(-3, -3)$ respectively both give $\tan \theta = 1$. As Fig. 3 shows, P is in the first quadrant, so $\theta = \pi/4$ for P, but Q is in the third quadrant, so $\theta = \pi/4 + \pi = 5\pi/4$ for Q. The polar coordinates of P and Q are $(2\sqrt{2}, \pi/4)$ and $(3\sqrt{2}, 5\pi/4)$ respectively.

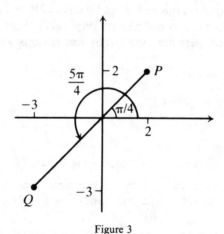

Figure 3

Exercise 2A

Throughout this exercise O is the pole.

1 Plot the points A, B, C, D with polar co-ordinates $(4, \pi/6), (2, 2\pi/3), (4, 7\pi/6), (2, 5\pi/3)$ respectively. What shape is $ABCD$?

2 The point P has polar coordinates $(3, 5\pi/6)$, and $OPQR$ is a square. Find the polar coordinates of Q and R. (There are two possible sets of answers.)

3 Show on separate sketch diagrams the sets of points with polar coordinates (r, θ) subject to the following conditions: (a) $r = 3$; (b) $r < 3$; (c) $3 \leqslant r \leqslant 4$; (d) $\theta = \pi/4$; (e) $\pi \leqslant \theta \leqslant 3\pi/2$; (f) $\theta = 5\pi/12$ and $r \geqslant 2$; (g) $\pi/4 \leqslant \theta \leqslant 3\pi/4$ and $1 \leqslant r \leqslant 3$.

4 Find the Cartesian coordinates of the points whose polar coordinates are (a) $(4, \pi)$; (b) $(3, 7\pi/4)$; (c) $(5, 3\pi/2)$; (d) $(8, 5\pi/6)$; (e) $(7, 4)$.

5 Find the polar coordinates (with $0 \leqslant \theta < 2\pi$) of the points whose Cartesian coordinates are (a) $(-3, 0)$; (b) $(\sqrt{3}, 1)$; (c) $(\sqrt{18}, -\sqrt{18})$; (d) $(-5, -12)$; (e) $(-6.9, 2.1)$.

6 Taking the pivot as the pole and ignoring the curvature of the windscreen, suggest possible conditions on r and θ which define the region swept clear by a car windscreen wiper.

7 Check that you know how to use your calculator to convert from polar to rectangular coordinates and back, using the P → R and R → P functions.

2.2 THE POLAR EQUATION OF A CURVE

If f is a function and $C = \{(r, \theta):r = f(\theta)\}$ then $r = f(\theta)$ is called the *polar equation* of C. The polar equation of a curve may be simpler than the Cartesian equation, particularly when the curve has rotational symmetry.

The definition $r = |OP|$ given in §2.1 implies that r is never negative. But when we work with polar equations of curves it may be convenient to allow r to take negative values, using the obvious interpretation that $(-r, \theta)$ is the same as $(r, \theta + \pi)$. This will apply in this section and Exercise 2B, and in §3.3 and Exercise 3B. Later we shall use polar coordinates in physical applications, and then r will remain positive, since there are usually physical reasons why r cannot change sign.

Example 1
Investigate the curve $r = 4 \cos \theta$.

Solution
Three methods are given.
  (i) Make a table of values, with θ increasing by $\pi/12$ (i.e. 15°).

θ	0	$\pi/12$	$\pi/6$	$\pi/3$	$\pi/4$	$5\pi/12$	$\pi/2$	$7\pi/12$	$2\pi/3$	$3\pi/4$	$5\pi/6$	$11\pi/12$	π
r	4	3.9	3.5	2.8	2	1.0	0	−1.0	−2	−2.8	−3.5	−3.9	−4

For values of θ from π to 2π we get the same points again; for example $\theta = 13\pi/12 \Rightarrow r = -3.9$, which gives the same point as $(3.9, \pi/12)$. Plotting these points gives the graph of Fig. 4.

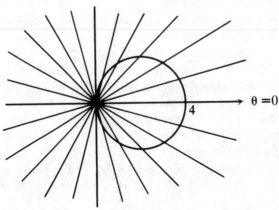

Figure 4

(ii) If $r \neq 0$, $r = 4 \cos \theta \Leftrightarrow r^2 = 4r \cos \theta$

$$\Leftrightarrow x^2 + y^2 = 4x.$$

If $r = 0$, then $x = y = 0$, which also satisfies $x^2 + y^2 = 4x$.
Therefore the Cartesian equation is

$$x^2 + y^2 = 4x$$
$$\Leftrightarrow \quad x^2 - 4x + y^2 = 0$$
$$\Leftrightarrow x^2 - 4x + 4 + y^2 = 4$$
$$\Leftrightarrow \quad (x - 2)^2 + y^2 = 4.$$

This shows that the curve is a circle with centre at the (Cartesian) point $(2, 0)$ and radius 2.

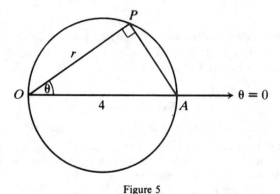

Figure 5

(iii) If P is the point on this circle with polar coordinates (r, θ) then angle OPA is a right angle (Fig. 5), and so $r = 4 \cos \theta$ as required. (What happens if P is on the lower semicircle?) □

Example 2
Describe the motion of a point along the curve $r = 3/(1 + 2 \cos \theta)$ as θ increases from 0 to 2π.

Solution
As θ increases from 0 to $\pi/2$, $1 + 2 \cos \theta$ decreases from 3 to 1, so r increases from 1 to 3 and the point (r, θ) moves from A to B (Fig. 6). As θ increases to $2\pi/3$, $1 + 2 \cos \theta$ decreases to zero (since $\cos (2\pi/3) = -\frac{1}{2}$), so r increases without limit and the point moves away through C. There is no point for which $\theta = 2\pi/3$, but for θ just greater than $2\pi/3$, $1 + 2 \cos \theta$ is negative and nearly zero, so r is numerically large and negative, giving D. When $\theta = \pi$, $r = 3/-1 = -3$ (at E). As θ increases to $4\pi/3$, $1 + 2 \cos \theta$ remains negative but approaches zero, so r remains negative and increases in magnitude without limit; the point moves away through F. There is no point for $\theta = 4\pi/3$. When θ is just greater than $4\pi/3$,

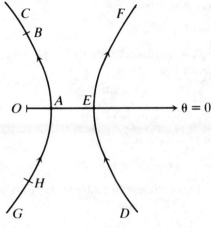

Figure 6

$1 + 2 \cos \theta$ is small and positive, so r is large and positive (at G). As θ increases to 2π the point completes its journey via H $(3, 3\pi/2)$ back to A. This curve is called a *hyperbola*; it has two separate branches.   □

Exercise 2B

In questions 1–4 polar graph paper should be used, with $\frac{1}{2}$ cm unit for r.

1   Make a table of values of $10 \sin \theta$ for θ from 0 to π at intervals of $\pi/12$ ($=15°$), and consider what happens when $\pi \leqslant \theta \leqslant 2\pi$. Hence draw the curve $r = 10 \sin \theta$. Identify this curve, and find its Cartesian equation.

2   Draw on a single graph the curves $r = k + 5 \sin \theta$ for $k = 3, 5, 7$. These curves are called *limaçons* (snail curves). Without detailed plotting, sketch the limaçons obtained when k is very large and when k is close to zero.

3   Draw the four-petal *rhodonea* (rose curve) whose equation is $r = 10 \cos 2\theta$. Without detailed plotting, sketch the curve $r = 10 \cos 3\theta$.

4   Draw on a single graph (a) the *ellipse* $r = 6/(2 + \cos \theta)$; (b) the *parabola* $r = 6/(2 + 2 \cos \theta)$; (c) the *hyperbola* $r = 6/(2 + 3 \cos \theta)$.

5   Prove that the curves $r = a \sec \theta$, $r = a \operatorname{cosec} \theta$ (where a is a non-zero constant) are both straight lines. Find the Cartesian equation of each.

6   The straight line l passes through the point A with polar coordinates (p, α) and is perpendicular to OA. Show that the polar equation of l is $r \cos (\theta - \alpha) = p$. By using the expansion of $\cos (\theta - \alpha)$ show that the Cartesian equation of l is $x \cos \alpha + y \sin \alpha = p$.

7   The point P (r, θ) lies on the circle with centre A (a, α) and radius b.
   (i) By using the cosine rule with triangle OAP, show that
   $$r^2 - 2ar \cos (\theta - \alpha) + a^2 - b^2 = 0.$$
   (ii) Check that the result in (i) fits with previously known results in the special cases $a = 0$ and $a = b$.
   (iii) Obtain the Cartesian equation of the circle.

8   The point P moves so that its distance from a fixed point O is always equal to its distance PM from a fixed line l which is 4 units from O (Fig. 7). Taking O as the pole

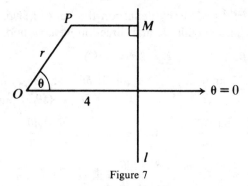

Figure 7

and the perpendicular from O to l as the line $\theta = 0$, find the polar equation of the locus of P. Draw the locus, and find its Cartesian equation.

2.3 MOTION IN A CIRCLE

When a point P moves in a circle of radius k with centre O its polar coordinates at time t are $r = k$, $\theta = f(t)$. If we want to find the velocity and acceleration of P we can use Cartesian components

$$\mathbf{OP} = \mathbf{r} = \begin{bmatrix} k \cos (f(t)) \\ k \sin (f(t)) \end{bmatrix}$$

and then differentiate with respect to t. But this differentiation can be complicated, and the result may not be easy to interpret. It is often better to split the velocity and acceleration vectors into components which are in the direction of $\mathbf{OP}$ (called the *radial* component) and at right angles to $\mathbf{OP}$ (the *transverse* component).

We start by differentiating a variable *unit* vector $\hat{\mathbf{r}}$, i.e. a vector whose length is always one unit, but whose direction changes with t. This is both the simplest example of differentiating a vector, and also the key to dealing with the general case. Because of its importance we do the work by two methods, from first principles and then using known calculus results.

Suppose that $\hat{\mathbf{r}}$ changes by $\delta\hat{\mathbf{r}}$ when t changes by δt. The initial $\hat{\mathbf{r}}$ and subsequent $\hat{\mathbf{r}} + \delta\hat{\mathbf{r}}$ are both unit vectors, so the vector triangle OAB showing them is isosceles (Fig. 8); let the angle AOB between the unit sides be $\delta\theta$ (Note 2.1).

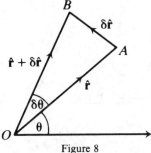

Figure 8

The derivative $d\hat{\mathbf{r}}/dt$ $(=\dot{\hat{\mathbf{r}}})$ is by definition the limit of $\delta\hat{\mathbf{r}}/\delta t$ as $\delta t \to 0$. This limit is a vector, whose magnitude and direction we now find.

From triangle OAB, $|\delta\hat{\mathbf{r}}| = 2 \sin(\delta\theta/2)$,

and so $\left|\dfrac{\delta\hat{\mathbf{r}}}{\delta t}\right| = \dfrac{2 \sin(\delta\theta/2)}{\delta t} = \dfrac{2\sin(\delta\theta/2)}{\delta\theta}\cdot\dfrac{\delta\theta}{\delta t} = \dfrac{\sin(\delta\theta/2)}{(\delta\theta/2)}\cdot\dfrac{\delta\theta}{\delta t}.$

As $\delta t \to 0$, $\delta\theta \to 0$, $\dfrac{\sin(\delta\theta/2)}{(\delta\theta/2)} \to 1$ (Note 2.2) and $\dfrac{\delta\theta}{\delta t} \to \dfrac{d\theta}{dt}.$

Therefore $\left|\dfrac{d\hat{\mathbf{r}}}{dt}\right| = \dfrac{d\theta}{dt} = \dot{\theta}.$

The direction of $\delta\hat{\mathbf{r}}/\delta t$ is the same as the direction of $\delta\hat{\mathbf{r}}$, which makes angle OAB with $\hat{\mathbf{r}}$.

But   angle $OAB = \pi/2 - \delta\theta/2 \to \pi/2$ as $\delta t \to 0$.

Therefore $d\hat{\mathbf{r}}/dt$ is perpendicular to $\hat{\mathbf{r}}$.

Thus $d\hat{\mathbf{r}}/dt$ is the vector of magnitude $\dot{\theta}$ at right angles to $\hat{\mathbf{r}}$. We can show this more directly by writing $\hat{\mathbf{r}} = \begin{bmatrix} \cos\theta \\ \sin\theta \end{bmatrix}$ and differentiating the components. When we differentiate with respect to t to find $\dot{\hat{\mathbf{r}}}$ we must use the chain rule (Note 2.3); for example,

$$\frac{d}{dt}(\cos\theta) = \frac{d}{d\theta}(\cos\theta) \times \frac{d\theta}{dt} = (-\sin\theta)\dot{\theta}.$$

So $\hat{\mathbf{r}} = \begin{bmatrix} \cos\theta \\ \sin\theta \end{bmatrix} \Rightarrow \dot{\hat{\mathbf{r}}} = \begin{bmatrix} -\sin\theta\,\dot{\theta} \\ \cos\theta\,\dot{\theta} \end{bmatrix}$

$$= \dot{\theta}\begin{bmatrix} -\sin\theta \\ \cos\theta \end{bmatrix}$$

$$= \dot{\theta}\hat{\mathbf{u}},$$

where $\hat{\mathbf{u}} = \begin{bmatrix} -\sin\theta \\ \cos\theta \end{bmatrix}$ is the unit vector obtained by rotating $\hat{\mathbf{r}}$ through $+\frac{1}{2}\pi$ (Fig. 9).

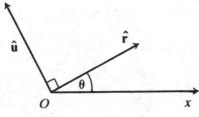

Figure 9

Thus to differentiate a *unit* vector with respect to t we turn the vector through $+\frac{1}{2}\pi$ and multiply by $\dot{\theta}$.

Q.1 Show that $\dot{\hat{\mathbf{u}}} = -\dot{\theta}\hat{\mathbf{r}}$.

Example 3
The to-and-fro motion of the end P of a windscreen wiper is described by the polar representation

$$r = 0.4, \qquad \theta = 1 + \sin 2t,$$

where r is in metres and t is the time in seconds. Find the velocity and acceleration of P.

Solution
We have

$$\mathbf{r} = 0.4\hat{\mathbf{r}} \quad \text{and} \quad \theta = 1 + \sin 2t$$

so that

$$\dot{\theta} = 2\cos 2t \quad \text{and} \quad \mathbf{v} = \dot{\mathbf{r}} = 0.4\dot{\hat{\mathbf{r}}}$$

$$= 0.4\dot{\theta}\hat{\mathbf{u}}$$

$$= 0.8\cos 2t\,\hat{\mathbf{u}}.$$

The velocity of P is therefore $0.8\cos 2t$ perpendicular to $\mathbf{r}$, i.e. tangential to the circular path of P.

To find the acceleration $\ddot{\mathbf{r}}$ we differentiate again, using the product rule (Note 2.4):

$$\mathbf{a} = \ddot{\mathbf{r}} = 0.4\ddot{\theta}\hat{\mathbf{u}} + 0.4\dot{\theta}\dot{\hat{\mathbf{u}}}$$

$$= 0.4\ddot{\theta}\hat{\mathbf{u}} - 0.4\dot{\theta}^2\hat{\mathbf{r}}, \quad \text{since} \quad \dot{\hat{\mathbf{u}}} = -\dot{\theta}\hat{\mathbf{r}}$$

$$= -1.6\sin 2t\,\hat{\mathbf{u}} - 1.6\cos^2 2t\,\hat{\mathbf{r}}, \quad \text{since} \quad \ddot{\theta} = -4\sin 2t.$$

These results are shown in Fig. 10.   □

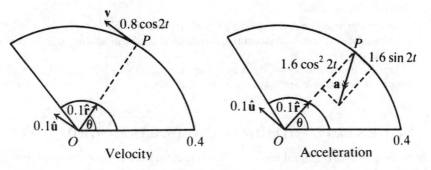

Figure 10

The velocity and acceleration of a point P moving in a circle of radius k are found by the same method:

$$\mathbf{r} = k\hat{\mathbf{r}}$$

$$\Rightarrow \mathbf{v} = \dot{\mathbf{r}} = k\dot{\hat{\mathbf{r}}} = k\dot{\theta}\hat{\mathbf{u}}$$

$$\Rightarrow \mathbf{a} = \ddot{\mathbf{r}} = k\ddot{\theta}\hat{\mathbf{u}} + k\dot{\theta}\dot{\hat{\mathbf{u}}}$$

$$= k\ddot{\theta}\hat{\mathbf{u}} - k\dot{\theta}^2\hat{\mathbf{r}}.$$

The point moves at right angles to OP with speed $k\dot{\theta}$; its acceleration has two components:

(i) $-k\dot{\theta}^2$ away from O, i.e. $k\dot{\theta}^2$ towards O (the radial component);
(ii) $k\ddot{\theta}$ at right angles to OP (the transverse component).

Exercise 2C

1 For the windscreen wiper of Example 3 find:
   (a) the magnitudes of the velocity and acceleration when $t = 0.2$ and when $t = 2$;
   (b) the times during a complete sweep when the speed is greatest, and the direction of the acceleration at these times.

2 Prove that, in the windscreen wiper example, the tangent of the angle between **OP** and the acceleration vector is $\tan 2t \sec 2t$.

3 As the string carrying a heavy weight unwinds from a pulley, a particular point P on the rim of the pulley has polar coordinates $(0.2, 1.5t^2)$, where r is in metres and t in seconds.
   (a) Find the radial and transverse components of acceleration when $t = 1$ and when $t = 3$.
   (b) Find when the magnitude of the acceleration is 10 m s^{-2}.

4 Show that the radial acceleration $k\dot{\theta}^2$ can be expressed as v^2/k, where v is the tangential speed.

5 A motor-cyclist crosses a hump-backed bridge which forms an arc of a vertical circle of radius 25 m. At the top of the hump he is travelling at 15 m s^{-1} and increasing speed at 2 m s^{-2}. Find the magnitude and direction of his acceleration at that instant. The greatest vertical component of acceleration his weight can produce is 10 m s^{-2}. What is the greatest speed he can have at the top of the bridge if he is not to lose contact with the road?

6 What can be said about the speed of a point moving in a circle
   (a) when the acceleration is tangential, (b) when the acceleration is towards the centre of the circle?
      Discuss in general terms the way in which the velocity and acceleration of a pendulum bob vary when it swings in a vertical plane.

2.4 GENERAL MOTION USING POLAR COORDINATES

In dealing with the general motion of a point P we have to take into account the fact that its position vector **r** changes in magnitude as well as direction. It is helpful to show the magnitude and direction separately by writing

$$\mathbf{r} = r\hat{\mathbf{r}};$$

We can then differentiate using the product rule.

Thus
$$\mathbf{v} = \dot{\mathbf{r}} = \dot{r}\hat{\mathbf{r}} + r\dot{\hat{\mathbf{r}}}$$

$$= \dot{r}\hat{\mathbf{r}} + r\dot{\theta}\hat{\mathbf{u}}.$$

We differentiate again to find $\mathbf{a}$, noting that the derivative of the product of three variables $r\dot{\theta}\hat{\mathbf{u}}$ has three terms:

$$\mathbf{a} = \ddot{\mathbf{r}} = (\ddot{r}\hat{\mathbf{r}} + \dot{r}\dot{\hat{\mathbf{r}}}) + (\dot{r}\dot{\theta}\hat{\mathbf{u}} + r\ddot{\theta}\hat{\mathbf{u}} + r\dot{\theta}\dot{\hat{\mathbf{u}}})$$

$$= \ddot{r}\hat{\mathbf{r}} + \dot{r}\dot{\theta}\hat{\mathbf{u}} + \dot{r}\dot{\theta}\hat{\mathbf{u}} + r\ddot{\theta}\hat{\mathbf{u}} - r\dot{\theta}^2\hat{\mathbf{r}}$$

$$= (\ddot{r} - r\dot{\theta}^2)\hat{\mathbf{r}} + (2\dot{r}\dot{\theta} + r\ddot{\theta})\hat{\mathbf{u}}.$$

This gives the following radial ($\hat{\mathbf{r}}$) and transverse ($\hat{\mathbf{u}}$) components.

	Radial	Transverse
Velocity $\mathbf{v}$	$\dot{r}$	$r\dot{\theta}$
Acceleration $\mathbf{a}$	$\ddot{r} - r\dot{\theta}^2$	$2\dot{r}\dot{\theta} + r\ddot{\theta}$

Note the following special cases.

(1) θ constant: the motion is in a straight line through the origin. $\dot{\theta} = \ddot{\theta} = 0$ and the velocity and acceleration reduce to $\dot{r}$ and $\ddot{r}$ radially, i.e. in the direction of motion.

(2) r and $\dot{\theta}$ constant ($r = k$ and $\dot{\theta} = \omega$ say): the motion is with constant speed v ($= k\omega$) round a circle. The acceleration reduces to $-k\omega^2$ radially, i.e. $k\omega^2$ towards the centre of the circle, which may also be written as v^2/k.

(3) r only is constant ($r = k$ say): the motion is circular but the speed is not constant. There is an acceleration $k\ddot{\theta}$ ($= \dot{v}$) transversely, i.e. tangential to the circle, as well as $-k\omega^2$ ($= -v^2/k$) radially.

Example 4

Show that, for a particle which moves so that $r = \sqrt{(at + b)}$, the radial acceleration is $-v^2/r$, whatever the function for θ.

Solution

The radial acceleration is $\ddot{r} - r\dot{\theta}^2$, so we need to find $\ddot{r}$.

To avoid complications with the square root we square before differentiating twice:

$$r^2 = at + b$$

$$\Rightarrow \qquad 2r\dot{r} = a \qquad \text{(using the chain rule)}$$

$$\Rightarrow 2\dot{r}^2 + 2r\ddot{r} = 0 \qquad \text{(using the product rule)}$$

$$\Rightarrow \qquad \ddot{r} = -\dot{r}^2/r.$$

The radial acceleration is

$$\ddot{r} - r\dot{\theta}^2 = -\dot{r}^2/r - r\dot{\theta}^2$$
$$= -(\dot{r}^2 + (r\dot{\theta})^2)/r.$$

But the radial and transverse components of $\mathbf{v}$ are $\dot{r}$ and $r\dot{\theta}$, so that $v^2 = \dot{r}^2 + (r\dot{\theta})^2$.

Therefore the radial acceleration is $-v^2/r$, as required.　　□

Exercise 2D

1　Find the velocity and acceleration vectors in terms of $\hat{\mathbf{r}}$ and $\hat{\mathbf{u}}$ when $r = 10 + \sin t$, $\theta = 2t$. Sketch the path of a particle moving in this way. Calculate the velocity and acceleration when $t = \pi/3$ and when $t = 2\pi/3$.

2　A gramophone record is rotating at $33\frac{1}{3}$ revolutions per minute. What is its angular velocity in radians per second? While the record is rotating, a spider crawls from the centre along a radius at 3 cm s^{-1}. Find the polar equation of the spider's path. Find the magnitude and direction of the spider's velocity when it is 12 cm from the centre.

3　A fairground roundabout is rotating with constant angular velocity ω. The attendant, having collected the fares, walks along a radius towards the centre with constant speed u relative to the roundabout. Find the magnitude and direction of his acceleration when his distance from the centre is r.

4　The position of a point after t seconds is given by $r = \cos\theta$, $\theta = t$. Show that the point traces out a circle with constant speed, but that the speed is not equal to $r\dot{\theta}$. Show that the acceleration is of constant magnitude and is always directed towards the centre of the circle, but is not equal to v^2/r.

5　The velocity of a particle is $ar\hat{\mathbf{r}} + b\theta\hat{\mathbf{u}}$, where a and b are constants. Prove that the acceleration is

$$\left(a^2 r - \frac{b^2\theta^2}{r}\right)\hat{\mathbf{r}} + b\theta\left(a + \frac{b}{r}\right)\hat{\mathbf{u}}.$$

6　A particle moves so that its velocity is $r^2\hat{\mathbf{r}} + \theta^2\hat{\mathbf{u}}$. Given that $r = \theta = 1$ when $t = 0$, find r and θ in terms of t. Deduce that

$$r = \left(\frac{\theta}{2 - \theta}\right)^{\frac{1}{2}}.$$

*7　Show that an alternative expression for the transverse acceleration $2\dot{r}\dot{\theta} + r\ddot{\theta}$ is $\dfrac{1}{r}\dfrac{d}{dt}(r^2\dot{\theta})$. (This is not merely a curiosity—see §4.2 and Exercise 14B, question 6.)

8　A particle moves along the curve $r\theta = a$ in such a way that the transverse acceleration is always zero. Show that the acceleration is inversely proportional to r^3.

9　Fig. 11 shows a particle on the end of a string which is unwinding in a horizontal plane from a cylindrical reel of radius b whose axis is vertical. Initially the particle is in contact with the reel and is given a velocity away from the axis of the reel; after a time t the radius to the point where the string leaves the reel has rotated through an angle θ. $\hat{\mathbf{u}}$ and $\hat{\mathbf{n}}$ are unit vectors along and at right angles to this radius. Express the position vector of the particle, relative to the point in the plane of motion on the axis of the reel, in terms of b, θ, $\hat{\mathbf{u}}$ and $\hat{\mathbf{n}}$, and deduce its velocity and acceleration.

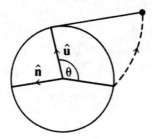

Figure 11

Supposing that the only force in the plane on the particle is the tension of the string, prove that θ is proportional to $\sqrt{t}$, and that the magnitude of the acceleration of the particle is inversely proportional to θ.   [SMP]

10   The position vector of a particle is given by

$$\mathbf{r} = \hat{\mathbf{r}} a \cos (3\theta), \qquad \theta = \omega t,$$

where a and ω are constants and t is time.

Show that when r is a maximum the speed of the particle is a minimum and its acceleration a maximum and that when r is a minimum the speed is a maximum and the acceleration a minimum. Find these maximum and minimum values in each case.   [MEI]

3

Conics

3.1 A PRELIMINARY INVESTIGATION

Fig. 1 consists of circles $C_1, C_2, \ldots, C_{12}$ with centre C_0, radii $1, 2, \ldots, 12$ units, and parallel lines $L_0, L_1, \ldots, L_{24}$ spaced at unit intervals. On A4 paper a unit of 1 cm is suitable.

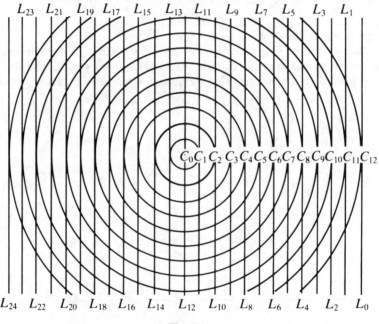

Figure 1

On a copy of this diagram mark the following points of intersection of lines and circles:

$$L_9 \cap C_3, \quad L_{12} \cap C_4, \quad L_{15} \cap C_5, \quad L_{18} \cap C_6.$$

These points are all of the form $L_p \cap C_q$ with $q = \frac{1}{3}p$, and it is fairly simple to plot intermediate points by eye. For example, $L_{13.5} \cap C_{4.5}$ is halfway between L_{13} and L_{14}, and halfway between C_4 and C_5. Plot some of these extra points, and then join all the points with a smooth curve. Label this curve (i).

In a similar way, plot the intersections $L_p \cap C_q$ and join them with a smooth

40

curve in each of the following cases:

(ii) $q = \frac{1}{2}p$, (iii) $q = p$, (iv) $q = 2p$, (v) $q = 3p$.

You should obtain curves as shown in Fig. 2. The closed curves (i) and (ii) are *ellipses*; curve (iii) is a *parabola*, and curves (iv) and (v) are parts of *hyperbolas*. From the method of drawing them it is clear that all these curves are symmetrical about the line through C_0 perpendicular to L_0; we call this the *axis*.

The diagram suggests a gradual transition from one curve to the next as the constant e in the defining equation $q = ep$ increases. You may wonder whether curves (iii), (iv), (v) would eventually close if they were extended, and why we distinguish between the parabola and hyperbola when they look so similar. These questions are investigated in the following exercise.

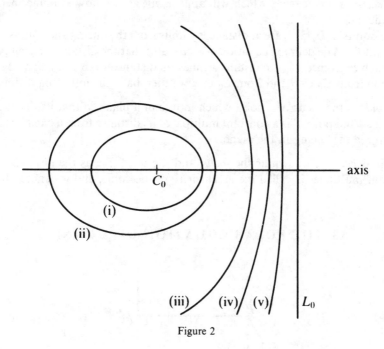

Figure 2

Exercise 3A

The curve in this exercise is the locus $\{L_p \cap C_q\}$, where L_p and C_q are as in §3.1.

1 Show that the curve meets the axis at points where either $p + q = 12$ or $p - q = 12$.

2 Given that $q = ep$, where $0 < e < 1$, find in terms of e the two values of p where the curve meets the axis. Check that your answers agree with your drawings for ellipses (i) and (ii) of §3.1.

3 For the case $0 < e < 1$, find in terms of e the distance between the two points where the curve meets the axis.

4 Find what happens to the results of questions 2 and 3 as $e \to 1$. Show that the parabola (curve (iii), with $e = 1$) meets the axis at only one point.

5 Given that $q = ep$, where $e > 1$, show that the equations of question 1 give two solutions for p in terms of e, one positive and the other negative. Suggest a meaning for lines L_p with negative p. Show on a diagram the two points of intersection with the axis for each of the hyperbolas (iv) and (v) of §3.1. (This indicates that when $e > 1$ the curve has two branches; further details come in the next section.)

3.2 THE FOCUS–DIRECTRIX DEFINITION OF A CONIC

The curves investigated in the previous section have many interesting geometrical properties, and many important practical applications, especially in connection with orbits (see Chapter 5). These curves are known as *conics*, or *conic sections*, for reasons which will appear in §3.6; we now examine them in more detail.

The points of $L_p \cap C_q$ are at distances p units from the line L_0 and q units from the point C_0. The defining equation $q = ep$ states that the distance of each point of the curve from C_0 is a constant e times its distance from L_0. Changing the notation from C_0 to S and from L_0 to d we then have the following definition.

A *conic* is the locus of a point which moves in a plane so that its distance from a fixed point S is a constant multiple of its distance from a fixed line d, both S and d being in the plane.

The fixed point is known as the *focus*, and the fixed line as the *directrix*. The constant multiplier is called the *eccentricity* of the conic, and is denoted by e.

3.3 THE POLAR EQUATION OF A CONIC

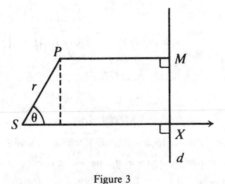

Figure 3

Choose the focus S to be the origin, and the perpendicular from S to the directrix d to be the initial line (Fig. 3). Then P lies on the conic

$$\Leftrightarrow \qquad SP = e\,PM$$

$$\Leftrightarrow \qquad r = e(SX - r\cos\theta)$$

$$\Leftrightarrow r(1 + e \cos \theta) = e\,SX$$

$$= \text{constant } (= l, \text{ say})$$

$$\Leftrightarrow \qquad \frac{l}{r} = 1 + e \cos \theta$$

which is the polar equation of a conic with the focus as pole.

When $\theta = \pi/2$, $\cos \theta = 0$ and so $l/r = 1$, i.e. $r = l$ (Fig. 4).

The chord of the conic through the focus parallel to the directrix is called the *latus rectum* (meaning 'upright side'). Thus the constant l in the polar equation equals half the length of the latus rectum.

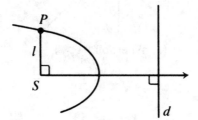

Figure 4

The polar equation can be written in the form

$$r = \frac{l}{1 + e \cos \theta},$$

from which we have the following three cases:

(a) If $0 < e < 1$ then $1 + e \cos \theta$ is never zero, so r is always finite. The conic is an ellipse, a closed curve (Fig. 5).

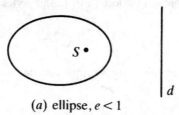

Figure 5   (a) ellipse, $e < 1$

(b) If $e = 1$ then $1 + e \cos \theta = 0$ when $\theta = \pi$, so that r increases without limit as θ approaches π. The conic is a parabola, open towards the $\theta = \pi$ direction (Fig. 6).

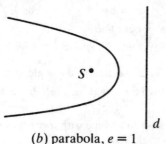

Figure 6   (b) parabola, $e = 1$

(c) If $e > 1$ then $1 + e \cos \theta = 0$ when $\cos \theta = -1/e$, which gives two values of θ for which r is undefined, and r can take negative values. The conic is a hyperbola, with two branches (Fig. 7). This has already been considered in detail in Example 2 of Chapter 2 (page 31).

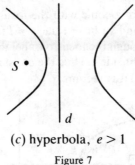

(c) hyperbola, $e > 1$

Figure 7

Exercise 3B

1   Find the polar equation of each of the five curves drawn in §3.1.

2   Find the values of l and e for each of the conics in Exercise 2B, question 4.

3   Find the polar equation of the directrix of the conic $l/r = 1 + e \cos \theta$.

4   Identify the curve with polar equation $l/r = 1 + e \cos \theta$ in the special cases (a) $e = 0$; (b) $l = 0$. (Because of these extreme cases, circles and line pairs are also counted as conics.)

5   The chord PQ passes through the focus S of a conic with semi-latus rectum l. Prove that

$$\frac{1}{PS} + \frac{1}{QS} = \frac{2}{l}.$$

6   The chords PQ, HK of an ellipse are perpendicular, and both pass through the focus S. Prove that

$$\frac{1}{PQ} + \frac{1}{HK}$$

is constant.

7   (a) By converting to Cartesian coordinates show that
$$l/r = \cos(\theta - \alpha) + e \cos \theta$$
is the polar equation of a straight line.
(b) Show that this line meets the conic $l/r = 1 + e \cos \theta$ where $\theta = \alpha$ and nowhere else.
(c) Deduce that this line is the tangent to the conic at $\theta = \alpha$.

8   The chord PQ passes through the focus of a conic. Prove that the tangents at P and Q meet on the directrix.

9   The tangents from a point T to a conic with focus S touch the conic at H and K. Prove that angle TSH = angle TSK.

3.4 CARTESIAN EQUATIONS OF CONICS

To find the Cartesian equations of conics we return to the original focus–directrix definition. All conics are clearly symmetrical about the perpendicular SX from the focus S to the directrix, and this line is taken as the x-axis. The most convenient position for the origin then depends on the type of conic, so we deal with the three cases separately.

1 Parabola (e = 1)

Here $PS = PM$, and in particular the midpoint O of SX is a point of the parabola. We take O as the origin. Then the focus is $(a, 0)$ and the directrix is $x = -a$, where a is a constant which fixes the size of the parabola (Fig. 8).

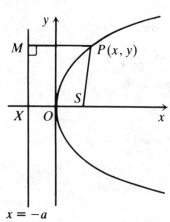

Figure 8

The point $P(x, y)$ is on the parabola

$$\Leftrightarrow \qquad PS = PM$$

$$\Leftrightarrow \qquad PS^2 = PM^2$$

$$\Leftrightarrow (x - a)^2 + y^2 = (x + a)^2$$

$$\Leftrightarrow \qquad y^2 = 4ax$$

which is the standard Cartesian equation of the parabola.

2 Ellipse (e < 1)

The curve meets the x-axis in two points, A and A'. Take the midpoint O of AA' as the origin, and let $AA' = 2a$, $OS = p$, $OX = q$ (Fig. 9). Using the focus–directrix property for A and A' gives

$$a - p = e(q - a)$$

and

$$a + p = e(q + a),$$

from which $p = ae$ and $q = a/e$.

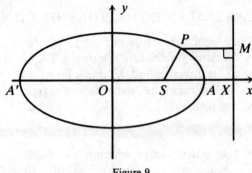

Figure 9

Thus the focus has coordinates $(ae, 0)$, and the equation of the directrix is $x = a/e$.

The point $P(x, y)$ is on the ellipse

$\Leftrightarrow$ $\qquad\qquad PS = e\,PM$

$\Leftrightarrow$ $\qquad\qquad PS^2 = e^2 PM^2$

$\Leftrightarrow$ $\qquad (x - ae)^2 + y^2 = e^2\left(\dfrac{a}{e} - x\right)^2$

$\Leftrightarrow x^2 - 2aex + a^2e^2 + y^2 = a^2 - 2aex + e^2x^2$ $\qquad$ (expanding the squares)

$\Leftrightarrow \qquad x^2(1 - e^2) + y^2 = a^2(1 - e^2)$ $\qquad$ (collecting like terms)

$\Leftrightarrow \qquad \dfrac{x^2}{a^2} + \dfrac{y^2}{a^2(1 - e^2)} = 1$ $\qquad$ (dividing by $a^2(1 - e^2)$) $\quad$ (1)

$\Leftrightarrow \qquad \dfrac{x^2}{a^2} + \dfrac{y^2}{b^2} = 1,$ where $b^2 = a^2(1 - e^2)$.

This is the standard equation of the ellipse.

Q.1 Where does the standard ellipse meet the y-axis?

Q.2 Prove that

$$a = \frac{l}{1 - e^2} \quad \text{and} \quad b^2 = \frac{l^2}{1 - e^2}.$$

(These results give the constants a and b in terms of the original constants e and l.)

3   Hyperbola ($e > 1$)

Exactly the same procedure as for the ellipse can be applied up to the stage marked (1). The diagram is different, with the directrix between the origin and the focus; you should draw your own.

Since $e > 1$ it is more convenient to write (1) as

$$\frac{x^2}{a^2} - \frac{y^2}{a^2(e^2 - 1)} = 1$$

and then define $b^2 = a^2(e^2 - 1)$. This gives the standard equation of the hyperbola

$$\frac{x^2}{a^2} - \frac{y^2}{b^2} = 1, \quad \text{where} \quad b^2 = a^2(e^2 - 1).$$

Q.3 Find a and b in terms of l and e for the hyperbola.

Exercise 3C

1 Use the focus–directrix definition to show that the equation of the parabola with focus $(2, 0)$ and directrix $x = -2$ is $y^2 = 8x$.

2 Find the equation of the parabola with focus $(4, 5)$ and directrix $x = 10$. Show this parabola with its focus and directrix on a sketch diagram.

3 Use $a^2(1 - e^2) = b^2$ to find the eccentricity of the ellipse

$$\frac{x^2}{25} + \frac{y^2}{16} = 1.$$

4 Show that the circle $x^2 + y^2 = 9$ transforms into the ellipse

$$\frac{x^2}{9} + \frac{y^2}{4} = 1$$

under a stretch, factor $\frac{2}{3}$, parallel to the y-axis. What is the area of the ellipse?

5 A transformation given by the matrix $\begin{bmatrix} 4 & 0 \\ 0 & 3 \end{bmatrix}$ is applied to the circle $x^2 + y^2 = 1$. Show that the resulting curve is an ellipse, and find its eccentricity.

6 Find the equation of the ellipse

$$\frac{x^2}{9} + \frac{y^2}{4} = 1$$

after a translation $\begin{bmatrix} -1 \\ 2 \end{bmatrix}$, and show that it can be written in the form

$$4x^2 + 9y^2 + 8x - 36y + 4 = 0.$$

7 A hyperbola has eccentricity 2, focus $S(1, 3)$ and directrix $x = 4$. If P is the point (x, y) on the hyperbola, write down expressions for SP^2 and the square of the distance from P to the directrix.

Use the focus–directrix property to show that the equation of the hyperbola is

$$3x^2 - y^2 - 30x + 6y + 54 = 0.$$

Write this in the form

$$\frac{(x - \lambda)^2}{a^2} - \frac{(y - \mu)^2}{b^2} = 1.$$

About which point does the hyperbola have point symmetry? Check that its eccentricity is 2 using $b^2 = a^2(e^2 - 1)$.

8   For the ellipse with eccentricity $\frac{1}{3}$, focus $(1, -2)$ and directrix $x = -3$, carry out steps similar to those in question 7.

9   Verify that the point $(at^2, 2at)$ lies on the parabola $y^2 = 4ax$, and show conversely that every point of this parabola can be written as $(at^2, 2at)$ by a suitable choice of t. Show on a diagram how the point $(at^2, 2at)$ describes the parabola as t increases from $-\infty$ to ∞.

10 Prove that the chord joining the points $(at_1^2, 2at_1)$ and $(at_2^2, 2at_2)$ has equation

$$2x - (t_1 + t_2)y + 2at_1t_2 = 0.$$

By letting $t_2 \to t_1$, deduce that the equation of the tangent to $y^2 = 4ax$ at $(at_1^2, 2at_1)$ is

$$x - t_1y + at_1^2 = 0.$$

11 Verify that the point $(a \cos \theta, b \sin \theta)$ lies on the ellipse

$$\frac{x^2}{a^2} + \frac{y^2}{b^2} = 1,$$

and show conversely that every point of this ellipse can be written as $(a \cos \theta, b \sin \theta)$ for exactly one θ with $0 \leqslant \theta < 2\pi$. Fig. 10 shows concentric circles of radii a and b with centre O. A variable line through O meets these circles at A and B, and P is the intersection of lines through A and B parallel to the y-axis and x-axis respectively. Prove that the locus of P is an ellipse.

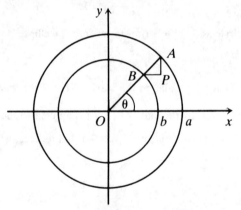

Figure 10

Use this method to draw accurately

$$\frac{x^2}{25} + \frac{y^2}{9} = 1.$$

12 Prove that the ellipse

$$\frac{x^2}{a^2} + \frac{y^2}{b^2} = 1$$

can be obtained by applying the one-way stretch $\begin{bmatrix} 1 & 0 \\ 0 & \dfrac{b}{a} \end{bmatrix}$ to the circle centre O radius a. Find the one-way stretch which transforms the circle centre O radius b into the same ellipse. What is the area of this ellipse?

13 By using the one-way stretch of question 12, or otherwise, prove that the equation of the tangent to

$$\frac{x^2}{a^2} + \frac{y^2}{b^2} = 1$$

at $(a \cos \theta, b \sin \theta)$ is

$$\frac{x \cos \theta}{a} + \frac{y \sin \theta}{b} = 1.$$

14 Show that $x = a \sec \theta$, $y = b \tan \theta$ are parametric equations of the hyperbola

$$\frac{x^2}{a^2} - \frac{y^2}{b^2} = 1.$$

Describe how $(a \sec \theta, b \tan \theta)$ moves along the curve as θ increases from 0 to 2π. What values of θ must be excluded?

15 Prove that the equation of the tangent to

$$\frac{x^2}{a^2} - \frac{y^2}{b^2} = 1$$

at $(a \sec \theta, b \tan \theta)$ is

$$\frac{x \sec \theta}{a} - \frac{y \tan \theta}{b} = 1.$$

3.5 SOME PROPERTIES OF CONICS

1   The parabolic reflector property
If P is any point on a parabola with focus S, and M is the foot of the perpendicular from P to the directrix, then the tangent at P bisects angle SPM (Fig. 11). This is the key to many other geometrical properties and most of the practical uses of parabolas. We give two proofs.

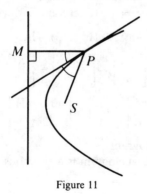

Figure 11

Proof (i)
Consider the motion of P along the curve. At any instant the velocity of P is directed along the tangent at P. But, since $e = 1$ for a parabola, SP always equals MP. Therefore, as P moves, SP and MP must change at the same rate, so that $\dot{r} = \dot{z}$, where $SP = r$ and $MP = z$.

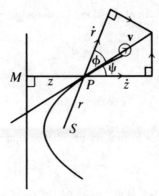

Figure 12

If the tangent at P makes angles ϕ and ψ with SP and MP respectively (Fig. 12), then

$$\dot{r} = v \cos \phi$$

(splitting $\mathbf{v}$ into components along and perpendicular to $\mathbf{SP}$) and

$$\dot{z} = v \cos \psi$$

(splitting $\mathbf{v}$ into components along and perpendicular to $\mathbf{MP}$). Since $\dot{r} = \dot{z}$ it follows that $\cos \phi = \cos \psi$, and so $\phi = \psi$. Therefore the tangent bisects angle SPM.

Proof (ii)
Let P be the point $(at^2, 2at)$ on the parabola $y^2 = 4ax$. Then the tangent at P has equation

$$x - ty + at^2 = 0 \quad \text{(Exercise 3C, question 10)}$$

and meets the x-axis at $T(-at^2, 0)$ (Fig. 13). Thus

$$\mathbf{TM} = \begin{bmatrix} -a \\ 2at \end{bmatrix} - \begin{bmatrix} -at^2 \\ 0 \end{bmatrix} = \begin{bmatrix} a(t^2 - 1) \\ 2at \end{bmatrix}$$

and

$$\mathbf{SP} = \begin{bmatrix} at^2 \\ 2at \end{bmatrix} - \begin{bmatrix} a \\ 0 \end{bmatrix} = \begin{bmatrix} a(t^2 - 1) \\ 2at \end{bmatrix} = \mathbf{TM},$$

so that $SPMT$ is a parallelogram.

But $SP = PM$, so this parallelogram is a rhombus, and therefore PT bisects angle SPM. $\qquad\square$

Q.4 Show that rays of light emitted from the focus and reflected by a parabolic mirror will emerge parallel to the axis, and that an incoming beam parallel to the axis will be focused at the focus (hence the name). (This is why parabolic reflectors are used in headlamps, electric fires and optical or radio telescopes.)

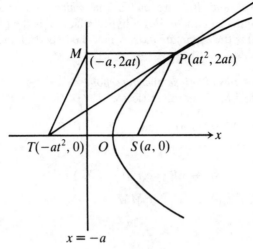

$$x = -a$$

Figure 13

2 Central conics; foci and directrices

Since the standard equations of the ellipse and hyperbola contain only even powers of x and y, both these curves have line symmetry about both coordinate axes, and hence have point symmetry about the origin. The ellipse and hyperbola are called *central conics*. The origin is called the *centre* of the ellipse or hyperbola; any chord through the centre is bisected there, and is called a *diameter*.

We saw in §3.4(2) that the ellipse $\dfrac{x^2}{a^2} + \dfrac{y^2}{b^2} = 1$ has focus $(ae, 0)$ and directrix $x = a/e$. By symmetry in $x = 0$ there is a second focus at $(-ae, 0)$, with the corresponding directrix $x = -a/e$ (Fig. 14). Similarly the hyperbola $\dfrac{x^2}{a^2} - \dfrac{y^2}{b^2} = 1$ has two foci, at $(\pm ae, 0)$, and two directrices, $x = \pm a/e$ (Fig. 15).

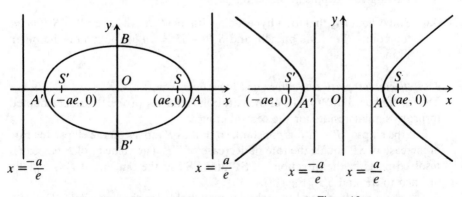

Figure 14   Figure 15

For an ellipse, AA' and BB' are called the *major axis* and *minor axis* respectively, with lengths $2a$ and $2b$. For a hyperbola, AA' is the *transverse axis* with length $2a$; $x = 0$ is the *conjugate axis*, which the hyperbola does not meet.

3   Focal length properties of ellipse and hyperbola
For an ellipse with foci S, S' and directrices d, d',

$$SP = e\, PM \quad \text{and} \quad S'P = e\, PM'$$

so that

$$SP + S'P = e(PM + PM')$$

$$= e\, MM'$$

$$= e \cdot \frac{2a}{e}$$

$$= 2a.$$

Thus the sum of the distances from the foci to any point of the ellipse is constant, and equals the length of the major axis.

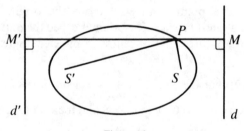

Figure 16

Q.5   Use this property to draw an ellipse with the aid of a loop of thread PSS' passing round pins at S and S'.

Q.6   Show similarly that for a hyperbola with foci S, S' we have $SP - S'P = 2a$ for points P on one branch, and $S'P - SP = 2a$ for points on the other branch.

4   Reflector properties of ellipse and hyperbola
The method used in Proof (i) of the parabolic reflector property can be adapted to prove similar results for the central conics.

For the ellipse $SP + S'P$ is constant, so that as P moves on the ellipse the rate of increase of SP equals the rate of decrease of $S'P$. The velocity of P has equal resolved parts in the directions of **SP** and **PS'**, so the tangent at P is equally inclined to SP and $S'P$ (Fig. 17).

The same result, proved in a similar way, holds for the hyperbola (Fig. 18).

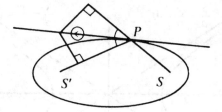

Figure 17

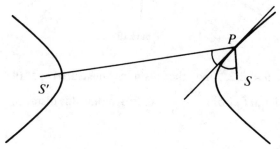

Figure 18

Q.7 Write out the proof of the hyperbolic reflector property.

5   The asymptotes of a hyperbola
We saw in Exercise 3C, questions 14 and 15 that $(a \sec \theta, b \tan \theta)$ lies on the hyperbola

$$\frac{x^2}{a^2} - \frac{y^2}{b^2} = 1,$$

that the equation of the tangent at this point is

$$\frac{x \sec \theta}{a} - \frac{y \tan \theta}{b} = 1,$$

and that the point moves to infinity along the curve as $\theta \to \pi/2$ or $\theta \to 3\pi/2$.

In order to see what happens to the tangent as the point moves to infinity we first multiply throughout the equation of the tangent by $\cos \theta$, giving

$$\frac{x}{a} - \frac{y}{b} \sin \theta = \cos \theta.$$

As $\theta \to \pi/2$, $\sin \theta \to 1$ and $\cos \theta \to 0$, so the tangent approaches the line $x/a - y/b = 0$. As $\theta \to 3\pi/2$, $\sin \theta \to -1$ and $\cos \theta \to 0$, so the tangent approaches the line $x/a + y/b = 0$. These two 'tangents at infinity' are called the *asymptotes* of the hyperbola; the hyperbola approaches arbitrarily close to them, but never meets them (Fig. 19).

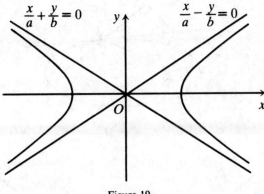

Figure 19

Q.8 For $0 < \theta < \pi/2$, find the distance measured parallel to $x = 0$ of $(a \sec \theta, b \tan \theta)$ from $\dfrac{x}{a} - \dfrac{y}{b} = 0$. Prove that this distance tends to zero as $\theta \to \pi/2$).

Exercise 3D

1   The point P is on a parabola with focus S; M is the foot of the perpendicular from P to the directrix. The tangent at P meets SM at Z. Prove that PZ is the perpendicular bisector of SM.

2   Mark a point S on a piece of paper about 5 cm from one straight edge l. Fold the paper so that l passes through S, and make a sharp crease. Repeat this several times, changing the direction of l but making sure that it always passes through S. Use question 1 to prove that all these creases touch a parabola.

3   With the notation of question 1, prove that Z lies on the tangent at the vertex O (where the axis meets the parabola).

4   Draw a straight line m and a point S not on it. Place a set square with the right angle on m and one arm of the right angle through S. Draw the other arm of the right angle. Repeat this several times, changing the position of the set square. Use question 3 to prove that all the lines you draw touch a parabola.

5   A radio telescope has a parabolic dish of radius 25 m, and its depth at the centre is 8 m. An aerial is situated at the focus of the dish; find its distance from the deepest point in the dish.

6   A *focal chord* of a parabola is a chord which passes through the focus. If P, Q have co-ordinates $(ap^2, 2ap)$, $(aq^2, 2aq)$ prove that PQ is a focal chord $\Leftrightarrow pq = -1$.
   Prove that the tangents at the ends of a focal chord meet at right angles on the directrix.

7   Prove that a circle which has a focal chord of a parabola as a diameter touches the directrix.

8   The width of a river is x, and A, B are points on the two river banks directly opposite each other. A swimmer starts from A and always aims towards B. The swimmer's speed in still water is u, and the speed of the current is v.

(a) Show that if $u = v$ then the swimmer's path is part of a parabola, and that the swimmer approaches the point $\frac{1}{2}x$ downstream from B.

(b) Give rough sketches of the swimmer's path
(i) when $u > v$; (ii) when $u < v$.

9   A paraboloid P is the set of points in three-dimensional space which are equidistant from a fixed point S and a fixed plane D. If, referred to rectangular Cartesian axes, S is the point $(0, 0, 2)$ and D is the plane $z = -2$, show that the equation of P is $x^2 + y^2 = 8z$.

Show that the plane $y = 4$ intersects P in a parabola, and find its focus and directrix.   [SMP]

10 An ellipse has foci S, S'. The perpendicular from S to the tangent at a point P of the ellipse meets that tangent at Q and meets $S'P$ produced at H. Prove that $HP = SP$, and deduce that the locus of H is a circle centre S'. What is the radius of this circle?

11 Mark a point S on a circular piece of paper. Fold the paper so that the circumference passes through S, and make a sharp crease. Repeat this several times, changing the position of the crease. Use question 10 to prove that all the creases touch an ellipse. Where are the foci? (Compare with question 2.)

12 With Q as in question 10, prove that Q lies on the circle which has diameter the major axis AA'.

13 Draw a circle and mark a point S inside it. Place a set square with the right angle on the circle and one arm of the right angle through S. Draw the other arm of the right angle. Repeat this several times, changing the position of the set square. Use question 12 to prove that all the lines you draw touch an ellipse. (Compare with question 4.)

14 Find results for the hyperbola which correspond to those in questions 12 and 13.

15 The tangent at a point P on a hyperbola meets the asymptotes at U, V. Prove that P is the midpoint of UV. Prove also that as P varies the area of triangle OUV is constant.

16 Prove that the directrices of the hyperbola $\dfrac{x^2}{a^2} - \dfrac{y^2}{b^2} = 1$ pass through the points where the circle $x^2 + y^2 = a^2$ meets the asymptotes.

17 A *rectangular hyperbola* is a hyperbola whose asymptotes are perpendicular. Prove that all rectangular hyperbolas have eccentricity $\sqrt{2}$.

Since the asymptotes of a rectangular hyperbola are perpendicular they can be used as coordinate axes. By rotating $x^2 - y^2 = a^2$ through $\pi/4$ about O prove that the equation of a rectangular hyperbola referred to its asymptotes as axes is $xy = c^2$, where $c^2 = a^2/2$.

18 Prove that $x = ct$, $y = c/t$ are parametric equations for a rectangular hyperbola. Prove that the equation of the chord joining $(ct_1, c/t_1)$ and $(ct_2, c/t_2)$ is $x + t_1 t_2 y = c(t_1 + t_2)$, and deduce the equation of the tangent at $(ct_1, c/t_1)$.

19 The vertices of a triangle are on a rectangular hyperbola. Prove that the orthocentre of the triangle (where the three altitudes meet) is also on the hyperbola.

20 A variable circle C touches two fixed circles C_1, C_2. Prove that the locus of the centre of C is:
(a) an ellipse if C_1 lies entirely inside C_2;
(b) both branches of a hyperbola if C_1 lies entirely outside C_2.
What is the locus if C_1 and C_2 intersect?

21 The equation $x^2 + 2\alpha xy + y^2 = 1$ represents a conic for any value of α. It can be written, because of its symmetry, as

$$p(x + y)^2 + q(x - y)^2 = 1. \tag{1}$$

Calculate the coefficients p and q in terms of α.

Use equation (1) to calculate the lengths of the axes of the conic and hence, or otherwise, determine the eccentricity of the conic for the cases (a) $0 < \alpha < 1$, (b) $\alpha > 1$.

What types of conic are represented by the cases (i) $\alpha = \frac{1}{2}$, (ii) $\alpha = 2$?   [SMP]

3.6 CONICS AS SECTIONS OF A CONE

As their name suggests, the conic sections were originally studied (by the Greeks, especially Apollonius of Perga, 247–205 B.C.) as sections of a cone.

Figs. 20–22 suggest how an inclined plane can cut a double circular cone in an ellipse, parabola, or hyperbola, depending on the angle of inclination of the plane.

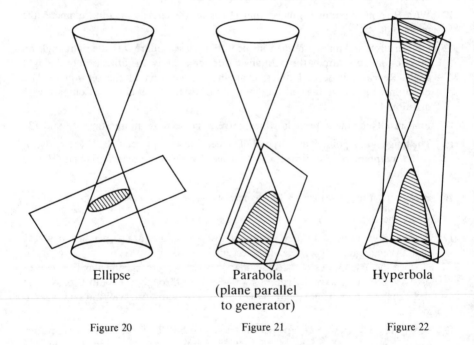

Ellipse	Parabola	Hyperbola
	(plane parallel	
	to generator)	
Figure 20	Figure 21	Figure 22

Q.9 Show how to obtain (a) a circle (b) a line pair as sections of a cone.

Project Exercise 3E

The following exercise uses a method devised by Dandelin in 1822 to show that these sections are indeed conics as defined in §3.2 (Note 3.1). The notation refers to Fig. 23 which shows a cone with a vertical axis and vertex V cut by a plane Π. The angle between any generator of the cone and the vertical is α; the angle between any line of greatest slope of Π and the vertical is β. A sphere touches Π at S, and touches the cone in a horizontal circle. The horizontal plane through this circle of contact meets Π in the line d. From any point P on the intersection of the cone and Π perpendiculars are drawn meeting d at M, and meeting the horizontal plane at N; PV meets the circle of contact at Q.

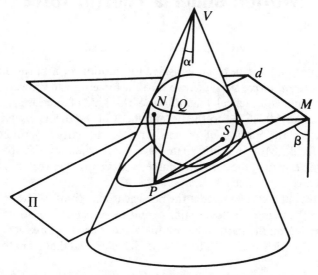

Figure 23

In questions 1–8 prove the following properties of the Dandelin figure.

1 $PS = PQ$.

2 $\angle NPQ = \alpha$.

3 $PN = PS \cos \alpha$.

4 $\angle NPM = \beta$.

5 $PN = PM \cos \beta$.

6 $PS = \dfrac{\cos \beta}{\cos \alpha} PM$.

7 P lies on the conic with focus S, directrix d, and eccentricity $\cos \beta / \cos \alpha$.

8 This conic is an ellipse if $\beta > \alpha$, a parabola if $\beta = \alpha$, and a hyperbola if $\beta < \alpha$.

9 Are there any other spheres which touch Π and the cone? Taking separately the three cases $\beta > \alpha$, $\beta = \alpha$, $\beta < \alpha$, describe the positions of these spheres if they exist, and identify their points of contact with Π.

10 Prove the focal distance properties ($SP + S'P =$ constant for the ellipse, $|SP - S'P| =$ constant for the hyperbola) directly from the Dandelin figure.

11 An ellipse has major axis AA' and foci S, S'. Prove that the locus of points from which this ellipse appears as a circle is a hyperbola with transverse axis SS' and foci A, A'.

   (*Hint*: at such a point the rays of light entering the eye from the ellipse form a circular cone.)

4

Motion under a central force

4.1 CENTRAL FORCES

In this chapter and the next we consider the motion of a particle under the action of a *central force*, by which we mean a force directed towards or away from a fixed point O. Practical illustrations of this kind of force are plentiful. The earliest examples, which led to the development of the theory by Newton and others, concern the motion of planets (treated as particles) round the sun (treated as fixed). More recently there have come satellites and space probes; relative to the centre of the earth, the force of attraction between a satellite and the earth is a central force.

Suppose that at a certain instant the particle is at a point P. Then the particle is moving in the plane which contains O and the tangent at P to its path. The only force acting on the particle lies in this plane, since the force acts along OP. Therefore the particle continues to move in this plane, so that its path must be a plane curve.

The only central forces we shall consider are those which depend only on the distance OP.

Taking O to be the origin for polar co-ordinates in the plane of the motion, let the force on the particle be $-F(r)\hat{\mathbf{r}}$. The minus sign is used here so that $F(r)$ is positive for a force attracting the particle towards O.

One simple example of motion under a central force should be familiar already: motion in a circle with constant speed (Note 4.1). For a particle of mass m moving with constant speed V round a circle of radius R the acceleration is V^2/R towards the centre of the circle, and the central force required to maintain the motion is mV^2/R.

Now
$$\frac{mV^2}{R} = F(R) \Leftrightarrow V = \sqrt{\left(\frac{RF(R)}{m}\right)}.$$

Therefore if the particle, moving under this central force, is projected from a point P, where $OP = R$, with this speed V and in a direction perpendicular to OP, it will move with this same constant speed V round the circle with centre O and radius R.

Exercise 4A

(Take the radius of the earth as 6400 km.)

1 A satellite of mass 1000 kg is moving in a circular orbit 480 km above the earth's surface with constant speed 27 300 km h^{-1}. Find the time for one orbit and the central force acting on the satellite.

2 A satellite is moving in a circular orbit around the earth. If the time for one orbit is 96 minutes and the height of the satellite above the earth is 500 km, find its constant speed. Find the force acting on it if its mass is 800 kg.

3 A particle of mass m subject to a central attraction $F(r)$ is made to move in a circular orbit by projecting it at the appropriate speed V at right angles to the radius vector. Given that V is the same whatever the initial point of projection, find an expression for $F(r)$.

4 The force acting on a space capsule orbiting the earth is inversely proportional to the square of its distance from the centre of the earth. Show that in circular orbit its distance from the centre of the earth is inversely proportional to the square of its speed.

Two space capsules of equal mass are in circular orbits around the earth at heights of 490 km and 320 km. The speed of the latter is 27 700 km h^{-1}; find the speed of the former.

5 Kepler's Third Law (see p. 71) states that the square of the time taken by a planet to orbit the sun varies as the cube of its mean distance from the sun. Assuming for the sake of simplicity that the planets move in circular orbits with constant speeds with the sun as centre, deduce from Kepler's Third Law that the forces with which the sun attracts the planets are proportional to their masses and inversely proportional to the squares of their distances from the sun. (A more exact argument, using the proper elliptical orbits, is given on p. 79.)

4.2 THE RADIAL AND TRANSVERSE EQUATIONS OF MOTION

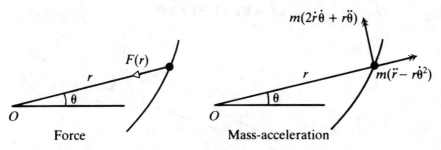

Figure 1

Equating force and mass-acceleration for a particular of mass m subject to a central force $-F(r)\hat{r}$ gives

radially $$-F(r) = m(\ddot{r} - r\dot{\theta}^2) \tag{1}$$

transversely $$0 = m(2\dot{r}\dot{\theta} + r\ddot{\theta}). \tag{2}$$

For the moment we shall concentrate on the transverse equation (2). Since $2\dot{r}\dot{\theta} + r\ddot{\theta} = \dfrac{1}{r}\dfrac{d}{dt}(r^2\dot{\theta})$ (Exercise 2D, question 7),

(2) $$\Leftrightarrow \frac{m}{r}\frac{d}{dt}(r^2\dot{\theta}) = 0$$

$$\Leftrightarrow \frac{d}{dt}(r^2\dot{\theta}) = 0$$

$$\Leftrightarrow r^2\dot{\theta} \text{ is constant, } h \text{ say,}$$

i.e. $$r^2\dot{\theta} = h. \tag{3}$$

This important and useful result holds for all motion under a central force, whatever the nature of $F(r)$. Conversely, if a particle moves so that $r^2\dot{\theta}$ is constant then the transverse component of acceleration is zero, so the only possible force on the particle is a central force.

Q.1 Show that if a particle moves in a circle when subject to a force directed towards the centre of the circle then it must move with constant speed.

Q.2 What are the SI units of h?

One immediate consequence of (3) is that $\dot{\theta} = h/r^2$, which is of constant sign. It is usual to choose the sense of rotation so that h is positive, in which case θ always increases for motion under a central force. In most practical problems r has a positive least value. If r becomes zero in a finite time (so that the particle reaches the centre of attraction) then the physical circumstances usually change drastically, and we are not concerned with the subsequent motion.

4.3 AREAL SPEED

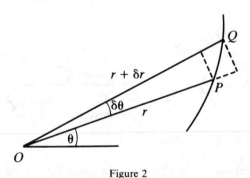

Figure 2

Suppose that the particle moves from P to Q in time δt under the action of a central force. Let P, Q have polar coordinates (r, θ), $(r + \delta r, \theta + \delta\theta)$, and let the area of sector POQ be δA (Fig. 2). Then

$$\tfrac{1}{2}r^2\delta\theta < \delta A < \tfrac{1}{2}(r + \delta r)^2\delta\theta$$

so that $\tfrac{1}{2}r^2\dfrac{\delta\theta}{\delta t} < \dfrac{\delta A}{\delta t} < \tfrac{1}{2}(r + \delta r)^2\dfrac{\delta\theta}{\delta t}$. As $\delta t \to 0$ the first and last terms tend to

$\frac{1}{2}r^2\dot\theta$, so $\delta A/\delta t$, which is sandwiched between them, must also tend to $\frac{1}{2}r^2\dot\theta$. Thus

$$\frac{dA}{dt} = \tfrac{1}{2}r^2\dot\theta = \tfrac{1}{2}h.$$

The quantity $\dfrac{dA}{dt}$ is called the *areal speed*. It follows that, for motion under any central force, the rate at which the radius vector sweeps out area is constant, and that h equals twice this areal speed.

Q.3 Consider how the above argument must be modifed if r decreases as θ increases.

Since the areal speed is constant, the time taken for the particle to move from an initial position P_0 to P_1 is proportional to the area A of the sector P_0OP_1. This area can be found by integration, for

$$\frac{dA}{d\theta} \times \dot\theta = \frac{dA}{dt} = \tfrac{1}{2}r^2\dot\theta \Rightarrow \frac{dA}{d\theta} = \tfrac{1}{2}r^2$$

and so
$$A = \int_{\theta_0}^{\theta_1} \tfrac{1}{2}r^2 d\theta.$$

This gives a straightforward method for finding the time taken to reach any point on the orbit.

Example 1
A particle describes the curve $r = 2 + \cos\theta$ under a central force acting towards O. Sketch the orbit. If the particle is initially at $\theta = 0$ with speed 5 m s^{-1}, find the time taken to reach $\theta = \pi/2$.

Solution
The orbit is as shown in Fig. 3 (a limaçon).

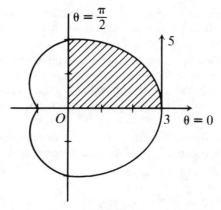

Figure 3

By symmetry, when $\theta = 0$ the velocity has zero radial component, and so the transverse component $r\dot\theta$ is 5 m s^{-1} when $\theta = 0$.

Thus $h = r^2\dot\theta = r \times r\dot\theta = 3 \times 5 = 15$ m^2 s^{-1}, and the areal speed is $15/2$ m^2 s^{-1}.

The shaded area (in m^2) $= \displaystyle\int_0^{\pi/2} \tfrac{1}{2}r^2 d\theta$

$$= \int_0^{\pi/2} \tfrac{1}{2}(2 + \cos\theta)^2 d\theta$$

$$= \int_0^{\pi/2} (2 + 2\cos\theta + \tfrac{1}{2}\cos^2\theta)d\theta$$

$$= \int_0^{\pi/2} (\tfrac{9}{4} + 2\cos\theta + \tfrac{1}{4}\cos 2\theta)d\theta$$

$$\text{using } \cos^2\theta = \tfrac{1}{2}(1 + \cos 2\theta)$$

$$= [\tfrac{9}{4}\theta + 2\sin\theta + \tfrac{1}{8}\sin 2\theta]_0^{\pi/2}$$

$$= \tfrac{9}{8}\pi + 2.$$

The time taken to move from $\theta = 0$ to $\theta = \pi/2$ is therefore

$$(\tfrac{9}{8}\pi + 2) \div \tfrac{15}{2} \ (\approx 0.74) \text{ seconds.} \qquad \square$$

Q.4 Find the time taken to move from $\theta = \pi/2$ to $\theta = \pi$.

Exercise 4B

1 A particle moves round the curve $r = 3 + 2\cos\theta$ under a central force acting towards O. Sketch the orbit. When $\theta = 0$ the particle has speed 4 m s^{-1}. Find the constant h and the time taken to move from $\theta = 0$ to $\theta = \pi/3$.

2 A particle moves round the curve $r = 4 + \sin 4\theta$ under a central force acting towards O. Sketch the orbit. If the particle takes 20 seconds to move once round the orbit, how long does it take to move from $\theta = 0$ to $\theta = \pi/4$?

3 The path of a particle of unit mass is given parametrically by the equations $r = t$, $\theta = 6\pi/t$. Sketch the curve for the values of t from 1 to 12. Find the velocity and acceleration vectors in terms of their radial and transverse components, and show that this motion is consistent with motion under a central force. Find this force when $t = 2$ and when $t = 3$.

4 A particle describes the curve $r = 1/\sqrt{t}$, $\theta = kt^2$. Show that this motion is consistent with motion under a central force. If the areal speed is 10 units find the value of k.

5 A particle moves along the equiangular spiral $r = ae^{k\theta}$ $(k < 0)$ under a central force towards O (Fig. 4).

Prove that the times taken to move along successive whorls (from P_1 to P_2, from P_2 to $P_3, \ldots$) form a geometric sequence, and find its common ratio.

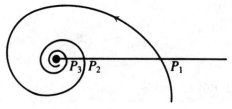

Figure 4

6 The diameter OA of a circle has length $2k$. A particle is projected with speed V from A perpendicular to OA, and moves round the circle under the action of a central force directed towards O (Fig. 5). Prove that the time taken to move from A to P, where $A\hat{O}P = \theta$, is $(k/V)(\theta + \sin\theta\cos\theta)$.

Find the time T taken by the particle to reach O. Use an approximate method to estimate the value of θ after time $\frac{1}{2}T$.

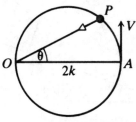

Figure 5

4.4 OTHER INTERPRETATIONS OF h

There are three further useful interpretations of the quantity h. As before, we suppose that the particle moves from P to Q in time δt.

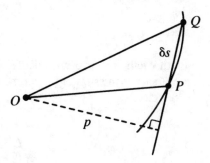

Figure 6

(a) Let the perpendicular from O to PQ be of length p, and let $PQ = \delta s$ (Fig. 6). Then the area of the triangle POQ is $\frac{1}{2}p\,\delta s$, so that

$$\frac{\delta A}{\delta t} \approx \frac{1}{2}p\,\frac{\delta s}{\delta t}.$$

In the limit as $\delta t \to 0$,

$$\frac{dA}{dt} = \tfrac{1}{2}p\frac{ds}{dt} = \tfrac{1}{2}pv,$$

where v is the speed. But

$$\frac{dA}{dt} = \tfrac{1}{2}h,$$

and therefore

$$pv = h.$$

Thus h equals the product of the speed and the perpendicular distance from O to the tangent to the path at P; this product is called the *moment of the velocity* about O. Similarly, the quantity mh, which equals the product $p \times mv$, is called the *moment of momentum*; there will be much more to say about this in Chapter 10.

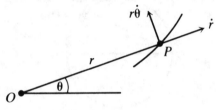

Figure 7

(b) The velocity at P has radial and transverse components $\dot{r}$ and $r\dot{\theta}$ (Fig. 7). The moments of these components about O are respectively:

zero (since the radial vector passes through O);

and

$$r \times r\dot{\theta} = r^2\dot{\theta} = h$$

(since the transverse vector through P is at perpendicular distance r from O).

Thus the moment of the velocity is the sum of the moments of the radial and transverse components of velocity.

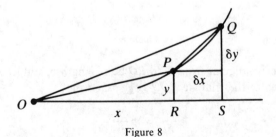

Figure 8

(c) Let P, Q have Cartesian coordinates (x, y), $(x + \delta x, y + \delta y)$ (Fig. 8). Then

$$\delta A \approx \triangle POQ$$
$$= \triangle OQS - \triangle OPR - RPQS$$
$$= \tfrac{1}{2}(x + \delta x)(y + \delta y) - \tfrac{1}{2}xy - \tfrac{1}{2}(y + y + \delta y)\delta x$$
$$= \tfrac{1}{2}(x\delta y - y\delta x).$$

Dividing by δt and taking the limit as $\delta t \to 0$ gives

$$\frac{dA}{dt} = \tfrac{1}{2}(x\dot{y} - y\dot{x})$$

and therefore $\qquad\qquad x\dot{y} - y\dot{x} = h.$

If the velocity of P is written in component form $\begin{bmatrix} \dot{x} \\ \dot{y} \end{bmatrix}$ then $x\dot{y}$ and $-y\dot{x}$ are the moments of the two components about O (Fig. 9), so their total $x\dot{y} - y\dot{x}$ is the moment of the velocity about O, as in (a).

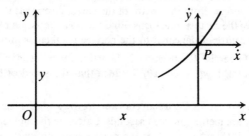

Figure 9

Q.5 Use the relations $x = r \cos \theta$, $y = r \sin \theta$ to show that $x\dot{y} - y\dot{x} = r^2\dot{\theta}$.

To summarise, for a particle moving under a central force the quantity $r^2\dot{\theta}$ is constant, and is called h (§4.2). This h equals twice the areal speed of the particle (§4.3), and also equals the moment of the particle's velocity about O, which can be calculated directly as pv or by using radial and transverse components or Cartesian components (§4.4).

4.5 APSES

A point A on a central orbit at which the particle is moving at right angles to OA is called an *apse*. The line OA is called an *apse line*, and the distance OA an *apsidal distance*. If the central force depends on r only, then the orbit will be symmetrical about any apse line.

At an apse the radial component of velocity is zero, i.e. $\dot{r} = 0$, and so r has a stationary value. The result $pv = h$ is particularly simple to use at an apse, since the radius vector there is itself perpendicular to the velocity. Therefore

$$h = \text{apsidal speed} \times \text{apsidal distance}.$$

For a body orbiting the earth the apse furthest from the earth is called the *apogee*, and the closest apse is the *perigee*. The corresponding terms for a body orbiting the sun are *aphelion* and *perihelion*.

Exercise 4C

1 Find the apsidal distances and apsidal speeds for the particle of Exercise 4B, question 1.

2 For motion along the curve $1/r = \frac{1}{2} + \frac{2}{5} \cos \theta$ under a central force, find the apsidal distances and hence the ratio of maximum to minimum speeds.

3 The planet Pluto moves in an elliptic orbit with the sun at one focus and eccentricity $\frac{1}{4}$. Find the ratio of Pluto's speeds at the perihelion and aphelion.

4 A satellite is in orbit round the earth with speeds at apogee and perigee in the ratio 7:8. The distance between the apogee and perigee is 15 000 km. Find the distances of the apogee and perigee from the centre of the earth, given that the orbit is an ellipse with the centre of the earth at one focus. Find the polar equation of the orbit when the line joining the centre of the earth to the perigee is taken as initial line.

5 With the data of Exercise 4B, question 6, show that the perpendicular distance from O to the tangent at P is $k(1 + \cos 2\theta)$. Deduce that the speed of the particle at P is $2V/(1 + \cos 2\theta)$.

6 A particle moves so that its Cartesian coordinates are $x = 3t + 2t^3$, $y = 5t^2$, where the units for x and y are metres and for t seconds. Calculate the moment of velocity about O, (a) when $t = 1$, (b) when $t = 3$. Is the particle moving under a central force with centre O?

7 The Cartesian coordinates of a particle at time t are given by $x = 4t \sin (10/t)$, $y = 6t \cos (10/t)$. Prove that the moment of velocity about the origin is constant. Make a deduction about the force acting on the particle.

4.6 THE ENERGY EQUATION

Having made good use of the transverse equation of motion $2\dot{r}\dot{\theta} + r\ddot{\theta} = 0$ and its consequence $r^2\dot{\theta} = h$, we now consider the radial equation

$$m(\ddot{r} - r\dot{\theta}^2) = -F(r).$$

On the left side we have

$$\ddot{r} = \frac{d}{dt}(\dot{r}) = \frac{d}{dr}(\dot{r}) \times \frac{dr}{dt} = \dot{r}\frac{d\dot{r}}{dr} = \frac{1}{2}\frac{d}{dr}(\dot{r}^2)$$

and

$$r\dot{\theta}^2 = r\left(\frac{h}{r^2}\right)^2 = \frac{h^2}{r^3},$$

so that the equation is

$$m\left(\frac{1}{2}\frac{d}{dr}(\dot{r}^2) - \frac{h^2}{r^3}\right) = -F(r).$$

Integrating with respect to r,

$$\tfrac{1}{2}m\left(\dot{r}^2 + \frac{h^2}{r^2}\right) = -\int F(r)dr$$

or

$$\tfrac{1}{2}m(\dot{r}^2 + (r\dot{\theta})^2) = -\int F(r)dr.$$

Now $\dot{r}$ and $r\dot{\theta}$ are the radial and transverse components of velocity, so that $\dot{r}^2 + (r\dot{\theta})^2 = v^2$, and therefore

$$\tfrac{1}{2}mv^2 = -\int F(r)dr.$$

This is called the *energy equation*. If we know $F(r)$ and the initial conditions we can use this to find the kinetic energy $\tfrac{1}{2}mv^2$ (Note 4.2), and hence the speed, at any subsequent position.

Example 2
A particle is moving under a central force of $5/r^2$ per unit mass acting towards the origin. Initially $r = 5$, $v = 1$, and the direction of motion is inclined at $\sin^{-1} 0.8$ to the radius vector. Find the apsidal distances and speeds.

Solution
For unit mass, the energy equation is

$$\tfrac{1}{2}v^2 = -\int \frac{5}{r^2}dr$$

$$\Rightarrow v^2 = \frac{10}{r} + C, \text{ where } C \text{ is a constant.}$$

Initially $r = 5$ and $v = 1$, so $C = -1$. Thus

$$v = \sqrt{\left(\frac{10}{r} - 1\right)}. \tag{1}$$

At an apse, $\dot{r} = 0$ and $v = r\dot{\theta} = h/r$. Therefore

$$\frac{h^2}{r^2} = \frac{10}{r} - 1, \text{ i.e. } r^2 - 10r + h^2 = 0 \text{ at an apse.} \tag{2}$$

To find the constant h we use the initial moment of velocity (Fig. 10):

$$h = 5\sin\alpha \times 1 = 4.$$

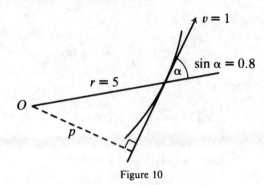

Figure 10

(2) is then

$$r^2 - 10r + 16 = 0$$
$$\Leftrightarrow (r - 2)(r - 8) = 0$$
$$\Leftrightarrow \qquad r = 2 \text{ or } 8.$$

From (1), $r = 2 \Rightarrow v = 2$

$$r = 8 \Rightarrow v = \tfrac{1}{2}.$$

These are the required apsidal distances and speeds.   □

Q.6 Check that $pv = h$ at each apse.

We can also use the energy equation to find the particular central force function $F(r)$ needed to make a particle move along a given curve.

Let the angle between OP and the tangent to the curve at P be ϕ (Fig. 11). The direction of the tangent is the direction of the velocity $\mathbf{v}$. Using the radial and transverse components of $\mathbf{v}$ we have

$$\tan \phi = \frac{r\dot\theta}{\dot r} = r\frac{d\theta}{dt} \times \frac{dt}{dr} = r\frac{d\theta}{dr},$$

from which we can find ϕ in terms of r for a given curve.

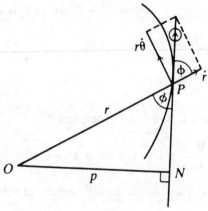

Figure 11

The length p of the perpendicular ON is $r \sin \phi$, and so from $pv = h$ we can obtain first v and then $\frac{1}{2}mv^2$ in terms of r. Finally we can find $F(r)$ by differentiating the energy equation:

$$F(r) = -\frac{d}{dr}\left(\tfrac{1}{2}mv^2\right).$$

Example 3
Find the central force needed to make a particle move along the equiangular spiral $r = ae^{k\theta}$.

Solution
With the notation of Fig. 11,

$$\tan \phi = r\frac{d\theta}{dr} = \frac{r}{dr/d\theta} = \frac{ae^{k\theta}}{kae^{k\theta}} = \frac{1}{k},$$

so ϕ is constant. (This is why the spiral is called equiangular.) Therefore

$$v = \frac{h}{p} = \frac{h}{r \sin \phi}$$

and

$$\tfrac{1}{2}mv^2 = \frac{\tfrac{1}{2}mh^2}{r^2 \sin^2 \phi} = \frac{A}{r^2}$$

say, where A is a constant. So

$$F(r) = -\frac{d}{dr}\left(\tfrac{1}{2}mv^2\right) = -\frac{2A}{r^3};$$

an inverse cube law of force is needed.   ☐

Exercise 4D

1   A particle is moving under a central force of $10/r^2$ per unit mass acting towards the origin. It is projected from an apse 2 units from O with speed 3 units. Find
   (a) the speed when $r = 4$,
   (b) the value of r when the speed is $\frac{1}{2}$ unit,
   (c) the other apsidal distance and apsidal speed.

2   As the particle in question 1 passes through the given apse its speed is increased to 4 units. Show that the new orbit has no other apse, and hence that the particle moves 'to infinity'. What are the speed and the perpendicular distance from O to the tangent when r is very large?

3   A particle of unit mass moves under a central attraction of $16/r^3$. With the usual notation $v = 1$ when $r = 2$, and $h = 3$. Show that there is just one apse, and find its distance from O.

4   A particle moves under a central force of k^2r per unit mass directed towards the origin.
   (a) Show that $v^2 + k^2r^2 = c$, where c is a constant.

(b) Show that the apsidal distances satisfy $k^2 r^4 - c r^2 + h^2 = 0$.

(c) Show that in general this fourth degree equation has two positive roots, whatever the initial conditions. Examine any exceptional cases.

5 With the data of Exercise 4B, question 6, and Exercise 4C, question 5, prove that $v = 4k^2 V/r^2$. Use the energy equation to deduce that the central force is proportional to $1/r^5$.

6 A particle describes the cardioid $r = a(1 + \cos \theta)$ under the action of a central force. The foot of the perpendicular from O to the tangent at P is N (Fig. 12).

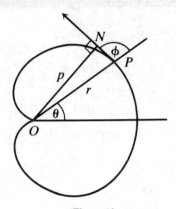

Figure 12

(a) Use the fact that $\tan \phi = r d\theta/dr$ to show that $P\hat{O}N = \theta/2$.

(b) Deduce that $p \propto r^{3/2}$.

(c) Show that the force is an attraction proportional to $1/r^4$.

5
Planetary orbits

5.1 KEPLER AND NEWTON

For twenty years the Danish nobleman Tycho de Brahe (1546–1601) worked in his island observatory near Copenhagen to produce an unbroken series of astronomical observations of unprecedented accuracy. By 1599, having moved with his instruments to a castle near Prague provided by the Emperor Rudolph II, Tycho realised that he was not good enough at theory to construct an adequate explanation of his observations, so he invited the eminent mathematician Johannes Kepler (1571–1630) to join him as his assistant. Eighteen months later Tycho died, and Kepler succeeded him as Imperial Mathematician, a post which included duties as Court Astrologer. For a further six years Kepler worked on Tycho's information about the orbit of Mars; in 1609 the results of this intense effort appeared in his book *Astronomia Nova* (New Astronomy), which includes the first two of Kepler's three planetary laws.

(1) The planets have elliptical orbits with the sun at one focus.

(2) The radius from the sun to a planet sweeps out equal areas in equal times.

Ten years later, in *Harmonice Mundi* (Harmony of the World), Kepler published his third law.

(3) The squares of the times which the planets take to complete their orbits are proportional to the cubes of their mean distances (Note 5.1) from the sun.

In his introduction to *Astronomia Nova* Kepler comes close to the idea of universal gravitation, but he fails to develop this coherently. In the next thirty years Galileo did much to make clear the basic laws of mechanics, though mainly in connection with the motion of bodies on earth. By 1684 three distinguished English scientists, Robert Hooke, Christopher Wren and Edmund Halley, had become convinced that the motion of each planet was caused by the gravitational attraction of the sun, and that this gravitational force is inversely proportional to the square of the planet's distance from the sun. They were unable however to prove that the orbit of a planet moving under such an attraction would be an ellipse. Because of Kepler's first law this was crucially important, so Halley went to Cambridge to ask Isaac Newton (1642–1727) if he could help. Newton replied that he had proved what they wanted some years before, but had lost the solution. Halley urged Newton to write out his results, and in 1687 these appeared, greatly expanded, as *Philosophiae Naturalis Principia Mathematica* (Mathematical Principles of Natural Philosophy), one of the greatest scientific works ever written.

5.2 KEPLER'S FIRST AND SECOND LAWS

In §4.2 and §4.3 we saw that the rate at which the radius vector sweeps out area is constant if and only if the particle is moving under a central force. Thus Kepler's second law is equivalent to stating that the planets are subject to a central attraction towards the sun, but it says nothing about the way in which this attraction varies with distance.

Next we prove the result which eluded Hooke, Wren and Halley, namely that the orbit under an inverse square law of attraction is a conic with a focus at the centre of attraction. The proof given here is very different from the one in *Principia*, where Newton uses elegant but now almost forgotten pure geometry.

If a particle is subject to a central attraction of μ/r^2 per unit mass, where μ is constant, then

radially
$$\ddot{r} - r\dot{\theta}^2 = -\mu/r^2 \tag{1}$$

transversely
$$r^2\dot{\theta} = h. \tag{2}$$

In order to obtain the equation of the orbit for this motion we take components in the x and y directions. (An alternative method is given in Exercise 5A, questions 6 and 7.)

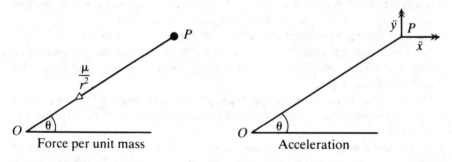

Force per unit mass   Acceleration

Figure 1

Equating components of acceleration and force per unit mass (Fig. 1) gives

$$\left.\begin{array}{l} \ddot{x} = -\dfrac{\mu}{r^2}\cos\theta \\[3mm] \ddot{y} = -\dfrac{\mu}{r^2}\sin\theta \end{array}\right\} \tag{3}$$

Now
$$\ddot{x} = \frac{d\dot{x}}{dt} = \frac{d\dot{x}}{d\theta} \times \frac{d\theta}{dt} = \frac{d\dot{x}}{d\theta} \times \frac{h}{r^2} \qquad \text{from (2)}$$

and similarly
$$\ddot{y} = \frac{d\dot{y}}{d\theta} \times \frac{h}{r^2}.$$

Substituting these expressions for $\ddot{x}$ and $\ddot{y}$ into (3) gives

$$\frac{d\dot{x}}{d\theta} = -\frac{\mu}{h}\cos\theta$$

$$\frac{d\dot{y}}{d\theta} = -\frac{\mu}{h}\sin\theta$$

which we integrate with respect to θ to get

$$\left.\begin{array}{l} \dot{x} = -\dfrac{\mu}{h}\,(\sin\theta + A) \\[2mm] \dot{y} = \dfrac{\mu}{h}\,(\cos\theta + B) \end{array}\right\} \tag{4}$$

where A and B are constants determined by the initial conditions. (We put these constants inside the brackets for later convenience.) From §4.4,

$$h = x\dot{y} - y\dot{x} = r(\dot{y}\cos\theta - \dot{x}\sin\theta), \quad \text{since} \quad x = r\cos\theta, \; y = r\sin\theta.$$

Using (4), $\qquad h = r\dfrac{\mu}{h}(\cos^2\theta + B\cos\theta + \sin^2\theta + A\sin\theta)$

so that $\qquad \dfrac{h^2/\mu}{r} = 1 + B\cos\theta + A\sin\theta, \quad \text{since} \quad \cos^2\theta + \sin^2\theta = 1,$

or $\qquad \dfrac{h^2/\mu}{r} = 1 + \sqrt{(A^2 + B^2)}\cos(\theta - \alpha),$

where $\qquad \alpha = \tan^{-1}\dfrac{A}{B}$ (Note 5.2).

If we write $l = \dfrac{h^2}{\mu}, \; e = \sqrt{(A^2 + B^2)}$ this equation becomes

$$l/r = 1 + e\cos(\theta - \alpha).$$

This is very similar to the polar equation of a conic

$$l/r = 1 + e\cos\theta$$

found in §3.3; the presence of $(\theta - \alpha)$ instead of θ simply means that the major axis makes an angle α with the initial line (Fig. 2).

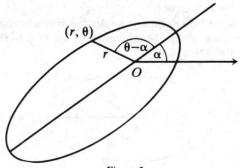

Figure 2

Q.1 What is the orbit if the constants A and B are both zero?

This completes the proof that the orbit of a particle moving under an inverse square law of attraction is a conic. The converse is also true; see Exercise 5A, question 4.

Exercise 5A

1 Table 1 gives the mean distance from the sun, a, and the time to complete one orbit, T, for the six planets known to Kepler. The *astronomical unit* (a.u.) is the earth's mean distance from the sun ($\approx 1.5 \times 10^{11}$ m)

Table 1

	a (a.u.)	T (years)
Mercury	0.387	0.241
Venus	0.723	0.615
Earth	1.000	1.000
Mars	1.524	1.881
Jupiter	5.208	
Saturn		29.457

Check Kepler's third law for Mercury, Venus and Mars, and complete the table.

2 A particle of unit mass is projected from the point $(5, 0)$ with initial velocity $\mathbf{v}_0$, and is then subject to a central attraction $20/r^2$ towards O. The polar equation of its orbit is $l/r = 1 + e \cos (\theta - \alpha)$. Find the constants l, e, α and sketch the orbit

(a) when $\mathbf{v}_0 = \begin{bmatrix} 0 \\ 1 \end{bmatrix}$, (b) when $\mathbf{v}_0 = \begin{bmatrix} 1 \\ 2 \end{bmatrix}$, (c) when $\mathbf{v}_0 = \begin{bmatrix} -1.2 \\ 2.5 \end{bmatrix}$.

3 Halley's comet completes an orbit once in 76.03 years. What is its mean distance from the sun in astronomical units? Its perihelion is distant 0.587 a.u. from the sun. Find the eccentricity of its orbit, and the distance of its aphelion from the sun.

4 Prove that $\dfrac{h^2/\mu}{r} = 1 + e \cos \theta$ and $r^2 \dot{\theta} = h$ together imply that $\ddot{r} - r\dot{\theta}^2 = \dfrac{-\mu}{r^2}$.

5 The centre of the ellipse $l/r = 1 + e \cos \theta$ is C, and $CA = a$. With the notation of Fig. 3 prove that $r = a - ez \cos \beta$.

(While searching for his second law Kepler found results equivalent to this, but failed to realise that they define the orbit as an ellipse; he then set off on a long and complicated false trail (Note 5.3)).

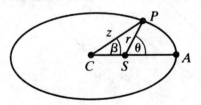

Figure 3

6 Given that $r^2\dot\theta = h$ and $u = 1/r$, prove that

(a) $\dot r = -h\dfrac{du}{d\theta}$; (b) $v^2 = h^2\left[\left(\dfrac{du}{d\theta}\right)^2 + u^2\right]$, where v is the speed;

(c) $\ddot r = -h^2 u^2 \dfrac{d^2 u}{d\theta^2}$; (d) $\ddot r - r\dot\theta^2 = -h^2 u^2\left[\dfrac{d^2 u}{d\theta^2} + u\right]$.

7 Use question 6 to show that, for motion under a central attraction μ/r^2 per unit mass, the substitution $u = 1/r$ in the equation of radial motion gives

$$\frac{d^2 u}{d\theta^2} + u = \frac{\mu}{h^2}.$$

Verify that $u = (\mu/h^2) + k\cos(\theta - \alpha)$ is a solution (Note 5.4) of this differential equation whatever the values of the constants k and α, and show that this leads to the same conical orbit as in §5.2.

8 A particle is subject to an inverse cube law of attraction, so that the attractive force is μ/r^3 per unit mass. Show that if $u = 1/r$ then

$$\frac{d^2 u}{d\theta^2} = \left(\frac{\mu}{h^2} - 1\right)u.$$

Assuming that $\mu > h^2$, let $c^2 = (\mu/h^2) - 1$. Verify that $u = Ae^{c\theta} + Be^{-c\theta}$ is a solution (Note 5.4) whatever the values of the constants A and B.

Show that if $h = 3$, $\mu = 25$, and the particle starts 2 units from O with speed $\frac{5}{2}$, then the orbit is an equiangular spiral.

5.3 THE SIZE AND SHAPE OF AN ORBIT

The size and shape of an orbit are determined by the semi-latus rectum l and the eccentricity e. We have already seen in §5.2 that

$$l = \frac{h^2}{\mu}. \tag{1}$$

Now we consider the eccentricity in more detail.

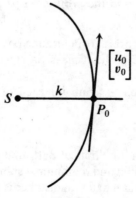

Figure 4

Suppose that when the planet passes through the point $P_0(k, 0)$ its velocity in Cartesian components is $\begin{bmatrix} u_0 \\ v_0 \end{bmatrix}$, and therefore $h = kv_0$ (Fig. 4). From equations (4) of §5.2,

$$u_0 = -\frac{\mu A}{h} \quad \text{and} \quad v_0 = \frac{\mu}{h}(1 + B)$$

so that

$$e^2 = A^2 + B^2$$

$$= \frac{h^2 u_0^2}{\mu^2} + \frac{h^2 v_0^2}{\mu^2} - \frac{2hv_0}{\mu} + 1$$

$$= 1 + \frac{h^2}{\mu^2}(u_0^2 + v_0^2) - \frac{2h^2}{k\mu} \quad \text{since} \quad h = kv_0$$

$$= 1 + \frac{h^2}{\mu^2}\left[(u_0^2 + v_0^2) - \frac{2\mu}{k}\right],$$

i.e.

$$e^2 = 1 + \frac{2h^2}{\mu^2}\left[\tfrac{1}{2}w^2 - \frac{\mu}{k}\right],$$

where $w = \sqrt{(u_0^2 + v_0^2)}$ is the speed at P_0.

Now the energy equation (§4.6) for attraction μ/r^2 per unit mass is $\tfrac{1}{2}v^2 = -\int \frac{\mu dr}{r^2} = \frac{\mu}{r} + C$, where C is a constant, so that the quantity $\tfrac{1}{2}v^2 - \frac{\mu}{r}$ remains constant throughout the motion. This constant C is called the *total energy* (per unit mass) in the motion (Note 5.5). In particular at P_0

$$C = \tfrac{1}{2}w^2 - \frac{\mu}{k}.$$

Therefore $e^2 = 1 + \dfrac{2h^2 C}{\mu^2}$, which shows that   (2)

if $\begin{matrix} C < 0 \\ C = 0, \\ C > 0 \end{matrix}$ then $\begin{matrix} e < 1 \\ e = 1, \\ e > 1 \end{matrix}$ and the orbit is $\begin{matrix} \text{an ellipse} \\ \text{a parabola} \\ \text{one branch of a hyperbola.} \end{matrix}$

The size and shape of the orbit are determined by the constants of moment of momentum h and energy C per unit mass via equations (1) and (2).

Q.2 Find C and hence find e again for each of the orbits of Exercise 5A, question 2.

Example 1

(a) A particle is moving in an elliptical path under an inverse square law of attraction so that its maximum and minimum distances from O are 5 units and 4 units respectively. Its speed at maximum distance is 16 units s^{-1}. Find the orbit, and the speed when 4 units from O.

(b) When the particle is 4 units from O its speed is instantaneously increased by 50%. Determine the new orbit.

(c) Find the direction which this new orbit approaches, and also the ultimate speed of the particle.

Solution

(a) With the usual notation the ellipse can be taken as

$$l/r = 1 + e \cos \theta.$$

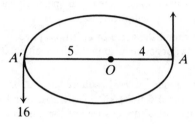

Figure 5

Now $r = 4$ when $\theta = 0$, and $r = 5$ when $\theta = \pi$ (Fig. 5)

$$\Rightarrow l/4 = 1 + e \quad \text{and} \quad l/5 = 1 - e,$$

giving $l = 40/9$, $e = 1/9$, so the ellipse has equation

$$40/r = 9 + \cos \theta.$$

Since $h = OA' \times$ speed at $A' = 80 = OA \times$ speed at A, the speed at A is 20 units s^{-1}. Also

$$\mu = \frac{h^2}{l} = \frac{6400}{40/9} = 1440.$$

(b) Using the suffix 1 for the new orbit,

$$h_1 = 4 \times 30 = 120$$

and

$$l_1 = \frac{h_1^2}{\mu} = \frac{120^2}{1440} = 10.$$

Putting $\theta = 0$ in the equation of the new orbit gives $\frac{10}{4} = 1 + e_1$, so that $e_1 = \frac{3}{2}$. The new orbit is the hyperbola

$$\frac{10}{r} = 1 + \tfrac{3}{2} \cos \theta.$$

(c) From the equation of the new orbit, $\cos \theta \to -\frac{2}{3}$ as $r \to \infty$, so the direction of motion makes an angle approaching $\cos^{-1}(-\frac{2}{3})$ with the initial line.

The energy in the new orbit (per unit mass) is

$$\tfrac{1}{2} \times 30^2 - \frac{1440}{4} = 90 \text{ (using values at } A)$$

and so $\qquad\qquad \frac{1}{2}v^2 - \dfrac{1440}{r} = 90$ throughout the motion.

As $r \to \infty$, $\frac{1}{2}v^2 \to 90$, so that the 'velocity at infinity' is $\sqrt{180} = 6\sqrt{5}$ units s^{-1}.   □

Exercise 5B

1   A satellite is in orbit round the earth in an ellipse of eccentricity $\frac{1}{2}$. When it is at the perigee the speed is increased by 10%. Find the eccentricity of the new orbit. What is the greatest permitted percentage increase in speed at the perigee of the original orbit if the new orbit is to be elliptical?

2   A satellite is in orbit round the earth in an ellipse of eccentricity $\frac{3}{4}$. It is desired to change the speed at the apogee so as to make the orbit circular. In what way should the speed be altered?

3   A particle moving under inverse square attraction along the hyperbola $3/r = 1 + 2\cos\theta$ has speed 5 units s^{-1} at the apse. Find the direction which the motion approaches and the ultimate speed of the particle.

4   A space craft is to be put into an orbit. In order to achieve this orbit the craft is given an initial velocity $\mathbf{v}_0$ of 10^4 m s^{-1} at right angles to its position vector $\mathbf{r}_0$ from the centre of the earth. If $r_0 = 7.5 \times 10^6$ m, find the polar equation of the orbit in the form $l/r = 1 + e\cos\theta$ (where θ is measured from the direction of $\mathbf{r}_0$) and determine whether the orbit is elliptic, parabolic, or hyperbolic. (Take the earth's radius to be 6×10^6 m and $r_0^2 v_0^2 = l\mu$, where the force per unit mass $(=\mu/r^2)$ is 10 N at the earth's surface.)   [SMP]

5   A comet is being observed. It is assumed that it is moving in a known plane under an inverse square law of attraction towards the sun. How many positional sightings (distance and direction) are required to fix the polar equation of the orbit of the comet referred to the sun as pole and focus?

Assuming that the direction of the major axis has been established and is being used for the initial line for the polar coordinate system describing the orbit, take as much of the following data as you need to estimate a polar equation of the comet's orbit.

r	2	2.29	2.67	3.20
θ	0	60	90	120

(r is measured in suitable astronomical units, and θ is measured in degrees from the initial line.)

Check how well any unused data fits your equation.   [SMP]

6   An ellipse has major axis $2a$, minor axis $2b$, latus rectum $2l$ and eccentricity e. Prove that

$$l = \frac{b^2}{a} = a(1 - e^2).$$

Deduce that, for an elliptic orbit with the notation of §5.3,

$$C = \frac{-\mu}{2a}.$$

Find the corresponding result for a hyperbolic orbit.

7   The orbit of a particle moving under a central attraction μ/r^2 per unit mass is an ellipse with semi-major axis a. Prove that the particle's speed, v, is given by

$$v^2 = \mu\left(\frac{2}{r} - \frac{1}{a}\right).$$

8   Find the speed of Halley's comet (Exercise 5A, question 3) when it is 10 a.u. from the sun, giving your answer (a) in a.u./year, (b) in m s^{-1}. (1 a.u. $\approx 1.5 \times 10^{11}$ m).

9   The eccentricity of the earth's orbit is 0.017. Find the greatest speed of the earth in m s^{-1}.

10   The equations of energy and of moment of momentum for a particle moving in an elliptical orbit are

$$\tfrac{1}{2}v^2 - \frac{\mu}{r} = C \quad \text{and} \quad pv = h.$$

At an apse $p = r$; by eliminating v in this case show that the quadratic equation whose roots are the apsidal distances is

$$2Cr^2 + 2\mu r - h^2 = 0.$$

(This is called the *apsidal quadratic*.)

Write down these apsidal distances in terms of a and e. Hence, by using the sum and product of the roots of the apsidal quadratic, obtain again the results

$$C = \frac{-\mu}{2a} \quad \text{and} \quad l = \frac{h^2}{\mu}.$$

11   A particle subject to a central attraction μ/r^2 per unit mass towards O is projected from a point K, distance k from O, with speed w in a direction at right angles to OK (so that K is an apse).

Using the result of question 6, show that if $kw^2 < \mu$ the orbit is an ellipse with O as the focus further from K, but if $\mu < kw^2 < 2\mu$ the orbit is an ellipse with O as the focus nearer to K.

What happens if (a) $kw^2 = \mu$, (b) $kw^2 = 2\mu$, (c) $kw^2 > 2\mu$?

12   A particle of mass m and charge q in the solar wind is approaching the upper atmosphere when it encounters a much heavier ion of charge nq which may be taken to be at rest throughout the interaction. When the distance between the particle and the ion is r, the force between them is a repulsion of magnitude nq^2/r^2. Initially (when r is large) the particle has speed V, and its moment of momentum about the ion is $nq^2\sqrt{3}/V$. Write down the equations of motion of the particle, using plane polar coordinates based on the ion, and show that

$$\dot\theta = \frac{nq^2\sqrt{3}}{mVr^2}.$$

Multiply the radial equation of motion by $\dot r$ and integrate to derive an expression for $\dot r^2$, and show that the minimum separation is $3nq^2/(mV^2)$.   [SMP]

5.4   KEPLER'S THIRD LAW AND UNIVERSAL GRAVITATION

We have seen in §4.3 that the rate at which the radius vector OP sweeps out area is $\tfrac{1}{2}h$, so that the time T which a planet takes to complete its elliptical orbit is

$$\frac{2 \times \text{area of ellipse}}{h} = \frac{2\pi ab}{h},$$

from which
$$T^2 = \frac{4\pi^2 a^2 b^2}{h^2}.$$

Now for any ellipse $l = b^2/a$ (Exercise 5B, question 6) and for this orbit $l = h^2/\mu$.

Therefore $b^2 = \dfrac{ah^2}{\mu}$ and $T^2 = \dfrac{4\pi^2 a^2}{h^2} \times \dfrac{ah^2}{\mu} = \left(\dfrac{4\pi^2}{\mu}\right) a^3.$

Kepler's third law, based on observations, states that T^2/a^3 is constant for all the planets; it follows then that the constant μ is the same for all the planets. Since μ/r^2 is the force per unit mass, the gravitational force between the sun and a planet is proportional to the mass of the planet and inversely proportional to the square of its distance from the sun. This is all consistent with Newton's Law of Gravitation, which states that:

The force of attraction between two particles is $\dfrac{\gamma m_1 m_2}{r^2}$, where m_1, m_2 are the masses of the particles, r is their distance apart, and γ is a universal constant.

The value of γ in SI units is 6.67×10^{-11} N m^2 kg^{-2}.

It is an example of Newton's genius that he realised and was able to demonstrate that this law governs not only the motion of the planets round the sun, but also the moon's orbit round the earth, and even the fall of an apple from tree to ground.

Three simplifying assumptions which we have made so far should be mentioned.

(1) We have ignored the gravitational forces between one planet and another. The mathematical treatment of the problem of even three mutually attracting bodies is exceedingly difficult; in practice numerical methods are used to make corrections to the elliptic orbits obtained for two body attraction. A celebrated example of this concerns the discovery of the planet Neptune in 1846. It was noticed that the orbit of Uranus had irregularities which could not be accounted for by the attractions of the other planets then known. The astronomers Adams and Leverrier, working independently, calculated where an unknown planet would have to be to produce this effect on Uranus. Observers then found the new planet very close to its predicted position, thus giving a convincing confirmation of the soundness of Newton's theory, on which the calculations were based.

(2) We have taken the centre of attraction, the sun, to be fixed. In fact the sun is attracted to each planet by a force equal and opposite to the force on that planet due to the sun. The consequence is that the sun also moves; the effect of this is discussed in Exercise 5C, question 4.

(3) We have treated all the bodies involved as particles of negligible size. For the motion of the planets the distances involved are very great, so this simplification seems reasonable. It is obviously more serious when dealing with the gravitational attraction of the earth on the moon or a satellite or an apple. Fortunately it turns out that, for a sphere whose mass is distributed with

spherical symmetry, the gravitational attraction exerted on an external particle is the same as if all the mass of the sphere were concentrated at its centre. The proof is given in Exercise 5C, questions 5 and 6.

Exercise 5C

1   Assuming that the earth attracts other bodies as though its whole mass were concentrated at its centre, show that the acceleration g of a body falling freely near the earth's surface is given by

$$g = \frac{\gamma M}{R^2},$$

where M and R are the mass and radius of the earth. Given that $g = 9.81 \text{ m s}^{-2}$, $R = 6.37 \times 10^6$ m and $\gamma = 6.67 \times 10^{-11} \text{ N m}^2 \text{ kg}^{-2}$, calculate the mass of the earth.

2   Newton first tested his theory of gravitation by the motion of the moon. Assuming for simplicity that the orbit of the moon is a circle of radius R_1 and that its period of revolution is T, show that the moon's acceleration is $4\pi^2 R_1/T^2$, and hence that

$$\frac{4\pi^2 R_1/T^2}{g} = \frac{R^2}{R_1^2},$$

where g and R are as in question 1.

Given that $T = 27.3$ days, calculate R_1 by this method, and compare your answer with the value 3.84×10^8 m found by observation.

3   A spaceship approaches a planet of mass M along the path

$$l/r = 1 + 2 \cos \theta$$

where l is a constant. Show that the closest approach is to $\frac{1}{3}l$ (provided this exceeds the planet's radius).

Differentiate the equation of the path with respect to time to show that $\dot{r} = 0$ when $\theta = 0$; differentiate again, and use the values of $\dot{r}$ and θ at the point of closest approach to show that then

$$\frac{l\ddot{r}}{r^2} = 2\dot{\theta}^2.$$

Now use the fact that the acceleration towards the planet is $\gamma M/r^2$, where γ is the gravitational constant, to find the speed at closest approach in terms of γ, M and l.   [SMP]

4   (a) Let the sun S, with mass M, and a planet P, with mass m, have position vectors $\mathbf{s}$, $\mathbf{p}$ with respect to a fixed origin O, and let $\mathbf{SP} = \mathbf{r}$ (Fig. 6).

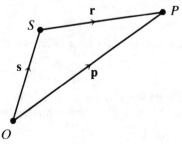

Figure 6

Show that the force on S due to P is

$$\frac{\gamma M m \mathbf{r}}{r^3}$$

and hence that

$$\ddot{\mathbf{s}} = \frac{\gamma m \mathbf{r}}{r^3}.$$

Find $\ddot{\mathbf{p}}$ similarly. Deduce that

$$\ddot{\mathbf{r}} = -\frac{\gamma(M + m)}{r^3} \mathbf{r}.$$

This differential equation can be solved as in §5.2, with μ replaced by $\gamma(M + m)$. Therefore it is still true to say that, relative to the sun, the planet moves in an ellipse with the sun at one focus.

(b) If two planets of masses m and m' have periods T and T', and their orbits relative to the sun have semi-major axes a and a', use the method of §5.4 to show that

$$\frac{T^2}{a^3} : \frac{T'^2}{a'^3} = (M + m') : (M + m).$$

This gives a correction to Kepler's third law, but, since the mass of the largest planet, Jupiter, is less than one-thousandth of the mass of the sun, the differences are very slight.

5   In this question we find the gravitational attraction of a uniform circular ring of radius c and mass m on a particle of unit mass at P on its axis and at distance p from its centre C (Fig. 7).

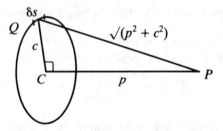

Figure 7

(a) Show that the attraction on the unit mass of a small element of the ring of length δs is

$$\frac{\gamma m \delta s}{2\pi c} \times \frac{1}{p^2 + c^2}.$$

(b) Show that the component of the force in (a) along the axis is

$$\frac{\gamma m \delta s}{2\pi c} \times \frac{p}{(p^2 + c^2)^{3/2}}.$$

(c) Explain why, when we integrate round the ring, the resultant of the components perpendicular to the axis is zero. Show that the attraction of the complete ring is

$$\frac{\gamma m p}{(p^2 + c^2)^{3/2}}$$ along the axis.

6   We now use the result of question 5 to find the attraction of a uniform spherical shell of radius a and mass M on a unit mass at P, distance r from the centre O ($r > a$). Consider an elementary ring of radius $a \sin \theta$ and thickness $a\delta\theta$, as shown in Fig. 8.

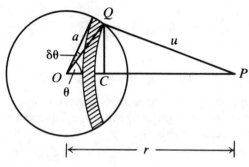

Figure 8

(a) Show that the mass of this ring is $\frac{1}{2}M \sin \theta \, \delta\theta$, and that the attraction due to this ring is

$$\gamma \times \tfrac{1}{2}M \sin \theta \, \delta\theta \times \frac{(r - a \cos \theta)}{u^3}, \text{ where } u = PQ.$$

(b) Using the cosine formula in triangle POQ, show that
$$u^2 = a^2 + r^2 - 2ar \cos \theta.$$
Deduce that   (i) $u\delta u = ar \sin \theta \, \delta\theta$,

(ii) $r - a \cos \theta = \dfrac{u^2 + r^2 - a^2}{2r}$.

(c) Using (b) (i) and (ii) in (a), show that the attraction of the ring is
$$\frac{\gamma M}{4ar^2}\left[1 + \frac{r^2 - a^2}{u^2}\right]\delta u.$$

(d) By integrating with respect to u from $u = r - a$ to $u = r + a$, show that the attraction of the whole shell is $\dfrac{\gamma M}{r^2}$.

(e) Deduce that the gravitational attraction of a sphere whose mass is distributed with spherical symmetry on a particle outside it is the same as if all the mass of the sphere were concentrated at its centre.

7   By making a suitable modification to question 6 (d), show that the gravitational attraction on a particle inside a uniform spherical shell is zero.

6

Arc length

6.1 LENGTH OF CURVE

If the position vector of a point P on a curve is given in terms of a parameter p then the *positive* sense of description of the curve is defined to be the sense in which P moves as p increases (Fig. 1).

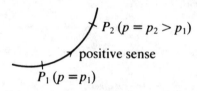

$P_2 \, (p = p_2 > p_1)$

positive sense

$P_1 \, (p = p_1)$

Figure 1

The positive sense on a curve depends on the particular parameter used. For example, the unit circle centred at the origin may be expressed parametrically as

$$(a) \quad \mathbf{r} = \begin{bmatrix} \cos \theta \\ \sin \theta \end{bmatrix} \quad \text{or as } (b) \quad \mathbf{r} = \begin{bmatrix} \sin \phi \\ \cos \phi \end{bmatrix}.$$

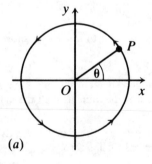

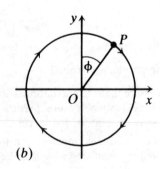

Figure 2

In case (a) the positive sense is anti-clockwise, whereas in (b) it is clockwise (Fig. 2).

When considering the arc length of a curve we shall normally restrict ourselves to cases where the curve has a continuously turning tangent, i.e. where $\dfrac{dx}{dp}$ and $\dfrac{dy}{dp}$ are continuous.

Let C be a fixed point on such a curve, and let P be the point on the curve with parameter p. Then it can be proved that to each p there corresponds a number s which gives the distance measured along the curve from C to P; s is positive if and only if the sense of motion from C to P is positive. The need to prove that s exists is shown by question 12 of Exercise 6A, which gives an example of a curve with no finite length. However, the details of this proof are beyond the scope of this book, so from now on we shall assume that the arc length s exists.

Our intuitive idea of arc length suggests that if two points P and Q on the curve are very close together then the arc length PQ is nearly the same as the length of the chord PQ. We shall therefore make the further assumption that

$$\frac{\text{arc } PQ}{\text{chord } PQ} \to 1 \quad \text{as} \quad Q \to P. \tag{1}$$

Let P and Q have position vectors $\mathbf{r}$ and $\mathbf{r} + \delta\mathbf{r}$, corresponding to parametric values p and $p + \delta p$ (Fig. 3).

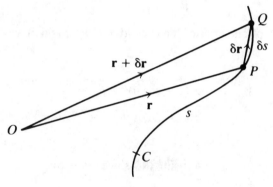

Figure 3

Then chord $PQ = |\mathbf{PQ}| = |\delta\mathbf{r}| = \sqrt{((\delta x)^2 + (\delta y)^2)}$. If arc $PQ = \delta s$ then our assumption (1) takes the form

$$\frac{\delta s}{|\delta\mathbf{r}|} \to 1 \quad \text{as} \quad \delta p \to 0.$$

Now
$$\frac{\delta s}{\delta p} = \frac{\delta s}{|\delta\mathbf{r}|} \times \frac{|\delta\mathbf{r}|}{\delta p}$$

$$= \frac{\delta s}{|\delta\mathbf{r}|} \sqrt{\left(\left(\frac{\delta x}{\delta p}\right)^2 + \left(\frac{\delta y}{\delta p}\right)^2\right)}.$$

As $\delta p \to 0$, $\frac{\delta s}{\delta p}, \frac{\delta x}{\delta p}, \frac{\delta y}{\delta p}$ tend to $\frac{ds}{dp}, \frac{dx}{dp}, \frac{dy}{dp}$ respectively, and $\frac{\delta s}{|\delta\mathbf{r}|} \to 1$. Therefore, taking limits as $\delta p \to 0$, we have the basic result

$$\frac{ds}{dp} = \sqrt{\left(\left(\frac{dx}{dp}\right)^2 + \left(\frac{dy}{dp}\right)^2\right)}$$

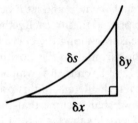

Figure 4

An easy way to remember this result is to apply Pythagoras to this right-angled 'triangle' (Fig. 4):

$$(\delta s)^2 \approx (\delta x)^2 + (\delta y)^2,$$

then divide by $(\delta p)^2$ and take the positive square root of each side. Notice that ds/dp is positive since by definition s increases with p.

Example 1
Find the length of one arch of the cycloid $x = a(\theta - \sin \theta)$, $y = a(1 - \cos \theta)$.

Solution
$$\left(\frac{ds}{d\theta}\right)^2 = \left(\frac{dx}{d\theta}\right)^2 + \left(\frac{dy}{d\theta}\right)^2 = a^2(1 - \cos \theta)^2 + a^2 \sin^2 \theta$$
$$= a^2(1 - 2 \cos \theta + \cos^2 \theta + \sin^2 \theta)$$
$$= 2a^2(1 - \cos \theta) \quad \text{since} \quad \cos^2 \theta + \sin^2 \theta = 1$$
$$= 4a^2 \sin^2 \tfrac{1}{2}\theta \quad \text{since} \quad 1 - \cos \theta = 2 \sin^2 \tfrac{1}{2}\theta.$$

Therefore $$\frac{ds}{d\theta} = 2a \sin \tfrac{1}{2}\theta. \tag{2}$$

The length of one arch is
$$\int_0^{2\pi} 2a \sin \tfrac{1}{2}\theta \, d\theta = [-4a \cos \tfrac{1}{2}\theta]_0^{2\pi}$$
$$= 4a(1 - (-1))$$
$$= 8a.$$

Note that when taking square roots at (2) we must choose the $\pm$ sign so that $\frac{ds}{d\theta} \geqslant 0$; here the $+$ sign is correct since $\sin \tfrac{1}{2}\theta$ is positive for the range of integration $0 \leqslant \theta \leqslant 2\pi$.   □
   If the independent variable is x then we put $p = x$ in the basic result, so that $\frac{dx}{dp} = \frac{dx}{dx} = 1$ and $\frac{dy}{dp} = \frac{dy}{dx}$. This gives
$$\frac{ds}{dx} = \sqrt{\left(1 + \left(\frac{dy}{dx}\right)^2\right)}.$$

Similarly $\dfrac{ds}{dy} = \sqrt{\left(1 + \left(\dfrac{dx}{dy}\right)^2\right)}$ when the independent variable is y. Finally, if the parameter is the time t then

$$\frac{ds}{dt} = \sqrt{\left(\left(\frac{dx}{dt}\right)^2 + \left(\frac{dy}{dt}\right)^2\right)}$$

or
$$\dot{s} = \sqrt{(\dot{x}^2 + \dot{y}^2)}$$
$$= |\mathbf{v}|,$$

showing, not surprisingly, that the rate of change of arc length is the speed of P.

Exercise 6A

1   Check that integration gives the correct arc length in the following simple cases:
   (a) the straight line $y = 4x + 3$ from $x = 1$ to $x = 6$;
   (b) the circle $x = 3 \sin p$, $y = 3 \cos p$ from $p = 0$ to $p = \pi$.

2   Calculate the length of the curve

$$x = \frac{1}{1 + p^2}, \; y = \frac{p}{1 + p^2}$$

   from $p = 0$ to $p = 1$.

3   Calculate the length of the semicubical parabola $x = 2p^3$, $y = 3p^2$ from $(2, 3)$ to $(16, 12)$.

4   Given that $x = 4\sqrt{2}p^3$, $y = 3(p^4 - p^2)$, where $p \geqslant 0$, show that $ds/dp = 6p(2p^2 + 1)$. Find the arc length S from $p = 0$ to $p = P$. If $x = X$ and $y = Y$ when $p = P$, show that $9X^2 = 8(S^2 - Y^2)$.

5   The flight path of an aeroplane immediately after take-off is given by $\mathbf{r} = t^2\mathbf{i} + 0.01t^3\mathbf{j}$, where $\mathbf{i}$ and $\mathbf{j}$ are respectively horizontal and vertical, and the units are metric. Calculate:
   (a) the position, velocity and acceleration after 100 s;
   (b) the (straight line) distance of the aeroplane from take-off point after 100 s;
   (c) the distance travelled by the aeroplane in the first 100 seconds of flight.

6   Show that, for the astroid $x = a \cos^3 p$, $y = a \sin^3 p$,

$$\frac{ds}{dp} = \frac{3a}{2} \sin 2p \quad \text{when} \quad 0 \leqslant p \leqslant \tfrac{1}{2}\pi.$$

   Find the arc length from $p = 0$ to $p = \tfrac{1}{2}\pi$, and deduce the length of the whole curve.
   What is $\displaystyle\int_0^{2\pi} \frac{3a}{2} \sin 2p \, dp$? Why does this integral fail to give the length of the astroid?

7   Show that, for the cardioid $\mathbf{r} = \begin{bmatrix} 2 \cos \theta + \cos 2\theta \\ 2 \sin \theta + \sin 2\theta \end{bmatrix}$,

$$\frac{ds}{d\theta} = 4 \cos \tfrac{1}{2}\theta \quad \text{when} \quad 0 \leqslant \theta \leqslant \pi.$$

   What is $ds/d\theta$ when $\pi \leqslant \theta \leqslant 2\pi$? Calculate the length of the cardioid.

8 Each cable supporting the central section of a suspension bridge forms part of a parabola. For the Severn bridge the equation of the parabola is approximately

$$y = \frac{x^2}{3000} \quad \text{for} \quad -500 \leqslant x \leqslant 500,$$

where the units are metres and the axes are as shown in Fig. 5. Show that the length of this part of a cable is

$$\int_{-500}^{500} \sqrt{\left(1 + \frac{x^2}{2\,250\,000}\right)} dx.$$

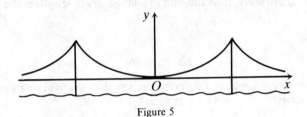

Figure 5

Use the fact that $1 + \frac{1}{2}h - \frac{1}{8}h^2 < \sqrt{(1 + h)} < 1 + \frac{1}{2}h$ for $0 < h < 1$ (Note 6.1) to evaluate this length to the nearest metre.

9 Show that the length of the perimeter of the ellipse $x = 5 \cos \theta$, $y = 4 \sin \theta$ is $20 \int_0^{\pi/2} \sqrt{(1 - \frac{9}{25} \cos^2 \theta)} d\theta$. Use the trapezium rule or Simpson's rule with four strips to evaluate this approximately.

10 Show that the arc length of one complete wave of $y = 3 \cos \frac{1}{4}x$ is exactly the same as the perimeter of the ellipse in question 9.

11 Sketch the curve $y = \frac{1}{2}(e^x + e^{-x})$ and find the arc length from $x = -1$ to $x = 1$.

12 Let $f(x) = x \cos \left(\dfrac{\pi}{2x^2}\right)$ for $x \neq 0$; $f(0) = 0$.

(a) Show that the curve $y = f(x)$ lies between the lines $y = \pm x$ and passes through the points $(1, 0)$, $(\sqrt{\frac{1}{2}}, -\sqrt{\frac{1}{2}})$, $(\sqrt{\frac{1}{3}}, 0)$, $(\sqrt{\frac{1}{4}}, \sqrt{\frac{1}{4}})$, $(\sqrt{\frac{1}{5}}, 0)$, $(\sqrt{\frac{1}{6}}, -\sqrt{\frac{1}{6}})$, $(\sqrt{\frac{1}{7}}, 0)$, ... Sketch the curve for $0 \leqslant x \leqslant 1$.

(b) Show that the length of the curve from $x = \dfrac{1}{\sqrt{(2m + 1)}}$ to $x = \dfrac{1}{\sqrt{(2m - 1)}}$ is greater than $\dfrac{2}{\sqrt{(2m)}} = \dfrac{\sqrt{2}}{\sqrt{m}}$.

(c) Deduce that the length of the curve from $x = \dfrac{1}{\sqrt{(2n + 1)}}$ to $x = 1$ is greater than $\sqrt{2}\left(\dfrac{1}{1} + \dfrac{1}{\sqrt{2}} + \dfrac{1}{\sqrt{3}} + \cdots + \dfrac{1}{\sqrt{n}}\right)$.

(d) By replacing each term of the sum by the smallest term, show that

$$\frac{1}{1} + \frac{1}{\sqrt{2}} + \frac{1}{\sqrt{3}} + \cdots + \frac{1}{\sqrt{n}} > \frac{n}{\sqrt{n}} = \sqrt{n}.$$

(e) Deduce that this curve does not have a finite length between $x = 0$ and $x = 1$.

6.2 ARC LENGTH WITH POLAR COORDINATES

Since
$$\mathbf{v} = \dot{r}\hat{\mathbf{r}} + r\dot{\theta}\hat{\mathbf{u}},$$

where $\hat{\mathbf{r}}$ and $\hat{\mathbf{u}}$ are perpendicular unit vectors (Fig. 6), the speed of P is

$$|\mathbf{v}| = \sqrt{(\dot{r}^2 + (r\dot{\theta})^2)}.$$

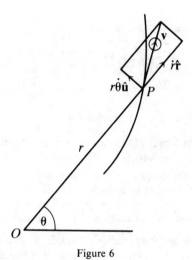

Figure 6

But, as we saw in §6.1, the speed is $\dot{s}$, where s is the arc length measured from some fixed point on the curve.

So
$$s = \int \sqrt{(\dot{r}^2 + (r\dot{\theta})^2)}\,dt.$$

Similarly, if r and θ are given in terms of a parameter p,

$$s = \int \sqrt{\left[\left(\frac{dr}{dp}\right)^2 + \left(r\frac{d\theta}{dp}\right)^2\right]}\,dp,$$

and in particular when $\theta = p$,

$$s = \int \sqrt{\left[\left(\frac{dr}{d\theta}\right)^2 + r^2\right]}\,d\theta, \quad \text{since} \quad \frac{d\theta}{d\theta} = 1.$$

Example 2
Find the length of the curve $r = \cos^2 p$, $\theta = 2p$ from $p = 0$ to $p = \frac{1}{2}\pi$.

Solution

$$\frac{dr}{dp} = -2 \cos p \sin p, \quad \frac{d\theta}{dp} = 2$$

$$\Rightarrow s = \int_0^{\pi/2} \sqrt{[4 \cos^2 p \sin^2 p + 4 \cos^4 p]} \, dp$$

$$= \int_0^{\pi/2} 2 \cos p \sqrt{[\sin^2 p + \cos^2 p]} \, dp$$

$$= \int_0^{\pi/2} 2 \cos p \, dp$$

$$= [2 \sin p]_0^{\pi/2}$$

$$= 2. \qquad \square$$

Exercise 6B

1   Find by integration the length of the curve $r = 2 \cos \theta$ from $\theta = 0$ to $\theta = \alpha$. Draw a diagram to explain your answer.

2   Find by integration the length of the curve $r = 5 \sec \theta$ from $\theta = 0$ to $\theta = \alpha$ $(0 < \alpha < \pi/2)$. Draw a diagram to explain your answer.

3   Sketch the curve whose polar equation is $r = \dfrac{a\theta}{2\pi}$, where a (constant) and r are measured in centimetres and θ is in radians. Find, in the form of an integral, the length of the curve from $\theta = 0$ to $\theta = 2n\pi$, where n is a positive integer. (You are not required to evaluate this integral.)   [SMP]

4   P is a point on the rim of a wheel with radius 1 and centre A which rolls without slipping round an equal fixed wheel with centre B. Initially B, A, P are in a straight line, and C is the point where the diameter PAB meets the fixed wheel again. Fig. 7 shows a later stage in the motion, when BA has turned through θ.

   (a) Explain why the angle between BA produced and AP is also θ.

   (b) Prove that $CBAP$ is an isosceles trapezium.

   (c) Hence show that, with C as pole, the polar equation of the locus of P is $r = 2(1 + \cos \theta)$. This locus is a *cardioid*.

   (d) Find the length of this cardioid.

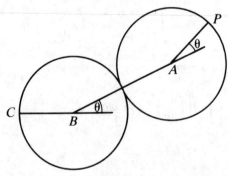

Figure 7

(Compare with Exercise 1B, question 8(*c*)(ii), where the centre *B* is called *O*, with Exercise 2B, question 2, which shows that a cardioid is a special limaçon, and with Exercise 6A, question 7.)

5 A particle moves so that $r = \cos t$, $\theta = \ln \sec t$. Find the distance travelled from $t = 0$ to $t = \pi/3$.

6 The curve *C* has polar equation $r = 2\pi a/\theta$. Show that for small values of θ the *y*-coordinate is approximately $2\pi a$. Sketch *C* between $\theta = 0$ and $\theta = 4\pi$.

Suppose θ is given in terms of the time *t* by $\theta = t(1 - t^2)^{-1/2}$, for $0 < t < 1$. Mark the points *L*, *M*, *N* at which $t = \frac{1}{2}$, $2^{-1/2}$, $\frac{4}{5}$ respectively.

It is given that for this parametrisation the speed of the point *P* whose coordinates are (r, θ) is $2\pi a/\{t^2(1 - t^2)\}$. Write (but do not evaluate) an integral in terms of *t* for the distance from *L* to *N* along the curve. [SMP]

7 (*a*) Sketch the *equiangular spiral* $r = ae^{k\theta}$:
  (i) when $k > 0$; (ii) when $k = 0$; (iii) when $k < 0$.
 (*b*) Find the length of the equiangular spiral from $\theta = \alpha$ to $\theta = \beta$.
 (*c*) With $k > 0$, what happens to (i) the curve, (ii) the length of the curve, as $\alpha \to -\infty$ in (*b*)?

8 The ellipse $l/r = 1 + e \cos \theta$ has eccentricity *e* so small that e^2 may be neglected. Show that, to this degree of approximation,

$$r = l(1 - e \cos \theta)$$

and $$s = l(\theta - e \sin \theta),$$

where *s* is the arc length measured from the point where $\theta = 0$.

9 Use the substitution $\theta = \tan u$ to show that the arc length of the spiral $r = a\theta$ from $\theta = 0$ to $\theta = \alpha$ is

$$\int_0^k a \sec^3 u \, du, \quad \text{where} \quad k = \tan^{-1} \alpha.$$

By writing $\sec^3 u = \sec u \times \sec^2 u$ and integrating by parts, show that this arc length is

$$\tfrac{1}{2}a\{\alpha\sqrt{(1 + a^2)} + \ln(\alpha + \sqrt{(1 + \alpha^2)})\}.$$

Project Exercise 6C

This sequence of questions deals first with the calculation of the area of a surface of revolution (questions 1–8), and then with the celebrated Pappus–Guldin Theorems (questions 9–18), which were first stated by Pappus of Alexandria in about AD 320, and then reappeared (without acknowledgement) in books written by Paul Guldin (1577–1643).

In this exercise all rotations are through four right angles.

1 Show that the curved surface area of a right circular cone of base radius *r* and slant height *l* is $\pi r l$.

2 A line segment of length δs makes angle α with the *x*-axis, and the *y*-coordinates of its endpoints and midpoint are y_1, y_2, y respectively (Fig. 8). When this line segment is rotated about the *x*-axis it forms a surface of revolution (called a *frustum*) with surface area δS (Fig. 9).

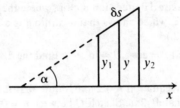

Figure 8

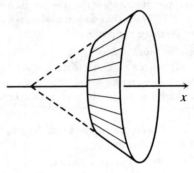

Figure 9

(a) Treating the frustum as the difference of two cones, show that

$$\delta S = \pi(y_2^2 - y_1^2)\operatorname{cosec}\alpha.$$

(b) Show by factorising that $\delta S = \pi(y_2 + y_1)\delta s$ and deduce that

$$\delta S = 2\pi y\delta s.$$

3   A surface of revolution is formed by rotating the arc AB of the curve $y = f(x)$ about the x-axis (Fig. 10). Prove that the area S of this surface is given by

$$S = \int_a^b 2\pi y\frac{ds}{dx}\,dx.$$

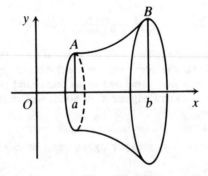

Figure 10

Write down the corresponding integral for S when x and y are given in terms of a parameter p.

4   For the parabola $x = ap^2$, $y = 2ap$, show that, when $p > 0$,

$$y\frac{ds}{dp} = 4a^2 p\sqrt{(1 + p^2)}.$$

Using the substitution $u = 1 + p^2$, find the area of the surface formed by rotating the part of the parabola from $x = a$ to $x = 4a$ about the x-axis.

5   For the circle $x^2 + y^2 = a^2$, show that

$$\frac{ds}{dx} = \frac{a}{\sqrt{(a^2 - x^2)}}.$$

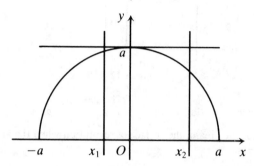

Figure 11

Fig. 11 shows the semicircle $x^2 + y^2 = a^2$, $y > 0$, the line segment $y = a$, $-a \leqslant x \leqslant a$, and two lines $x = x_1$, $x = x_2$. When these are all rotated about the x-axis we obtain a sphere with a circumscribing cylinder cut by two planes perpendicular to the axis of the cylinder (try to sketch this).

Prove that the portions of the sphere and cylinder between the two planes have equal curved surface areas. (This is said to have been the discovery which most pleased Archimedes (287–212 BC); at his request the figure of a sphere circumscribed by a cylinder was carved on his tombstone.)

6   Use the 'Archimedes tombstone' theorem to find
   (*a*) the surface area of a sphere of radius a;
   (*b*) the surface area of the region north of the Arctic Circle (latitude 66.53°N), taking the Earth to be a sphere of radius 6370 km.

7   One arch of the cycloid $x = a(\theta - \sin \theta)$, $y = a(1 - \cos \theta)$ is rotated about the x-axis. Show that the area of the surface generated is $64\pi a^2/3$.

8   The region bounded by the curve $y = 1/x$ and the lines $y = 0$, $x = 1$, $x = k$ (where $k > 1$) is rotated about the x-axis.
   (*a*) Prove that the volume V of the body formed is $\pi(1 - 1/k)$.
   (*b*) Prove that the curved surface area S is

$$\int_1^k \frac{2\pi}{x} \sqrt{\left(1 + \frac{1}{x^4}\right)} dx.$$

Use the fact that $1 + \dfrac{1}{x^4} > 1$ to show that $S > 2\pi \ln k$.

   (*c*) Deduce that, as $k \to \infty$, $V \to \pi$ but $S \to \infty$.

(This gives a paradox. Imagine an infinitely long vessel of this shape placed with its axis vertical. Then a volume π of paint poured into the vessel would completely fill it, but no quantity of paint however great would be enough to cover the surface!)

9   Consider a curve defined parametrically by $x = f(p)$, $y = g(p)$ and such that the arc for which $p_1 \leqslant p \leqslant p_2$ does not cut the x-axis (Fig. 12). Let s_0 be the length of this arc, and let $\bar{y}$ be the distance of the centroid of this arc from the x-axis.

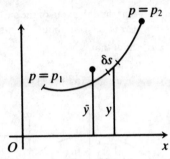

Figure 12

(a) Explain why $\displaystyle \bar{y}s_0 = \lim_{\delta s \to 0} \sum y\delta s = \int_{p_1}^{p_2} y \frac{ds}{dp} dp.$

(b) Show that the area of the surface of revolution when the arc is rotated about the x-axis is $2\pi\bar{y}s_0$.

(c) Deduce that

area of surface of revolution = length of arc

× distance moved by centroid of arc.

This is the Pappus–Guldin theorem for areas. The theorem still applies if the arc is a closed loop; in this case p varies from p_1 to p_2 as (x, y) makes a complete circuit of the loop.

10 Verify the formula for the curved surface area of a cone by using the Pappus–Guldin theorem for the line in Fig. 13 rotating about the x-axis.

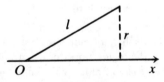

Figure 13

11 A torus (anchor ring) is formed by rotating about the x-axis the circle of radius a and centre $(0, b)$, where $b > a$. Find the surface area of this torus.

12 Use question 6(a) and the Pappus–Guldin theorem to find the centroid of a semicircular arc of radius a.

13 Use question 7 and Example 1 to find the centroid of one arch of a cycloid.

14 A solid of volume V is formed by rotating about the x-axis a region of area A which does not cut the x-axis (Fig. 14). The distance of the centroid of the region from the x-axis is $\bar{y}$.

(a) Explain why $\displaystyle V = \int_a^b \pi(y_2^2 - y_1^2)dx$

and $\displaystyle \bar{y}A = \lim_{\delta x \to 0} \sum \frac{y_1 + y_2}{2}(y_2 - y_1)\delta x = \int_a^b \tfrac{1}{2}(y_2^2 - y_1^2)dx.$

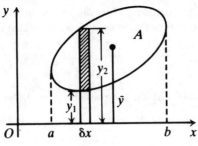

Figure 14

(b) Show that $2\pi\bar{y}A = V$.

(c) Deduce that

volume of solid of revolution = area of region

> × distance moved by centroid of region.

This is the Pappus–Guldin theorem for volumes.

15   The rectangle in Fig. 15 is rotated about AB to form a solid. Use the Pappus–Guldin theorems to find the surface area and volume of this solid. Check your results by other methods.

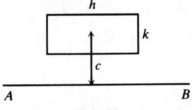

Figure 15

16   Find the volume of the torus in question 11.

17   Find the centroid of a semicircular region of radius a.

18   Fig. 16 shows a circular arc AB of radius a subtending angle 2α at the centre O of the circle.

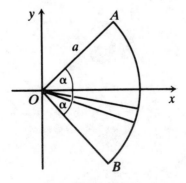

Figure 16

(*a*) Use 'Archimedes tombstone' (question 5) to find the surface area generated when this arc is rotated about the *y*-axis. Hence show that the centroid of the arc is $\left(\dfrac{a \sin \alpha}{\alpha}, 0 \right)$.

(*b*) By dividing the region *OAB* into thin sectors, which may be treated as thin isosceles triangles, show that the centroid of region *OAB* is $\left(\dfrac{2a \sin \alpha}{3\alpha}, 0 \right)$.

(*c*) Now rotate region *OAB* about *OA*. Show that the volume generated is $\frac{4}{3}\pi a^3 \sin^2 \alpha$.

(*d*) Deduce that the volume common to a cone of semivertical angle *β*, vertex *O*, and a sphere of radius *a*, centre *O*, is

$$\tfrac{2}{3}\pi a^3 (1 - \cos \beta).$$

7

Curvature

7.1 CURVATURE

Anyone who has driven along a winding country lane will have felt that the forces on the steering depend on how much and how suddenly the direction of motion changes. In this chapter we shall first make precise this intuitive idea of 'the rate at which a curve curves', and then apply our ideas to the motion of a particle along a curve.

Let the distance measured along a curve from a fixed point P_0 to another point P be s. The *positive tangent* at P is the tangent with the same sense as the positive sense of description at P, as defined in §6.1. Let ψ be the angle between the positive tangent at P and the positive x-axis. Let the increases in s and ψ when moving from P to Q on the curve be δs and $\delta\psi$ (Fig. 1).

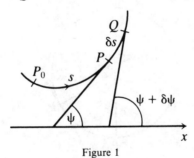

Figure 1

The *average curvature* from P to Q is defined to be $\dfrac{\delta\psi}{\delta s}$; a large change of direction when travelling a small distance then gives a large average curvature, as we would expect intuitively.

Taking the limit as $Q \to P$ and $\delta s \to 0$ leads to the following definition.

The *curvature* at a point P is the rate of change of ψ with respect to s at P. Curvature is denoted by κ (kappa), and thus $\kappa = \dfrac{d\psi}{ds}$.

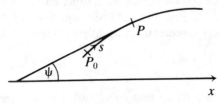

Figure 2

For the curve in Fig. 1, ψ increases as s increases, so κ is positive. In Fig. 2 κ is negative.

Q.1   Draw similar sketches for other cases to check that if $\kappa > 0$ the curve curves to the left of the positive tangent, but if $\kappa < 0$ it curves to the right.

Q.2   Sketch a curve for which $\kappa < 0$ when $x < a$, $\kappa = 0$ when $x = a$, and $\kappa > 0$ when $x > a$.

Two simple special cases can be dealt with immediately. For a straight line ψ is constant, and so $\kappa = 0$ at every point. For a circle of radius a described anticlockwise and with P_0 the minimum point (Fig. 3),

$$s = a\psi$$

$$\Rightarrow \frac{ds}{d\psi} = a$$

$$\Rightarrow \kappa = \frac{1}{a}.$$

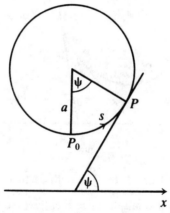

Figure 3

A circle therefore has constant curvature $1/a$. Note that, as expected, if the radius is large then the curvature is small, whereas a small circle has large curvature.

It is not so simple to find the curvature of other curves. If we have an equation connecting s and ψ (called the *intrinsic* equation of the curve) we can differentiate to find κ (Example 1), but usually we have to take a less direct route (Example 2).

Example 1

A uniform flexible chain hangs in a curve called a *catenary*. Find the intrinsic equation of a catenary. Find the curvature when $\psi = \pi/4$.

Solution
Let the chain have weight w per unit length. Consider the portion of the chain from the lowest point P_0 to another point P, where arc $P_0 P = s$. This portion is in equilibrium under the action of three forces: the weight ws, the horizontal tension T_0 at P_0, and the tension T at P, which makes angle ψ with the horizontal (Fig. 4).

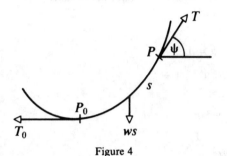

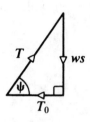

Figure 4   Figure 5

From the triangle of forces (Fig. 5)

$$ws = T_0 \tan \psi$$

or $\qquad s = c \tan \psi$, where c is the constant T_0/w.

This is the intrinsic equation. Differentiating,

$$\frac{ds}{d\psi} = c \sec^2 \psi$$

so that $\qquad\qquad \kappa = \frac{d\psi}{ds} = \frac{1}{c} \cos^2 \psi,$

and $\qquad\qquad \psi = \frac{\pi}{4} \Rightarrow \kappa = \frac{1}{2c}.$ $\qquad\qquad \square$

Q.3   What is the greatest curvature of this catenary, and where does it occur?

Example 2
Find the curvature of the parabola $x = 5t^2$, $y = 10t$ in terms of the parameter t.

Solution
Both s and ψ depend on the parameter t, so we eventually want to use

$$\kappa = \frac{d\psi}{ds} = \frac{\dot{\psi}}{\dot{s}}.$$

We know (§6.1) that

$$\dot{s} = \sqrt{(\dot{x}^2 + \dot{y}^2)}$$
$$= \sqrt{(100t^2 + 100)} = 10\sqrt{(t^2 + 1)}.$$

Since ψ is the angle between the positive tangent and the positive x-axis, to find $\dot{\psi}$ we can use

$$\tan \psi = \frac{dy}{dx} = \frac{\dot{y}}{\dot{x}} = \frac{10}{10t} = \frac{1}{t} \qquad (t \neq 0)$$

or alternatively $\cot \psi = t$.

In this particular example the point given by $t = 0$ is significant as it is the vertex of the parabola, so we prefer to use $\cot \psi$.

Differentiating with respect to t.

$$(-\operatorname{cosec}^2 \psi)\dot{\psi} = 1.$$

But $\qquad \operatorname{cosec}^2 \psi = 1 + \cot^2 \psi = 1 + t^2.$

Therefore $\qquad \dot{\psi} = \dfrac{-1}{t^2 + 1},$

and $\qquad \kappa = \dfrac{\dot{\psi}}{\dot{s}} = \dfrac{-1}{10(t^2 + 1)^{3/2}}.$

Q.4   Account for the negative sign in this answer. What is the greatest value of $|\kappa|$, and where does this occur?

A similar method can be used to find the curvature whenever x and y are given in terms of a parameter t.

For then $\qquad \dot{s} = \sqrt{(\dot{x}^2 + \dot{y}^2)}$

and $\qquad \tan \psi = \dfrac{\dot{y}}{\dot{x}} \Rightarrow (\sec^2 \psi)\dot{\psi} = \dfrac{\dot{x}\ddot{y} - \dot{y}\ddot{x}}{\dot{x}^2}$

$$\Rightarrow \left(1 + \frac{\dot{y}^2}{\dot{x}^2}\right)\dot{\psi} = \frac{\dot{x}\ddot{y} - \dot{y}\ddot{x}}{\dot{x}^2}$$

$$\Rightarrow \qquad \dot{\psi} = \frac{\dot{x}\ddot{y} - \dot{y}\ddot{x}}{\dot{x}^2 + \dot{y}^2}$$

so that $\qquad \kappa = \dfrac{\dot{\psi}}{\dot{s}} = \dfrac{\dot{x}\ddot{y} - \dot{y}\ddot{x}}{(\dot{x}^2 + \dot{y}^2)^{3/2}}.$

If $\dot{x} = 0$ then $\tan \psi$ is undefined, but we can obtain the same formula for κ starting from $\cot \psi = \dfrac{\dot{x}}{\dot{y}}$, as in Example 2.

Q.5   Write out the details of this method.

If $\dot{x} = \dot{y} = 0$ then κ is undefined, as we might expect since the point is then a cusp (unless we have a 'bad parametrisation', as in Note 1.4).

Q.6   Write down the formula for κ when x and y are given in terms of a parameter p.

Q.7 Check that this formula gives the curvature of the circle $x = a \cos \theta$, $y = a \sin \theta$ correctly.

As an important special case, if $t = x$ then $\dot{x} = 1$, $\ddot{x} = 0$,

$$\dot{y} = \frac{dy}{dx}, \quad \ddot{y} = \frac{d^2 y}{dx^2}$$

and so

$$\kappa = \frac{\dfrac{d^2 y}{dx^2}}{\left(1 + \left(\dfrac{dy}{dx}\right)^2\right)^{3/2}}$$

Q.8 Write down the formula for κ when x is given in terms of y.

Example 3
Find the curvature at $(1, \frac{1}{4})$ for the curve $4y = x^3$.

Solution

$$\frac{dy}{dx} = \tfrac{3}{4}x^2, \quad \frac{d^2 y}{dx^2} = \tfrac{3}{2}x.$$

At $(1, \frac{1}{4})$

$$\frac{dy}{dx} = \tfrac{3}{4}, \quad \frac{d^2 y}{dx^2} = \tfrac{3}{2}.$$

Therefore

$$\kappa = \frac{3/2}{(1 + 9/16)^{3/2}} = \frac{96}{125}. \qquad \square$$

The expression for curvature in polar coordinates is cumbersome and rarely used. Instead it is better to use θ as a parameter for Cartesian coordinates:

$$r = f(\theta) \Rightarrow \begin{cases} x = f(\theta) \cos \theta \\ y = f(\theta) \sin \theta \end{cases}.$$

Exercise 7A

Find the curvature at a general point for each of the curves of questions 1–6.

1   $y = 4x^2 + 3$.   2 $x = 2t^3$, $y = 3t^2$.   3 $y = \sin x$.

4   The astroid, $x = a \cos^3 p$, $y = a \sin^3 p$.

5   The cardioid, $r = a(1 + \cos \theta)$.

6   The equiangular spiral $r = 2e^\theta$.

7   Find the curvature at $(4, 9)$ on the hyperbola $xy = 36$.

8   Find the curvature of the parabola $y^2 = 4ax$ at the origin.

9   Find the curvature at the point $\theta = \pi/4$ on the ellipse $x = a \cos \theta$, $y = b \sin \theta$.

10   Find κ in terms of x when $y = x^3$. Show that κ is greatest when $x = 45^{-1/4}$.

11   Show that, for the curve $y = \frac{1}{2}(e^x + e^{-x})$, $\kappa = 1/y^2$.

12 (a) Show that $\kappa \approx \dfrac{d^2y}{dx^2}$ if $\dfrac{dy}{dx}$ is small.

(b) Show that if the angle between the tangent and the x-axis is less than $15°$ then $\dfrac{d^2y}{dx^2}$ may be used instead of κ with an error of less than 10%.

13 Find the curvature when $\psi = \alpha$ for the curve with intrinsic equation

$$s = c \ln \sec \psi.$$

14 For the cycloid $x = a(\theta - \sin \theta)$, $y = a(1 - \cos \theta)$ (as in Example 3 of Chapter 1, p. 5) use half-angle formulae to show that

$$\psi = \frac{\pi}{2} - \frac{\theta}{2}.$$

Deduce from the fact that $\dfrac{ds}{d\theta} = 2a \sin \dfrac{\theta}{2}$ (Example 1 of Chapter 6, p. 86)

that

$$\kappa = -\frac{1}{4a} \sec \psi.$$

Hence find the intrinsic equation of the cycloid.

15 The coordinates of the point P are (x, y) referred to one pair of Cartesian axes, and (X, Y) referred to a second pair of axes obtained by rotating the first pair through angle α about O (Fig. 6).

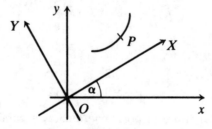

Figure 6

Show that
$$\begin{bmatrix} X \\ Y \end{bmatrix} = \begin{bmatrix} \cos \alpha & \sin \alpha \\ -\sin \alpha & \cos \alpha \end{bmatrix} \begin{bmatrix} x \\ y \end{bmatrix}.$$

Verify that the curvature at P is unchanged by this rotation of axes. (Hint: suppose that x and y are given in terms of a parameter t, and check that

$$(\dot{X}\ddot{Y} - \dot{Y}\ddot{X})/(\dot{X}^2 + \dot{Y}^2)^{3/2} = (\dot{x}\ddot{y} - \dot{y}\ddot{x})/(\dot{x}^2 + \dot{y}^2)^{3/2}.)$$

16 If x and y are given in terms of the arc length s, prove that

(a) $\kappa = -x''/y' = y''/x'$,

(b) $\kappa^2 = (x'')^2 + (y'')^2$,

where dashes denote differentiation with respect to s.

7.2 RADIUS AND CENTRE OF CURVATURE

Since a circle with curvature κ has radius $1/\kappa$, we define the *radius of curvature* at a point on a curve to be $1/\kappa$; this is denoted by ρ (rho), so that

$$\rho = \frac{1}{\kappa} = \frac{ds}{d\psi}.$$

A family of circles can be drawn which pass through a point P of a curve and touch the tangent at P (Fig. 7). All these circles have at P the same values of y and dy/dx as the curve.

The particular circle with radius $|\rho|$ and on the concave side of the curve also has the same curvature as the curve at P, and is in this sense the best fitting circle of the family. This circle is called the *circle of curvature* at P. If the steering wheel of a car being driven along the curve jams at P, the car will then move round the circle of curvature. The centre C of the circle of curvature is called the *centre of curvature* at P.

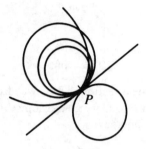

Figure 7

We now introduce two standard *unit* vectors (Fig. 8). The unit vector in the direction of the positive tangent is called $\hat{t}$. By definition the direction angle of $\hat{t}$ is ψ, and so

$$\hat{t} = \begin{bmatrix} \cos \psi \\ \sin \psi \end{bmatrix}.$$

The unit vector $\hat{n}$ is obtained by rotating $\hat{t}$ through $+\pi/2$, so that the direction angle of $\hat{n}$ is $\psi + \pi/2$, and

$$\hat{n} = \begin{bmatrix} -\sin \psi \\ \cos \psi \end{bmatrix}.$$

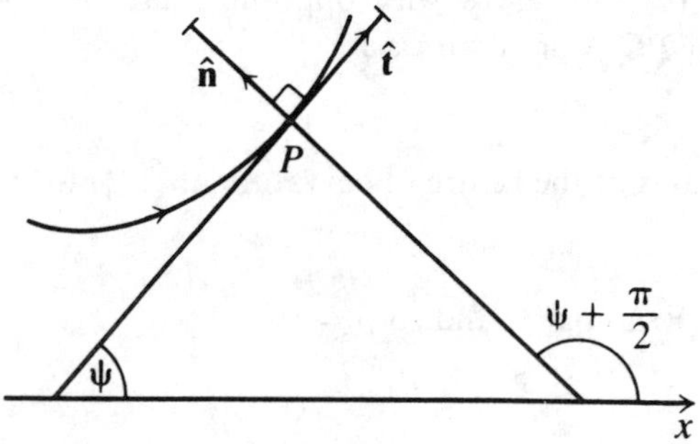

Figure 8

Q.9   Show that $\dot{\hat{t}} = \dot{\psi}\hat{n}$ and $\dot{\hat{n}} = -\dot{\psi}\hat{t}$.

If $\kappa > 0$ then $\rho > 0$ and the direction of $\hat{n}$ is towards the concave side of the curve

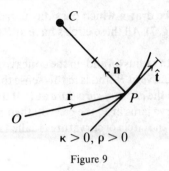

Figure 9

(Fig. 9). Therefore

$$\mathbf{PC} = \rho\hat{\mathbf{n}}.$$

If $\kappa < 0$ then $\rho < 0$ and the direction of $\hat{\mathbf{n}}$ is away from the concave side of the curve (Fig. 10). To get from P to C we go a distance $-\rho$ in the direction of $-\hat{\mathbf{n}}$, so that $\mathbf{PC} = (-\rho)(-\hat{\mathbf{n}}) = \rho\hat{\mathbf{n}}$ again.

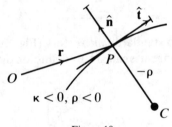

Figure 10

Therefore in both cases

| the position vector of the centre of curvature is $\mathbf{r} + \rho\hat{\mathbf{n}}$. |

Q.10 Draw diagrams similar to Figs. 9 and 10, (a) for curves with negative gradients, (b) for curves with opposite sense of description positive. Check that $\mathbf{PC} = \rho\hat{\mathbf{n}}$ in all cases.

Example 4

Find the coordinates of the centre of curvature at $(1, \frac{1}{4})$ for the curve $4y = x^3$.

Solution

At $(1, \frac{1}{4})$ $\kappa = \frac{96}{125}$ (Example 3) and so $\rho = \frac{125}{96}$.

Also

$$\tan\psi = \frac{dy}{dx} = \tfrac{3}{4}x^2$$

$$= \tfrac{3}{4} \text{ at } (1, \tfrac{1}{4}),$$

so that

$$\hat{\mathbf{t}} = \begin{bmatrix} \frac{4}{5} \\ \frac{3}{5} \end{bmatrix} \quad \text{and} \quad \hat{\mathbf{n}} = \begin{bmatrix} -\frac{3}{5} \\ \frac{4}{5} \end{bmatrix}.$$

Therefore $\qquad \mathbf{OC} = \mathbf{r} + \rho\hat{\mathbf{n}} = \begin{bmatrix} 1 \\ \frac{1}{4} \end{bmatrix} + \frac{125}{96} \begin{bmatrix} -\frac{3}{5} \\ \frac{4}{5} \end{bmatrix} = \begin{bmatrix} \frac{7}{32} \\ \frac{11}{24} \end{bmatrix}.$

The centre of curvature is $(\frac{7}{32}, \frac{11}{24})$. $\qquad\qquad\qquad\qquad\qquad$ □

Exercise 7B

1 Find the coordinates of the centre of curvature of the hyperbola $xy = 25$ at $(5, 5)$.

2 A curve $\mathscr{C}$ is defined by $\mathbf{r} = \begin{bmatrix} \frac{1}{2}t^2 \\ t + \frac{1}{3}t^3 \end{bmatrix}$ for a real parameter t. Calculate a unit tangent vector at $t = 0$, a unit normal vector at $t = 1$, and the curvatures at $t = 0$ and $t = 1$. Hence sketch $\mathscr{C}$ between $t = -2$ and $t = 2$. $\qquad$ [SMP]

3 Given that $x = a\cos 3p + 3a\cos p$, $y = a\sin 3p + 3a\sin p$,

(a) prove that $\hat{\mathbf{t}} = \begin{bmatrix} -\sin 2p \\ \cos 2p \end{bmatrix}$ and hence that $\psi = \frac{\pi}{2} + 2p$,

(b) prove that $ds/dp = 6a\cos p$.

Deduce that $\rho = 3a\cos p$, and find the coordinates of the centre of curvature.

4 (a) Find the radius and centre of curvature at the point P with parameter p on the curve $x = 2p^3$, $y = 3p^2$.

(b) Repeat (a), using the following method:

Let the equation of the circle of curvature be

$$(x - a)^2 + (y - b)^2 = \rho^2.$$

The circle and the curve must both

(i) pass through P, (ii) have the same gradient at P,

(iii) have the same value of d^2y/dx^2 at P.

These three conditions determine the values of a, b, ρ. (This method can be used for any curve.)

5 The position vector $\mathbf{r}$ of a point on an ellipse is given by $\mathbf{r} = \begin{bmatrix} 2\cos\theta \\ \sin\theta \end{bmatrix}$. Find the radius of curvature, and prove that the position vector $\mathbf{c}$ of the centre of curvature is given by $\mathbf{c} = \frac{3}{2}\begin{bmatrix} \cos^3\theta \\ -2\sin^3\theta \end{bmatrix}$. Find $\mathbf{c}$ when $\theta = 0$, $\tan^{-1}(\frac{3}{4})$ and $\pi/2$.

Sketch on the same axes the ellipse and the locus of its centre of curvature. (The locus of the centre of curvature of a curve is called the *evolute* of the curve.)

6 Prove that, for the parabola $y^2 = 4x$,

$$\mathbf{r} = \begin{bmatrix} t^2 \\ 2t \end{bmatrix} \Rightarrow \mathbf{c} = \begin{bmatrix} 2 + 3t^2 \\ -2t^3 \end{bmatrix}.$$

Deduce that the equation of the evolute is $27y^2 = 4(x - 2)^3$. Sketch the parabola and its evolute in a single diagram.

7 (a) Show that the centre of curvature has coordinates

$$\left(x - \frac{dy}{d\psi}, y + \frac{dx}{d\psi} \right)$$

(b) Find ψ in terms of θ for the curve

$$x = a(\cos\theta + \theta\sin\theta), \qquad y = a(\sin\theta - \theta\cos\theta),$$

and use (a) to find the centre of curvature. What is the evolute?

8 Obtain an expression for the arc length s of the curve

$$\mathbf{r} = \frac{e^{\theta}}{\sqrt{2}} \, (\mathbf{i} \cos \theta + \mathbf{j} \sin \theta)$$

measured from the point $(1/\sqrt{2}, 0)$ on the curve. Hence find $\mathbf{r}$ in terms of s. Check your answer by showing that $|d\mathbf{r}/ds| = 1$.

Show that the tangent unit vector $\hat{\mathbf{t}}$ at the point with parameter s is given by

$$\hat{\mathbf{t}}\sqrt{2} = (p - q)\mathbf{i} + (p + q)\mathbf{j}.$$

where $p = \cos \{\ln (1 + s)\}$ and $q = \sin \{\ln (1 + s)\}$. Find also the normal unit vector $\hat{\mathbf{n}}$ at s and deduce that the curvature κ at s is inversely proportional to $|\mathbf{r}|$.

[SMP]

9 Prove that (a) $\dfrac{d\mathbf{r}}{ds} = \hat{\mathbf{t}}$, (b) $\dfrac{d\hat{\mathbf{t}}}{ds} = \kappa\hat{\mathbf{n}}$, (c) $\dfrac{d\hat{\mathbf{n}}}{ds} = -\kappa\hat{\mathbf{t}}$.

10 The centre of curvature has position vector $\mathbf{c}$. Prove that $\dfrac{d\mathbf{c}}{dp} = \dfrac{d\rho}{dp} \, \hat{\mathbf{n}}$, where p is a parameter. (Hint: Start by differentiating $\mathbf{c} = \mathbf{r} + \rho\mathbf{n}$ with respect to the arc length s.)

Deduce that

(a) every normal to a curve touches its evolute;

(b) with the notation of Fig. 11, arc $C_1C_2 = \rho_2 - \rho_1$.

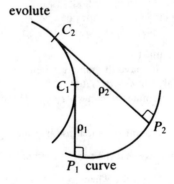

Figure 11

11 Use 10(b) to find the total length of the evolute of the ellipse of question 5.

12 Prove that the evolute of the cycloid $x = a(\theta - \sin \theta)$, $y = a(1 - \cos \theta)$ is a congruent cycloid, and show them both in a sketch. Try to find another curve whose evolute is congruent to itself.

7.3 TANGENTIAL AND NORMAL COMPONENTS OF ACCELERATION

The velocity $\mathbf{v}$ of a particle moving along a curve is given by

$$\mathbf{v} = v\hat{\mathbf{t}}.$$

We differentiate with respect to time to find the acceleration $\mathbf{a}$:

$$\mathbf{a} = \dot{\mathbf{v}} = \dot{v}\hat{\mathbf{t}} + v\dot{\psi}\hat{\mathbf{n}}.$$

But
$$\dot{\psi} = \frac{d\psi}{dt} = \frac{d\psi}{ds} \times \frac{ds}{dt} = \kappa v = \frac{v}{\rho}.$$

Therefore
$$\mathbf{a} = \dot{v}\hat{\mathbf{t}} + \frac{v^2}{\rho}\hat{\mathbf{n}}.$$

This gives the following tangential ($\hat{\mathbf{t}}$) and normal ($\hat{\mathbf{n}}$) components for a particle moving along a curve with speed v.

	Tangential	Normal
Velocity **v**	v	0
Acceleration **a**	$\dot{v}$	v^2/ρ

(Compare §2.4.) These components are, of course, the same as if the particle were at this moment moving around the circle of curvature.

Example 5
A hump-backed bridge has a road surface in the shape of the curve $y = 1 - x^2/16$ ($-4 \leqslant x \leqslant 4$, x and y in metres). What is the greatest speed a car may have at the top of the hump if it is not to leave the road there?

Solution
The top of the hump is $(0, 1)$.
$$\frac{dy}{dx} = -\frac{x}{8}, \quad \frac{d^2y}{dx^2} = -\tfrac{1}{8}$$

so when $x = 0$, $\rho = -8$.

The acceleration at the top is $v^2/8$ downwards. If the car has mass M then the vertical forces are its weight Mg and the normal contact force R (Fig. 12).

Resolving vertically,
$$Mg - R = Mv^2/8 \Rightarrow R = Mg - Mv^2/8.$$

For the car not to leave the road, $R \geqslant 0$
$$\Rightarrow Mg \geqslant Mv^2/8 \Rightarrow v^2 \leqslant 8g$$

so the greatest speed is $\sqrt{(8g)}$ (≈ 8.9) m s^{-1}. $\qquad\square$

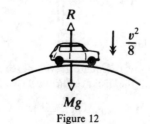

Figure 12

Exercise 7C

1 A particle moves along the curve $4y = x^3$ (x and y in metres) with constant speed 12 m s^{-1}. Find its acceleration at $(1, \frac{1}{4})$.

2 A particle moves along a curve in such a way that the tangent rotates uniformly. Prove that the normal acceleration is proportional to the radius of curvature.

3 A railway track has to pass smoothly from a straight section AO to a curved section joining O and B. Axes and units are chosen so that AO is part of the negative x-axis, O is the origin, and B is $(3, 1)$. Show that, for $0 \leqslant x \leqslant 3$, both the curves $y = x^2/9$ and $y = x^3/27$ will satisfy the requirements. Comment on what the passengers would feel at O for each track layout.

4 When cornering, a vehicle is liable to skid if the force normal to the wheels reaches a certain (fixed) limit. Show that for the most rapid cornering the speed should be kept proportional to the square root of the radius of curvature.

5 A road consists of a straight section (the negative x-axis) followed by a curve (starting at the origin). It is required that a car moving into the curved part at constant speed shall experience an acceleration whose magnitude increases at a constant rate. Find the intrinsic equation of the curve.

6 Two straight stretches of road at right angles to each other are joined by a quarter-circle of radius r. A car approaches the bend with speed v_0, and whilst negotiating the bend the driver regulates the speed so that the acceleration vector makes a constant angle α with the velocity vector. Prove that the car comes out of the bend with a speed of $v_0 e^{\frac{1}{2}\pi \cot \alpha}$.

   Obtain an expression for the time that the car takes to round the bend.

   [SMP, adapted]

7 An object of mass m near the surface of the earth is projected horizontally from a point O. The resistance, mR, of the atmosphere has a direction opposite to that of the velocity of the object. If, at a subsequent instant, ψ is the angle which the direction of motion makes with the horizontal, ρ the radius of curvature of the trajectory at that point and s the length of the trajectory traversed from O (Fig. 13), show that

$$g \cos \psi = v^2/\rho \quad \text{and} \quad g \sin \psi - R = v \, dv/ds.$$

Hence show that
$$\tan \psi - \frac{R}{g \cos \psi} = \frac{1}{v} \frac{dv}{d\psi}.$$

   [SMP]

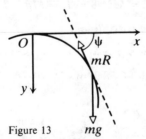

Figure 13

8 In planetary motion under inverse square gravity (force μ/r^2 per unit mass) it may be shown that the speed v and the distance r from S (see Fig. 14) are related by

$$v^2 = \mu \left(\frac{2}{r} - \frac{1}{a} \right),$$

where a is the semi-major axis. Calculate the radius of curvature ρ of this orbit at A by using the formula for normal acceleration, the above formula for v^2, and the inverse square law.

Name which two of A, S, C, A' the centre of curvature at A lies between, and give your reason. **[SMP]**

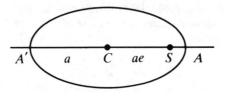

Figure 14

9　The curve C has parametric equations

$$x = a \sec^2 \theta, \qquad y = 2a \tan \theta \qquad (0 \leqslant \theta < \tfrac{1}{2}\pi).$$

Sketch C, by eliminating θ or otherwise. Mark on it the points given by $\theta = 0$ and $\theta = \tfrac{1}{4}\pi$.

A particle moves along C (in the direction of increasing θ) in such a way that its speed v is given by $v^2 = k^2 x^3/a$, where k is a positive constant. Show that $\dot\theta = \tfrac{1}{2}k$.

Find the x- and y-components of the particle's acceleration, and hence show that the acceleration along the normal to the curve is

$$\tfrac{1}{2}k^2 a \sec^3 \theta.$$

Use a formula on normal acceleration and radius of curvature to find the radius of curvature at any point of the curve, and find the centre of curvature at $\theta = \tfrac{1}{4}\pi$.

[SMP]

10　*The Cycloidal Pendulum*

(a) Fig. 15 shows a pendulum string BP which is fixed at B. As it swings the string wraps around the arcs AB and BC which are parts of a cycloid. The length of the pendulum string is $4a$, which is half the arc length of one complete arch of the cycloid (Example 1 on page 86). Use Exercise 7B questions 10 and 12 to show that the pendulum bob moves along an equal cycloid AOC.

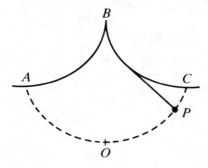

Figure 15

(b) Use Exercise 7A question 14 to show that, with the origin at O, the intrinsic equation of cycloid AOC is $s = 4a \sin \psi$.

(c) Prove that the equation of tangential motion of P is

$$\ddot{s} = \frac{-g}{4a} s.$$

Hence show that P moves with *exact* SHM along its path, with period $4\pi\sqrt{(a/g)}$ which is independent of the amplitude.

[Christiaan Huygens (1629–1695) discovered this and made some pendulum clocks with the cycloidal guides, but because of other mechanical difficulties they were no more accurate than ordinary pendulum clocks.]

Miscellaneous exercise A

1 Describe the curve given by

$$\mathbf{r} = \begin{bmatrix} 5 \cos (t^2) \\ 5 \sin (t^2) \end{bmatrix},$$

where t denotes time.

Find $\mathbf{a} \,(= \ddot{\mathbf{r}})$ and deduce the radial and transverse components of the acceleration.

A boy slides down a banister such that his path is given by

$$\mathbf{r} = \begin{bmatrix} 5 \cos (t^2) \\ 5 \sin (t^2) \\ kt^2 \end{bmatrix},$$

where the units are metres and k is a constant. Indicate on a diagram the shape of the banister and the magnitudes of the boy's acceleration components in the directions (*a*) towards the axis of the curve, (*b*) vertically downwards, (*c*) in a direction perpendicular to those in (*a*) and (*b*).

(*Note*: the unit vectors for $\mathbf{r}$ are horizontal south, horizontal west, and vertically downwards.)

2 Find the points of intersection of the curves

$$1/r = 1 + \cos \theta, \qquad 3/r = 1 - \cos \theta.$$

Show that the curves intersect at right angles.

3 A particle P of mass m moves in a plane under the action of a force which is directed towards the fixed point O. The magnitude of the force is $m\omega^2 r$, where ω is a constant and r is the distance OP. The particle is projected from the point $r = 2a$, $\theta = 0$ with velocity $a\omega$ in a direction perpendicular to the radius vector to that point.

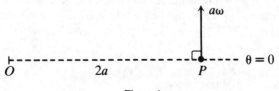

Figure 1

Write down a vector equation of motion for P, and show that both this equation and the initial conditions can be satisfied by

$$\mathbf{r} = \begin{bmatrix} c \cos \omega t \\ a \cos (\omega t + \delta) \end{bmatrix}$$

if the constants c and δ are chosen correctly.

Show that the orbit of P round O is an ellipse, and find its eccentricity. What is the least distance of P from O?

111

4

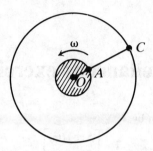

Figure 2

A space station C is orbiting the earth in a circular orbit so that it is always above the point A on the equator. The gravitational force exerted by the earth on a particle at distance r from the centre O is μ/r^2 per unit mass, and ω is the angular velocity of rotation of the earth. Show that

$$OC = (\mu/\omega^2)^{1/3}.$$

The station ejects a small satellite forwards with speed $\frac{1}{4}\omega OC$ relative to the space station, along a path parallel (at the instant of ejection) to its motion. Sketch the orbit of this satellite.

Show that the orbit of the satellite has eccentricity $e = \frac{9}{16}$.

(You may assume the formula $r = h^2/\mu(1 + e \cos \theta)$.)

5   A curve has parametric equation

$$\begin{bmatrix} x \\ y \end{bmatrix} = a \begin{bmatrix} \cos^3 t \\ \sin^3 t \end{bmatrix}, \qquad 0 \leqslant t \leqslant 2\pi.$$

Show that $dy/dx = -\tan t$. Identify the tangents at $t = 0$ and $t = \frac{1}{2}\pi$ and sketch the complete curve.

Show that the length of the curve is $6a$.

6   A cycloid is traced out by a point K on the circumference of a circle of radius c which rolls along a line (see Fig. 3). Initially K coincides with a point O on the line. If $\hat{\imath}$ and $\hat{\jmath}$ denote unit vectors along and perpendicular to the line, and $\hat{\mathbf{u}}$ and $\hat{\mathbf{n}}$ denote unit vectors along and perpendicular to the radius through K when the circle has rotated through an angle p ($0 < p < 2\pi$), find an expression for the vector $\mathbf{r} = \mathbf{OK}$ and deduce that

$$\frac{d\mathbf{r}}{dp} = c(\hat{\imath} + \hat{\mathbf{n}}).$$

Give the direction of this vector.

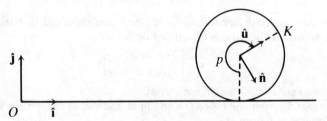

Figure 3

7   Sketch the curve C which has polar equation

$$r = a(2 - \sin \theta), \qquad 0 \leqslant \theta < 2\pi.$$

A point P moves around C in such a way that OP has a constant angular velocity ω. Find the velocity of P; and find the acceleration of P when $\theta = \frac{1}{2}\pi$.

8   A stone is dropped down a deep well. The effect of the well's atmosphere on the stone's motion (which is vertical) is to produce a retardation per unit mass proportional to its speed. If y is the distance fallen by the stone in time t, show that the equation of motion of the stone can be written in the form

$$\frac{d^2 y}{dt^2} + k \frac{dy}{dt} = g,$$

where k is a constant.

Solve this differential equation to obtain the relation between y, g, k and t, given that both y and $\dfrac{dy}{dt}$ are zero when t is zero.

9   A spacecraft is returning to the earth along a hyperbolic path of eccentricity 1.2. At the point of this hyperbola nearest the earth the engines are fired so as to reduce the velocity by 25% (but not to change its direction). Find the eccentricity of the new orbit.

(You may quote the formulae

$$h^2 = \mu l, \qquad l/r = 1 + e \cos \theta.)$$

10

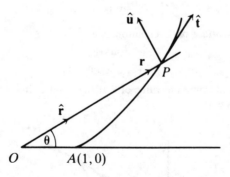

Figure 4

A curve is defined by the equation $\mathbf{r} = e^{2\theta}\hat{\mathbf{r}}$. Write down an expression for

$$\frac{ds}{d\theta}\hat{\mathbf{t}}$$

in terms of $\hat{\mathbf{r}}$, $\hat{\mathbf{u}}$ and θ and hence, or otherwise, find the arc length of the part of the curve for which $0 \leqslant \theta \leqslant 2\pi$.

($\hat{\mathbf{t}}$, $\hat{\mathbf{r}}$ and $\hat{\mathbf{u}}$ are unit vectors. They are illustrated in Fig. 4, part of the curve in which θ is measured from OA. You may quote the result

$$\frac{d\mathbf{r}}{d\theta} = \frac{ds}{d\theta}\hat{\mathbf{t}}.)$$

11

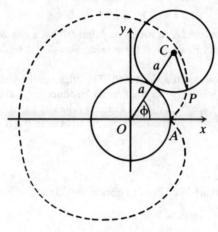

Figure 5

Fig. 5 illustrates a mechanism for generating a cardioid (dashed). The circle centre O, radius a, is fixed. A second circle, also of radius a, rolls without slipping round the outside of the first circle. If P is a point fixed on the circumference of the second circle then, as C makes a complete revolution about O, the point P describes the cardioid. Axes Ox and Oy are taken as shown and the moving circle starts with P at A and C initially on Ox. If the angle $AOC = \phi$, as in the figure, show that

$$OP = a \begin{bmatrix} 2\cos\phi - \cos 2\phi \\ 2\sin\phi - \sin 2\phi \end{bmatrix}.$$

12 Draw the curves whose polar equations are

$$4r = 3a\sec\theta$$

and

$$r = a(\cos\theta + 1)$$

for $0 \leqslant \theta \leqslant \pi$. Determine the value of θ at the point of intersection, and the angle between the curves there.

13

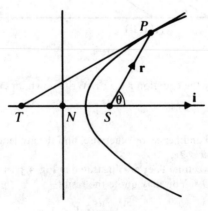

Figure 6

State the focus–directrix definition of a parabola. In the diagram, P lies on a parabola whose focus is S and whose axis is in the direction of the unit vector $\mathbf{i}$; the distance SN from the focus to the directrix is $2a$, and TP is the tangent at P. Show from Fig. 6 that

$$r = 2a + \mathbf{r} \cdot \mathbf{i}$$

where r denotes the magnitude of $\mathbf{r}$.

By differentiating this equation and also the equation

$$r^2 = \mathbf{r} \cdot \mathbf{r}$$

with respect to θ (shown in Fig. 6) show that

$$\hat{\mathbf{r}} \cdot d\mathbf{r}/d\theta = \mathbf{i} \cdot d\mathbf{r}/d\theta.$$

Identify the direction of the vector $d\mathbf{r}/d\theta$. Hence deduce that

$$\text{angle } STP = \text{angle } SPT.$$

14 An interstellar spaceway is being planned for the vicinity of the solar system. The path of the spaceway is a hyperbola with the Sun at its focus, as in Fig. 7 which also shows the asymptotes meeting at P, and its nearest approach to the Sun is 0.5 astronomical units. The spaceway turns through 60° as it passes the Sun. Show that the equation of the spaceway is

$$\tfrac{1}{3}r = (2 + 4\cos\theta)^{-1}$$

in a suitable system of polar coordinates.

What is the eccentricity of this path? Show (using standard formulae) that the distance from the Sun to P is 1 astronomical unit.

A spaceship moving along the spaceway has constant moment of momentum about the Sun. If its speed at a large distance from the Sun is V, find its speed at its closest approach to the Sun.

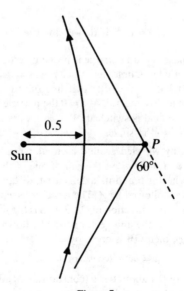

Figure 7

15 The curve
$$r = a \sin^3 \tfrac{1}{3}\theta$$
for $0 \leqslant \theta \leqslant 3\pi$ is sketched in Fig. 8. Show that
$$dx/d\theta = a \sin^2 \tfrac{1}{3}\theta \cos \tfrac{4}{3}\theta$$
at any point P on the curve. Use this and a similar expression for $dy/d\theta$ to show that the tangent at P makes an angle $4\theta/3$ with the x-axis.

By using the formula
$$\kappa = d\psi/ds,$$
or otherwise, calculate the radius of curvature of the curve at P (in terms of a and θ).

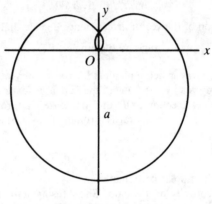

Figure 8

16 Show, by using an integrating factor or otherwise, that the solution of
$$dv/dt + kv = a \sin \omega t$$
which has $v(0) = 0$ is
$$v(t) = e^{-kt} \int_0^t (a + b \sin \omega s)e^{ks} \, ds.$$

A particle of unit mass and unit charge is moving vertically under gravity, with a resistance to motion equal to k times its velocity. At $t = 0$ an electric field $E \sin \omega t$ is switched on, and after half a cycle it is switched off; this applies an upward force $E \sin \omega t$ to the particle in this interval. At $t = 0$ the particle is instantaneously at rest. Find its speed when the field is switched off.

(*Note:* $\int e^{kz} \sin \omega z \, dz = e^{kz}(k \sin \omega z - \omega \cos \omega z)/(k^2 + \omega^2)$.)

17 A perambulator is being wheeled around a circular road island. Fig. 9 is to help illustrate the motion of a point B on the rim of one of the wheels.

The radius of the wheel is b and its axle is at A, distance a from O which is the centre of the circle being followed by A. The wheel rolls without slipping at a steady speed. The unit vector in the direction of OA is $\mathbf{e}$, $\mathbf{m}$ is the unit vector in the direction of the velocity of A and $\mathbf{k}$ is the unit vector vertically downwards. If the angle which AB makes with $\mathbf{m}$ is ϕ, then $\mathbf{OB}$ is given by
$$\mathbf{p} = a\mathbf{e} + b \cos \phi \mathbf{m} + b \sin \phi \mathbf{k}.$$
If the angular velocity of OA about $\mathbf{k}$ is $\dot\theta$ (constant), write down $\dot{\mathbf{e}}$ in terms of $\mathbf{m}$, and $\dot{\mathbf{m}}$ in terms of $\mathbf{e}$. Differentiate $\mathbf{p}$ with respect to time and rearrange your expression

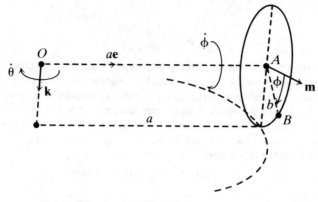

Figure 9

for $\dot{\mathbf{p}}$ in terms of $\mathbf{e}$, $\mathbf{m}$, $\mathbf{k}$, $\dot{\theta}$ and $\dot{\phi}$ in the form

(velocity of A relative to O) + (velocity of B relative to A).

18 A particle P of mass m moves in a plane under the influence of a force $\mathbf{F}$. At time t the particle has position vector

$$\mathbf{r}(t) = \begin{bmatrix} a \cos 2\omega t \\ \omega^{-1} u \sin \omega t \end{bmatrix}$$

where ω, u, a are constants. Find the force $\mathbf{F}$.

Show that the motion of P is periodic and state its period.

Show that the path of P is part of the parabola

$$y^2 = -\tfrac{1}{2}u^2(x - a)/(a\omega^2).$$

Indicate on a rough sketch how P moves on this curve over one complete period.

19 A fixed planet exerts a gravitational force μ/r^2 per unit mass, where r is distance from the centre O of the planet. You are given that under gravity any object (not dropping straight) moves in the curve

$$\frac{1}{r} = \frac{\mu}{h^2}(1 + e \cos \theta),$$

where e is a constant, h is the moment of the velocity about O, and the initial line $\theta = 0$ has been chosen suitably. A satellite of mass m is moving in an ellipse round the planet, and has velocity v at its nearer apse where $\theta = 0$ and $r = d$. Show that

$$v < (2\mu/d)^{1/2}.$$

At the apse the satellite ejects a capsule of mass $\tfrac{1}{4}m$ in a forward direction with a speed $(2\mu/d)^{1/2}$ (relative to the planet). Show that the satellite now has speed

$$v_1 = \tfrac{1}{3}\{4v - (2\mu/d)^{1/2}\},$$

and determine the eccentricity of its new orbit.

20 Show that the tangent to the spiral given by the polar equation

$$r = a\theta, \qquad a > 0, \qquad 0 < \theta < \tfrac{1}{2}\pi$$

makes an angle

$$\psi = \theta + \tan^{-1}\theta$$

with the line $\theta = 0$. Hence show that the radius of curvature, defined as $ds/d\psi$, is given by

$$\rho = \frac{(a^2 + r^2)^{3/2}}{2a^2 + r^2}.$$

21 A computer programmer is devising a computer game of football in which a 'football' B moves over the field of play with a constant velocity **u**, until it reaches the boundaries of the field. As part of the program, a 'defender' P is programmed to move with a constant speed $u = |\mathbf{u}|$ directly towards a point Q midway between B and a fixed point G representing the goal (see Fig. 10). If θ is the angle between the directions of the motions of P and B (and hence Q), show that the distance r of P from Q satisfies the equations

$$\dot{r} = \tfrac{1}{2}u \cos \theta - u, \qquad r\dot{\theta} = -\tfrac{1}{2}u \sin \theta.$$

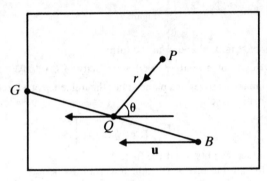

Figure 10

Using the result

$$\int \operatorname{cosec} \theta \, d\theta = -\ln |\operatorname{cosec} \theta + \cot \theta| + \text{const.},$$

deduce that when $0 < \theta < \pi$ the path of P relative to Q satisfies the equation

$$r = \frac{a \sin \theta}{(1 + \cos \theta)^2},$$

where a is a constant. Given that at time $t = 0$, $\theta = \pi/2$ and $r = a$, sketch the path of P relative to Q. (Assume that B continues in a straight line within the field of play until P reaches Q.)

22 A rabbit R runs from the origin O along the y-axis with constant speed u. A dog D starts from position $(-a, 0)$ when the rabbit is at O and runs towards the rabbit with constant speed v. Let r be the distance DR and let θ be the angle which the direction of the dog's velocity makes with the x-axis.

(a) Show that

$$\dot{r} = u \sin \theta - v, \qquad r\dot{\theta} = u \cos \theta.$$

(b) Form a differential equation for $dr/d\theta$ and solve it to show that

$$r = \frac{a(\cos \theta)^{k-1}}{(1 + \sin \theta)^k},$$

where $k = v/u$.

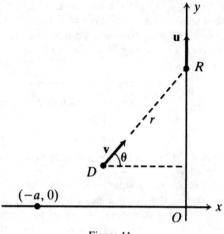

Figure 11

(c) In the case $v = u$ show that the path of R *relative to D* is part of a certain conic, and sketch it in a separate diagram, with D as origin.

23 Sketch the curve whose polar equation is

$$\frac{1}{r} = 1 + 2 \cos \theta,$$

indicating clearly which parts of the curve correspond to various sub-intervals of $-\pi \leqslant \theta \leqslant \pi$.

An object describes the part of this path over which θ increases from $-\tfrac{1}{2}\pi$ to $+\tfrac{1}{2}\pi$ at a rate determined by the equation

$$r^2 \dot{\theta} = 10,$$

where $\dot{\theta}$ denotes the time derivative $d\theta/dt$. Prove that its acceleration is directed towards the origin with magnitude k/r^2, and find the value of k. Write down in the form of an integral the time taken to travel between the points $[1, -\tfrac{1}{2}\pi]$ and $[1, \tfrac{1}{2}\pi]$.

24 (a) A particle moves under the action of a central force. Derive Kepler's second law, that $r^2\dot{\theta}$ is constant.

(b) It used to be believed that there was another planet following the same orbit as the Earth round the Sun, but at the opposite side of the Sun. Suppose that this hypothetical 'anti-Earth' planet E' was furthest from the Sun S ($\phi = 0$ in Fig. 12) when the Earth E was nearest S ($\theta = 0$ in Fig. 12).

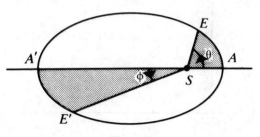

Figure 12

Show that at any subsequent time the two areas ASE and $A'SE'$ must be equal. Assuming that the common orbit is an ellipse of eccentricity e and semi-latus rectum l, write this result as an equality between two integrals.

(c) Find $d\phi/d\theta$ (from (a) or (b) or otherwise) and show that the angle $E'SE$ can only have a stationary value when

$$1 + e \cos \theta = 1 - e \cos \phi.$$

25 A curve R is the locus of a point whose position vector $\mathbf{r}$ is given by

$$\mathbf{r} = \begin{bmatrix} 2p^2 \\ 4p \end{bmatrix},$$

where p is a parameter. Verify that R is the parabola with focus at $(2, 0)$ and directrix $x = -2$. Sketch the curve.

Show that the radius of curvature, ρ, at the point with parameter p is $-4(1 + p^2)^{3/2}$ and explain the significance of the negative sign.

The position of the centre of curvature C for the point with parameter p is given by $\mathbf{c} = \mathbf{r} + \rho\hat{\mathbf{n}}$, where $\hat{\mathbf{n}}$ is the unit vector obtained by rotating $\hat{\mathbf{t}}$ through $90°$ anticlockwise ($\hat{\mathbf{t}}$ being the unit tangent in the direction of increasing p). Write down $d\mathbf{r}/dp$ and hence show that

$$\hat{\mathbf{n}} = \frac{1}{(1 + p^2)^{\frac{1}{2}}} \begin{bmatrix} -1 \\ p \end{bmatrix}.$$

Find $\mathbf{c}$ and sketch the locus of C.

26 A wooden stick is of square section, and long compared to its section. When it is projected horizontally, perpendicular to its length and with a 'back spin' (i.e. the top side moving back relative to the axis of the stick), it is observed to start its flight by *rising*, if the spin is large enough.

This situation is modelled by the motion of a particle of mass m under the action of two forces, one being gravity and the other being a force L perpendicular to the velocity of the particle and equal to kv (where v is the speed of the particle and k is a constant proportional to the spin of the original stick).

The particle, whose position is given by the complex number $z = x + jy$, is projected horizontally from $z = 0$ at time $t = 0$ with speed u. Show that the equation of motion is

$$m\ddot{z} - jk\dot{z} = -jmg,$$

and solve it under the assumption that $k = 2mg/u$.

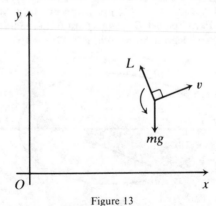

Figure 13

Show that, for this value of k and for small values of t,

$$x \approx ut, \qquad y \approx \tfrac{1}{2}gt^2.$$

27 The position vector of a point P relative to a fixed point O is expressed in polar coordinates. State the radial and transverse components of the velocity of P relative to O in terms of r, $\dot{r}$ and $\dot{\theta}$.

An aircraft moving at constant speed v, relative to the air, and keeping at a constant height, passes round a radio beacon. Although the air is moving at a steady speed u, the pilot keeps the beacon dead abeam. Obtain the equation

$$\frac{1}{r}\dot{r} = \left(\frac{u \cos \theta}{v - u \sin \theta}\right)\dot{\theta}.$$

(In Fig. 14 A represents the aircraft, B the beacon and (r, θ) are the polar coordinates of A relative to B where θ is measured from the downwind direction through B.)

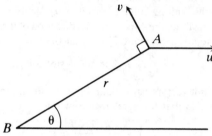

Figure 14

Hence, or otherwise, show that the path of the aircraft is a conic. State the direction of the major axis in relation to the direction of the wind and the significance of the ratio u/v. Under what circumstances will the aircraft make an elliptical circuit of the beacon?

28 A particle P of mass m is attracted to a fixed point O by a central force

$$\mathbf{F} = -mf(r)\hat{\mathbf{r}},$$

where r is the distance of P from O and $\hat{\mathbf{r}}$ is a unit vector in the direction of OP. Show that the motion of P lies in a fixed plane through O. Write down the radial and tangential components of the equations of motion for P, and show that they may be put in the form

$$r^2\dot{\theta} = h, \qquad \ddot{r} = \frac{h^2}{r^3} - f(r),$$

where h is a constant. Using the relation

$$\frac{d}{dt} = \dot{\theta}\frac{d}{d\theta}$$

prove that

$$\dot{r} = -h\frac{d}{d\theta}\left(\frac{1}{r}\right), \qquad \ddot{r} = -\frac{h^2}{r^2}\frac{d^2}{d\theta^2}\left(\frac{1}{r}\right).$$

Hence show that $u = 1/r$ satisfies the equation

$$\frac{d^2u}{d\theta^2} + u = \frac{1}{h^2u^2}f\left(\frac{1}{u}\right).$$

P is projected from the point $r = a$ on the line $\theta = 0$ with a speed $v > \mu^{1/2}/a$ in a direction perpendicular to the radius vector OP. Show that if the central force is

$$f(r) = \frac{\mu}{r^3}$$

then the path of P is

$$r = a \sec k\theta,$$

where $k^2 = 1 - \dfrac{\mu}{v^2 a^2}$.

29 A curve C has polar equation

$$r = \frac{a}{\sinh k\theta} \quad (0 < \theta),$$

where a and k are positive constants. Show that as $\theta \to 0$ C approaches the line $y = a/k$. Find also the limiting value of r as $\theta \to \infty$. Hence sketch C for $0 < \theta \leqslant 3\pi$.

A particle P moves along the curve C in the direction of increasing θ in such a way that $\dot\theta = h/r^2$, where h is a constant. Show that the velocity of P is

$$\dot{\mathbf{r}} = \frac{h}{a}(-k \cosh k\theta \hat{\mathbf{r}} + \sinh k\theta \hat{\mathbf{u}}),$$

where $\hat{\mathbf{r}}$ and $\hat{\mathbf{u}}$ are unit vectors parallel, and at right angles to, the position vector $\mathbf{r}$, respectively. Show also that the acceleration of P is

$$\ddot{\mathbf{r}} = -\frac{h^2(1 + k^2)}{r^3}\hat{\mathbf{r}}.$$

Hence describe the resultant force acting on P. Show that for large values of θ the speed of P is approximately inversely proportional to its distance from O.

30 The orbit of a satellite moving about a planet under a gravitational attraction $f(r) = \mu/r^2$ per unit mass is, in standard notation and suitable axes,

$$r = \frac{h^2}{\mu(1 + e \cos \theta)}.$$

State *briefly* the significance of the constants h and e.

A space-station is moving in a circular orbit about the earth at a speed of 25 400 km h^{-1} and at an altitude of 1600 km above the earth's surface. The earth's radius may be assumed to be 6400 km. A space-shuttle is launched into an orbit at A, 600 km above the earth's surface, with a velocity perpendicular to the line OA (as in Fig. 15). It then moves only under gravity and is intended to rendezvous with the space-station at B, approaching it on a tangential path (although at a different

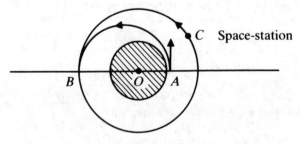

Figure 15

velocity). Use the above equation to show that the orbit of the shuttle has eccentricity $e = \frac{1}{15}$, and that the areal speed of the shuttle is $\sqrt{(14/15)}$ times that of the space-station. Hence show that the velocity of the shuttle at A is approximately $28\,044$ km h^{-1}. What is the relative velocity of the space-station and shuttle at the rendezvous point B? If C is the position of the space-station when the shuttle is at A, find the value of the angle $\alpha = \angle COB$ if the rendezvous is to be achieved. (You may assume the formula $\pi a^2 \sqrt{(1 - e^2)}$ for the area of an ellipse.)

8
Rigid body statics

8.1 FORCES ON A PARTICLE

When two forces, represented by vectors $\mathbf{F}_1$, $\mathbf{F}_2$, act on a particle, their effect is the same as if the single *resultant* force, represented by the vector sum $\mathbf{R} = \mathbf{F}_1 + \mathbf{F}_2$, were acting (Note 8.1). Similarly, the effect on a particle of n forces, represented by $\mathbf{F}_1, \mathbf{F}_2, \ldots, \mathbf{F}_n$, is the same as the effect of the single resultant force, represented by the vector sum $\mathbf{R} = \mathbf{F}_1 + \mathbf{F}_2 + \cdots + \mathbf{F}_n$. In this chapter we are dealing with systems of forces acting in a plane.

There are basically two methods for finding $\mathbf{R}$ when $\mathbf{F}_1, \mathbf{F}_2, \ldots, \mathbf{F}_n$ are known (Note 8.2).

(1) Choose a suitable scale and draw a vector polygon $A_0A_1A_2 \ldots A_n$, where the directed line segment $A_{r-1}A_r$ represents $\mathbf{F}_r$. Then the directed line segment from A_0 to A_n represents $\mathbf{R}$, and may be found either by drawing and measurement or by calculation (Fig. 1).

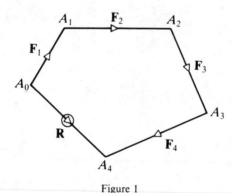

Figure 1

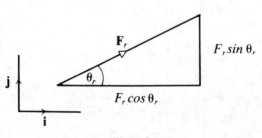

Figure 2

124

(2) Choose suitable perpendicular unit vectors **i**, **j**, and express each $\mathbf{F}_r$ in component form (Fig. 2):

$$\mathbf{F}_r = F_r \cos \theta_r \mathbf{i} + F_r \sin \theta_r \mathbf{j}$$

$$= \begin{bmatrix} F_r \cos \theta_r \\ F_r \sin \theta_r \end{bmatrix}.$$

Then $\mathbf{R} = \begin{bmatrix} X \\ Y \end{bmatrix}$, where $X = \sum_{r=1}^{n} F_r \cos \theta_r$ and $Y = \sum_{r=1}^{n} F_r \sin \theta_r$.

The acceleration **a** of the particle is linked to the resultant force **R** by Newton's second law

$$\mathbf{R} = m\mathbf{a},$$

where m is the mass of the particle. If any two of **R**, m, **a** are known then the third can be found from this equation.

As an important special case, if the particle is moving with constant velocity, and in particular if it is at rest, then its acceleration is zero and so $\mathbf{R} = \mathbf{0}$. The forces then balance, and are said to be *in equilibrium*. In this case the vector polygon formed by $\mathbf{F}_1, \mathbf{F}_2, \ldots, \mathbf{F}_n$ will itself be closed, since the resultant needed to complete it has zero magnitude (Fig. 3). (We shall see in §8.7 that if the forces act on a *large body* then $\mathbf{R} = \mathbf{0}$ is *not* sufficient to ensure equilibrium.)

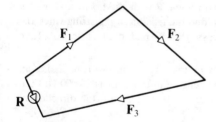

Three forces not in equilibrium, with their resultant.

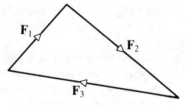

Three forces in equilibrium (when acting on a particle).

Figure 3

Exercise 8A

1 Forces of 10 N and 24 N at right angles to each other act on a particle. Find the magnitude of the resultant, and the angle which it makes with the direction of the larger force.

2 Three forces, measured in newtons, acting on a particle of mass 5 kg are represented by the vectors $5\mathbf{i} + 2\mathbf{j}$, $-7\mathbf{i} + 3\mathbf{j}$, $4\mathbf{i} + 6\mathbf{j}$. Find the acceleration of the particle in the form $p\mathbf{i} + q\mathbf{j}$. Find the magnitude of the acceleration, and the angle its direction makes with the **i**-direction.

3 Horizontal forces of 2 N, 4 N, 9 N act on a particle in directions 017°, 069°, 339° respectively. Find the magnitude and direction of their resultant
    (a) by drawing and measurement,
    (b) by components, taking **i** due East,
    (c) by components, taking **i** in the direction 069°.

4 The following forces act on a particle: 30 N at 050°, 25 N at 215°, and 50 N at 270°. Find their resultant.

5 Find, without undue labour, the resultant of forces $2F$ units at 150°, F units at 210°, and F units at 330° acting on a particle.

6 (a) Fig. 4 shows a particle of mass 2 kg at rest on a plane inclined at 30° to the horizontal. The forces (in newtons) on the particle are its weight W, the normal contact force N, and the friction force F. Using $g = 9.8 \text{ m s}^{-2}$, find these three forces.

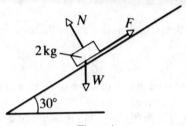

Figure 4

(b) When the inclination of the slope is increased to 60° the particle slides down the slope with acceleration 3 m s^{-2}. Find the friction force in this case.

7 A truck, which may be treated as a particle of mass 6 kg, is pulled along horizontal ground by means of a string which makes an angle θ with the horizontal, where $\tan \theta = \frac{3}{4}$. If the frictional resistance is 15 N, find the tension in the string when the truck accelerates at $1\frac{1}{2} \text{ m s}^{-2}$, and find also the normal contact force. (Take $g = 9.8 \text{ m s}^{-2}$.)

8 A ship is being towed with constant velocity by two tugs. One tow rope makes an angle of 35° with the direction of motion; the tension in this rope is 60 000 N. Find the tension in the other rope, which makes an angle of 40° with the direction of motion. Find also the resistance to motion.

9 The cable supporting a hanging lantern weighing 70 N is drawn aside by means of a force F so that the upper part of the cable makes an angle of 40° with the vertical. Find the magnitude of F when the direction of F is (a) horizontal, (b) at 20° above the horizontal, (c) such as to make the magnitude of F as small as possible.

10 A wire of length 42 m is fixed between two points at the same height on opposite sides of a street, 30 m apart. A Christmas street decoration weighing 560 N is hung from the wire 18 m from one end. Find the two tensions in the wire.

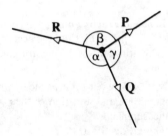

Figure 5

11   Fig. 5 shows three forces **P**, **Q**, **R** in equilibrium acting on a particle. Sketch the triangle of forces, and find its angles in terms of α, β, γ. Hence show that

$$\frac{P}{\sin \alpha} = \frac{Q}{\sin \beta} = \frac{R}{\sin \gamma}.$$

(This is called Lami's Theorem, after Bernard Lami who published it in 1679.) Use Lami's Theorem to solve questions 9 and 10 again.

8.2   RIGID BODIES

So far we have been concerned with the effects of forces on *particles* only, which means that in our mathematical model we have neglected the size of the bodies in question (even when they are as large as the planets). Now we consider bodies of appreciable size, but for simplicity restrict these to bodies which are not deformed when forces act upon them. These are called *rigid bodies*; the rigidity condition can be expressed by saying that the distance between any two points of the body remains constant no matter what forces are applied to it. In practice all bodies deform to some extent when subjected to forces, so assuming rigidity is part of the process of forming the mathematical model.

In this chapter all the forces and bodies are in two dimensions; a two-dimensional rigid body (such as a plane metal sheet of negligible thickness) is called a *lamina*.

8.3   TRANSMISSIBILITY OF FORCE

Suppose that a single external force **F** acts at the point A of a rigid body (Fig. 6). Choose any point B of the body on the line through A in the direction of **F**, and introduce at B the force **F′**, with **F′** = − **F** (Fig. 7); these two forces are said to be equal and opposite.

It is simple to verify experimentally that these two forces cancel, i.e. they do not disturb the equilibrium of the body. (For example, a polystyrene tile on a table could be pulled by horizontal strings attached to pegs at A and B.)

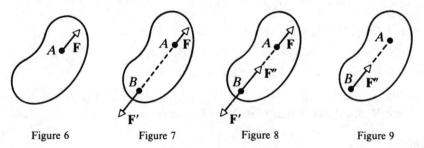

Figure 6   Figure 7   Figure 8   Figure 9

If a third force **F″**, equal to **F**, is now applied at B (Fig. 8), the set of three forces can be considered as either (*a*) **F** plus equal and opposite forces **F′** and **F″** or (*b*) **F″** plus equal and opposite forces **F** and **F′**. In both cases the equal and opposite forces cancel, leaving (*a*) **F** acting at A (Fig. 6) or (*b*) **F″** acting at B (Fig. 9).

This gives the following *principle of transmissibility of force*:

The effect of the force **F** on the rigid body is unchanged if its point of application is transferred from *A* to any other point *B* lying on the line through *A* in the direction of **F**.

The line *AB* is called the *line of action* of **F**. When a force is applied to a rigid body its line of action is important, but the particular point of this line at which it acts does not matter.

8.4 FORCES ON A RIGID BODY

Suppose that non-parallel forces $\mathbf{F}_1$, $\mathbf{F}_2$ act at points A_1, A_2 of a rigid body (Fig. 10). Let their lines of action meet at *B*. Then, as in §8.3, the effect of these forces is the same as if they were both acting at *B* (Fig. 11), and is therefore the same as if their resultant $\mathbf{R} = \mathbf{F}_1 + \mathbf{F}_2$ were acting at *B* (Fig. 12).

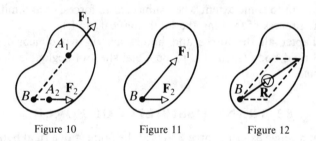

Figure 10   Figure 11   Figure 12

We say that the original system of forces is *equivalent* to the force **R** acting at *B*.

If there are more than two forces acting, this procedure can be used repeatedly, reducing the total number of equivalent forces by one at each stage, as in Example 1.

Example 1
Forces $\mathbf{F}_1$, $\mathbf{F}_2$, $\mathbf{F}_3$, $\mathbf{F}_4$ represented by vectors

$$\begin{bmatrix} 1 \\ 2 \end{bmatrix}, \begin{bmatrix} 1 \\ 0 \end{bmatrix}, \begin{bmatrix} -2 \\ 1 \end{bmatrix}, \begin{bmatrix} -2 \\ 2 \end{bmatrix}$$

act at the points $(1, 0)$, $(0, 2)$, $(6, 3)$, $(2, 3)$ respectively of a rigid body. Find their resultant **R** and the equation of its line of action.

Solution
Fig. 13 shows the four forces with their points of application. (There is no need to show the outline of the body, as this does not affect the solution.) The lines of action of $\mathbf{F}_1$ and $\mathbf{F}_2$ meet at $(2, 2)$, so we can replace $\mathbf{F}_1$ and $\mathbf{F}_2$ by $\mathbf{R}_1 = \mathbf{F}_1 + \mathbf{F}_2$
$= \begin{bmatrix} 2 \\ 2 \end{bmatrix}$ acting at $(2, 2)$, as in Fig. 14. (It is a coincidence that $\mathbf{R}_1 = \begin{bmatrix} 2 \\ 2 \end{bmatrix}$ acts at

(2, 2)!) The lines of action of $\mathbf{R}_1$ and $\mathbf{F}_3$ meet at (4, 4), and in Fig. 15 these two forces are replaced by $\mathbf{R}_2 = \mathbf{R}_1 + \mathbf{F}_3 = \begin{bmatrix} 0 \\ 3 \end{bmatrix}$ acting there. Finally, in Fig. 16, $\mathbf{R}_2$ and $\mathbf{F}_4$ are replaced by $\mathbf{R} = \mathbf{R}_2 + \mathbf{F}_4 = \begin{bmatrix} -2 \\ 5 \end{bmatrix}$ acting at (4, 1), where the lines of action of $\mathbf{R}_2$ and $\mathbf{F}_4$ meet.

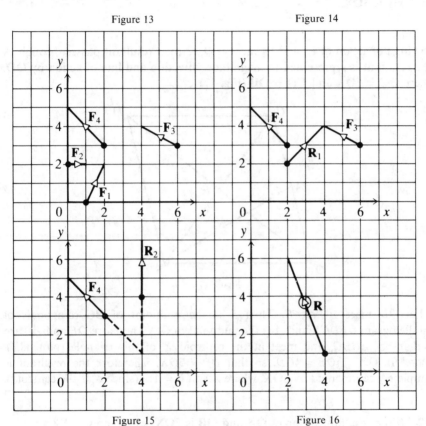

Figure 13   Figure 14

Figure 15   Figure 16

The vector equation of the line of action of $\mathbf{R}$ is

$$\begin{bmatrix} x \\ y \end{bmatrix} = \begin{bmatrix} 4 \\ 1 \end{bmatrix} + \lambda \begin{bmatrix} -2 \\ 5 \end{bmatrix},$$

from which

$$\frac{x - 4}{-2} = \frac{y - 1}{5} \ (= \lambda)$$

so that

$$5x + 2y - 22 = 0.$$

This is the Cartesian equation of the resultant's line of action.   □

Q.1   Solve Example 1 again, this time combining the forces in the order $\mathbf{F}_2, \mathbf{F}_3,$ $\mathbf{F}_1, \mathbf{F}_4$.

Example 2
O, A, B, are non-collinear points of a rigid body. With a fixed scale the force $\mathbf{F}_1$ is represented in magnitude, direction and line of action by $2\mathbf{OA}$, and force $\mathbf{F}_2$ is similarly represented by $\mathbf{OB}$. Show that their resultant is similarly represented by $3\mathbf{OX}$, where X is the point on AB such that $AX:XB = 1:2$. (In future we abbreviate this by saying that the resultant of the forces $2\mathbf{OA}$ and $\mathbf{OB}$ acting on the body is $3\mathbf{OX}$.)

Solution
The lines of action of $\mathbf{F}_1$ and $\mathbf{F}_2$ meet at O, so their resultant passes through O. The resultant is represented in magnitude, direction and line of action by $\mathbf{OD}$, where $\mathbf{OC} = 2\mathbf{OA}$ and $\mathbf{CD} = \mathbf{OB}$ (Fig. 17).

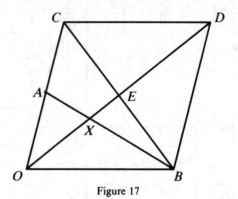

Figure 17

Let OD meet BC at E. Then E is the midpoint of BC (diagonals of parallelogram $OBDC$), and A is the midpoint of OC. Therefore OE and AB are medians of $\triangle OBC$, and meet at the centroid X of this triangle (Note 8.3). Therefore $OX = \frac{2}{3}OE = \frac{1}{3}OD$, so that $OD = 3OX$. Therefore the resultant is completely represented by $3\mathbf{OX}$, where $AX:XB = 1:2$ (since X is the centroid).   □

Q.2 If the resultant of forces $\mathbf{OA}$ and $\mathbf{OB}$ is $2\mathbf{OX}$, where now is X?

It is worth generalising Example 2 by finding the resultant of forces $p\mathbf{OA}$ and $q\mathbf{OB}$ acting on a rigid body (Fig. 18).

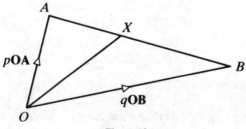

Figure 18

Considering first just magnitudes and directions, for any fixed point X on AB we have

$$\mathbf{OA} = \mathbf{OX} + \mathbf{XA} \quad \text{and} \quad \mathbf{OB} = \mathbf{OX} + \mathbf{XB},$$

so that
$$p\mathbf{OA} + q\mathbf{OB} = p(\mathbf{OX} + \mathbf{XA}) + q(\mathbf{OX} + \mathbf{XB})$$

$$= (p + q)\mathbf{OX} + (p\mathbf{XA} + q\mathbf{XB}).$$

If we take X to be the point on AB such that $AX:XB = q:p$ then

$$p\mathbf{AX} = q\mathbf{XB}$$

and so
$$p\mathbf{XA} + q\mathbf{XB} = 0 \quad \text{(since } \mathbf{XA} = -\mathbf{AX}\text{).}$$

Therefore with this choice of X

$$p\mathbf{OA} + q\mathbf{OB} = (p + q)\mathbf{OX}.$$

This gives the magnitude and direction of the resultant. Moreover, since the two given lines of action meet at O, the resultant's line of action passes through O. Therefore

The resultant of forces $p\mathbf{OA}$ and $q\mathbf{OB}$, where $p + q \neq 0$, is $(p + q)\mathbf{OX}$, where X is the point of AB such that $AX:XB = q:p$.

This is equivalent to the ratio theorem of vector geometry (Note 8.4).

Q.3   What values of p and q give the results of Example 2 and Q.2?

Q.4   Draw   diagrams   to   illustrate   the   cases   (a) $p = 2$, $q = -1$, (b) $p = -2$, $q = 1$, (c) $p = -2$, $q = -1$.

Q.5   Investigate the special case when $p + q = 0$.

Example 3
Find the resultant of forces $\mathbf{AC}$, $\mathbf{AB}$ and $3\mathbf{CB}$ acting on a rigid triangle ABC (Fig. 19).

Solution
First use the theorem just proved to replace the forces $\mathbf{AC}$ and $\mathbf{AB}$ by the single force $2\mathbf{AM}$, where M is the midpoint of BC. Next replace $3\mathbf{CB}$ by $6\mathbf{CM}$, so that both remaining forces are given in terms of segments which terminate at M (Fig. 20). Finally use the theorem again to replace $2\mathbf{AM}$ and $6\mathbf{CM}$ by the resultant $8\mathbf{PM}$, where P is the point on AC such that $AP:PC = 6:2 = 3:1$ (Fig. 21).

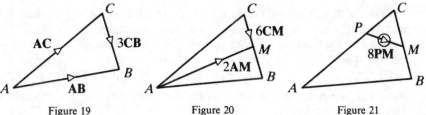

Figure 19   Figure 20   Figure 21

Note that at the final stage we use the theorem with both forces pointing towards the common point M; we can interpret this as combining $-2\mathbf{MA}$ and $-6\mathbf{MC}$ to give $-8\mathbf{MP}$. $\qquad\qquad\qquad\qquad\qquad\square$

Exercise 8B

Questions 1–4 should be done with the aid of graph paper.

1   A rectangular table $ABCD$ with $AB = 1$ m and $BC = 2$ m is moved by three people. One pushes at A with a force 30 N along AB, one pushes at C with a force of 30 N along CB, and one pushes at D with a force of 50 N parallel to AC. Find by drawing and measurement how much and where a single person must push in order to produce the same effect.

2   Forces $3\mathbf{i} + 2\mathbf{j}$ and $2\mathbf{i} - \mathbf{j}$ act at the points $(2, 3)$ and $(4, -1)$ respectively of a rigid body. Find their resultant in the form $X\mathbf{i} + Y\mathbf{j}$, and give the equation its line of action.

3   Forces $\begin{bmatrix} 0 \\ 3 \end{bmatrix}$, $\begin{bmatrix} -1 \\ -1 \end{bmatrix}$, $\begin{bmatrix} 2 \\ 3 \end{bmatrix}$, $\begin{bmatrix} 2 \\ -1 \end{bmatrix}$ act at the points $(6, 0)$, $(7, 9)$, $(2, 3)$, $(4, -2)$ respectively of a rigid body. Find their resultant and the equation of its line of action.

4   Show that the forces $\begin{bmatrix} 4 \\ 1 \end{bmatrix}$, $\begin{bmatrix} -1 \\ -2 \end{bmatrix}$, $\begin{bmatrix} -3 \\ 1 \end{bmatrix}$ acting at the points $(-2, 1)$, $(4, 6)$, $(8, 0)$ respectively of a rigid body are in equilibrium. What is the effect of these forces if the point of application of the third is moved to $(4, 0)$?

5   Forces $2\mathbf{AB}$, $\mathbf{BC}$, $\mathbf{AC}$ act on a rigid body. Prove that their resultant is $6\mathbf{PQ}$, where P is the midpoint of AB and Q is the point of trisection of BC nearer B.

6   Find the resultant of forces $\mathbf{AB}$, $4\mathbf{BC}$, $2\mathbf{AC}$ acting on a rigid triangle ABC.

7   Investigate the effect of forces $\mathbf{AB}$, $\mathbf{BC}$, $\mathbf{CA}$, acting on a rigid triangle ABC.

8   Forces $\mathbf{AB}$, $\mathbf{AD}$, $\mathbf{CB}$, $\mathbf{CD}$ act on a rigid plane quadrilateral $ABCD$. Prove that their resultant is $4\mathbf{HK}$, where H, K are the midpoints of AC, BD respectively.

9   Suppose that it is possible to draw a circle inside quadrilatereral $ABCD$ of question 8 touching the sides AB, BC, CD, DA at P, Q, R, S respectively. Replace each of the given forces by an equivalent pair:

$$\mathbf{AB} = \mathbf{AP} + \mathbf{PB}, \qquad \mathbf{AD} = \mathbf{AS} + \mathbf{SD}, \qquad \text{and so on.}$$

By taking these eight forces in suitable pairs and considering their resultant, prove that the centre of the circle lies on HK.

10   The sides of the quadrilateral of question 8 are extended so that AB, CD meet at E and AD, BC meet at F. (The figure is now called a complete quadrilateral.) The midpoint of the third diagonal EF is L. Replace each of the given forces by an equivalent pair:

$$\mathbf{AB} = \mathbf{AE} + \mathbf{EB}, \qquad \mathbf{AD} = \mathbf{AF} + \mathbf{FD}, \qquad \mathbf{CB} = \mathbf{CF} + \mathbf{FB}, \qquad \mathbf{CD} = \mathbf{CE} + \mathbf{ED}.$$

By taking these eight forces in suitable pairs and considering their resultant, prove that H, K, L are collinear.

8.5 PARALLEL FORCES

The methods of §8.4 make use of the point where the lines of action of two forces meet, and therefore cannot be applied if the forces are parallel. We now deal with this important special case.

Let F_1 and F_2 be parallel forces with the same sense acting on a rigid body, and let any transversal meet their lines of action at A_1 and A_2. By the transmissibility of force we can suppose that F_1 acts at A_1 and F_2 at A_2. Without changing the resultant we introduce a force P acting along A_2A_1 at A_1, and an equal and opposite force $-P$ acting at A_2. Combining F_1 and P gives a force through A_1, and combining F_2 and $-P$ gives a force through A_2; these forces are not parallel, so let their lines of action meet at B (Fig. 22).

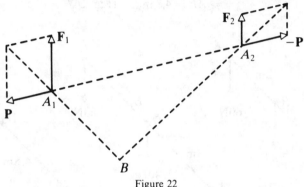

Figure 22

Transmit these forces to B, and then split them back into their original components (Fig. 23). The forces P and $-P$ cancel, and we are left with the resultant $F_1 + F_2$ acting through B. If the line of action of the resultant meets A_1A_2 at X then, by similar triangles,

$$\frac{A_1X}{XB} = \frac{P}{F_1} \quad \text{and} \quad \frac{XA_2}{XB} = \frac{P}{F_2}$$

so that

$$\frac{A_1X}{XA_2} = \frac{(XB \cdot P/F_1)}{(XB \cdot P/F_2)} = \frac{F_2}{F_1},$$

i.e. X divides A_1A_2 in the ratio $F_2:F_1$, where F_1 and F_2 are the magnitudes of F_1 and F_2 respectively.

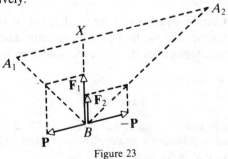

Figure 23

Example 4
Particles with weights 10 N, 30 N, 60 N are attached to a straight rod of negligible weight at the points *A*, *B*, *C* respectively, where $AB = 4$ m and $BC = 2$ m (Fig. 24). Find where the resultant weight acts.

Solution
The resultant of the weights at *A* and *B* is a vertical force of 40 N acting through the point *D* on the rod, where $AD:DB = 30:10$, so that $AD = 3$ m (Fig. 25).

The resultant of this 40 N force and the 60 N weight at *C* is a vertical force of 100 N acting through the point *E* on the rod, where $DE:EC = 60:40$

$$\Rightarrow DE = \tfrac{3}{5} \times DC = 1.8 \text{ m}$$

$$\Rightarrow AE = 4.8 \text{ m} \qquad \text{(Fig. 26)}$$

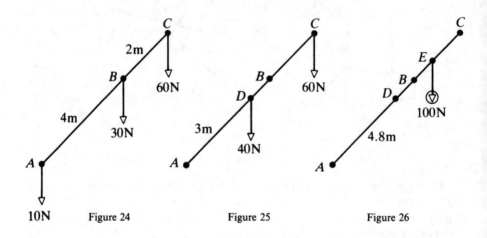

10N   Figure 24   Figure 25   Figure 26

Note that the point of the rod through which the resultant weight acts is independent of the inclination of the rod. This point is the centre of gravity of the three particles.   □

Q.6 Work through Example 4 again, starting by combining the weights at *B* and *C*. Check that the final result is the same.

A similar argument can be used to find the resultant of two parallel forces with opposite senses (Exercise 8C, question 6), with an important special case when the forces have equal magnitudes (Exercise 8C, question 9).

Exercise 8C

1   Two parallel forces with the same sense act on a rigid body. Their magnitudes are 7 N and 13 N, and their lines of action are 2 m apart. How far is the line of action of the resultant from that of the smaller force?

2 Find the resultant of forces $12\mathbf{j}$ and $18\mathbf{j}$ acting along the lines $x = 3$ and $x = 8$ respectively.

3 Particles of weights 20 N, 5 N, 25 N are attached to a weightless straight rod at the points A, B, C respectively, where $AB = 3$ m and $BC = 1$ m. The line of action of the resultant weight meets the rod at G. Find AG.

4 (a) Particles of weights w_1, w_2 are attached to a weightless straight rod at distances x_1, x_2 from one end O of the rod. The line of action of the resultant weight meets the rod at G. Prove that

$$OG = \frac{w_1 x_1 + w_2 x_2}{w_1 + w_2}.$$

(b) An extra weight w_3 is attached to the rod at a distance x_3 from O. The line of action of the resultant now meets the rod at G'. Prove that

$$OG' = \frac{w_1 x_1 + w_2 x_2 + w_3 x_3}{w_1 + w_2 + w_3}.$$

5 Particles of weights $w_1, w_2, \ldots, w_n$ are attached to a weightless straight rod at distances $x_1, x_2, \ldots, x_n$ respectively from one end O of the rod. The line of action of the resultant weight meets the rod at G. Use mathematical induction to prove that

$$OG = \frac{w_1 x_1 + w_2 x_2 + \cdots + w_n x_n}{w_1 + w_2 + \cdots + w_n}.$$

6 Parallel forces $\mathbf{F}_1$, $\mathbf{F}_2$ with *opposite* senses act at points A_1, A_2 of a rigid body. Adapt the method of §8.5 to show that the line of action of the resultant divides $A_1 A_2$ *externally* in the ratio $F_2 : F_1$.

7 Two boys push horizontally with forces 75 N and 150 N at points A and B 1.5 m apart on a bench which rests on the ground. Both forces are at right angles to the bench. Find the resultant force and the position of its line of action (a) when the boys push from the same side of the bench, (b) when they push from opposite sides.

8 Find the resultant of forces $11\mathbf{j}$, $-4\mathbf{j}$, $-2\mathbf{j}$ acting along the lines $x = 3$, $x = 7$, $x = 10$ respectively.

*9 Show that two non-collinear parallel forces of equal magnitude but opposite senses acting on a rigid body have no resultant, but are not in equilibrium. Such a set of forces is called a *couple*.

10 (a) Show that the forces $5\mathbf{j}$, $-3\mathbf{j}$, $-2\mathbf{j}$, acting along the lines $x = 4$, $x = 6$, $x = 9$ respectively form a couple.

(b) Show that if the forces $5\mathbf{j}$ and $-3\mathbf{j}$ in (a) are interchanged then the system is in equilibrium.

(c) Investigate all the other permutations of these three forces acting along these three lines.

8.6 MOMENTS

Since a rigid body has an appreciable size it is capable of rotating as well as shifting from one position to another.

Consider for example a uniform plank of weight 80 N and length 3 m which can turn freely about one end A. We want to keep the plank horizontal by applying an upward force of 60 N. Where should this force be applied (Fig. 27)?

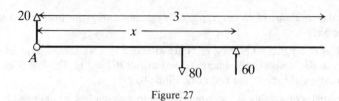

Figure 27

For equilibrium the resultant force on the plank must be zero, so there must be an upward force of 20 N on the plank at A due to the pivot. Moreover, the resultant of the two upward forces must act along the line of action of the weight, since otherwise there would be a couple (as in Exercise 8C, questions 9 and 10). If the 60 N force acts at a distance x metres from A then, dividing x in the ratio $60:20$, the resultant of the upward forces acts at a distance $\frac{3}{4}x$ metres from A. Therefore $\frac{3}{4}x = 1\frac{1}{2}$, so that $x = 2$. The 60 N force must be applied 2 m from A.

Q.7   Repeat this calculation when the upward force applied to maintain equilibrium is (a) 50 N, (b) 80 N, (c) 120 N.

Q.8   To maintain equilibrium, what upward force must be applied (a) 2.5 m from A, (b) 0.5 m from A?

Q.9   What is the least upward force which can maintain equilibrium? Where should this be applied? Is there an upper limit on the upward force which can be applied?

The results of Q.7, Q.8 and Q.9 show that the larger the upward force applied the nearer it must be to the pivot. We can make this precise by considering the general case, in which the upward force is F newtons. Then the upward force on the plank at A is $(80 - F)$ newtons (with the obvious interpretation if $F > 80$). Dividing x in the ratio $F:(80 - F)$ gives

$$\frac{F}{80} \times x = 1\frac{1}{2},$$

i.e. $Fx \qquad = 120.$ (1)

The quantity Fx, the product of the magnitude of the force and the perpendicular distance of its line of action from the pivot, is called the *moment* of the force about the pivot, and is measured in newton-metres (N m) (Note 8.5). The moment is a measure of the turning effect of the force. With the diagram as drawn the moment of F about A is anticlockwise; this is conventionally taken to be the positive sense for moments. The moment for the weight of the plank about A is $-80 \times 1\frac{1}{2} = -120$ N m (i.e. 120 N m clockwise). The force at A due to the pivot has zero moment about A.

Equation (1) can be written.

$$Fx + (-120) + 0 = 0$$

and is then an example of the use of the *principle of moments*:

The algebraic sum of the moments about any point of the forces acting on a rigid body in equilibrium is zero.

Q.10   Check that in the original example the sum of the moments about the other end of the plank is zero.

From §8.3 we know that the particular point at which a force is applied to a rigid body is unimportant; what matters is the line of action of the force. Therefore when finding the moment of a force about a point A it is essential to use the *perpendicular* distance from A to the line of action of the force. This is illustrated in the next example, where we take moments of forces which are not all parallel.

Example 5
An inn sign is supported by a rigid light framework ABC attached to a vertical wall at A and C, such that $\angle ABC = 30°$. The sign, of weight 100 N, is equally supported at B and D, where $BD = 40$ cm and $DA = 20$ cm. Find the tension in BC.

Solution
Fig. 28 shows the forces on the rod AB. The direction of the force at A is unknown; this is indicated by using a wavy arrow. Let the tension in BC be T N.

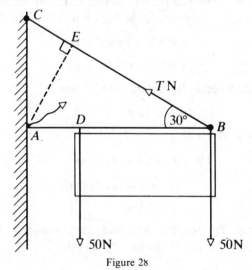

Figure 28

The perpendicular distance of BC from A is $AE = 0.6 \sin 30° = 0.3$ m. Taking moments about A and applying the principle of moments:

$$0 + (-50 \times 0.2) + (-50 \times 0.6) + T \times 0.3 = 0$$

$$\Rightarrow T = \frac{50 \times 0.8}{0.3} = 133\tfrac{1}{3}.$$

The tension is $133\tfrac{1}{3}$ newtons.   □

Sometimes finding the perpendicular distance to the line of action of a force is complicated, and it may be easier to use an alternative method, based on the result which follows.

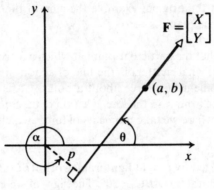

Figure 29

Suppose that the force $\mathbf{F} = \begin{bmatrix} X \\ Y \end{bmatrix}$ acts at the point (a, b) of a rigid body, and that we want to find the moment of $\mathbf{F}$ about O. Let the line of action of $\mathbf{F}$ and the perpendicular from O to this line make angles θ, α respectively with Ox, as shown in Fig. 29. Let the perpendicular distance from O to the line of action be p. Then, as in Exercise 2B, question 6, the equation of the line of action of $\mathbf{F}$ is

$$x \cos \alpha + y \sin \alpha = p$$

or
$$x \sin \theta - y \cos \theta = p,$$

since $\alpha = \theta + 3\pi/2$. As (a, b) lies on this line of action,

$$p = a \sin \theta - b \cos \theta.$$

So the moment of $\mathbf{F}$ about O is

$$Fp = Fa \sin \theta - Fb \cos \theta$$

$$= (F \sin \theta)a - (F \cos \theta)b$$

$$= Ya - Xb.$$

Now $-Xb$ and Ya are the anticlockwise moments about O of the perpendicular components of $\mathbf{F}$, $X\mathbf{i}$ and $Y\mathbf{j}$ (Fig. 30).

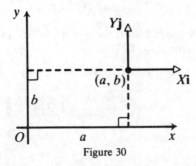

Figure 30

Therefore the moment about O of **F** equals the sum of the moments about O of the perpendicular components of **F**. (Compare this with §4.4, where we found similar results for the moments of velocities.)

Example 6
A uniform rectangular block of stone 1 m long and 0.4 m high weighs 300 N. It is held tilted at an angle of 20° to the horizontal by a rope attached to the centre of the top edge of one end face, the rope making an angle of 30° with the vertical. Find the tension in the rope.

Solution

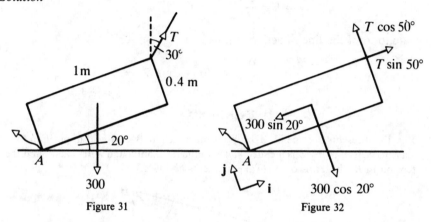

Figure 31   Figure 32

Let the tension be T N. The forces on the block are the weight, the tension, and the contact force due to the ground (Fig. 31). Since this last force need not be found, we take moments about the edge of the block in contact with the ground (which appears in the diagrams as the point A). The distances of the lines of action from A are difficult to find, so we replace the weight and tension by their perpendicular components, taking **i**, **j** parallel to the edges of the block (Fig. 32). Then, using the principle of moments,

$$T \cos 50° \times 1 - T \sin 50° \times 0.4 + 300 \sin 20° \times 0.2 - 300 \cos 20° \times 0.5 = 0$$

$$\Rightarrow T = \frac{150 \cos 20° - 60 \sin 20°}{\cos 50° - 0.4 \sin 50°} = 358.$$

The tension is 358 N.   □

Example 7
Solve Example 1 (page 128) again, using moments.

Solution
The resultant **R** is the vector sum of the given forces,

$$\mathbf{R} = \begin{bmatrix} 1 \\ 2 \end{bmatrix} + \begin{bmatrix} 1 \\ 0 \end{bmatrix} + \begin{bmatrix} -2 \\ 1 \end{bmatrix} + \begin{bmatrix} -2 \\ 2 \end{bmatrix} = \begin{bmatrix} -2 \\ 5 \end{bmatrix},$$

and it only remains to find the equation of its line of action. Let this line meet the x-axis at $(h, 0)$; by transmissibility we can take **R** to act at this point. Since the given forces and **R** are equivalent, the sum of the moments about O of the given forces equals the moment of **R** about O.

Using the component form $Ya - Xb$ for the moments,

$$5 \times h - (-2) \times 0 = (2 \times 1 - 1 \times 0) + (0 \times 0 - 1 \times 2)$$
$$+ (1 \times 6 + 2 \times 3) + (2 \times 2 + 2 \times 3)$$
$$= 22$$
$$\Rightarrow h = \frac{22}{5}.$$

The equation of the line of action is thus

$$\frac{x - \frac{22}{5}}{-2} = \frac{y - 0}{5} \quad \text{or} \quad 5x + 2y - 22 = 0. \qquad \square$$

Exercise 8D

1   Fig. 33 represents a crane jib AB supporting a weight W and held in position by a stay BC. Given that AB is inclined at 45° to the horizontal and $ABC = 30°$, find the tension in BC in terms of W. (Take moments about A.)

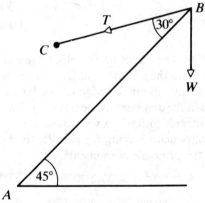

Figure 33

2   A uniform ladder of length 3 m and mass 15 kg rests on rough horizontal ground against a smooth vertical wall. By taking moments about the lower end find the reaction at the wall, given that the lower end of the ladder is 1 metre from the wall.

3   A uniform rod AB of length 2 m and weight 30 N is free to turn in a vertical plane about a hinge at its upper end A. When a force P N is applied at B the rod is in equilibrium at an angle of 30° to the vertical. Find P (a) when **P** is horizontal, (b) when **P** is perpendicular to AB, (c) when **P** is inclined at 20° to the upward vertical.

4   The distance between the back wheels of a coach is 2 m. The coach must be able to rest on a slope of 45° without toppling. Find the maximum height of the centre of gravity (assumed to be symmetrically positioned).

5   A cabin trunk 0.8 m long and 0.4 m high has weight 400 N, uniformly distributed. It is dragged along the floor at a constant speed, tilted at an angle of 30° to the horizontal, by means of a force applied to a handle in the centre of one end. Find this force if it is inclined at 40° to the vertical. Find also the friction force on the trunk.

6   Answer questions 2 and 3 of Exercise 8B again, using moments.

7   A uniform diving board of mass m and length $4a$ is supported by rigid bars running across the width of the board at points A, B, C, as shown in Fig. 34.

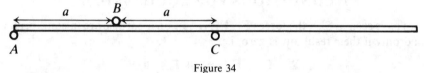

Figure 34

A man of mass M walks the length of the board from left to right before diving off. Find expressions for the forces exerted by the three bars as functions of the distance x that the man is from the end A of the board.

If the strengths of the bars are such that the forces at A, B and C must not exceed $3mg$, $5mg$ and $10mg$ respectively, find the maximum safe value of M.   [MEI]

8   A couple is formed by equal and opposite forces $\mathbf{F}$ and $-\mathbf{F}$ acting along parallel lines which are a distance d apart. Prove that the total moment of these forces about any point is constant, and has magnitude Fd.

9   A rigid body is acted upon by a set of forces. Prove that the total moment of these forces is the same about all points if, and only if, the resultant of these forces is zero.

$\Bigg($ *Suggested method*: Let the forces be $\begin{bmatrix} X_r \\ Y_r \end{bmatrix}$ acting at (a_r, b_r), where $r = 1, 2, \ldots, n$.

Show that the total moment about (p, q) is

$$\sum_{r=1}^{n} [Y_r(a_r - p) - X_r(b_r - q)]$$

and that this is independent of p and q if, and only if,

$$\sum_{r=1}^{n} X_r = \sum_{r=1}^{n} Y_r = 0. \Bigg)$$

If the resultant is zero but the total moment is not zero the system is a couple, and the total moment about any point is called the *moment of the couple* (question 8 gives the simplest example).

10 It takes a couple of moment 8 N m to unscrew a bottle top of diameter 4 cm. I supply this moment by pinching the top with my thumb and first finger, and then turning it. What inward force must I use with thumb and finger if the coefficient of friction between them and the top is 0.7?

11 Andrew, weighing 400 N, and Belinda, weighing 300 N, sit on a seesaw at opposite sides of a pivot P. They find that when Belinda sits 1.2 m from P, Andrew can move up to 1.5 m from P before the seesaw starts to tip. Find the greatest frictional couple that the pivot can produce. Assuming that this couple is available in the opposite sense and that Andrew stays 1.5 m from P, how far from P can Belinda move now before the seesaw tips?

12 (a) Prove that forces $k\mathbf{AB}$, $k\mathbf{BC}$, $k\mathbf{CA}$ acting on a rigid triangle ABC form a couple with moment of magnitude $2k\Delta$, where Δ is the area of the triangle.

(b) Generalise (a) by considering forces $k\mathbf{AB}$, $k\mathbf{BC}$, ..., $k\mathbf{NA}$ acting on a rigid closed polygon $ABC \ldots N$.

13   Forces of 8, 3, 2, 6 N act along the sides AB, BC, CD, AD respectively of a square of side 2 m. Show that this system is equivalent to a force at A together with a couple. Find the magnitude and direction of the force, and the moment of the couple. Find also where the line of action of the resultant of this system meets AD.

8.7 CONDITIONS FOR EQUILIBRIUM

As we have seen in §8.1, the forces $\mathbf{F}_1$, $\mathbf{F}_2$, ..., $\mathbf{F}_n$ on a particle are in equilibrium if and only if their resultant is zero, i.e.

$$\mathbf{R} = \mathbf{F}_1 + \mathbf{F}_2 + \cdots + \mathbf{F}_n = \mathbf{0}.$$

We can use this condition either by drawing a closed force polygon with sides representing $\mathbf{F}_1$, $\mathbf{F}_2$, ..., $\mathbf{F}_n$, or by choosing perpendicular unit vectors $\mathbf{i}$, $\mathbf{j}$ (Note 8.6), expressing each $\mathbf{F}_r$ in components, $\mathbf{F}_r = X_r\mathbf{i} + Y_r\mathbf{j}$, and then using the two equations

$$\sum_{r=1}^{n} X_r = 0, \qquad \sum_{r=1}^{n} Y_r = 0.$$

If these forces are acting on a rigid body the condition $\mathbf{R} = \mathbf{0}$ is necessary for equilibrium, but it is not now sufficient, since, as we have seen in Exercise 8D, question 9, the forces may still have a turning effect, i.e. they may form a couple. To show that this does not happen we need to check that the total moment of the forces about one point is zero.

Therefore a set of forces acting on a rigid body is in equilibrium if and only if
    (a) their resultant is zero
and (b) their total moment about one point is zero.

An alternative condition, which is sometimes easier to use, is that

There is equilibrium if the total moment is zero about each of three non-collinear points.

For then the system cannot form a couple; nor can it reduce to a resultant force since this would have to pass through each of the three points to give zero moments, which is impossible since the points are not collinear.

Notice that either set of conditions for equilibrium involves three equations, from which at most three unknowns can be found.

Q.11   Show that a set of forces on a rigid body is in equilibrium if $\sum X_r = 0$ and the sum of the moments about each of two points A and B is zero, provided that $\mathbf{AB}$ is not perpendicular to $\mathbf{i}$.

It is worth noting two simple particular cases, which occur frequently.
   (1) *Two force system*. If a rigid body is in equilibrium under the action of only two forces then those forces have equal magnitudes and opposite senses along

the same line of action. For if not, the two forces would either have a resultant or form a couple.

(2) *Three force system.* If a rigid body is in equilibrium under the action of only three forces then their lines of action meet at a point, unless they are parallel. For if not, the total moment about the point of intersection of two of the forces would be non-zero, since the third force would not pass through this point.

Q.12 Give a simple example of a rigid body in equilibrium under the action of four forces whose lines of action are not concurrent or parallel.

8.8 THE ANGLE OF FRICTION

In a first discussion of friction (Note 8.7) the contact force $\mathbf{R}$ on a body due to a surface is usually replaced by its components perpendicular and parallel to the surface. These are the normal reaction $\mathbf{N}$ and the friction force $\mathbf{F}$. The friction model used can then be summarised by saying that

$$F \leqslant \mu N \qquad \text{where } \mu \text{ is the coefficient of friction,}$$

with equality when the body is sliding or in limiting equilibrium (just about to slide).

If instead of using components we use the total contact force $\mathbf{R}$, then the angle θ between $\mathbf{R}$ and the normal to the surface is given by $\tan\theta = F/N$ (Fig. 35).

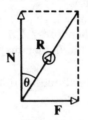

Figure 35

Since $F \leqslant \mu N$, it follows that $\tan\theta \leqslant \mu$ and hence that there is a limit to the size of the angle θ. The greatest possible angle is usually denoted by λ, where $\tan\lambda = \mu$, and is called the *angle of friction*. The principle $F \leqslant \mu N$ can be restated simply as

$$\theta \leqslant \lambda, \qquad \text{where } \tan\lambda = \mu,$$

with equality when the body is sliding or in limiting equilibrium.

By using $\mathbf{R}$ instead of $\mathbf{F}$ and $\mathbf{N}$ we reduce the number of forces in the problem. This can lead to simpler solutions, as in the following example.

Example 8

A uniform ladder rests with its top against a vertical wall and its foot on horizontal ground. The angle of friction between the ladder and both surfaces is λ. What is the least angle the ladder can make with the horizontal?

Solution
Fig. 36 shows the forces when equilibrium is limiting. The total contact forces at A and B then each make an angle λ with the respective normals. Therefore AC is perpendicular to CB, and so C lies on the circle with diameter AB. The centre of this circle is the midpoint G of AB, through which the weight $\mathbf{W}$ acts.

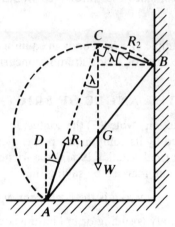

Figure 36

The ladder is in equilibrium under three forces $\mathbf{R}_1$, $\mathbf{R}_2$, $\mathbf{W}$, and so the line of action of $\mathbf{W}$ also passes through C.

Hence CG is parallel to AD, and $\angle ACG = \lambda$. But $AG = GC$ (radii), so that triangle AGC is isosceles, and therefore $\angle CAG = \lambda$ also.

Therefore $\angle DAG = 2\lambda$, and the ladder makes an angle $90° - 2\lambda$ with the horizontal.

Note that if we had used normal and friction forces we should have had to deal with five forces instead of three.   □

Exercise 8E

1   A uniform ladder of length 2.6 m rests with its top against a smooth vertical wall and its foot on the rough horizontal floor. When its foot is 1 m from the wall the ladder is in limiting equilibrium. Find the coefficient of friction between the ladder and the floor. What difference does it make if the wall is rough and the floor is smooth?

2   A light rigid square $ABCD$ rests on a horizontal table. Strings are attached to the corners A, B, C and pulled horizontally away from the square. The angle between the string at A and AD is 120°, the angle between the string at B and BC is 140°, and the tension in the string at C is 10 N. Find by accurate drawing
   (a) the angle between the string at C and CD,
   (b) the tensions in the other two strings.

3   A gate is supported by two hinges 0.6 m apart. The lower hinge bears all the weight, so that the force exerted by the upper hinge is horizontal. The gate's weight of 200 N acts along a line 0.8 m from the line of the hinges. Find the force exerted by each hinge.

4 A uniform spar AB of length 8 m and weight 500 N has light wires of lengths 6 m and 10 m fastened to it at A and B. The other ends of the wires are attached to a fixed hook C so that the spar hangs in equilibrium from C by the two wires. What angle does the spar make with the vertical, and what are the tensions in the wires?

5 The centre of gravity of a plank AB 3 m long and of weight 250 N is 1 m from B. The plank is freely attached to a fixed point at A, and is held horizontal by means of a light string fastened between B and the point C 2 m vertically above A. Find the tension in the string and the magnitude and direction of the force at A.

6 A modern substitute for an office paper-clip is shown in section in Fig. 37. The frame, fastened to a wall as shown, has three inner plane surfaces of which one is vertical and another inclined at 30° to the vertical; lodged between these is a cylinder of negligible weight with its axis horizontal. Papers inserted between the cylinder and the vertical face become jammed and cannot be released by a downward pull. Determine the least angle of friction between the cylinder and the surfaces in contact with it for the apparatus to work, explaining your argument carefully. [MEI]

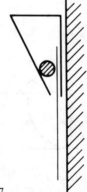

Figure 37

7 A drawer of depth d jams shut when only one of its handles is pulled. If this handle is at a distance h from the centre of the front, prove that the coefficient of friction at the sides of the drawer is not less than $d/2h$.

8 A man is using a uniform ladder while painting the outside of his house. His weight is three times that of the ladder. In one place, shown in Fig. 38, the ladder cannot be

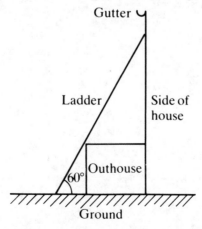

Figure 38

inclined at an angle greater than 60° to the horizontal because of an obstructing outhouse. At this inclination the ladder is just *not* in contact with the outhouse. The man finds that he can reach the gutter at this point only by standing on the top rung of the ladder (whose distance from the top of the ladder is so small that it can be ignored). If the side of the house is smooth, show that the coefficient of friction between the ladder and the ground is greater than 0.505.

Before the man is able to complete painting the gutter at this place, a thunderstorm causes the ground to become muddy so that the coefficient of friction between the ladder and the ground is reduced to 0.4. Unfortunately the man resumes without realising this. How far up the ladder is he before it slips?   [MEI]

9   Fig. 39 shows the end view of a cylinder of radius r resting on the horizontal floor. A uniform plank of length $2x$ rests across the cylinder (perpendicular to the axis of the cylinder) with its centre B in contact with the cylinder and its lower end C resting on the floor. The coefficient of friction μ is the same at all three points of contact.

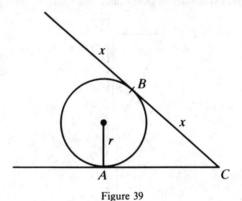

Figure 39

(a) By considering the forces on the cylinder, show that if the cylinder slips it will slip at B but not at A.

(b) Show that if friction is limiting at both B and C then $\mu = r/x = 1/\sqrt{3}$.

(c) Show that if friction is limiting at just one of B or C then the point at which friction is limiting is B or C according as r/x is greater or lesser than $1/\sqrt{3}$. What can be said about μ in these cases?

9

Moments of inertia

9.1 THE KINETIC ENERGY OF A RIGID BODY ROTATING ABOUT A FIXED AXIS

When dealing with the motion of a rigid body we shall often consider the body to be composed of a large number of pieces, each of which is small enough to be regarded as a particle.

The kinetic energy (KE) of a particle of mass m moving with speed v is $\frac{1}{2}mv^2$ (Note 9.1). If a rigid body moves without rotating then all the particles of the body move with the same speed in the same direction. The kinetic energy T of the body is then the sum of the kinetic energies of its component particles, i.e.

$$T = \sum \tfrac{1}{2}mv^2$$

$$= \tfrac{1}{2}(\sum m)v^2, \text{ since all the particles have the same speed } v,$$

$$= \tfrac{1}{2}Mv^2, \text{ where } M \text{ is the total mass.}$$

When the body rotates, different particles move with different velocities, so it is no longer possible to speak of 'the velocity of the body'. But we can still find the kinetic energy of the body by summing the kinetic energies of its component particles.

Example 1
A light straight rod $OABC$ has masses 1 kg, 2 kg, 3 kg attached to it at A, B, C respectively, where $OA = 0.5$ m, $AB = 0.3$ m, $BC = 0.1$ m. It rotates with angular velocity 5 rad s^{-1} about an axis through O perpendicular to the rod (Fig. 1). Find the kinetic energy.

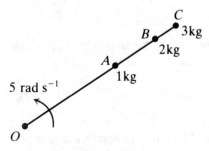

Figure 1

Solution
The particles A, B, C move in concentric circles round O, with speeds $0.5 \times 5\,\text{m s}^{-1}$, $0.8 \times 5\,\text{m s}^{-1}$, $0.9 \times 5\,\text{m s}^{-1}$ respectively. The total KE is therefore

$$\tfrac{1}{2} \times 1 \times 2.5^2 + \tfrac{1}{2} \times 2 \times 4^2 + \tfrac{1}{2} \times 3 \times 4.5^2 \text{ J}$$
$$= 49.5 \text{ J}. \qquad \square$$

Often the summing process involves integration, as in Example 2.

Example 2
The three masses in Example 1 are replaced by a uniform bar AC of mass 6 kg. What is the kinetic energy now?

Solution

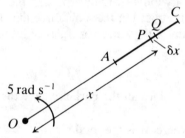

Figure 2

Consider a small portion PQ of the bar, where $OP = x$ m and $PQ = \delta x$ m (Fig. 2). Since the bar is uniform, the mass of PQ is

$$6 \times \frac{\delta x}{0.4} = 15\delta x \text{ kg}.$$

We approximate by treating the portion PQ as a particle of mass $15\delta x$ kg placed at P. This particle moves with speed $x \times 5\,\text{m s}^{-1}$ and so has KE

$$\tfrac{1}{2} \times 15\delta x \times (5x)^2 = 187.5x^2\delta x \text{ J}.$$

The total KE is approximately

$$\sum_{x=0.5}^{x=0.9} 187.5x^2\delta x \text{ J}.$$

The exact KE is the limit of this sum as $\delta x \to 0$, which is found by integration (Note 9.2). Therefore the total KE is

$$\int_{0.5}^{0.9} 187.5x^2 \, dx = \left[\frac{187.5x^3}{3} \right]_{0.5}^{0.9} = 37.75 \text{ J}. \qquad \square$$

Q.1 If all the mass of 6 kg in Example 2 where concentrated at the centre of mass of the bar, would the KE be the same?

These are examples of the simplest general case, when a rigid body rotates about
a fixed axis. Each particle of the body then moves in a plane perpendicular to
this axis; the diagrams show one such plane, which the axis meets at O. The axis
is then perpendicular to the page.

Let P, Q be two points of the body, and let OA be a line fixed in space. If
$\angle AOP = \theta$ and $\angle AOQ = \phi$, then $\phi - \theta = \angle POQ$, which is constant since
the body is rigid (Fig. 3).

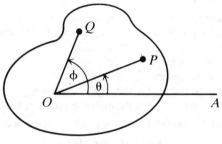

Figure 3

Therefore $\dot{\phi} - \dot{\theta} = 0$, and so $\dot{\phi} = \dot{\theta}$, so that the angular velocities of P and Q about
the axis are equal.

Furthermore, the common angular velocity of any one plane section must be
equal to that of any other, since otherwise the distance between two points of the
body, one in each plane, would vary. Therefore all points of the rigid body have a
common angular velocity about the axis; this is denoted by ω.

A particle of mass m at the point P of the body moves in a circle centre O, since
the distance OP is constant (Fig. 4). If $OP = r$ then the speed of P is $r\omega$, and the
KE of the particle is $\frac{1}{2}m(r\omega)^2 = \frac{1}{2}mr^2\omega^2$.

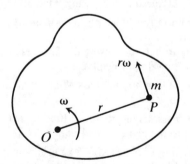

Figure 4

The total KE is $\sum \frac{1}{2}mr^2\omega^2 = \frac{1}{2}(\sum mr^2)\omega^2$, since ω is the same for all particles.
The quantity $\sum mr^2$, which is independent of ω, is called the *moment of inertia*
(MI) of the body about the axis, and is usually denoted by I. In the SI system I is
measured in kg m^2.

Thus the KE of a rigid body rotating about a fixed axis with angular
velocity ω is $\frac{1}{2}I\omega^2$, where $I = \sum mr^2$ is the moment of inertia about the axis.

The role of the moment of inertia in rotational motion is similar to that of the mass in linear motion, though it is important to remember that a body has different moments of inertia about different axes.

Exercise 9A

1 Find the MI of the body of Example 1, (a) about the axis through O; (b) about the parallel axis through A.

2 A light rigid square of side 1 m has eight 1 kg masses attached to it, one at each corner and one at the midpoint of each edge. Find the MI when the axis of rotation is:
   (a) an edge of the square;
   (b) a diagonal of the square;
   (c) perpendicular to the square through one corner;
   (d) perpendicular to the square through the centre of the square.

3 A flywheel rotating at 100 rad s^{-1} has KE 1.2 kJ. What is its MI?

4 The heavy turntable of a record player has MI 0.2 kg m^2 about its spindle. What is the increase in KE when its angular velocity changes from $33\frac{1}{3}$ to 45 revolutions per minute?

5 Find the MI of the bar in Example 2 about the axis through O.

6 A light rod of length l has n equal particles, each of mass M/n, attached to it, equally spaced at distances $l/n, 2l/n, 3l/n, \ldots, l$ from one end A. Prove that the MI about an axis through A perpendicular to the rod is $\frac{1}{6}Ml^2(1 + 1/n)(2 + 1/n)$.

   (You will need to use the fact that $\sum_{i=1}^{n} i^2 = \frac{1}{6}n(n + 1)(2n + 1)$; Note 9.3.)

   Deduce that the MI of a uniform rod of length l and mass M about an axis through one end perpendicular to the rod is $\frac{1}{3}Ml^2$.

7 Prove the final result of question 6 by using integration.

8 Find the MI of a uniform rod of length l and mass M about a perpendicular axis through its midpoint:
   (a) by combining two half-rods, using the final result of question 6;
   (b) by integration from first principles.

9 Find the MI of a rod of length l and mass M about an axis parallel to the rod at a distance d from the rod.

10 A circular hoop has mass M and radius a. Find its MI about an axis through its centre perpendicular to the plane of the hoop.

11 A wooden wheel of radius 0.5 m has MI 1.8 kg m^2 about its axle. Find the MI after a metal band of mass 15 kg has been fitted round the circumference of the wheel.

12 For similar solid bodies made from material of constant density, how does the MI about a particular axis vary with the linear dimensions?

9.2 CALCULATING MOMENTS OF INERTIA

In Exercise 9A we have obtained the following standard results:

   (a) The MI of a uniform rod of length l and mass M about an axis perpendicular to the rod is

(i) $\frac{1}{3}Ml^2$ if the axis goes through one end of the rod,

(ii) $\frac{1}{12}Ml^2$ if the axis goes through the centre of the rod.

(b) The MI of a circular hoop of mass M and radius a about the axis through its centre perpendicular to the plane of the hoop is Ma^2.

From (b) we can find the MI of a uniform disc of mass M and radius a about the axis through the centre perpendicular to the disc.

Consider the ring bounded by circles of radii r and $(r + \delta r)$ (Fig. 5). The area of this ring is

$$\pi(r + \delta r)^2 - \pi r^2 \approx 2\pi r \delta r \quad \text{(neglecting } (\delta r)^2)$$

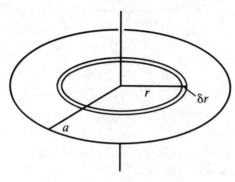

Figure 5

and its mass is approximately

$$2\pi r \delta r \times \frac{M}{\pi a^2} = \frac{2Mr\delta r}{a^2}$$

Therefore the MI of this ring is approximately

$$\frac{2Mr\delta r}{a^2} \times r^2.$$

The MI of the disc is found by summing such terms from $r = 0$ to $r = a$, and then taking the limit as $\delta r \to 0$. Therefore, for this disc

$$I = \int_0^a \frac{2Mr^3}{a^2} \, dr$$

$$= \frac{2M}{a^2} \left[\frac{r^4}{4} \right]_0^a$$

$$= \frac{1}{2}Ma^2.$$

Since a moment of inertia is defined as a sum $\sum mr^2$, it follows that if two parts of a composite body have moments of inertia I_1 and I_2 about the same axis then the MI about this axis of the body formed from these parts is $I_1 + I_2$. This *additive principle* is used in the next example.

Example 3
A letter 'T' is formed by fastening a rod AC of length 0.5 m across the top of a rod BD of length 0.6 m, as shown in Fig. 6. Each rod has linear density 2 kg m^{-1}. The small fastening at B has mass 0.1 kg. Find the MI about the axis through D parallel to AC.

Solution
The body is composed of three parts: AC, BC, and the fastening (Fig. 6). The masses of AC, BD are 1 kg, 1.2 kg respectively.

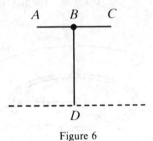

Figure 6

The MI of AC about the axis is $1 \times 0.6^2 = 0.36$ kg m^2.
The MI of BD is $\frac{1}{3} \times 1.2 \times 0.6^2 = 0.144$ kg m^2.
The MI of the fastening is $0.1 \times 0.6^2 = 0.036$ kg m^2.
The MI of the composite body is therefore

$$0.36 + 0.144 + 0.036 = 0.54 \text{ kg m}^2. \qquad \square$$

The MI of a body about an axis depends only on the way the mass is distributed with respect to distance from the axis. Therefore if one body is transformed into another body in a way which does not alter the distance of each particle from the axis then the moments of inertia of the two bodies are the same. This is known as the *stretching property*, since stretching parallel to the axis is one obvious type of transformation which has the required property (shearing with the axis invariant is another).

For example, the rod of (*a*) (i) above can be transformed by stretching parallel to the axis into a uniform rectangular lamina of mass M with the axis along one edge. (Think of lowering a venetian blind: Fig. 7.)

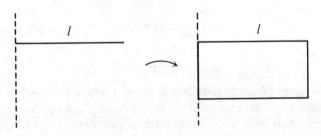

Figure 7

The MI is $\frac{1}{3}Ml^2$, where l is the length of edge perpendicular to the axis; this MI is independent of the length of edge parallel to the axis.

Q.2 Prove this result about the rectangular lamina directly by integration.

Q.3 Describe the body formed by stretching the circular ring of (b) above in the direction of the axis. State the MI of this body about this axis.

Q.4 Use the stretching property to find the MI of a circular cylinder of mass M and radius a about its axis of symmetry.

Example 4
Find the MI of the 'T' of Example 3 about the axis through B bisecting $\angle ABD$.

Solution

Figure 8

By shearing with the axis invariant, rod AC can be transformed into $A'C'$ perpendicular to the axis, where $A'C' = \dfrac{1}{\sqrt{2}}AC = \dfrac{0.5}{\sqrt{2}}$ (Fig. 8).

Similarly, BD can be sheared to BD' perpendicular to the axis, with $BD' = \dfrac{1}{\sqrt{2}}BD = \dfrac{0.6}{\sqrt{2}}$.

The fastening at B does not contribute to the MI.

Using results (a) (ii) for $A'C'$ and (a) (i) for BD', the required MI is

$$\tfrac{1}{12} \times 1 \times \left(\frac{0.5}{\sqrt{2}}\right)^2 + \tfrac{1}{3} \times 1.2 \times \left(\frac{0.6}{\sqrt{2}}\right)^2 = 0.0824 \text{ kg m}^2. \qquad \square$$

Exercise 9B

1 Find the MI of a thin uniform washer of mass M bounded by concentric circles of radii a and $2a$ about an axis through the centre perpendicular to the plane of the washer.

2 Find the MI of a uniform rod of mass M and length l about an axis through one end making an angle α with the rod.

3 A uniform lamina of mass M is in the shape of a rhombus with each side of length l and one angle $60°$. Find its MI about an axis along one edge.

4 Fig. 9 shows a shop sign of mass 8 kg which is a lamina bounded by two horizontal edges 1.2 m long and 1.5 m apart and by two identical curves. Find its MI about the upper edge.

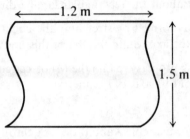

Figure 9

5 (a) A uniform semicircular lamina has mass M and radius l. Find its MI about the axis through the midpoint of its diameter perpendicular to the lamina.

(b) A rod AB of length l has mass M. The mass per unit length at a distance x from A is kx, where k is constant. Find the MI of the rod about the axis through A perpendicular to AB. (*Hint*: Consider transforming the lamina of (a) into the rod of (b) by closing it up like a fan.)

6 Find the MI of a uniform triangular lamina of mass M, base b and height h about the axis through its vertex parallel to the base. (*Hint*: Consider transforming the rod of 5(b).)

7 Find by integration the MI of a semicircular arc of mass M and radius a made of uniform wire, about the diameter joining its ends.

8 A uniform spherical shell has mass M and radius r. Referred to rectangular axes with the origin at its centre, a point of the sphere has coordinates (x, y, z), where $x^2 + y^2 + z^2 = r^2$. Show that the MI of the sphere about the z-axis, I_z, is given by $I_z = \sum m(x^2 + y^2)$.

Write down similar expressions for I_x and I_y, the moments of inertia about the other coordinate axes.

Deduce that $I_x + I_y + I_z = 2Mr^2$.

Hence show that the MI about any diameter is $\frac{2}{3}Mr^2$.

9 A uniform solid sphere of mass M has radius a. By considering it to be made from spherical shells, or otherwise, prove that its MI about any diameter is $\frac{2}{5}Ma^2$.

10 Taking the Earth to be a uniform sphere of mass 6×10^{24} kg and radius 6400 km, find its kinetic energy due to the rotation about its axis.

In fact the Earth's density increases towards its centre. Is the real kinetic energy of rotation more or less than your calculated value?

9.3 THE PERPENDICULAR AXIS RULE

This rule applies only to bodies whose mass is in one plane, i.e. to laminas.

Take perpendicular axes Ox, Oy in the plane of the lamina, and Oz perpendicular to this plane (Fig. 10). Let the moments of inertia of the lamina about these axes be I_x, I_y, I_z respectively.

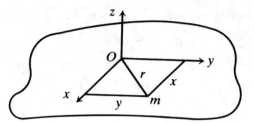

Figure 10

Then $I_x = \sum my^2$, $I_y = \sum mx^2$, and $I_z = \sum mr^2$.
But $r^2 = x^2 + y^2$. Therefore

$$I_z = I_x + I_y.$$

This is the *perpendicular axis rule*.

Example 5
Find the MI of a uniform circular disc of mass M and radius a about a diameter.

Solution
Take O at the centre of the disc. We know from §9.2 that

$$I_z = \tfrac{1}{2}Ma^2, \quad \text{so that} \quad I_x + I_y = \tfrac{1}{2}Ma^2.$$

But by symmetry $I_x = I_y$. Therefore $I_x = \tfrac{1}{4}Ma^2$. □

Example 6
A uniform lamina of mass M is bounded by the ellipse $x^2/a^2 + y^2/b^2 = 1$. Find its MI about the axis through its centre perpendicular to its plane.

Solution

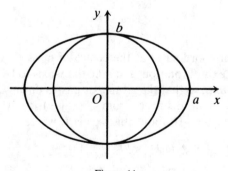

Figure 11

The ellipse can be obtained by stretching the circle $x^2 + y^2 = b^2$ parallel to the x-axis (Fig. 11). Therefore

$$I_x = \tfrac{1}{4}Mb^2.$$

Similarly, by squashing the circle $x^2 + y^2 = a^2$ parallel to the y-axis,

$$I_y = \tfrac{1}{4}Ma^2.$$

By the perpendicular axis rule,

$$I_z = \tfrac{1}{4}M(a^2 + b^2). \qquad \qquad \square$$

9.4 THE PARALLEL AXIS RULE

This very useful rule connects the MI of a body about a particular axis with the MI about a parallel axis through the centre of mass. The centre of mass is the point with position vector $\mathbf{r}_G$, where

$$\mathbf{r}_G = \frac{\sum m\mathbf{r}}{\sum m} \qquad \text{(Note 9.4).}$$

The parallel axis rule applies to three-dimensional bodies as well as laminas.

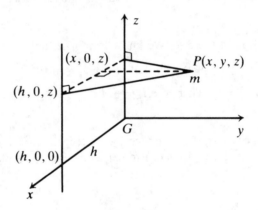

Figure 12

With the origin of coordinates at the centre of mass G, we take the z-axis parallel to the given axis of rotation, and take the x-axis to be the perpendicular from G to the given axis, so that the given axis passes through $(h, 0, 0)$ (Fig. 12). Then the perpendicular distance from $P(x, y, z)$ to the given axis is $\sqrt{[(x - h)^2 + y^2]}$, and the MI about this axis is I, where

$$I = \sum m[(x - h)^2 + y^2]$$
$$= \sum m[x^2 - 2xh + h^2 + y^2]$$
$$= \sum m(x^2 + y^2) + \sum mh^2 - \sum 2mxh.$$

The first term of this final expression is I_G, the MI about the parallel axis through G (the z-axis). Since h is constant, the second term is $(\sum m)h^2 = Mh^2$, where M is the total mass. The third term is $2h \sum mx$, which is zero since

$\sum mx/M$ is the x-component of $\mathbf{r}_G$, and we have chosen the origin so that $\mathbf{r}_G = \mathbf{0}$. Therefore

$$I = I_G + Mh^2.$$

This is the *parallel axis rule*, which shows that to find the MI about the given axis we just have to add Mh^2 to the MI about the parallel axis through the centre of mass, where M is the total mass and h is the distance between the axes.

Q.5 Check that results (*a*) (i) and (ii) of §9.2 agree with this rule.

Q.6 Show that, for a set of parallel axes, the MI is least when the axis passes through the centre of mass.

Example 7
Find the MI of a uniform circular disc of mass M and radius a about a tangent.

Solution
The centre of mass is at the centre of the disc, so

$$I_G = \text{MI about parallel diameter} = \tfrac{1}{4}Ma^2.$$

The distance between this diameter and the tangent is a. Therefore $I = \tfrac{1}{4}Ma^2 + Ma^2 = \tfrac{5}{4}Ma^2.$ □

9.5   RADIUS OF GYRATION

The *radius of gyration*, k, of a body rotating about an axis is the distance from the axis at which a single particle of the same mass as the body would have to be placed in order to have the same MI.

Therefore $Mk^2 = I$, and so $k = \sqrt{(I/M)}$ (Note 9.5).

For example, the radius of gyration of a uniform disc of radius a rotating about a perpendicular axis through its centre is

$$\sqrt{\left(\frac{\tfrac{1}{2}Ma^2}{M}\right)} = \frac{a}{\sqrt{2}}.$$

Q.7 Show that, with the obvious notation, the perpendicular axis rule may be stated as

$$k_z^2 = k_x^2 + k_y^2,$$

and the parallel axis rule as

$$k^2 = k_G^2 + h^2.$$

Exercise 9C

1 Find the MI of a rectangular lamina of mass M and sides a, b about an axis perpendicular to its plane (*a*) through its centre; (*b*) through one vertex.

2 Four equal rods, each of mass M and length l, are fastened together to form a rhombus. Prove that the MI about an axis through the centre perpendicular to the plane of the rhombus is independent of the shape of the rhombus. Find this MI.

3 Use the additive property and the perpendicular axis rule to solve Exercise 9B question 7 again.

4 Find the radius of gyration of a uniform solid sphere of radius a about a tangent.

5 The radius of gyration of a uniform spherical shell of radius r is r. How far is the axis from the centre?

6 Find the MI of the triangle of Exercise 9B question 6 about its base.

7 A square lamina has mass M and side l. Prove that the MI about any axis in the plane of the lamina through its centre is $\frac{1}{12}Ml^2$. (Hint: Take a second axis in the plane, perpendicular to the given one, and use symmetry.)

8 A pendulum consists of a circular disc of radius a and mass M rigidly attached to a rod of length l and mass m; the rod extends radially from the disc so that one end A of the rod is a distance $(l + a)$ from the centre of the disc. Find the MI of the pendulum about an axis through A perpendicular to the plane of the disc.

9 A uniform triangular lamina ABC of mass M has sides of lengths a, b, c and centre of mass G. The midpoints of BC, CA, AB are D, E, F, and $AD = l, BE = m, CF = n$. The centres of mass of triangles AFE, BDF, CED are P, Q, R (Fig. 13). Let I_G be the MI of $\triangle ABC$ about G, and I_P the MI of $\triangle AFE$ about P, both axes being perpendicular to the plane of the triangle.

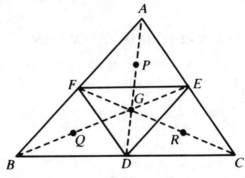

Figure 13

(a) Show that $I_P = \frac{1}{16}I_G$.

(b) Using the four small triangles, show that

$$I_G = \tfrac{1}{4}I_G + \frac{M}{4}\left(\frac{l^2 + m^2 + n^2}{9}\right)$$

and hence that $\qquad I_G = \frac{1}{27}M(l^2 + m^2 + n^2)$.

(c) Use $\mathbf{AB} = \mathbf{AD} + \frac{1}{2}\mathbf{CB}$ and $\mathbf{AC} = \mathbf{AD} + \frac{1}{2}\mathbf{BC}$ to show that

$$b^2 + c^2 = 2l^2 + a^2/2$$

(d) Hence show finally that $I_G = \frac{1}{36}M(a^2 + b^2 + c^2)$.

10

Rotation about a fixed axis

10.1 APPLICATIONS OF THE ENERGY PRINCIPLE

The Energy Principle (Note 10.1) states that the work done by the resultant force acting on a particle equals the change in kinetic energy of the particle. When applying this principle to the motion of a large body we sum over all the particles of which the body is composed. We have already seen that for a rigid body rotating about a fixed axis the total kinetic energy is $\frac{1}{2}I\omega^2$. Each force acting on any one particle of the body is either an internal force, due to other particles of the body, or an external force. By Newton's third law the internal forces occur in equal and opposite pairs, and for a *rigid* body the total work done by all the internal forces is zero; we shall prove this later, in §14.5. The change in the total kinetic energy is therefore equal to the total work done by the external forces.

If the rigid body is rotating freely under gravity about a fixed axis then the only external forces doing work are the weights of its component particles. Let a typical particle of the body have mass m. Suppose that the body moves so that the height of this particle above a fixed horizontal plane changes from z to z'. Then the work done by this particle's weight is $mg(z - z')$, and the total work done by the weights of all the particles is

$$\sum mg(z - z') = \sum mgz - \sum mgz'.$$

But
$$\sum mz = Mz_G,$$

where M is the mass of the body and z_G is the height of the centre of mass G above the fixed horizontal plane. Therefore the total work done when the body moves is

$$Mgz_G - Mgz'_G,$$

which is the same as if the total weight Mg were a single force acting on G.

If the angular velocity changes from ω to ω' because of this movement, then

$$\tfrac{1}{2}I\omega'^2 - \tfrac{1}{2}I\omega^2 = Mgz_G - Mgz'_G,$$

i.e.
$$\tfrac{1}{2}I\omega'^2 + Mgz'_G = \tfrac{1}{2}I\omega^2 + Mgz_G.$$

Therefore, for a rigid body rotating freely under gravity about a fixed axis,

$$\tfrac{1}{2}I\omega^2 + Mgz_G \text{ is constant.}$$

In this context the quantity Mgz_G is called the *potential energy* (PE) of the body. An alternative way of stating this result is to say that for a rigid body rotating freely under gravity about a fixed axis, the gain in KE = loss in PE.

159

Example 1
A uniform rod of mass M and length l can turn freely about a horizontal axis
through one end. From a horizontal position it is projected downwards with
initial angular velocity ω_0 (Fig. 1).
   (a) Find its angular velocity when it is vertically below the axis.
   (b) Find how large ω_0 must be for the rod to make complete rotations.

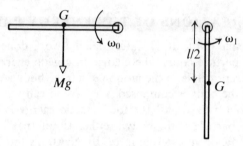

Figure 1

Solution
(a) The MI of the rod about this axis is $\frac{1}{3}Ml^2$. Let the angular velocity when the
rod is vertically down be ω_1. Then gain of KE = loss of PE

$$\Rightarrow \tfrac{1}{6}Ml^2\omega_1^2 - \tfrac{1}{6}Ml^2\omega_0^2 = Mg \times \frac{l}{2}$$

$$\Rightarrow \omega_1^2 = \omega_0^2 + \frac{3g}{l}$$

$$\Rightarrow \omega_1 = \sqrt{\left(\omega_0^2 + \frac{3g}{l}\right)}.$$

(b) The rod will make complete rotations provided that its initial KE exceeds
the PE the rod would gain in rising from the horizontal to the top position, i.e.
provided that

$$\tfrac{1}{6}Ml^2\omega_0^2 > \frac{Mgl}{2}$$

$$\Leftrightarrow \omega_0 > \sqrt{\frac{3g}{l}}. \qquad \square$$

To deal with cases in which the body is not rotating freely under gravity, we
need to take into account also the work done by other external forces acting on
the body.
   Suppose that **F** is one such force, and let OA be the perpendicular from the
fixed axis to the line of action of **F**. By the principle of transmissibility we can
take A as the point of application of **F**.
   Let ϕ be the angle between OA and some fixed direction, and let $OA = p$ (Fig.
2). When the body turns through a small angle $\delta\phi$ the displacement of A is

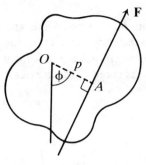

Figure 2

approximately $p\delta\phi$ in the direction of $\mathbf{F}$, and so the work done by $\mathbf{F}$ on the body is approximately

$$F p \delta\phi = L \delta\phi,$$

where $L (= Fp)$ is the moment of $\mathbf{F}$ about the axis. By summing from $\phi = \phi_0$ to $\phi = \theta$ and taking the limit as $\delta\phi \to 0$ we deduce that:

> The total work done by $\mathbf{F}$ when ϕ increases from θ_0 to θ is $\displaystyle\int_{\theta_0}^{\theta} L\, d\phi$, where L is the moment of $\mathbf{F}$ about the axis.

In particular, if the moment of $\mathbf{F}$ about the axis is constant, then the work done is $L(\theta - \theta_0)$.

Q.1   Taking $\mathbf{F}$ to be the weight $M\mathbf{g}$, use $\displaystyle\int_{\theta_0}^{\theta} L\, d\phi$ to prove again that the work done by the body's weight is $Mgz_G - Mgz'_G$.

Example 2
A record player turntable has MI 0.2 kg m^2 about its spindle. It is turning at $33\frac{1}{3}$ r.p.m. when the power is switched off. It then turns through $4\frac{1}{2}$ revolutions before stopping. What constant frictional couple is acting on the turntable?

Solution
The initial angular velocity is $\dfrac{33\frac{1}{3} \times 2\pi}{60}$ (≈ 3.49) rad s^{-1}, so the initial KE is $\frac{1}{2} \times 0.2 \times 3.49^2$ J. If the frictional couple has moment L N m, then the work done by this couple is $L \times 4\frac{1}{2} \times 2\pi$ J.

Therefore
$$L \times 4\tfrac{1}{2} \times 2\pi = \tfrac{1}{2} \times 0.2 \times 3.49^2$$

$$\Rightarrow L = \frac{\frac{1}{2} \times 0.2 \times 3.49^2}{4\frac{1}{2} \times 2\pi}$$

$$\approx 0.043 \text{ N m.} \qquad \square$$

Example 3
A heavy pulley, of MI I about its horizontal axle and radius r, has a light string hanging over it. Attached to the ends of the string are masses m and $2m$ (Fig. 3). The system is released from rest. Assuming that the pulley turns freely and that the string does not slip, find the speed of the heavier mass when it has descended a distance d.

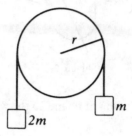

Figure 3

Solution
Let the required speed be v. Then the angular velocity of the pulley is v/r, since the string does not slip.
   The total kinetic energy is

$$\tfrac{1}{2}mv^2 + \tfrac{1}{2}.2mv^2 + \tfrac{1}{2}I\left(\frac{v}{r}\right)^2 = \tfrac{1}{2}\left(3m + \frac{I}{r^2}\right)v^2.$$

The lighter mass has gained potential energy mgd, the heavier mass has lost potential energy $2mgd$, and the potential energy of the pulley is unchanged. Thus the total loss of PE is mgd, and so

$$\tfrac{1}{2}\left(3m + \frac{I}{r^2}\right)v^2 = mgd$$

$$\Rightarrow v = \sqrt{\left(\frac{2mgdr^2}{3mr^2 + I}\right)}. \qquad \square$$

Q.2 Why is the work done by the tensions in the string not involved in this solution?

Exercise 10A

1 A uniform metre rule can turn freely about a horizontal axis through one end. The rod is held at rest vertically up above the axis, and then slightly displaced. It then rotates freely under gravity. Find the angular velocity of the rule (*a*) when it is horizontal, (*b*) when it is vertically below the axis.

2 Repeat question 1 for a metre rule which turns freely about a horizontal axis through the point 0.2 m along the rule from one end.

3 A uniform solid sphere of mass 0.5 kg and radius 0.1 m can turn freely about a fixed horizontal diameter AB. A particle of mass 0.2 kg is attached to the surface of the

sphere at a point as far as possible from *AB*. The sphere is held at rest with the particle at the same horizontal level as *AB*, and then released. What is the greatest angular velocity of the sphere in the subsequent motion? How far below its original level is the particle when the angular velocity has half this greatest value?

4   A rigid body of mass *M* turns freely about a horizontal axis at a distance *h* from its centre of mass. Its greatest and least angular velocities when it makes complete turns are ω and $\frac{3}{5}\omega$. Prove that the MI about the axis is $25Mgh/4\omega^2$.

5   A pendulum consists of a uniform rod of length *l* and mass *m* carrying a concentrated mass *M* at one end and freely pivoted at the other end. When the pendulum is hanging vertically below the pivot the mass *M* is given the horizontal velocity *v* which is just sufficient to cause complete rotations. Find *v* in terms of *m*, *M*, *l*, *g*. Sketch a graph to show how *v* changes as *M/m* increases from zero.

6   The lid of a kitchen waste bin is composed of two square sheets of plastic of side *a*, small thickness δ and uniform density ρ. They are fixed together at right angles along an edge of each square, and the resulting L-shaped lid swings freely about a horizontal axle through *A* (see Fig. 4). Find the moment of inertia of the lid about the axle.

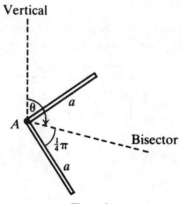

Figure 4

The lid is balanced in its position of unstable equilibrium ($\theta = 0$ in the diagram), and then displaced very slightly. Derive the equation

$$\sqrt{2}a\dot{\theta}^2 = 3g(1 - \cos \theta),$$

where θ is the angle between the upward vertical and the inner bisector of the lid angle.

Hence find the largest angular velocity of the lid.   [SMP]

7   When there is a record on the turntable of Example 2 the turntable and record take $4\frac{3}{4}$ revolutions to stop. Find the MI of the record about the spindle.

8   The flywheel of a gyroscope consists of a disc 6 cm in diameter and 0.2 cm thick. It is made of metal of density 8000 kg/m³. Determine its MI about the axle, ignoring the inertia of the axle. The gyroscope is started by pulling on a cord wrapped around the axle with a force of 100 N for 0.5 m. Neglecting friction, find the resulting angular velocity of the gyroscope.

9   A wheel of radius 6 cm rotating freely about a horizontal axis is set in motion by a light string wrapped round the edge of the wheel and supporting a mass of 0.7 kg.

When released from rest the mass takes 5 seconds to descend 80 cm. Find the MI of the wheel about the axis.

10   A revolving door consists of four uniform rectangles of width 1 m, each attached by one long side to a central vertical axis. A child pushing halfway between the axis and an outside edge with a force of 150 N turns the door through two complete revolutions, by which time it is turning at 3 rad s^{-1}, and then leaves it. The door comes to rest after turning through one more revolution. Find the constant frictional couple and the mass of the door.

10.2 THE EQUATION OF ROTATIONAL MOTION

We have seen in §10.1 that, for a rigid body rotating about a fixed axis, the energy principle takes the form

$$\int_{\theta_0}^{\theta} L \, d\phi = \tfrac{1}{2}I\omega^2 - \tfrac{1}{2}I\omega_0^2,$$

where L is the total moment about the axis of the external forces, ω_0 and ω are the angular velocities when $\phi = \theta_0$ and when $\phi = \theta$ respectively, and I is the MI about the axis.

Differentiating this equation with respect to θ gives

$$\frac{d}{d\theta} \int_{\theta_0}^{\theta} L \, d\phi = I\omega \frac{d\omega}{d\theta}.$$

Now
$$\omega \frac{d\omega}{d\theta} = \frac{d\theta}{dt} \times \frac{d\omega}{d\theta} = \frac{d\omega}{dt} = \dot{\omega},$$

by the chain rule, and

$$\frac{d}{d\theta} \int_{\theta_0}^{\theta} L \, d\phi = L,$$

by the fundamental theorem of analysis (Note 10.2). Therefore

$$L = I\dot{\omega}.$$

This is the *equation of rotational motion* for a rigid body rotating about a fixed axis (Note 10.3). It is similar in form to Newton's second law $\mathbf{F} = m\mathbf{a}$, with the moment L replacing the force $\mathbf{F}$, the moment of inertia I replacing the mass m, and the angular acceleration $\dot{\omega}$ $(= \ddot{\theta})$ replacing the acceleration $\mathbf{a}$. Here we have derived the equation of rotational motion from the energy principle; later (§16.1) we shall also obtain it directly from Newton's second law.

Example 4
Find the angular acceleration of the pulley of Example 3, and the tension in the part of the string attached to the heavier mass.

Solution

Let the tensions in the string attached to the heavier and lighter masses be T_1 and T_2 respectively, and let the angular acceleration of the pulley be $\dot{\omega}$. Then, since the string does not slip, the heavier and lighter masses have accelerations $r\dot{\omega}$ downward and upward respectively (Fig. 5).

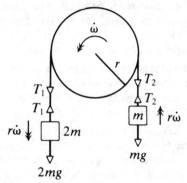

Figure 5

The equations of motion are

for the heavier mass $\qquad 2mg - T_1 = 2mr\dot{\omega}$ $\qquad\qquad$ (1)

for the lighter mass $\qquad T_2 - mg = mr\dot{\omega}$ $\qquad\qquad$ (2)

The equation of rotational motion for the pulley is

$$rT_1 - rT_2 = I\dot{\omega} \qquad\qquad (3)$$

Substituting for T_1 and T_2 from (1) and (2) in (3):

$$r(2mg - 2mr\dot{\omega}) - r(mg + mr\dot{\omega}) = I\dot{\omega}$$

$$\Leftrightarrow mgr - 3mr^2\dot{\omega} = I\dot{\omega}$$

$$\Leftrightarrow \qquad\qquad \dot{\omega} = \frac{mgr}{3mr^2 + I}.$$

Substituting for $\dot{\omega}$ in (1) gives

$$2mg - T_1 = 2m\frac{mgr^2}{3mr^2 + I}$$

$$\Rightarrow T_1 = 2mg\left(1 - \frac{mr^2}{3mr^2 + I}\right) = 2mg\left(\frac{2mr^2 + I}{3mr^2 + I}\right). \qquad\square$$

Q.3 Find T_2.

Exercise 10B

1 A couple of 0.1 N m is applied for 2 minutes to a flywheel of MI 0.005 kg m^2 about its axis. What is the change in angular speed of the flywheel?

2   Find the angular acceleration of a uniform sphere of mass M and radius r about an axis of symmetry when a couple L is applied about this axis and a frictional couple G opposes motion.

3   Find the ratio of the angular accelerations of a uniform rod when it is pivoted (a) about its centre, (b) about an end.

4   A wheel (which may be considered to be a uniform disc) of radius r and mass M has a driving belt round part of its circumference. If the tensions in the belt at the points where it leaves the wheel are T_1 and T_2, with $T_1 > T_2$, and friction may be neglected, find the angular acceleration of the wheel.

5   A uniform pulley wheel of radius r and mass m, mounted on a horizontal axis, has a light string hung over it, to one end of which is attached a mass $2m$ and to the other end a mass $3m$. Determine the angular acceleration of the wheel if the string does not slip and there is no friction at the axis.

6   A wheel with light spokes can be considered as having its mass of 1 kg concentrated round its rim. It is free to rotate about a horizontal axis through its centre, and a string passes over it with masses of 5 kg and 4 kg attached to its ends. Find the ratio of the angular acceleration in this case to the angular acceleration if the mass of the wheel is neglected.

7   The rear wheel of a bicycle is held off the ground and is assumed to have mass 1.5 kg concentrated at the rim of radius 0.4 m. A force of 45 N is applied at right angles to the crank (of length 12 cm). If the gear wheels are 9 cm and 4 cm in radius at the crank and the wheel respectively, find the angular acceleration of the wheel. What assumptions have you made?

8   The turntable and record of Exercise 10A, question 7, are turning at $33\frac{1}{3}$ r.p.m. with the pick-up stylus in contact with the record at a distance of 15 cm from the spindle. When the power is switched off the turntable and record turn through $4\frac{1}{4}$ revolutions before stopping. What is the angular retardation? What is the horizontal tangential force between the stylus and the record?

9   The 'rising hinges' of a uniform door of width 0.7 m raise the door through 4 cm when the door is opened through a right angle. The door takes 5 seconds to shut itself from this position. What percentage of the potential energy is wasted through friction?

10   The couple on a shaft of moment of inertia I kg m² increases uniformly with time for T seconds, from 0 to L N m. Find the angular velocity reached in this time.

11   At time t seconds a flywheel is acted on by a couple $L \sin t$ N m, where L is constant. The flywheel's MI is I kg m², and it has initial angular velocity Ω rad s⁻¹. Find its angular velocities after $2n\pi$ seconds and $(2n + 1)\pi$ seconds, where n is an integer.
     Find also its greatest and least angular velocities.
     If instead the couple is $L \sin^2 t$ N m, what constant resisting couple is needed to make the angular velocity oscillate between fixed limits, and what will these limits be?

10.3   MOMENT OF MOMENTUM

By differentiating the energy equation with respect to θ we have obtained the equation of motion $L = I\dot{\omega}$ for a rigid body rotating about a fixed axis. Now we derive another important result by integrating this equation of motion with respect to t:

$$\int_{t_0}^{t_1} L \, dt = \int_{t_0}^{t_1} I\dot{\omega} \, dt$$

$$= \int_{\omega_0}^{\omega_1} I \, d\omega$$

$$\Rightarrow \int_{t_0}^{t_1} L \, dt = I\omega_1 - I\omega_0,$$

where ω_0 and ω_1 are the values of ω when $t = t_0$ and $t = t_1$ respectively.

The expression $\int_{t_0}^{t_1} L \, dt$ is called the *impulsive moment* of the resultant force about the axis; its unit is N m s.

Note the following special cases.

(1) If L is constant then the impulsive moment is simply $L(t_1 - t_0)$.
(2) If L is the moment of a force $\mathbf{F}$ acting at a *constant* distance p from the axis (for example, a tension in a string round a pulley) then

$$\int L \, dt = \int pF \, dt = p \int F \, dt,$$

which is the moment of the impulse $\int F \, dt$ about the axis.

(3) A large force acting for a short time produces an impulse which is called a *jerk*. The change in the distance of the force from the axis during this short time is negligible, so that, as in (2), the impulsive moment equals the moment of the jerk about the axis.

The quantity $I\omega$ is called the *moment of momentum* of the body about the axis; since this is so closely linked to impulsive moment it is also measured in N m s (rather than kg m^2 s^{-1}). The reason for the name 'moment of momentum' is seen by considering a particle P of mass m of the body, at a distance r from the axis. Since the body is rigid, this particle moves with speed $r\omega$ at right angles to OP (Fig. 6). Its momentum is therefore $mr\omega$ perpendicular to OP, and the moment of its momentum about O is $r \times mr\omega = mr^2\omega$.

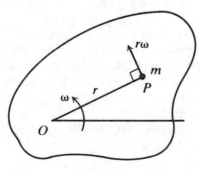

Figure 6

The total moment of a momentum for the whole body is

$$\sum mr^2\omega = \left(\sum mr^2\right)\omega, \text{ since } \omega \text{ is the same for all points of the body,}$$

$$= I\omega.$$

An alternative name for moment of momentum is *angular momentum*. The main result of this section can now be restated as:

Impulsive moment of resultant force = change in moment of momentum

or, in abbreviated form, $\int L\, dt = [I\omega]$.

This corresponds to the impulse–momentum equation for linear motion. (Note 10.4) and, like that equation, is very often used to deal with interacting bodies. In particular, if for a system the total impulsive moment about an axis is zero then the total moment of momentum about that axis is conserved.

Example 5
Two cog wheels A, B have radii a, b respectively and moments of inertia I_A, I_B about their axes. They are freely mounted on parallel axes of negligible inertia. When A is rotating with angular velocity ω it is brought into mesh with B, which is stationary. Find the final angular velocities of the wheels.

Solution

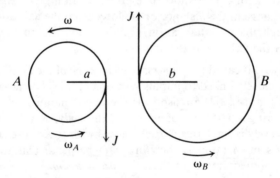

Figure 7

Let the final angular velocities be ω_A, ω_B as shown in Fig. 7. During the meshing there will be a force between the two wheels. The force on A due to B at any instant is equal and opposite to the force on B due to A. Therefore the impulse on A due to B is equal and opposite to the impulse on B due to A. Let the tangential components of these impulses have magnitude J. (What effect does any radial component have?)

Then, taking the anticlockwise sense positive, and applying

$$\int L\, dt = [I\omega]$$

for A: $-aJ = I_A(\omega_A - \omega)$

for B: $-bJ = I_B\omega_B.$

Eliminating J,

$$bI_A(\omega_A - \omega) = aI_B\omega_B. \tag{1}$$

But since the wheels are meshed after impact, the velocities at the point of contact on each are the same.

Hence $a\omega_A = -b\omega_B.$

Using this in (1) gives

$$b^2 I_A(\omega_A - \omega) = -a^2 I_B\omega_A$$

$$\Rightarrow \omega_A = \frac{b^2 I_A\omega}{b^2 I_A + a^2 I_B}, \qquad \omega_B = -\frac{abI_A\omega}{b^2 I_A + a^2 I_B}. \qquad \square$$

Q.4   What is the sum of the moments of momentum of A and B about their respective axes, (*a*) initially, (*b*) finally? Why are these not the same?

Exercise 10C

1   The couple applied to a wheel, initially at rest, varies with time as follows:

Time (s)	0	3	6	9	12	15	18
Couple (N m)	0	65	90	110	120	85	55

The wheel has MI $12 \, \text{kg m}^2$ and turns freely. Estimate its angular velocity after 18 s.

2   A flywheel has MI $25 \, \text{kg m}^2$ about its axis. It is accelerated from rest by a couple which varies between 0 and 40 N m over a period of 30 seconds as shown in Fig. 8. Find the angular velocity at the end of this period, (*a*) when there is no friction, (*b*) when there is a frictional couple which cannot exceed 16 N m.

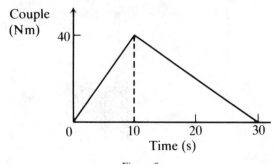

Figure 8

3   A flat disc is spinning freely with angular velocity ω_1 about a vertical axis through its centre. Its MI about this axis is I. A uniform ring of mass m and radius R spins about its centre, in its own horizontal plane with angular velocity ω_2 in the opposite sense to ω_1. The ring is lowered onto the disc so that the two centres coincide. The coefficient of friction between the ring and the disc is μ. Find an expression for the time during which relative slipping continues.

4   Two flywheels, of moments of inertia I_1 and I_2 about their axis, are rotating on the same axis with angular speeds ω_1 and ω_2 in the same sense when they are brought in contact so that they continue with a common speed. Determine this common speed. If the connection between the flywheels is by means of a friction clutch which slips as long as the couple applied to it is greater than L, determine the time for which slipping persists.

5   A meteor of mass m and speed v strikes the earth. What is the greatest resulting fractional change in the earth's speed of rotation? Assume the earth is of radius R and uniform density ρ.

6   A metre rule of mass M is freely pivoted about a horizontal axis through its centre. It is initially horizontal and stationary. A lump of putty of mass m falls through a height h and sticks to the end of the rule. Determine (a) the subsequent angular speed, (b) the minimum value of h for the rule to make complete revolutions.

7   Two spheres, A and B, each of radius a, are mounted on axles (through their centres) which produce equal constant resisting couples. They are set rotating with equal initial angular velocities. Sphere A comes to rest in half the time taken by B. One sphere is solid and the other is hollow (the cavity being a concentric sphere), although the material used in both spheres is uniform and of equal density.
   Determine which sphere is hollow. Find the radius of the cavity in terms of a.
                                                                              [SMP]

8   In a fairground shooting gallery a target has to be knocked over for a prize to be won. The target consists of a rectangular metal plate of mass M, height $2l$ and small thickness. To the bottom of the target plate is rigidly fixed, at right angles, another plate of negligible mass and thickness and of length l; the latter plate can rotate freely about a fixed horizontal axle A. When the target is ready for a shot it stands vertically on a fixed wall, as shown in Fig. 9. Calculate the moment of inertia of the target about the axle.

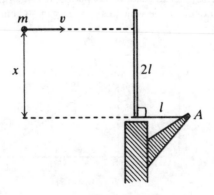

Figure 9

A small bullet of mass m is fired with speed v to hit the plate horizontally at a distance x above the level of the axle. The bullet flattens on impact and then drops vertically. Show that the angular velocity of the target just after impact is

$$\frac{3mvx}{7Ml^2},$$

and write down the energy acquired by the target.

Find the value of x (assumed to be less than $2l$) for which the target just fails to be tipped over.   [SMP]

11

Vector product in mechanics

11.1 MOMENTS IN THREE DIMENSIONS

When a rigid body rotates about a fixed axis, each point of the body moves in a plane perpendicular to the axis; we have shown this by a typical plane section, with the axis perpendicular to the page. The only 'directional' consideration which then arises when we take moments is to distinguish between clockwise and anticlockwise turning effects.

Suppose now that we have a rigid body which can turn about a fixed point O. Examples are an airship attached to its mooring tower, a fairground wheel that can tilt as well as turn, or the bell-shaped type of roundabout found in children's playgrounds (Fig. 1).

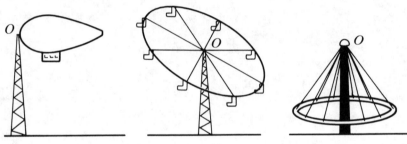

Figure 1

Let the body be initially at rest, but free to turn about O. It is found by experiment that if a force $\mathbf{F}$ acts at a point P of the body then the body will turn about the line through O perpendicular to the plane containing O and $\mathbf{F}$. The magnitude of the turning effect of $\mathbf{F}$ about O equals the magnitude of $\mathbf{F}$ times the perpendicular distance of O from the line of action of $\mathbf{F}$, which is

$$|\mathbf{F}| \times |\mathbf{r}| \sin \theta,$$

where $\mathbf{OP} = \mathbf{r}$, and θ is the angle between $\mathbf{r}$ and $\mathbf{F}$ (Fig. 2). The line about which the body turns is perpendicular to both $\mathbf{r}$ and $\mathbf{F}$. There are two unit vectors in this direction, with opposite senses, so to be precise we define $\hat{\mathbf{e}}$ to be the unit vector perpendicular to $\mathbf{r}$ and $\mathbf{F}$ in the sense in which a right-hand corkscrew would move if it were rotated under the action of $\mathbf{F}$.

Then the turning effect is completely represented by the vector

$$|\mathbf{r}||\mathbf{F}| \sin \theta \hat{\mathbf{e}},$$

which we call the (*vector*) *moment* of $\mathbf{F}$ about O.

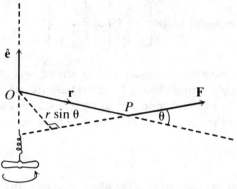

Figure 2

Q.1 If O and F lie in the plane of the page and F has a positive (anticlockwise) moment about O, does $\hat{e}$ point towards or away from the reader?

Example 1
A body is free to turn about the origin of coordinates. Find the vector moment of the force

$$\mathbf{F} = \begin{bmatrix} 0 \\ 0 \\ 8 \end{bmatrix}$$

acting at the point $(3, 4, 6)$.

Solution
The line of action of F meets the x-y-plane at $Q(3, 4, 0)$. The perpendicular distance from O to the line of action is $OQ = \sqrt{(3^2 + 4^2)} = 5$. The magnitude of the moment is therefore $5 \times 8 = 40$.

Unit vector $\hat{e}$ is perpendicular to $\mathbf{OQ}$ and $\mathbf{k}$, in the sense shown in Fig. 3, so

$$\hat{e} = \begin{bmatrix} 4/5 \\ -3/5 \\ 0 \end{bmatrix}.$$

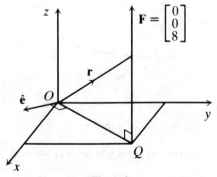

Figure 3

Thus the vector moment is $40 \begin{bmatrix} 4/5 \\ -3/5 \\ 0 \end{bmatrix} = \begin{bmatrix} 32 \\ -24 \\ 0 \end{bmatrix}.$ □

So far the vector moment is merely a convenient way of packaging the information about the turning effect of **F**. In the following sections we shall find that it makes sense to add such moments using vector addition, and to multiply them by scalars. In other words, we shall find that moment is a vector quantity.

Exercise 11A

1   A cube of side 1 m has one corner at the origin and three edges as **i**, **j**, **k**. Find the vector moment about O of each of these forces (measured in N):

(a) $\begin{bmatrix} 7 \\ 0 \\ 0 \end{bmatrix}$ at $(1, 0, 1)$;   (b) $\begin{bmatrix} 0 \\ 0 \\ 5 \end{bmatrix}$ at $(0, 1, 0)$;   (c) $\begin{bmatrix} 0 \\ 9 \\ 9 \end{bmatrix}$ at $(1, 1, 0)$.

2   The force $\begin{bmatrix} 1 \\ 4 \\ 2 \end{bmatrix}$ has moment $\begin{bmatrix} 8 \\ -1 \\ -2 \end{bmatrix}$ about the origin. What is the magnitude of the moment? How far from the origin is the line of action of the force?

3   The moment of a force about O is $\begin{bmatrix} 4 \\ 12 \\ 3 \end{bmatrix}$, and the distance of the line of action from O is 5. Find the magnitude of the force. What can be said about the direction of the force?

4   Find the vector moments about $(0, 1, 1)$ of the forces in question 1.

11.2 THE VECTOR PRODUCT

The method of combining vectors **r** and **F** to give the vector $|\mathbf{r}||\mathbf{F}| \sin \theta \hat{\mathbf{e}}$ leads directly to the definition of the vector product. We work now with unspecified vectors **a** and **b**, since the vector product has important applications in geometry and kinematics as well as in connection with moments.

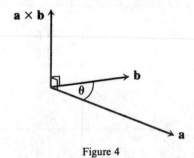

Figure 4

The *vector product* **a** × **b** (read as 'a cross b') is defined to be the vector

$$|\mathbf{a}||\mathbf{b}| \sin \theta \hat{\mathbf{e}},$$

where θ is the angle between **a** and **b**, and **ê** is the unit vector perpendicular to both **a** and **b** with the sense of **ê** such that a rotation through angle θ from **a** to **b** will move a right-hand screw along **ê** (Fig. 4). If **a** or **b** is **0**, or if **a** and **b** are parallel, then **ê** cannot be specified; in these cases we naturally define **a** × **b** to be **0**. The alternative notation **a** ∧ **b** is also used for the vector product. Reversing the order of **a** and **b** reverses the sense of **ê**, so that **b** × **a** = −**a** × **b**. The vector product is therefore not commutative, and so it is important to be careful about the order of vectors in a vector product.

Q.2   Prove that $(h\mathbf{a}) \times \mathbf{b} = h(\mathbf{a} \times \mathbf{b})$. (Take the cases $h > 0$, $h = 0$, $h < 0$ separately.) Deduce that $(h\mathbf{a}) \times (k\mathbf{b}) = hk(\mathbf{a} \times \mathbf{b})$.

Q.3   What is **a** × **a**? (Note 11.1).

Q.4   Find the nine vector products which can be formed using two of the unit vectors **i**, **j**, **k** (including repetitions).

Q.5   Is it true that $\mathbf{i} \times (\mathbf{i} \times \mathbf{j}) = (\mathbf{i} \times \mathbf{i}) \times \mathbf{j}$? Is the vector product operation associative?

Q.6   Prove that $\mathbf{a} \times \mathbf{b} = \mathbf{0} \Leftrightarrow \mathbf{a} = \mathbf{0}$ or $\mathbf{b} = \mathbf{0}$ or **a** is parallel to **b**.

Q.7   Interpret the results of Q.2 and Q.6 in the case of **r** × **F**.

11.3   THE DISTRIBUTIVE PROPERTY OF VECTOR PRODUCTS

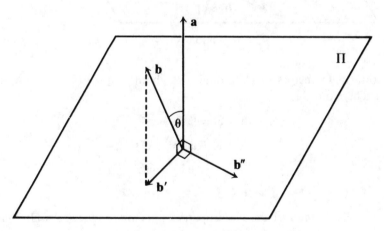

Figure 5

Taking **a** and **b** as position vectors from an origin O, let Π be the plane through O perpendicular to **a**, and let **b**′ be the projection of **b** onto Π (Fig. 5). Then

$$|\mathbf{b}'| = |\mathbf{b}| \sin \theta,$$

so that
$$|\mathbf{a} \times \mathbf{b}| = |\mathbf{a}||\mathbf{b}| \sin \theta$$
$$= |\mathbf{a}||\mathbf{b}'|$$
$$= |\mathbf{a} \times \mathbf{b}'|,$$

since $\mathbf{a}$ and $\mathbf{b}'$ are perpendicular.

Also $\mathbf{a} \times \mathbf{b}$ and $\mathbf{a} \times \mathbf{b}'$ have the same direction and sense, in Π at right angles to $\mathbf{b}'$. Therefore $\mathbf{a} \times \mathbf{b} = \mathbf{a} \times \mathbf{b}'$.

Now $\mathbf{a} \times \mathbf{b}'$ is particularly easy to find; all we have to do is rotate $\mathbf{b}'$ in Π through 90° about O to give $\mathbf{b}''$, and then enlarge $\mathbf{b}''$ by scale factor $|\mathbf{a}|$. Then $\mathbf{a} \times \mathbf{b} = |\mathbf{a}|\mathbf{b}''$.

If $\mathbf{c}$ is another position vector then the projection of $(\mathbf{b} + \mathbf{c})$ onto Π is the sum of the projections of $\mathbf{b}$ and $\mathbf{c}$, i.e. $(\mathbf{b} + \mathbf{c})' = \mathbf{b}' + \mathbf{c}'$.

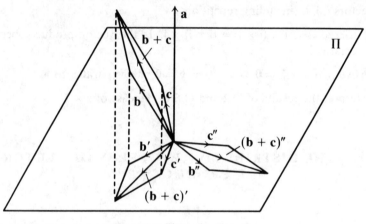

Figure 6

Rotating these vectors in Π through 90° about O gives $(\mathbf{b} + \mathbf{c})'' = \mathbf{b}'' + \mathbf{c}''$ (Fig. 6). Therefore
$$\mathbf{a} \times (\mathbf{b} + \mathbf{c}) = |\mathbf{a}|(\mathbf{b} + \mathbf{c})''$$
$$= |\mathbf{a}|(\mathbf{b}'' + \mathbf{c}'')$$
$$= |\mathbf{a}|\mathbf{b}'' + |\mathbf{a}|\mathbf{c}'',$$

i.e.
$$\mathbf{a} \times (\mathbf{b} + \mathbf{c}) = \mathbf{a} \times \mathbf{b} + \mathbf{a} \times \mathbf{c}$$

which establishes the distributive property of vector products. An alternative proof is given in Example 1 of Chapter 12 (p. 194).

Q.8   Deduce that $(\mathbf{a} + \mathbf{b}) \times \mathbf{c} = \mathbf{a} \times \mathbf{c} + \mathbf{b} \times \mathbf{c}$.

Q.9   What is wrong with the following?
$$(\mathbf{a} - \mathbf{b}) \times (\mathbf{a} + \mathbf{b}) = \mathbf{a} \times \mathbf{a} - \mathbf{b} \times \mathbf{b} = 0 - 0 = 0.$$

11.4 COMPONENT FORM OF THE VECTOR PRODUCT

The result of Q.4 can be written in this anti-symmetric array

		Second		
$\times$		**i**	**j**	**k**
First	**i**	**0**	**k**	$-\mathbf{j}$
	j	$-\mathbf{k}$	**0**	**i**
	k	**j**	$-\mathbf{i}$	**0**

With $\mathbf{a} = a_1\mathbf{i} + a_2\mathbf{j} + a_3\mathbf{k}$, $\mathbf{b} = b_1\mathbf{i} + b_2\mathbf{j} + b_3\mathbf{k}$ we can now use the distributive property and Q.2 to expand the vector $\mathbf{a} \times \mathbf{b}$; after simplifying we obtain

$$\mathbf{a} \times \mathbf{b} = (a_2b_3 - a_3b_2)\mathbf{i} + (a_3b_1 - a_1b_3)\mathbf{j} + (a_1b_2 - a_2b_1)\mathbf{k}.$$

Q.10 Check the details of this.

Q.11 Solve Example 1 again, using this component form.

This result can be written formally as the expansion of a determinant.

$$\mathbf{a} \times \mathbf{b} = \begin{vmatrix} \mathbf{i} & a_1 & b_1 \\ \mathbf{j} & a_2 & b_2 \\ \mathbf{k} & a_3 & b_3 \end{vmatrix}$$

or in column vector form

$$\mathbf{a} = \begin{bmatrix} a_1 \\ a_2 \\ a_3 \end{bmatrix}, \qquad \mathbf{b} = \begin{bmatrix} b_1 \\ b_2 \\ b_3 \end{bmatrix} \Rightarrow \mathbf{a} \times \mathbf{b} = \begin{bmatrix} a_2b_3 - a_3b_2 \\ a_3b_1 - a_1b_3 \\ a_1b_2 - a_2b_1 \end{bmatrix}.$$

Exercise 11B

1 Given that $\mathbf{a} = \begin{bmatrix} 6 \\ 9 \\ 1 \end{bmatrix}$, $\mathbf{b} = \begin{bmatrix} 7 \\ -5 \\ 2 \end{bmatrix}$, $\mathbf{c} = \begin{bmatrix} 0 \\ 3 \\ -6 \end{bmatrix}$, check by direct evaluation that

$\mathbf{a} \times (\mathbf{b} + \mathbf{c}) = \mathbf{a} \times \mathbf{b} + \mathbf{a} \times \mathbf{c}$ and $(\mathbf{a} + \mathbf{b}) \times \mathbf{c} = \mathbf{a} \times \mathbf{c} + \mathbf{b} \times \mathbf{c}$.

2 Given that $\mathbf{a} = \begin{bmatrix} 2 \\ 4 \\ 5 \end{bmatrix}$, $\mathbf{b} = \begin{bmatrix} -1 \\ 5 \\ -7 \end{bmatrix}$, work out $\mathbf{a} \times \mathbf{b}$. Use the scalar product to check that $\mathbf{a} \times \mathbf{b}$ is perpendicular to both $\mathbf{a}$ and $\mathbf{b}$.

3 Find a unit vector perpendicular to both $4\mathbf{i} + 3\mathbf{j} - \mathbf{k}$ and $7\mathbf{i} + 10\mathbf{k}$.

4 Prove that $|\mathbf{a} \times \mathbf{b}|^2 + (\mathbf{a} \cdot \mathbf{b})^2 = |\mathbf{a}|^2|\mathbf{b}|^2$.

Verify this in the particular case $\mathbf{a} = \begin{bmatrix} 8 \\ 2 \\ 5 \end{bmatrix}$, $\mathbf{b} = \begin{bmatrix} -3 \\ 7 \\ 11 \end{bmatrix}$.

5   Find the moment about the origin of

(a) a force $\begin{bmatrix} 2 \\ 0 \\ -1 \end{bmatrix}$ acting at the point $(1, 1, 0)$,

(b) a force $7\mathbf{i} + 4\mathbf{j} + 2\mathbf{k}$ acting at the point $(2, -1, 6)$.

6   An unknown force $\begin{bmatrix} F_1 \\ F_2 \\ 0 \end{bmatrix}$ has a vector moment $\begin{bmatrix} 4 \\ 1 \\ -1 \end{bmatrix}$ about the origin and acts on a

body at the point $(1, 3, 7)$. Find F_1 and F_2.

7   Prove that $\mathbf{a} + \mathbf{b} + \mathbf{c} = \mathbf{0} \Rightarrow \mathbf{a} \times \mathbf{b} = \mathbf{b} \times \mathbf{c} = \mathbf{c} \times \mathbf{a}$.
Find whether or not the converse is true.

*8   Let $\mathbf{w} = \mathbf{u} \times \mathbf{v}$, where $\mathbf{u}$, $\mathbf{v}$ are vectors which depend on the scalar variable t. Let the
changes in $\mathbf{u}$, $\mathbf{v}$, $\mathbf{w}$ when t changes by δt be $\delta\mathbf{u}$, $\delta\mathbf{v}$, $\delta\mathbf{w}$ respectively.
(a) Show that $\delta\mathbf{w} = \delta\mathbf{u} \times \mathbf{v} + \mathbf{u} \times \delta\mathbf{v} + \delta\mathbf{u} \times \delta\mathbf{v}$.
(b) By dividing by δt and letting $\delta t \to 0$, show that

$$\frac{d\mathbf{w}}{dt} = \frac{d\mathbf{u}}{dt} \times \mathbf{v} + \mathbf{u} \times \frac{d\mathbf{v}}{dt},$$

assuming that these derivatives exist.

9   Given that $\mathbf{u} = \begin{bmatrix} 2t \\ 3t^2 \\ t^3 \end{bmatrix}$, $\mathbf{v} = \begin{bmatrix} -t^2 \\ 5t \\ 4 \end{bmatrix}$ and $\mathbf{w} = \mathbf{u} \times \mathbf{v}$, find $\dfrac{d\mathbf{w}}{dt}$

(a) by working out $\mathbf{u} \times \mathbf{v}$ and then differentiating,
(b) by using the result of question 8.

11.5 SUMMING VECTOR MOMENTS

The vector moment of $\mathbf{F}$ about O may now be written concisely as $\mathbf{r} \times \mathbf{F}$, where
$\mathbf{r} = \mathbf{OP}$ is the position vector of an arbitrary point P on the line of action of $\mathbf{F}$.
We saw in §8.6 (for the two-dimensional case) that this moment is independent
of the choice of P on the line of action. The proof of this in the general case is
simplified by using the vector product.

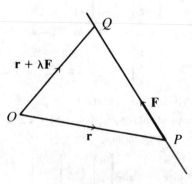

Figure 7

Any other point $\mathbf{Q}$ on the line of action of $\mathbf{F}$ has position vector $\mathbf{r} + \lambda\mathbf{F}$, where λ is a number (Fig. 7). The moment taking Q as the point of application is

$$(\mathbf{r} + \lambda\mathbf{F}) \times \mathbf{F} = \mathbf{r} \times \mathbf{F} + (\lambda\mathbf{F}) \times \mathbf{F}, \quad \text{using distributivity,}$$

$$= \mathbf{r} \times \mathbf{F} + \lambda(\mathbf{F} \times \mathbf{F})$$

$$= \mathbf{r} \times \mathbf{F}, \quad \text{since } \mathbf{F} \times \mathbf{F} = \mathbf{0},$$

which equals the moment with P as the point of application, as required.

We can now prove the important result mentioned in §11.1, that vector moments can be added by vector addition. That is, we shall show that:

The total turning effect about O of two forces, $\mathbf{F}_1$ acting at P_1 and $\mathbf{F}_2$ acting at P_2, is

$$\mathbf{r}_1 \times \mathbf{F}_1 + \mathbf{r}_2 \times \mathbf{F}_2,$$

where $\mathbf{r}_1 = \mathbf{OP}_1$ and $\mathbf{r}_2 = \mathbf{OP}_2$.

The proof is in three parts, covering the cases in which the lines of action of $\mathbf{F}_1$ and $\mathbf{F}_2$ are (a) intersecting, (b) parallel, (c) skew.

(a) Let the lines of action meet at the point A, with position vector $\mathbf{a}$. Then the line of action of the resultant $\mathbf{F}_1 + \mathbf{F}_2$ passes through A, and so the total turning effect about O is

$\mathbf{a} \times (\mathbf{F}_1 + \mathbf{F}_2) = \mathbf{a} \times \mathbf{F}_1 + \mathbf{a} \times \mathbf{F}_2$, using distributivity,

$\qquad\qquad = \mathbf{r}_1 \times \mathbf{F}_1 + \mathbf{r}_2 \times \mathbf{F}_2$, using transmissibility, as proved above.

(This case is known as Varignon's Theorem, after Pierre Varignon, 1654–1722).

(b) If $\mathbf{F}_1$ and $\mathbf{F}_2$ are parallel we can take $\mathbf{F}_1 = k_1\mathbf{F}$ and $\mathbf{F}_2 = k_2\mathbf{F}$, where $\mathbf{F}$ is in the direction of $\mathbf{F}_1$ and $\mathbf{F}_2$, and k_1, k_2 are suitable numbers. Then, as in §8.5, the resultant of these forces is a force $(k_1 + k_2)\mathbf{F}$ acting through the point P which divides P_1P_2 in the ratio $k_2 : k_1$.

The position vector of P is $\dfrac{k_1\mathbf{r}_1 + k_2\mathbf{r}_2}{k_1 + k_2}$.

The total turning effect about O is

$$\frac{k_1\mathbf{r}_1 + k_2\mathbf{r}_2}{k_1 + k_2} \times (k_1 + k_2)\mathbf{F} = (k_1\mathbf{r}_1 + k_2\mathbf{r}_2) \times \mathbf{F}$$

$$= (k_1\mathbf{r}_1) \times \mathbf{F} + (k_2\mathbf{r}_2) \times \mathbf{F}$$

$$= \mathbf{r}_1 \times (k_1\mathbf{F}) + \mathbf{r}_2 \times (k_2\mathbf{F})$$

$$= \mathbf{r}_1 \times \mathbf{F}_1 + \mathbf{r}_2 \times \mathbf{F}_2.$$

(c) For the case in which the lines of action of $\mathbf{F}_1$ and $\mathbf{F}_2$ are skew you should construct for yourself a three-dimensional diagram by copying Fig. 8 and folding along the line AB. The paper then forms two planes, one containing $\mathbf{F}_1$ and O, the other containing $\mathbf{F}_2$ and O; these planes meet in the fold line AB. Let the lines of action of $\mathbf{F}_1$, $\mathbf{F}_2$ meet AB at Q_1, Q_2 respectively; Q_1 and Q_2 are

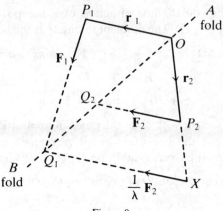

Figure 8

distinct since the lines of action are skew. Draw the line through Q_1 parallel to F_2, and let this line meet OP_2 (produced if necessary) at X. Then $OX = \lambda r_2$, where λ is a number. Now replace the force F_2 acting through P_2 by the parallel force $\frac{1}{\lambda} F_2$ through X. This does not change the turning effect, since

$$(\lambda r_2) \times \left(\frac{1}{\lambda} F_2 \right) = \left(\lambda . \frac{1}{\lambda} \right)(r_2 \times F_2), \quad \text{as in Q.2,}$$

$$= r_2 \times F_2.$$

But now the lines of action of the two forces F_1 and $\frac{1}{\lambda} F_2$ intersect at Q_1, and so by (a) the turning effect is

$$r_1 \times F_1 + (\lambda r_2) \times \left(\frac{1}{\lambda} F_2 \right) = r_1 \times F_1 + r_2 \times F_2,$$

as required. This completes the proof.

11.6   EQUIVALENT SYSTEMS OF FORCES

Now that the machinery of the vector product is available for dealing with moments we can extend the work of Chapter 8 to three-dimensional systems.

Equal forces acting on a body have different effects unless they have a common line of action. In order to represent a force completely we therefore need to use a *localised vector*, which is a vector with an associated line of action. Two localised vectors are said to be *equal* if they have the same magnitude, direction and sense; they are *equivalent* if they are equal and have the same line of action.

Thus, for example, forces P and Q acting at a point O are equivalent to the resultant R found by the parallelogram method (Fig. 9) but if a vector triangle is used (Fig. 10) the line of action of R does not pass through O, so R and $P + Q$ are then equal but not equivalent.

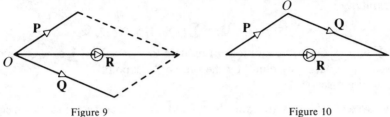

Figure 9   Figure 10

Other quantities which need localised vectors for their representation are, for example, impulse and the linear momentum of a particle. If X is a localised vector, and r is the position vector of a point on its line of action, then the *moment* of X about O is defined to be $r \times X$; in this way we obtain the moment of an impulse, or the moment of momentum of a particle. The results of this section apply similarly to any localised vector quantities, though they are presented here in terms of forces.

Suppose there are two systems of forces:

A: forces $F_1, F_2, \ldots, F_m$ acting at the points whose position vectors are $r_1, r_2, \ldots, r_m$ respectively;

B: forces $Q_1, Q_2, \ldots, Q_n$ acting at points $s_1, s_2, \ldots, s_n$.

The systems A and B are said to be *equivalent* if
(a) the vector sums of their forces are equal;
(b) the vector sums of their moments about any point are equal.

Condition (a) states that $\sum\limits_{i=1}^{m} F_i = \sum\limits_{j=1}^{n} Q_j$.

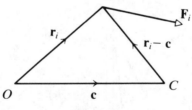

Figure 11

For moments about the point C with position vector c (Fig. 11), condition (b) states that

$$\sum (r_i - c) \times F_i = \sum (s_j - c) \times Q_j$$

(Note 11.2). But

$$\sum (r_i - c) \times F_i = \sum (r_i \times F_i - c \times F_i)$$
$$= \sum r_i \times F_i - \sum c \times F_i$$
$$= \sum r_i \times F_i - c \times \sum F_i,$$

and similarly

$$\sum (s_j - c) \times Q_j = \sum s_j \times Q_j - c \times \sum Q_j.$$

So if $\sum F_i = \sum Q_j$ then condition (b) reduces to $\sum r_i \times F_i = \sum s_j \times Q_j$, and in (b) we may replace 'any point' by the simpler 'one point'.

To summarise:

> Two systems of forces are equivalent if and only if their vector sums are equal and the vector sums of their moments about one point are equal.

Given a system of forces it is natural to seek a simple equivalent system. The simplest possible equivalent system is the system of no forces at all. In this case the given system is in equilibrium, so we see that (as for the two-dimensional case in §8.7):

> A system of forces is in equilibrium if and only if its vector sum is zero and the vector sum of the moments about one point is zero.

Example 2

A vertical television mast is held in place by three stays joined to the mast 12 m above the ground. Taking the base of the mast as the origin and the mast as the z-axis, the coordinates of the bottoms of the stays are $(0, -5, 0)$, $(-3, 1, 0)$ and $(3, 1, 0)$ (Fig. 12). If the mast weighs 80 N, and the tension in the first stay is 20 N, find the tensions (assumed equal) in the other two stays, and the reaction of the ground on the mast.

Solution

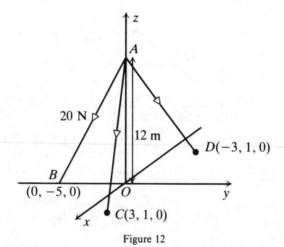

Figure 12

The forces acting on the mast are its weight, the reaction of the ground and the tensions in the stays. Let the unknown tensions be of magnitude T N each.

Taking moments about O does not involve the weight or the reaction at O. We first find *unit* vectors in the directions of the stays.

$$\widehat{AB} = \frac{1}{\sqrt{169}}\begin{bmatrix} 0 \\ -5 \\ -12 \end{bmatrix}, \quad \widehat{AC} = \frac{1}{\sqrt{154}}\begin{bmatrix} 3 \\ 1 \\ -12 \end{bmatrix}, \quad \widehat{AD} = \frac{1}{\sqrt{154}}\begin{bmatrix} -3 \\ 1 \\ -12 \end{bmatrix}.$$

Therefore the tensions in the stays are represented by the vectors

$$\frac{20}{13}\begin{bmatrix} 0 \\ -5 \\ -12 \end{bmatrix}, \quad \frac{T}{\sqrt{154}}\begin{bmatrix} 3 \\ 1 \\ -12 \end{bmatrix}, \quad \frac{T}{\sqrt{154}}\begin{bmatrix} -3 \\ 1 \\ -12 \end{bmatrix}.$$

The total moment about O is zero:

$$\mathbf{0} = \begin{bmatrix} 0 \\ 0 \\ 12 \end{bmatrix} \times \frac{20}{13}\begin{bmatrix} 0 \\ -5 \\ -12 \end{bmatrix} + \begin{bmatrix} 0 \\ 0 \\ 12 \end{bmatrix} \times \frac{T}{\sqrt{154}}\begin{bmatrix} 3 \\ 1 \\ -12 \end{bmatrix}$$

$$+ \begin{bmatrix} 0 \\ 0 \\ 12 \end{bmatrix} \times \frac{T}{\sqrt{154}}\begin{bmatrix} -3 \\ 1 \\ -12 \end{bmatrix}$$

$$= \begin{bmatrix} 0 \\ 0 \\ 12 \end{bmatrix} \times \begin{bmatrix} 0 \\ -\frac{100}{13} + \frac{2T}{\sqrt{154}} \\ -\frac{240}{13} - \frac{24T}{\sqrt{154}} \end{bmatrix} = \begin{bmatrix} \frac{1200}{13} - \frac{24T}{\sqrt{154}} \\ 0 \\ 0 \end{bmatrix}.$$

Therefore $\quad \dfrac{24T}{\sqrt{154}} = \dfrac{1200}{13} \Rightarrow T = \dfrac{50\sqrt{154}}{13} \approx 48.$

The tensions in these two stays are thus $\dfrac{50}{13}\begin{bmatrix} \pm 3 \\ 1 \\ -12 \end{bmatrix}$, and the weight is $\begin{bmatrix} 0 \\ 0 \\ -80 \end{bmatrix}$.

Let the reaction of the ground be $\mathbf{P}$. Then, using $\sum \mathbf{F}_i = \mathbf{0}$,

$$\mathbf{P} + \begin{bmatrix} 0 \\ 0 \\ -80 \end{bmatrix} + \frac{20}{13}\begin{bmatrix} 0 \\ -5 \\ -12 \end{bmatrix} + \frac{50}{13}\begin{bmatrix} 3 \\ 1 \\ -12 \end{bmatrix} + \frac{50}{13}\begin{bmatrix} -3 \\ 1 \\ -12 \end{bmatrix} = \mathbf{0}$$

$$\Rightarrow \mathbf{P} = \begin{bmatrix} 0 \\ 0 \\ \frac{2480}{13} \end{bmatrix} \approx \begin{bmatrix} 0 \\ 0 \\ 191 \end{bmatrix}.$$

The reaction of the ground is therefore 191 N vertically upward. $\qquad\square$

Q.12 Show that the reaction of the ground must be vertically upward, whatever the tensions in the stays.

Next we consider the possibility that the system A is equivalent to a single resultant force $\mathbf{R}$. If this is so, and the resultant acts through the point with position vector **a**, then

$$\text{(i)} \ \mathbf{R} = \sum \mathbf{F}_i \quad \text{and} \quad \text{(ii)} \ \mathbf{a} \times \mathbf{R} = \sum \mathbf{r}_i \times \mathbf{F}_i.$$

Conversely, if we can find a vector **a** for which $\mathbf{a} \times \mathbf{R} = \sum \mathbf{r}_i \times \mathbf{F}_i$ then the system is equivalent to a single force.

Let $\sum \mathbf{r}_i \times \mathbf{F}_i = \mathbf{L}$. Then $\mathbf{L} = \mathbf{0} \Rightarrow \mathbf{a} \times \mathbf{R} = \mathbf{0} = \mathbf{0} \times \mathbf{R}$, so $\mathbf{a} = \mathbf{0}$ is a solution; the line of action of **R** passes through the origin. If $\mathbf{L} \neq \mathbf{0}$ then, since $\mathbf{a} \times \mathbf{R}$ is perpendicular to **R**, there cannot be a solution for **a** unless **L** is perpendicular to **R**. If **L** is perpendicular to **R** then we can always find a suitable **a**. For example let l be the line which is

(a) in the plane through O perpendicular to **L**,
(b) in the direction of **R**,
(c) at a perpendicular distance $|\mathbf{L}|/|\mathbf{R}|$ from O,
(d) such that the effect of **R** about O is to turn a right-hand screw along **L**.

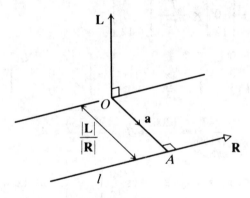

Figure 13

Let A be the foot of the perpendicular from O to l, and let $\mathbf{OA} = \mathbf{a}$ (Fig. 13). Then $|\mathbf{a} \times \mathbf{R}| = \dfrac{|\mathbf{L}|}{|\mathbf{R}|} \cdot |\mathbf{R}| \cdot \sin 90° = |\mathbf{L}|$, and **L** is perpendicular to **a** and **R**, and in the correct sense. Therefore $\mathbf{a} \times \mathbf{R} = \mathbf{L}$, as required. The position vector of any other point of l would do just as well for **a**.

Thus a system of forces is equivalent to a single resultant force $\mathbf{R} = \sum \mathbf{F}_i (\neq \mathbf{0})$ if and only if $\sum \mathbf{r}_i \times \mathbf{F}_i$ is either zero or perpendicular to **R**.

Example 3

Find the resultant of forces $\begin{bmatrix} 3 \\ 0 \\ 2 \end{bmatrix}, \begin{bmatrix} 4 \\ 2 \\ 1 \end{bmatrix}, \begin{bmatrix} 2 \\ 1 \\ 1 \end{bmatrix}$ acting at $(1, 1, 0), (0, -1, 1), (1, 1, 1)$ respectively.

Solution

$$\mathbf{R} = \sum \mathbf{F}_i = \begin{bmatrix} 3 \\ 0 \\ 2 \end{bmatrix} + \begin{bmatrix} 4 \\ 2 \\ 1 \end{bmatrix} + \begin{bmatrix} 2 \\ 1 \\ 1 \end{bmatrix} = \begin{bmatrix} 9 \\ 3 \\ 4 \end{bmatrix}.$$

$$\mathbf{L} = \sum \mathbf{r}_i \times \mathbf{F}_i = \begin{bmatrix} 1 \\ 1 \\ 0 \end{bmatrix} \times \begin{bmatrix} 3 \\ 0 \\ 2 \end{bmatrix} + \begin{bmatrix} 0 \\ -1 \\ 1 \end{bmatrix} \times \begin{bmatrix} 4 \\ 2 \\ 1 \end{bmatrix} + \begin{bmatrix} 1 \\ 1 \\ 1 \end{bmatrix} \times \begin{bmatrix} 2 \\ 1 \\ 1 \end{bmatrix}$$

$$= \begin{bmatrix} 2 \\ -2 \\ -3 \end{bmatrix} + \begin{bmatrix} -3 \\ 4 \\ 4 \end{bmatrix} + \begin{bmatrix} 0 \\ 1 \\ -1 \end{bmatrix} = \begin{bmatrix} -1 \\ 3 \\ 0 \end{bmatrix}.$$

$\mathbf{R} . \mathbf{L} = 9 \times (-1) + 3 \times 3 + 4 \times 0 = 0 \Rightarrow \mathbf{R}$ is perpendicular to $\mathbf{L}$

$\Rightarrow$ the system is equivalent to a resultant $\begin{bmatrix} 9 \\ 3 \\ 4 \end{bmatrix}$.

It remains to find the line of action of the resultant. This line is in the direction of $\begin{bmatrix} 9 \\ 3 \\ 4 \end{bmatrix}$; let it meet the plane $z = 0$ at $(a, b, 0)$. Then, taking moments about O for the resultant and for the original system,

$$\begin{bmatrix} a \\ b \\ 0 \end{bmatrix} \times \begin{bmatrix} 9 \\ 3 \\ 4 \end{bmatrix} = \mathbf{L} = \begin{bmatrix} -1 \\ 3 \\ 0 \end{bmatrix}$$

$$\Leftrightarrow \begin{bmatrix} 4b \\ -4a \\ 3a - 9b \end{bmatrix} = \begin{bmatrix} -1 \\ 3 \\ 0 \end{bmatrix} \Leftrightarrow a = -\tfrac{3}{4}, b = -\tfrac{1}{4}.$$

(Note that the three equations for a and b are consistent.)

Therefore the resultant is $\begin{bmatrix} 9 \\ 3 \\ 4 \end{bmatrix}$ acting through $(-\tfrac{3}{4}, -\tfrac{1}{4}, 0)$. $\qquad \square$

If the system is not in equilibrium but $\sum \mathbf{F}_i = \mathbf{0}$ then $\mathbf{L} = \sum \mathbf{r}_i \times \mathbf{F}_i \neq \mathbf{0}$; the system has no translational effect, but it has a turning effect. Such a system of forces is called a *couple*; see Exercise 8D, questions 8, 9.

The total moment of the system about the point with position vector $\mathbf{c}$ is

$$\sum (\mathbf{r}_i - \mathbf{c}) \times \mathbf{F}_i = \sum \mathbf{r}_i \times \mathbf{F}_i - \mathbf{c} \times \sum \mathbf{F}_i$$

$$= \mathbf{L}, \quad \text{since } \sum \mathbf{F}_i = \mathbf{0}.$$

Thus the total moment of the forces forming a couple is the same about all points. This total moment is called the *moment of the couple*; it is a vector quantity, but not localised, since there is no particular axis about which the couple acts.

Q.13 Show that two systems of forces which reduce to couples of equal moment are equivalent.

We have now dealt with the special cases in which a system of forces is equivalent to no forces (equilibrium), or to a single force, or to a couple. In general it is not possible to reduce a system to a force or to a couple. But of all the possible systems equivalent to a given system there are two particularly simple ones, which are useful in practice.

(1) Any system of forces can be reduced to a force acting at an arbitrary specified point together with a couple.

(2) Any system of forces can be reduced to a force together with a couple whose moment has the same direction as the force (this combination is called a *wrench*).

(In both cases the force or the couple in the reduced system may be zero.)

These results are illustrated in Example 4; general proofs are given in Exercise 11C, questions 8, 15.

Example 4

Reduce the system of forces $\begin{bmatrix} 0 \\ 1 \\ 1 \end{bmatrix}$, $\begin{bmatrix} 2 \\ -1 \\ -3 \end{bmatrix}$, $\begin{bmatrix} -1 \\ 0 \\ 2 \end{bmatrix}$ acting at $(1, 1, 0)$, $(2, 1, 0)$, $(0, 0, 2)$ respectively to

(*a*) a force acting at $(1, 2, 3)$ and a couple,

(*b*) a wrench.

Solution

(*a*) $\mathbf{R} = \sum \mathbf{F}_i = \begin{bmatrix} 0 \\ 1 \\ 1 \end{bmatrix} + \begin{bmatrix} 2 \\ -1 \\ -3 \end{bmatrix} + \begin{bmatrix} -1 \\ 0 \\ 2 \end{bmatrix} = \begin{bmatrix} 1 \\ 0 \\ 0 \end{bmatrix}.$

$\mathbf{L} = \sum \mathbf{r}_i \times \mathbf{F}_i = \begin{bmatrix} 1 \\ 1 \\ 0 \end{bmatrix} \times \begin{bmatrix} 0 \\ 1 \\ 1 \end{bmatrix} + \begin{bmatrix} 2 \\ 1 \\ 0 \end{bmatrix} \times \begin{bmatrix} 2 \\ -1 \\ -3 \end{bmatrix} + \begin{bmatrix} 0 \\ 0 \\ 2 \end{bmatrix} \times \begin{bmatrix} -1 \\ 0 \\ 2 \end{bmatrix}$

$= \begin{bmatrix} 1 \\ -1 \\ 1 \end{bmatrix} + \begin{bmatrix} -3 \\ 6 \\ -4 \end{bmatrix} + \begin{bmatrix} 0 \\ -2 \\ 0 \end{bmatrix} = \begin{bmatrix} -2 \\ 3 \\ -3 \end{bmatrix}.$

The moment of $\mathbf{R}$ acting at $(1, 2, 3)$ is $\begin{bmatrix} 1 \\ 2 \\ 3 \end{bmatrix} \times \begin{bmatrix} 1 \\ 0 \\ 0 \end{bmatrix} = \begin{bmatrix} 0 \\ 3 \\ -2 \end{bmatrix}$, so to produce the

required moment $\mathbf{L}$ an additional couple of moment $\begin{bmatrix} -2 \\ 0 \\ -1 \end{bmatrix}$ is required.

(b) As before, $\mathbf{R} = \begin{bmatrix} 1 \\ 0 \\ 0 \end{bmatrix}$, so to form a wrench we need a couple of moment

$\begin{bmatrix} \lambda \\ 0 \\ 0 \end{bmatrix}$. This, together with $\mathbf{R}$ acting at the point (a, b, c), must produce the

moment $\mathbf{L} = \begin{bmatrix} -2 \\ 3 \\ -3 \end{bmatrix}$. That is, we want (a, b, c) and λ such that

$$\begin{bmatrix} a \\ b \\ c \end{bmatrix} \times \begin{bmatrix} 1 \\ 0 \\ 0 \end{bmatrix} + \begin{bmatrix} \lambda \\ 0 \\ 0 \end{bmatrix} = \begin{bmatrix} -2 \\ 3 \\ -3 \end{bmatrix}$$

$$\Rightarrow \begin{bmatrix} a \\ b \\ c \end{bmatrix} \times \begin{bmatrix} 1 \\ 0 \\ 0 \end{bmatrix} = \begin{bmatrix} -2 - \lambda \\ 3 \\ -3 \end{bmatrix};$$

$\begin{bmatrix} -2 - \lambda \\ 3 \\ -3 \end{bmatrix}$ is therefore perpendicular to $\begin{bmatrix} 1 \\ 0 \\ 0 \end{bmatrix}$,

and so $(-2 - \lambda) \times 1 + 3 \times 0 + (-3) \times 0 = 0 \Rightarrow \lambda = -2$.
Therefore

$$\begin{bmatrix} a \\ b \\ c \end{bmatrix} \times \begin{bmatrix} 1 \\ 0 \\ 0 \end{bmatrix} = \begin{bmatrix} 0 \\ 3 \\ -3 \end{bmatrix} \Leftrightarrow \begin{bmatrix} 0 \\ c \\ -b \end{bmatrix} = \begin{bmatrix} 0 \\ 3 \\ -3 \end{bmatrix} \Leftrightarrow b = c = 3,$$

with a arbitrary.

The given system is therefore equivalent to the wrench composed of the force $\begin{bmatrix} 1 \\ 0 \\ 0 \end{bmatrix}$ acting at $\begin{bmatrix} 0 \\ 3 \\ 3 \end{bmatrix}$ and the couple $\begin{bmatrix} -2 \\ 0 \\ 0 \end{bmatrix}$. ☐

Exercise 11C

1   Are the forces $3\mathbf{i} - 2\mathbf{j} - 4\mathbf{k}$, $-\mathbf{i} + \mathbf{j}$, $-\mathbf{i} + \mathbf{j}$, $-\mathbf{i} + 4\mathbf{k}$, acting at $(1, 0, 1)$, $(0, 0, 1)$, $(0, 1, 1)$, $(1, 1, 1)$ respectively, in equilibrium?

2   A cube with edges of length a is placed with one vertex at the origin O and its edges parallel to the coordinate axes. There are six edges which do not meet the diagonal through O. Forces, each of magnitude F, act along these six edges. Find the force or couple needed to keep the cube in equilibrium if the senses in which these forces act are consecutively (a) $+ + + + + +$, (b) $+ - + - + -$, (c) $+ + - + + -$, with the first force $F\mathbf{i}$ through $(0, 0, a)$ in each case.

3   A vertical flagpole is held in place by three taut cables. Taking the base of the pole as the origin, the cables are fastened to the ground at $(1, 3, 0)$, $(-2, 0, 0)$, $(1, -3, 0)$, and they are fastened 5 m up the flagpole. The tensions in the cables are 50 N, T N and 50 N respectively. Find T.

4   Find T in question 3 if (*a*) the cables are attached 3 m up the flagpole, (*b*) the middle cable is fixed 3 m up, and the other two 5 m up the flagpole.

5   An unsprung four-wheeled trailer of mass M has length (between axles) $2a$, width (between wheel mid-planes) a, and is loaded so that its mass centre is on the centre line at a perpendicular distance $\frac{1}{2}a$ from the road, and at distance $\frac{3}{2}a$ behind the front axle. The brakes are applied and the trailer stands at rest on a slope of angle α to the horizontal with its front down the slope. A jack is now placed midway between front and rear axles, and in the plane of the wheels on one side of the trailer. The jack is normal to the slope, and is extended by a small amount so that the two wheels on its side of the trailer just leave the ground. Show by symmetry (or otherwise) that the normal force on the jack is $\frac{1}{2}Mg \cos \alpha$.

Split the weight Mg into two components $Mg \cos \alpha$ and $Mg \sin \alpha$, and take moments suitably, to find the normal force on the front wheel that is still in contact with the slope.   [SMP]

6   (*a*) Prove that a system of forces is in equilibrium if and only if the total moments about three non-collinear points are all zero.

(*b*) Prove that a system of forces is equivalent to a couple if and only if the total moments about three non-collinear points are equal but not zero.

7   The three forces $\begin{bmatrix} 0 \\ 2 \\ 3 \end{bmatrix}$, $\begin{bmatrix} 7 \\ -6 \\ 0 \end{bmatrix}$, $\begin{bmatrix} 0 \\ 0 \\ 5 \end{bmatrix}$ act at the points $(2, 4, 0)$, $(0, 1, 3)$, $(0, 3, 0)$ respectively. Find an equivalent system consisting of a couple and a force acting at (*a*) the origin, (*b*) the point $(5, 5, 6)$.

8   A system of forces is equivalent to a single force $\mathbf{R} = \sum \mathbf{F}_i$ acting at the point with position vector $\mathbf{a}$ together with a couple of moment $\mathbf{G}$. Find $\mathbf{G}$ in terms of $\mathbf{R}$, $\mathbf{a}$ and $\mathbf{L}$, where $\mathbf{L} = \sum \mathbf{r}_i \times \mathbf{F}_i$.

9   Find a single force equivalent to forces $\mathbf{i} + \mathbf{k}$, $\mathbf{i} + \mathbf{j}$, $-3\mathbf{j} + \mathbf{k}$ acting at $(1, 1, 0)$, $(1, 1, 1)$, $(1, 0, 1)$ respectively.

10   A triangular lamina has its three vertices A, B, C at $\mathbf{i} + \mathbf{j}$, $\mathbf{j} + \mathbf{k}$, $\mathbf{i} + \mathbf{k}$ respectively. Forces $\mathbf{F}_A = \mathbf{j} + \mathbf{k}$, $\mathbf{F}_B = \mathbf{i} + \mathbf{k}$, $\mathbf{F}_C = \mathbf{i} + \mathbf{j}$ act at A, B, C respectively. Is it possible to choose a single force to keep the triangle in equilibrium? Give your reasons.   [SMP]

11   A regular tetrahedron of side $2a$ is smoothly pivoted about a fixed axle through the fixed vertex A and the centroid B of the opposite face. Equal forces of magnitude F act along the edges in the directions shown in Fig. 14.

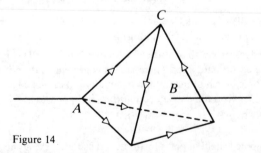

Figure 14

Reduce the forces to a single force at B together with a couple. What is the least single force at C which can hold the tetrahedron in equilibrium?   [SMP]

12   Find a wrench equivalent to a force $\begin{bmatrix} 1 \\ 0 \\ -1 \end{bmatrix}$ acting at the origin together with a

couple of moment $\begin{bmatrix} 2 \\ 1 \\ 0 \end{bmatrix}$.

13   Find a wrench equivalent to forces $2\mathbf{i} + 3\mathbf{j} + 4\mathbf{k}$, $4\mathbf{i} + 2\mathbf{j} + \mathbf{k}$, $6\mathbf{i} + \mathbf{j} + 3\mathbf{k}$ acting at $(1, 0, 0)$, $(0, 1, 0)$, $(0, 0, 1)$ respectively.

14   Find a wrench equivalent to forces $\begin{bmatrix} 2 \\ 1 \\ 1 \end{bmatrix}$, $\begin{bmatrix} 1 \\ -1 \\ -1 \end{bmatrix}$, $\begin{bmatrix} -2 \\ -3 \\ 1 \end{bmatrix}$ acting at $(2, 1, 2)$, $(0, 1, 2)$, $(2, 2, 2)$ respectively.

15   A system of forces is such that $\mathbf{R} = \sum \mathbf{F}_i$ and $\mathbf{L} = \sum \mathbf{r}_i \times \mathbf{F}_i$; we wish to find the equivalent wrench, i.e. to find $\mathbf{a}$ and λ so that the system is equivalent to a force $\mathbf{R}$ through the point with position vector $\mathbf{a}$ together with a couple $\lambda \mathbf{R}$.

(a)   Show that $\mathbf{L} = \mathbf{a} \times \mathbf{R} + \lambda \mathbf{R}$.

(b)   By taking scalar products, show that $\lambda = \dfrac{\mathbf{R} . \mathbf{L}}{\mathbf{R} . \mathbf{R}}$.

(c)   With this value of λ we have

$$\mathbf{a} \times \mathbf{R} = \mathbf{L} - \lambda \mathbf{R}, \tag{1}$$

from which we have to find $\mathbf{a}$.

Show that if $\mathbf{a} = \mathbf{a}_0$ is any particular solution of (1) then $\mathbf{a} = \mathbf{a}_0 + t\mathbf{R}$ is also a solution for all values of t, and every solution can be written in the form $\mathbf{a} = \mathbf{a}_0 + t\mathbf{R}$.

(d)   Show that if $\mathbf{a}_0$ is perpendicular to $\mathbf{R}$ then $\mathbf{a}_0 = \mu \mathbf{R} \times \mathbf{L}$.

(e)   By using components in (d), show that $\mu = 1/\mathbf{R} . \mathbf{R}$.

(f)   Deduce that the general solution of (1) is

$$\mathbf{a} = \frac{\mathbf{R} \times \mathbf{L}}{\mathbf{R} . \mathbf{R}} + t\mathbf{R}.$$

This gives a line of points in the direction of $\mathbf{R}$, at any one of which $\mathbf{R}$ may act together with the couple $\lambda \mathbf{R}$ so as to form an equivalent wrench. This line is called *Poinsot's central axis*, after Louis Poinsot (1777–1859).

12

Scalar triple product

12.1 MOMENT ABOUT AN AXIS

In Chapter 11 we found that the turning effect of a force on a rigid body is described by the vector moment $\mathbf{r} \times \mathbf{F}$. We can now see that in our earlier discussion (§8.6, where the body rotates about a fixed axis and all the forces act in a plane perpendicular to this axis) the vectors $\mathbf{r}$ and $\mathbf{F}$ lie in a fixed plane, and so the vector moment is perpendicular to this plane, i.e. parallel to the axis. In such cases we can treat moments as scalars, since we need only specify the magnitude and sense of the vector moment – its direction is already known.

Now we consider what happens when the body is constrained to move about a fixed axis (as commonly happens with flywheels and other parts of machines), but the forces on the body are not necessarily perpendicular to the axis.

A few seconds' experimenting with a record player turntable should confirm that a force parallel to the axis (spindle) has no turning effect (Fig. 1). This simple observation is the key to what follows.

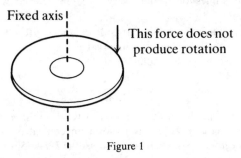

Figure 1

Let P be a point on the line of action of a force $\mathbf{F}$ acting on a rigid body which can rotate about a fixed axis. Let $\hat{\mathbf{e}}$ be a unit vector in the direction of the axis, and let O be the foot of the perpendicular from P to the axis, with $\mathbf{OP} = \mathbf{r}$ (Fig. 2).

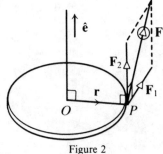

Figure 2

Split **F** into components $\mathbf{F}_1$ and $\mathbf{F}_2$ which are respectively perpendicular and parallel to $\hat{\mathbf{e}}$, so that $\mathbf{F} = \mathbf{F}_1 + \mathbf{F}_2$. As we have just seen, $\mathbf{F}_2$ has no turning effect about the axis, and so may be ignored. Moreover, since $\hat{\mathbf{e}}$ is perpendicular to both **r** and $\mathbf{F}_1$, if the body were free to turn about the point O under the action of $\mathbf{F}_1$ then it would turn about the line in the direction of $\hat{\mathbf{e}}$, so none of the turning effect of $\mathbf{F}_1$ is hindered by the presence of the fixed axis.

It would be reasonable therefore to define the moment of **F** about the axis to be $\mathbf{r} \times \mathbf{F}_1$, which is a vector in the direction of $\hat{\mathbf{e}}$. But since this direction is fixed it is more convenient (as in §8.6) to define the moment about the axis to be the *scalar* which gives the magnitude and sense of $\mathbf{r} \times \mathbf{F}_1$. This scalar is

$$\hat{\mathbf{e}} \cdot (\mathbf{r} \times \mathbf{F}_1).$$

There are two immediate advantages of doing this.

(1) We can find this scalar without finding $\mathbf{F}_1$. For since $\mathbf{F}_2$ is parallel to $\hat{\mathbf{e}}$, $\mathbf{F}_2 = k\hat{\mathbf{e}}$ and $\mathbf{F}_1 = \mathbf{F} - \mathbf{F}_2 = \mathbf{F} - k\hat{\mathbf{e}}$.

Therefore $\qquad\qquad \mathbf{r} \times \mathbf{F}_1 = \mathbf{r} \times (\mathbf{F} - k\hat{\mathbf{e}}) = \mathbf{r} \times \mathbf{F} - k\mathbf{r} \times \hat{\mathbf{e}}$

and $\qquad\qquad \hat{\mathbf{e}} \cdot (\mathbf{r} \times \mathbf{F}_1) = \hat{\mathbf{e}} \cdot (\mathbf{r} \times \mathbf{F}) - \hat{\mathbf{e}} \cdot (k\mathbf{r} \times \hat{\mathbf{e}}).$

But $k\mathbf{r} \times \hat{\mathbf{e}}$ is perpendicular to $\hat{\mathbf{e}}$, so the final term is zero.

Thus $\qquad\qquad\qquad \hat{\mathbf{e}} \cdot (\mathbf{r} \times \mathbf{F}_1) = \hat{\mathbf{e}} \cdot (\mathbf{r} \times \mathbf{F})$

and so we can use **F** directly, and not bother with $\mathbf{F}_1$.

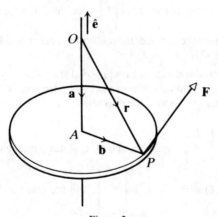

Figure 3

(2) We can use any other point on the axis as the origin O. With the notation of Fig. 3, the moment about the axis is

$$\hat{\mathbf{e}} \cdot (\mathbf{b} \times \mathbf{F}).$$

But $\qquad\qquad\qquad\qquad \mathbf{b} = \mathbf{r} - \mathbf{a} = \mathbf{r} - \lambda\hat{\mathbf{e}}$

so $\qquad\qquad\qquad\qquad \mathbf{b} \times \mathbf{F} = (\mathbf{r} - \lambda\hat{\mathbf{e}}) \times \mathbf{F}$

$$= \mathbf{r} \times \mathbf{F} - \lambda\hat{\mathbf{e}} \times \mathbf{F}$$

and $\hat{\mathbf{e}}.(\mathbf{b} \times \mathbf{F}) = \hat{\mathbf{e}}.(\mathbf{r} \times \mathbf{F}) - \hat{\mathbf{e}}.(\lambda\hat{\mathbf{e}} \times \mathbf{F})$

$$= \hat{\mathbf{e}}.(\mathbf{r} \times \mathbf{F})$$

since $\lambda\hat{\mathbf{e}} \times \mathbf{F}$ is perpendicular to $\hat{\mathbf{e}}$.

Therefore the moment about the axis is independent of the particular point of the axis which is taken as the origin.

Q.1 What vector properties have been used in (1) and (2)?

So finally we have the simple result:

The moment of a force $\mathbf{F}$ about an axis is the scalar

$$\hat{\mathbf{e}}.(\mathbf{r} \times \mathbf{F})$$

where $\hat{\mathbf{e}}$ is a unit vector in the direction of the axis, and $\mathbf{r} = \mathbf{OP}$, with O any point on the axis and P any point on the line of action of $\mathbf{F}$.

Notice that this moment is the resolved part of the vector moment $\mathbf{r} \times \mathbf{F}$ in the direction of $\hat{\mathbf{e}}$ (Note 12.1).

Exercise 12A

1   A millstone fixed to rotate about a vertical axis is acted on by a force represented in magnitude and direction by the vector $\begin{bmatrix} 2 \\ 1 \\ 3 \end{bmatrix}$. If the force is applied at the point $(3, 5, 0)$ relative to axes having the centre of the millstone as origin and $\mathbf{k}$ vertical, calculate the moment about the axis.

2   Suppose that the force in question 1 is applied at the point $(-4, 2, 0)$, what is now the moment? At what point on the rim of the stone (distance 10 units from the centre) should the same force be applied for the magnitude of the moment to be (*a*) greatest, (*b*) least?

3   Given that a force $\begin{bmatrix} F \\ F \\ 2F \end{bmatrix}$ acting through $(2, 1, 3)$ has a moment of 18 units about an axis through $(1, 1, 2)$ with direction $\begin{bmatrix} -1 \\ 1 \\ 1 \end{bmatrix}$, find the value of F.

4   A force of magnitude 10 units acts along a diagonal of a face of a cube whose edges have length 2 units. Calculate the moment of the force about one of the diagonals of the cube which it does not intersect.   [SMP]

5   A force of magnitude 26 N acts along the line AB from $A(-8, 6, 1)$ to $B(4, 3, 5)$. Find the moment of this force about the axis passing though the points $(6, 9, 1)$ and $(8, 7, 0)$. All coordinates are in metres.

6   A regular tetrahedron with edges of length 3 m can spin about the altitude from one vertex A to the opposite face. Find the moment about this axis of a force of magnitude 12 N acting along an edge which does not pass through A. (*Hint*: the diagonals of six faces of cube form a regular tetrahedron.)

7   A force of magnitude 4 N acts along the line PQ, where P lies in the plane $z = 0$ and Q is $(0, 1, 1)$. The coordinates are in metres. This force has moment 2 N m about the z-axis. Find the equation of the locus of P, and sketch the locus.

12.2   SCALAR TRIPLE PRODUCT

The moment about an axis $\hat{\mathbf{e}} . (\mathbf{r} \times \mathbf{F})$ is an example of a *scalar triple product* of three vectors. Such products are useful not only in mechanics, so we now explore their general properties.

Let $\mathbf{a}, \mathbf{b}, \mathbf{c}$ be the position vectors of points, A, B, C with respect to an origin O. The three edges OA, OB, OC define the parallelepiped $OAPBCQRS$ (Fig. 4); let this have volume V.

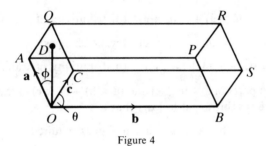

Figure 4

The area of parallelogram $OBSC$ is

$$|\mathbf{b}||\mathbf{c}| \sin \theta = |\mathbf{b} \times \mathbf{c}|.$$

With this parallelogram as the base, the height of the parallelepiped is OD, where D is the foot of the perpendicular from O to the plane $APRQ$. If angle $AOD = \phi$ then $OD = |\mathbf{a}| \cos \phi$ and

$$V = |\mathbf{a}||\mathbf{b} \times \mathbf{c}| \cos \phi.$$

If $\mathbf{a}, \mathbf{b}, \mathbf{c}$ is a right-handed triple of vectors (see §11.2), as in Fig. 4, then $\mathbf{b} \times \mathbf{c}$ has the same direction and sense as $\mathbf{OD}$. In this case

$$V = \mathbf{a} . (\mathbf{b} \times \mathbf{c}).$$

On the other hand (literally), if $\mathbf{a}, \mathbf{b}, \mathbf{c}$ is a left-handed triple then $\mathbf{b} \times \mathbf{c}$ has the opposite sense to $\mathbf{OD}$, the scalar triple product is negative and $V = -\mathbf{a} . (\mathbf{b} \times \mathbf{c})$.

Thus $\mathbf{a} . (\mathbf{b} \times \mathbf{c}) = \pm$ volume of parallelepiped with edges $\mathbf{a}, \mathbf{b}, \mathbf{c}$, with + or − according as $\mathbf{a}, \mathbf{b}, \mathbf{c}$ is a right- or a left-handed triple.

Since the volume is independent of which parallelogram is taken as the base,

$$\mathbf{a} . (\mathbf{b} \times \mathbf{c}) = \mathbf{b} . (\mathbf{c} \times \mathbf{a}) = \mathbf{c} . (\mathbf{a} \times \mathbf{b}) = -\mathbf{a} . (\mathbf{c} \times \mathbf{b}) = -\mathbf{b} . (\mathbf{a} \times \mathbf{c}) = -\mathbf{c} . (\mathbf{b} \times \mathbf{a}).$$

Cyclic interchange of $\mathbf{a}, \mathbf{b}, \mathbf{c}$ does not change the scalar triple product, whereas non-cyclic interchange reverses its sign.

The notation $[\mathbf{a}, \mathbf{b}, \mathbf{c}]$ is sometimes used for any of the scalar triple products of $\mathbf{a}, \mathbf{b}, \mathbf{c}$ in this cyclic order. Thus

$$[\mathbf{a}, \mathbf{b}, \mathbf{c}] = -[\mathbf{a}, \mathbf{c}, \mathbf{b}].$$

Example 1
Use scalar triple products to prove the distributive property of vector products,

$$\mathbf{a} \times (\mathbf{b} + \mathbf{c}) = \mathbf{a} \times \mathbf{b} + \mathbf{a} \times \mathbf{c} \qquad \text{(see §11.3)}$$

Solution
Let $\hat{\mathbf{e}}$ be an arbitrary unit vector. Then

$$\hat{\mathbf{e}} \cdot (\mathbf{a} \times (\mathbf{b} + \mathbf{c})) = (\mathbf{b} + \mathbf{c}) \cdot (\hat{\mathbf{e}} \times \mathbf{a}) \qquad \text{(cyclic change)}$$

$$= \mathbf{b} \cdot (\hat{\mathbf{e}} \times \mathbf{a}) + \mathbf{c} \cdot (\hat{\mathbf{e}} \times \mathbf{a}) \quad \text{(distributivity of scalar products)}$$

$$= \hat{\mathbf{e}} \cdot (\mathbf{a} \times \mathbf{b}) + \hat{\mathbf{e}} \cdot (\mathbf{a} \times \mathbf{c}) \quad \text{(cyclic changes)}$$

$$= \hat{\mathbf{e}} \cdot ((\mathbf{a} \times \mathbf{b}) + (\mathbf{a} \times \mathbf{c})) \quad \text{(distributivity of scalar products)}$$

Thus the resolved parts of $\mathbf{a} \times (\mathbf{b} + \mathbf{c})$ and $(\mathbf{a} \times \mathbf{b}) + (\mathbf{a} \times \mathbf{c})$ in the direction of $\hat{\mathbf{e}}$ are equal. Since $\hat{\mathbf{e}}$ is arbitrary it follows that

$$\mathbf{a} \times (\mathbf{b} + \mathbf{c}) = \mathbf{a} \times \mathbf{b} + \mathbf{a} \times \mathbf{c}, \text{ as required.} \qquad \square$$

Exercise 12B

1   Prove that interchanging 'dot' and 'cross' does not alter the scalar triple product, i.e. that $\mathbf{a} \cdot (\mathbf{b} \times \mathbf{c}) = (\mathbf{a} \times \mathbf{b}) \cdot \mathbf{c}$.

2   Find $[\mathbf{a}, \mathbf{a}, \mathbf{b}]$.

3   Prove that $\mathbf{a} \cdot (\mathbf{b} \times \mathbf{c}) = 0 \Leftrightarrow O, A, B, C$ are coplanar. State a similar condition for the moment about an axis $\mathbf{e} \cdot (\mathbf{r} \times \mathbf{F})$ to be zero, and give a mechanical argument to justify it.

4   Prove that the volume of the tetrahedron $OABC$ is $\pm\frac{1}{6}\mathbf{a} \cdot (\mathbf{b} \times \mathbf{c})$, with + or − as for the parallelepiped.
    Show how to split the parallelepiped with edges $\mathbf{a}, \mathbf{b}, \mathbf{c}$ into six tetrahedra with equal volumes.

5   Prove that $[\mathbf{a}, \mathbf{b}, \mathbf{c} + \mathbf{d}] = [\mathbf{a}, \mathbf{b}, \mathbf{c}] + [\mathbf{a}, \mathbf{b}, \mathbf{d}]$.
    Express $[\mathbf{a} + \mathbf{b}, \mathbf{c} + \mathbf{d}, \mathbf{e} + \mathbf{f}]$ as the sum of eight scalar triple products.

6   Three faces of a parallelepiped meet at the vertex O. The diagonals through O of these faces are three edges of a second parallelepiped. Prove that the volume of this second parallelepiped is twice the volume of the first.

7   The vectors $\mathbf{a}, \mathbf{b}, \mathbf{c}, \mathbf{d}$ are given, with $[\mathbf{a}, \mathbf{b}, \mathbf{c}] \neq 0$, and $x\mathbf{a} + y\mathbf{b} + z\mathbf{c} = \mathbf{d}$. By taking the scalar product of each side of this equation with $\mathbf{b} \times \mathbf{c}$, prove that

$$x = \frac{[\mathbf{d}, \mathbf{b}, \mathbf{c}]}{[\mathbf{a}, \mathbf{b}, \mathbf{c}]}.$$

Find similar expressions for y and z.

8   Write the simultaneous equations

$$5x + 3y - 5z = 3$$
$$3x - 9y + 7z = 7$$
$$7x - y - 2z = 8$$

as the vector equation $x\mathbf{a} + y\mathbf{b} + z\mathbf{c} = \mathbf{d}$, where $\mathbf{a} = \begin{bmatrix} 5 \\ 3 \\ 7 \end{bmatrix}$ and so on. Use the results of question 7 to find x, y, z.

9   Four forces in three dimensions acting at a point are in equilibrium. Prove that the magnitude of each force is proportional to the volume of the parallelepiped defined by unit vectors in the directions of the other three forces. (Compare this with Lami's theorem, Exercise 8A, question 11.)

12.3   COMPONENT FORM OF THE SCALAR TRIPLE PRODUCT

If $\mathbf{a} = \begin{bmatrix} a_1 \\ a_2 \\ a_3 \end{bmatrix}$, $\mathbf{b} = \begin{bmatrix} b_1 \\ b_2 \\ b_3 \end{bmatrix}$, $\mathbf{c} = \begin{bmatrix} c_1 \\ c_2 \\ c_3 \end{bmatrix}$ then $\mathbf{b} \times \mathbf{c} = \begin{bmatrix} b_2c_3 - b_3c_2 \\ b_3c_1 - b_1c_3 \\ b_1c_2 - b_2c_1 \end{bmatrix}$ and

$$\mathbf{a} \cdot (\mathbf{b} \times \mathbf{c}) = a_1(b_2c_3 - b_3c_2) + a_2(b_3c_1 - b_1c_3) + a_3(b_1c_2 - b_2c_1).$$

This expression for the scalar triple product in terms of components is the expansion of the 3×3 *determinant*

$$\begin{vmatrix} a_1 & b_1 & c_1 \\ a_2 & b_2 & c_2 \\ a_3 & b_3 & c_3 \end{vmatrix}.$$

We shall sometimes use the abbreviated notation $|\mathbf{a} \ \mathbf{b} \ \mathbf{c}|$ for this determinant.

Since $|\mathbf{a} \ \mathbf{b} \ \mathbf{c}|$ is the volume of the parallelepiped with edges $\mathbf{a}$, $\mathbf{b}$, $\mathbf{c}$ (with sign depending on handedness), the determinant is the volume scale factor of the transformation with matrix

$$\begin{bmatrix} a_1 & b_1 & c_1 \\ a_2 & b_2 & c_2 \\ a_3 & b_3 & c_3 \end{bmatrix} \quad \text{(Note 12.2)}.$$

The idea of the determinant as the volume of a parallelepiped leads directly to many of the standard properties of 3×3 determinants, as in the following exercise.

Exercise 12C

1   Evaluate these determinants:

(a) $\begin{vmatrix} -4 & 0 & 1 \\ 1 & -3 & 2 \\ 1 & -2 & 1 \end{vmatrix}$ (b) $\begin{vmatrix} 4 & 3 & 2 \\ 2 & 1 & 6 \\ 7 & 5 & 4 \end{vmatrix}$ (c) $\begin{vmatrix} 1 & 4 & 7 \\ 2 & 5 & 8 \\ 3 & 6 & 9 \end{vmatrix}$.

2 The points A, B, C have coordinates $(-1, -1, 2)$, $(1, -2, 4)$, $(-2, 1, -5)$ respectively. Find the volume of the parallelepiped of which OA, OB, OC are three edges.

3 Find the volume of the tetrahedron with vertices $(-3, -1, 2)$, $(3, 1, 4)$, $(-1, 2, 3)$, $(2, 4, 1)$.

4 Prove that the points $(2, 1, 3)$, $(5, 5, 4)$, $(2, -2, 4)$, $(5, -1, 6)$ are coplanar.

5 Four planes are defined in terms of the two non-zero, non-parallel vectors $\mathbf{a}$, $\mathbf{b}$. They are

$$\Pi_1 : \mathbf{a} . \mathbf{x} = 0, \quad \Pi_3 : (\mathbf{a} \times \mathbf{b}) . \mathbf{x} = 0$$
$$\Pi_2 : \mathbf{b} . \mathbf{x} = 0, \quad \Pi_4 : [\mathbf{a} + \mathbf{b} + (\mathbf{a} \times \mathbf{b})] . \mathbf{x} = s,$$

where s is a constant. For the case $\mathbf{a} = 3\mathbf{i}$, $\mathbf{b} = 2\mathbf{i} + 4\mathbf{j}$ and $s = 6$, find the vertices of the figure formed by the four planes, and hence find its volume.   [SMP]

6 Give geometrical arguments in terms of volumes to establish the following properties of 3×3 determinants.

(*a*) The sign of the determinant is reversed if two columns are interchanged, e.g. $|\mathbf{b}\ \mathbf{a}\ \mathbf{c}| = -|\mathbf{a}\ \mathbf{b}\ \mathbf{c}|$.

(*b*) The determinant is zero if two columns are proportional, e.g. $|\mathbf{a}\ \lambda\mathbf{a}\ \mathbf{c}| = 0$.

(*c*) If the elements of one column are all multiplied by a constant λ then the determinant is multiplied by λ, e.g. $|\lambda\mathbf{a}\ \mathbf{b}\ \mathbf{c}| = \lambda|\mathbf{a}\ \mathbf{b}\ \mathbf{c}|$.

(*d*) The determinant is unchanged if any multiple of one column is added to another column, e.g. $|\mathbf{a} + \lambda\mathbf{b}\ \mathbf{b}\ \mathbf{c}| = |\mathbf{a}\ \mathbf{b}\ \mathbf{c}|$.

7 Show by expanding that $\begin{vmatrix} a_1 & a_2 & a_3 \\ b_1 & b_2 & b_3 \\ c_1 & c_2 & c_3 \end{vmatrix} = \begin{vmatrix} a_1 & b_1 & c_1 \\ a_2 & b_2 & c_2 \\ a_3 & b_3 & c_3 \end{vmatrix}$, and hence that there are row properties corresponding to all the column properties of question 6.

8 Use property (*c*) of question 6 to express $\begin{vmatrix} 245 & 48 & 39 \\ 98 & 176 & 104 \\ 343 & 64 & 65 \end{vmatrix}$ as the product of prime factors.

9 Discuss this 'proof' that every determinant is zero.

$$|\mathbf{a}\ \mathbf{b}\ \mathbf{c}| = |\mathbf{a} + \mathbf{b}\ \ \mathbf{b} + \mathbf{c}\ \ \mathbf{c} - \mathbf{a}| \qquad \text{(using property (d) of question 6 three times)}$$
$$= |\mathbf{a} + \mathbf{b}\ \ \mathbf{b} + \mathbf{c} - (\mathbf{a} + \mathbf{b})\ \ \mathbf{c} - \mathbf{a}| \quad \text{(property (d) again)}$$
$$= |\mathbf{a} + \mathbf{b}\ \ \mathbf{c} - \mathbf{a}\ \ \mathbf{c} - \mathbf{a}|$$
$$= 0 \quad \text{(property (b))}.$$

10 Let P_1, P_2, P_3 be the points (x_1, y_1), (x_2, y_2), (x_3, y_3) in two dimensions, and let the area of the triangle $P_1 P_2 P_3$ be Δ. Consider this x-y-plane as the plane $z = 0$ in three dimensions, and then apply the translation $\begin{bmatrix} 0 \\ 0 \\ 1 \end{bmatrix}$, so that P_i now has coordinates $(x_i, y_i, 1)$ for $i = 1, 2, 3$.

Explain why tetrahedron $OP_1 P_2 P_3$ has volume $\frac{1}{3}\Delta$, and deduce that

$$\Delta = \pm\tfrac{1}{2} \begin{vmatrix} x_1 & x_2 & x_3 \\ y_1 & y_2 & y_3 \\ 1 & 1 & 1 \end{vmatrix}$$

where the sign is chosen to give a positive result.

11 How are P_1, P_2, P_3 in question 10 related if $\Delta = 0$? Show that the equation of the line through the points (x_1, y_1), (x_2, y_2) may be written as

$$\begin{vmatrix} x_1 & x_2 & x \\ y_1 & y_2 & y \\ 1 & 1 & 1 \end{vmatrix} = 0.$$

12 (a) The points A, B, C on the curve $y = x^2$ have x-coordinates $a - h$, a, $a + h$ respectively. Find the area of triangle ABC, and comment on your answer.

(b) The points A, B, C, D on the curve $y = x^2$ have x-coordinates in arithmetic progression. The chords AC, BD meet at E. Prove that $\triangle ABE = \triangle CDE$.

*13 If $\mathbf{a}$, $\mathbf{b}$, $\mathbf{c}$ are vectors in three dimensions then the *vector triple product* is the vector $\mathbf{a} \times (\mathbf{b} \times \mathbf{c})$.

(a) Show that this vector lies in the plane of $\mathbf{b}$ and $\mathbf{c}$, and hence that

$$\mathbf{a} \times (\mathbf{b} \times \mathbf{c}) = \lambda\mathbf{b} + \mu\mathbf{c}, \tag{1}$$

where λ, μ are scalars.

(b) By taking the scalar product of (1) with $\mathbf{a}$, show that

$$\lambda : \mu = (\mathbf{a}.\mathbf{c}) : -(\mathbf{a}.\mathbf{b}),$$

and hence that

$$\mathbf{a} \times (\mathbf{b} \times \mathbf{c}) = k[(\mathbf{a}.\mathbf{c})\mathbf{b} - (\mathbf{a}.\mathbf{b})\mathbf{c}].$$

(c) Use components to show that $k = 1$, so that

$$\mathbf{a} \times (\mathbf{b} \times \mathbf{c}) = (\mathbf{a}.\mathbf{c})\mathbf{b} - (\mathbf{a}.\mathbf{b})\mathbf{c}.$$

(d) Find a similar expression for $(\mathbf{a} \times \mathbf{b}) \times \mathbf{c}$.

14 Prove that $\mathbf{a} \times (\mathbf{b} \times \mathbf{c}) + \mathbf{b} \times (\mathbf{c} \times \mathbf{a}) + \mathbf{c} \times (\mathbf{a} \times \mathbf{b}) = \mathbf{0}$.

15 Prove that $(\mathbf{a} \times \mathbf{b}).(\mathbf{c} \times \mathbf{d}) = \begin{vmatrix} \mathbf{a}.\mathbf{c} & \mathbf{a}.\mathbf{d} \\ \mathbf{b}.\mathbf{c} & \mathbf{b}.\mathbf{d} \end{vmatrix}$.

16 A sequence of vectors $\mathbf{v}_1$, $\mathbf{v}_2$, ..., is defined inductively by the equations

$$\begin{cases} \mathbf{v}_1 = \mathbf{a} \times \mathbf{b} \\ \mathbf{v}_{n+1} = \mathbf{v}_n \times \mathbf{b} \text{ for } n = 1, 2, ..., \end{cases}$$

where $\mathbf{a}$ and $\mathbf{b}$ are two given non-parallel vectors. Prove that, for $n = 1, 2, ...$,
(a) $\mathbf{v}_{n+2} = k\mathbf{v}_n$, where k is a scalar; (b) $\mathbf{v}_{2n} = \lambda_n\mathbf{a} + \mu_n\mathbf{b}$, where λ_n and μ_n are scalars depending on n.

Prove also that, if $\mu_n = 0$ for some n, then $\mathbf{a}.\mathbf{b} = 0$ and $\mu_n = 0$ for all n.
(*Note*: It is not necessary to calculate the values of k, λ_n, μ_n.)   [SMP]

Project Exercise 12D

Central orbits
In this sequence of questions vector methods are used to prove again the main results on orbits given in Chapters 4 and 5. As usual, $\mathbf{r}$ is the position vector of a particle P under the action of a central force of attraction $F(r)$ per unit mass towards the origin O.

1 Prove that the equation of motion can be written as $\ddot{\mathbf{r}} = \dfrac{-F(r)\mathbf{r}}{r}$.

2 The moment of velocity of P about O is defined to be the vector $\mathbf{h}$, where $\mathbf{h} = \mathbf{r} \times \dot{\mathbf{r}}$.
Prove that $\dot{\mathbf{h}} = \mathbf{0}$, and hence that $\mathbf{h}$ is a constant vector.

3 Prove that $\mathbf{h}.\mathbf{r} = 0$, and hence that P moves in the plane through O perpendicular to $\mathbf{h}$.

4 Suppose now that $F(r) = \mu/r^2$ (inverse square attraction). Show that

$$\ddot{\mathbf{r}} = -\frac{\mu}{r^3}\,\mathbf{r}.$$

Taking the vector product of both sides of this with $\mathbf{r} \times \dot{\mathbf{r}}$, use Exercise 12C, question 13 to show that

$$\mathbf{h} \times \ddot{\mathbf{r}} = -\frac{\mu}{r^3}\left\{(\mathbf{r}.\mathbf{r})\dot{\mathbf{r}} - (\mathbf{r}.\dot{\mathbf{r}})\mathbf{r}\right\}.$$

Use the fact that $\mathbf{r}.\dot{\mathbf{r}} = \frac{1}{2}\dfrac{d}{dt}(\mathbf{r}.\mathbf{r}) = \frac{1}{2}\dfrac{d}{dt}(r^2) = r\dot{r}$ to simplify the right-hand side to

$$-\mu\frac{d}{dt}\left(\frac{\mathbf{r}}{r}\right).$$

5 Since $\mathbf{h}$ is constant, $\mathbf{h} \times \ddot{\mathbf{r}} = \dfrac{d}{dt}(\mathbf{h} \times \dot{\mathbf{r}})$. Deduce from question 4 that

$$\mathbf{h} \times \dot{\mathbf{r}} = -\frac{\mu\mathbf{r}}{r} + \text{a constant vector,}$$

which can be written as

$$\mathbf{h} \times \dot{\mathbf{r}} = -\mu\left\{\frac{\mathbf{r}}{r} + \mathbf{e}\right\}, \quad \text{where } \mathbf{e} \text{ is constant.}$$

6 Prove that $\mathbf{e}.\mathbf{h} = 0$, and deduce that $\mathbf{e}$ is in the plane of the motion.

7 Prove that $\mathbf{r}.(\mathbf{h} \times \dot{\mathbf{r}}) = -(\mathbf{r} \times \dot{\mathbf{r}}).\mathbf{h} = -h^2$.
   Deduce from question 5 that

$$h^2 = \mu\{r + \mathbf{e}.\mathbf{r}\}$$

and so, finally, that

$$l/r = 1 + e\cos\theta,$$

where $l = h^2/\mu$ and θ is the angle between $\mathbf{r}$ and $\mathbf{e}$.

This shows that the orbit is a conic with semi-latus rectum l, eccentricity e, and major axis in the direction of $\mathbf{e}$.

8 Use the first result of question 7 and the fact that $\mathbf{h}$ is perpendicular to $\dot{\mathbf{r}}$ to deduce from question 5 that

$$e^2 = \frac{2h^2}{\mu^2}\left(\tfrac{1}{2}\dot{r}^2 - \frac{\mu}{r}\right) + 1.$$

Hence show that

$$e^2 = 1 + \frac{2h^2 C}{\mu^2},$$

where $C = \frac{1}{2}\dot{r}^2 - \mu/r$ is the total energy per unit mass, as in §5.3.

13

Vector product in geometry

13.1 EQUATIONS OF PLANES AND LINES

This chapter shows some of the uses of the vector product in the coordinate geometry of planes and lines. Knowledge of the basic work is assumed, leading to the following main results (Note 13.1).

(a) The equation of the plane with normal vector $\mathbf{n}$ through the point with position vector $\mathbf{p}$ (Fig. 1) is

$$(\mathbf{r} - \mathbf{p}).\mathbf{n} = 0 \quad \text{or} \quad \mathbf{r}.\mathbf{n} = k, \quad \text{where } k = \mathbf{p}.\mathbf{n}.$$

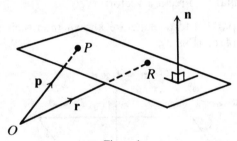

Figure 1

If
$$\mathbf{r} = \begin{bmatrix} x \\ y \\ z \end{bmatrix} \quad \text{and} \quad \mathbf{n} = \begin{bmatrix} a \\ b \\ c \end{bmatrix}$$

this equation may be written

$$ax + by + cz = k.$$

(b) The equation of the line with the direction vector $\mathbf{d}$ through the point with position vector $\mathbf{p}$ (Fig. 2) is

$$\mathbf{r} = \mathbf{p} + t\mathbf{d}, \quad \text{where } t \text{ is a real parameter.}$$

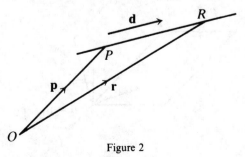

Figure 2

If
$$\mathbf{r} = \begin{bmatrix} x \\ y \\ z \end{bmatrix}, \qquad \mathbf{p} = \begin{bmatrix} x_1 \\ y_1 \\ z_1 \end{bmatrix}, \qquad \mathbf{d} = \begin{bmatrix} u \\ v \\ w \end{bmatrix}$$

this equation may be written

$$\begin{bmatrix} x \\ y \\ z \end{bmatrix} = \begin{bmatrix} x_1 \\ y_1 \\ z_1 \end{bmatrix} + t \begin{bmatrix} u \\ v \\ w \end{bmatrix}$$

or (by elimination of t)

$$\frac{x - x_1}{u} = \frac{y - y_1}{v} = \frac{z - z_1}{w}, \quad \text{provided that } uvw \neq 0.$$

The broad strategy when finding the equation of a plane is to find a point on the plane and a normal vector $\mathbf{n}$. Likewise, to deal with a line we need to know a point on it and a direction vector $\mathbf{d}$. The vector product often gives a quick way of obtaining a normal or direction vector:

(i) if two vectors parallel to a plane are known then their vector product is normal to the plane (Fig. 3);

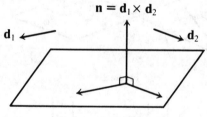

Figure 3

(ii) if the normal vectors of two planes are known then their vector product is perpendicular to both normals, and so is in the direction of the line of intersection of the planes (Fig. 4).

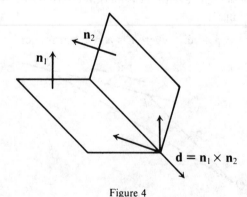

Figure 4

Example 1
Find the equation of the plane passing through the points $(1, 1, 1)$, $(2, 0, 2)$ and $(2, -1, 1)$.

Solution

The position vectors of the given points are $\begin{bmatrix} 1 \\ 1 \\ 1 \end{bmatrix}$, $\begin{bmatrix} 2 \\ 0 \\ 2 \end{bmatrix}$, $\begin{bmatrix} 2 \\ -1 \\ 1 \end{bmatrix}$, so the vectors

$\begin{bmatrix} 2 \\ 0 \\ 2 \end{bmatrix} - \begin{bmatrix} 1 \\ 1 \\ 1 \end{bmatrix} = \begin{bmatrix} 1 \\ -1 \\ 1 \end{bmatrix}$ and $\begin{bmatrix} 2 \\ -1 \\ 1 \end{bmatrix} - \begin{bmatrix} 1 \\ 1 \\ 1 \end{bmatrix} = \begin{bmatrix} 1 \\ -2 \\ 0 \end{bmatrix}$ are parallel to the plane.

Therefore $\begin{bmatrix} 1 \\ -1 \\ 1 \end{bmatrix} \times \begin{bmatrix} 1 \\ -2 \\ 0 \end{bmatrix} = \begin{bmatrix} 2 \\ 1 \\ -1 \end{bmatrix}$ is a normal vector. The equation of the

plane is $\begin{bmatrix} x \\ y \\ z \end{bmatrix} . \begin{bmatrix} 2 \\ 1 \\ -1 \end{bmatrix} = \begin{bmatrix} 1 \\ 1 \\ 1 \end{bmatrix} . \begin{bmatrix} 2 \\ 1 \\ -1 \end{bmatrix}$ or $2x + y - z = 2$. $\square$

Q.1   Check that $(2, 0, 2)$ and $(2, -1, 1)$ lie in this plane.

Example 2

Find the equation of the plane containing the line $\begin{bmatrix} x \\ y \\ z \end{bmatrix} = \begin{bmatrix} 1 \\ 5 \\ 0 \end{bmatrix} + s \begin{bmatrix} -1 \\ 2 \\ 1 \end{bmatrix}$ and

parallel to the line $\begin{bmatrix} x \\ y \\ z \end{bmatrix} = \begin{bmatrix} 3 \\ 4 \\ 2 \end{bmatrix} + t \begin{bmatrix} 1 \\ 1 \\ 2 \end{bmatrix}$.

Solution

The direction vectors $\begin{bmatrix} -1 \\ 2 \\ 1 \end{bmatrix}$ and $\begin{bmatrix} 1 \\ 1 \\ 2 \end{bmatrix}$ are parallel to the plane, so

$\begin{bmatrix} -1 \\ 2 \\ 1 \end{bmatrix} \times \begin{bmatrix} 1 \\ 1 \\ 2 \end{bmatrix} = \begin{bmatrix} 3 \\ 3 \\ -3 \end{bmatrix} = 3 \begin{bmatrix} 1 \\ 1 \\ -1 \end{bmatrix}$ is a normal vector.

The plane contains the first line, and so contains the point $(1, 5, 0)$. The

equation of the plane is therefore $\begin{bmatrix} x \\ y \\ z \end{bmatrix} . \begin{bmatrix} 1 \\ 1 \\ -1 \end{bmatrix} = \begin{bmatrix} 1 \\ 5 \\ 0 \end{bmatrix} . \begin{bmatrix} 1 \\ 1 \\ -1 \end{bmatrix}$ or $x + y - z = 6$.

$\square$

Q.2   Find the coordinates of another point on the first line, and check that it lies in the plane.

Example 3

Find the equation of the line of intersection of the planes $3x + 2y - z = 1$, $x - 4y + 2z = 5$.

Solution

The normal vectors of the planes are $\begin{bmatrix} 3 \\ 2 \\ -1 \end{bmatrix}$ and $\begin{bmatrix} 1 \\ -4 \\ 2 \end{bmatrix}$, and $\begin{bmatrix} 3 \\ 2 \\ -1 \end{bmatrix} \times \begin{bmatrix} 1 \\ -4 \\ 2 \end{bmatrix} =$

$\begin{bmatrix} 0 \\ -7 \\ -14 \end{bmatrix} = -7 \begin{bmatrix} 0 \\ 1 \\ 2 \end{bmatrix}$, so $\begin{bmatrix} 0 \\ 1 \\ 2 \end{bmatrix}$ is a direction vector of the line of intersection.

To find a point of intersection of the planes, choose any value for z, and solve the resulting equations for x and y.

For example, $z = 0 \Rightarrow \begin{cases} 3x + 2y = 1 \\ x - 4y = 5 \end{cases} \Rightarrow x = 1, y = -1$,

so $(1, -1, 0)$ is on the line of intersection.

The required line is $\begin{bmatrix} x \\ y \\ z \end{bmatrix} = \begin{bmatrix} 1 \\ -1 \\ 0 \end{bmatrix} + t \begin{bmatrix} 0 \\ 1 \\ 2 \end{bmatrix}$. ☐

Q.3   Find another point on this line, and check that it lies on both planes.

Q.4   On the line of intersection of Example 3, $x = 1$ always, so we are not at liberty to 'choose any value' for x when finding a point on both planes. The zero component in the direction vector should draw attention to this, but see what happens if x is chosen to be (*a*) the correct value 1, (*b*) any other value.

Exercise 13A

1   Find the equation of the plane containing the points $(0, 1, 4)$, $(0, -4, 2)$ and $(1, 2, 1)$.

2   Do the points $(-1, 2, 3)$, $(4, 3, -2)$, $(-1, -3, -4)$, $(1, 1, 0)$ lie on one plane?

3   The tetrahedron $ABCD$ has vertices A $(2, 2, 1)$, B $(4, 1, 2)$, C $(2, 1, 3)$, D $(2, 2, 4)$. Calculate to the nearest degree the angle between faces ABC, ABD.

4   Find the equation of the plane through the point $(2, 1, 0)$ parallel to the lines $\mathbf{r} = \mathbf{i} + p(2\mathbf{i} + 3\mathbf{j} + \mathbf{k})$ and $\mathbf{r} = \mathbf{k} + q(7\mathbf{i} + 4\mathbf{k})$.

5   With the data of question 3, find the equation of the plane through the point $(-3, 5, -1)$ parallel to AB and CD.

6   (*a*) Find the equation of the plane containing the line

$$L_1: \begin{bmatrix} x \\ y \\ z \end{bmatrix} = \begin{bmatrix} -2 \\ 0 \\ 6 \end{bmatrix} + s \begin{bmatrix} 1 \\ 2 \\ -1 \end{bmatrix}$$

and parallel to the line

$$L_2: \begin{bmatrix} x \\ y \\ z \end{bmatrix} = \begin{bmatrix} -5 \\ 0 \\ 0 \end{bmatrix} + t \begin{bmatrix} 1 \\ 1 \\ 3 \end{bmatrix}.$$

(b) Find the equation of the plane containing L_2 and perpendicular to L_1.

7 Find the general equation of the line through the point $(2, -1, -5)$ and perpendicular to the vector $3\mathbf{i} + 2\mathbf{j} - \mathbf{k}$.

8 Prove that the lines

$$\frac{x + 15}{-8} = \frac{y - 2}{4} = \frac{z - 8}{5} \quad \text{and} \quad \frac{x - 1}{-2} = \frac{y + 6}{1} = \frac{z + 2}{4}$$

intersect, and find the equation of the plane containing both lines.

9 Find the equation of the plane containing the point $(6, 9, 1)$ and the line $\mathbf{r} = 3\mathbf{i} + 5\mathbf{j} + 3\mathbf{k} + t(3\mathbf{i} - \mathbf{j} + 2\mathbf{k})$.

10 Find the direction of the line of intersection of the plane $\mathbf{r} \cdot (\mathbf{i} - 3\mathbf{j}) = 4$ and the plane through $(1, 1, 0)$ parallel to the vectors $3\mathbf{i} + \mathbf{j} + 2\mathbf{k}$ and $4\mathbf{i} + 2\mathbf{j} + 3\mathbf{k}$.

11 Find the equations of the line common to the planes $3x + 2y + z = 4$ and $x - 2y - 2z = 8$ in the form

$$\frac{x - a}{l} = \frac{y - b}{m} = \frac{z - c}{n}.$$

State the values of a, b, c, l, m, n. [SMP]

12 A pyramid has three faces which (taking the vertex as origin) have equations

$$3x + 2y + 4z = 0, \qquad 2x - 3y + 2z = 0, \qquad -3x - y + 3z = 0.$$

Find the three angles made by pairs of edges at the vertex.

13 A plane Π_1 is normal to the vector $\mathbf{n} = \mathbf{i} - \mathbf{j} + 2\mathbf{k}$ and passes through the point $A\,(1, -1, 2)$. A second plane Π_2 is perpendicular to Π_1 and passes through the points $B\,(1, 1, 0)$ and $C\,(2, 0, -1)$. Show that a normal $\mathbf{n}_2$ to Π_2 is given by

$$\begin{bmatrix} 1 \\ -1 \\ 2 \end{bmatrix} \times \begin{bmatrix} 1 \\ -1 \\ -1 \end{bmatrix}$$

and derive the equations of Π_1 and Π_2.

Calculate $\mathbf{n}_1 \times \mathbf{n}_2$, and hence find the vector equation of the line of intersection of Π_1 and Π_2. [SMP]

13.2 DISTANCES FROM LINES AND PLANES

Further geometrical results can be obtained by using vector moments. Let P, Q, R have position vectors $\mathbf{p}, \mathbf{q}, \mathbf{r}$ and let $\mathbf{d}$ be a non-zero localised vector acting along the line PR (Fig. 5).

Then the vector moment of $\mathbf{d}$ about Q is

$$\mathbf{QP} \times \mathbf{d} = (\mathbf{p} - \mathbf{q}) \times \mathbf{d}.$$

But the magnitude of this moment is

$$|\mathbf{d}| \times \text{distance of } Q \text{ from the line } PR$$

(of course 'distance' here means 'perpendicular distance').

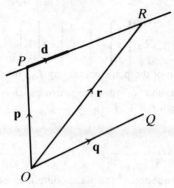

Figure 5

Therefore the distance of Q from PR is

$$\frac{|(\mathbf{q} - \mathbf{p}) \times \mathbf{d}|}{|\mathbf{d}|} = |(\mathbf{q} - \mathbf{p}) \times \hat{\mathbf{d}}|.$$

(Reversing the order of $\mathbf{p}$ and $\mathbf{q}$ makes no difference to the modulus of the vector product, and is more convenient later.)

Example 4
Find the distance of Q $(5, 3, 2)$ from the line joining P $(3, -1, 0)$ and R $(4, -3, 2)$.

Solution

$$\mathbf{q} - \mathbf{p} = \begin{bmatrix} 5 \\ 3 \\ 2 \end{bmatrix} - \begin{bmatrix} 3 \\ -1 \\ 0 \end{bmatrix} = \begin{bmatrix} 2 \\ 4 \\ 2 \end{bmatrix}.$$

For $\mathbf{d}$ we use $\mathbf{PR}$:

$$\mathbf{d} = \mathbf{r} - \mathbf{p} = \begin{bmatrix} 4 \\ -3 \\ 2 \end{bmatrix} - \begin{bmatrix} 3 \\ -1 \\ 0 \end{bmatrix} = \begin{bmatrix} 1 \\ -2 \\ 2 \end{bmatrix},$$

so

$$(\mathbf{q} - \mathbf{p}) \times \mathbf{d} = \begin{bmatrix} 2 \\ 4 \\ 2 \end{bmatrix} \times \begin{bmatrix} 1 \\ -2 \\ 2 \end{bmatrix} = \begin{bmatrix} 12 \\ -2 \\ -8 \end{bmatrix}.$$

$$|(\mathbf{q} - \mathbf{p}) \times \mathbf{d}| = \sqrt{(144 + 4 + 64)} = \sqrt{212}, |\mathbf{d}| = \sqrt{(1 + 4 + 4)} = 3.$$

The required distance $= \sqrt{212}/3 \approx 4.85.$ ☐

Taking an important special case,
$\qquad$ R is on the line through P with direction vector $\mathbf{d}$
$\qquad\qquad$ $\Leftrightarrow$ distance of R from this line is zero

$$\Leftrightarrow |(\mathbf{r} - \mathbf{p}) \times \mathbf{d}| = 0$$

$$\Leftrightarrow (\mathbf{r} - \mathbf{p}) \times \mathbf{d} = \mathbf{0}.$$

This gives a vector equation for the line through P with direction vector $\mathbf{d}$

which does not involve a parameter.

If
$$\mathbf{r} = \begin{bmatrix} x \\ y \\ z \end{bmatrix}, \qquad \mathbf{p} = \begin{bmatrix} x_1 \\ y_1 \\ z_1 \end{bmatrix}, \qquad \mathbf{d} = \begin{bmatrix} u \\ v \\ w \end{bmatrix}$$

then
$$(\mathbf{r} - \mathbf{p}) \times \mathbf{d} = \begin{bmatrix} x - x_1 \\ y - y_1 \\ z - z_1 \end{bmatrix} \times \begin{bmatrix} u \\ v \\ w \end{bmatrix} = \begin{bmatrix} (y - y_1)w - (z - z_1)v \\ (z - z_1)u - (x - x_1)w \\ (x - x_1)v - (y - y_1)u \end{bmatrix}.$$

This is the zero vector if and only if

$$\left. \begin{array}{c} (y - y_1)w = (z - z_1)v \\ (z - z_1)u = (x - x_1)w \\ (x - x_1)v = (y - y_1)u \end{array} \right\} \tag{1}$$

If $uvw \neq 0$ these equations give

$$\frac{x - x_1}{u} = \frac{y - y_1}{v} = \frac{z - z_1}{w}, \tag{2}$$

one familiar form of the equation of the line.

If $uvw = 0$ then one or two of u, v, w may be zero (but not all three, since $\mathbf{d} \neq \mathbf{0}$). Suppose for example that $u = 0$ and $v \neq 0$. Then the third equation (1) gives $x - x_1 = 0$, i.e. $x = x_1$. This can be incorporated into equation (2) by using the convention that if a zero denominator occurs then the corresponding numerator must also be zero. A line with $u = 0$ can then be written

$$\frac{x - x_1}{0} = \frac{y - y_1}{v} = \frac{z - z_1}{w}$$

as an alternative to

$$x = x_1, \qquad \frac{y - y_1}{v} = \frac{z - z_1}{w}.$$

The vector equation of a line $(\mathbf{r} - \mathbf{p}) \times \mathbf{d} = \mathbf{0}$ is similar in form to the equation of the plane through P with normal vector $\mathbf{n}$, which is $(\mathbf{r} - \mathbf{p}).\mathbf{n} = 0$.

With the notation of Fig. 6, the perpendicular distance of Q from this plane is

$$QM = PQ|\cos\theta|$$

$$= \frac{|\mathbf{q} - \mathbf{p}||\mathbf{n}||\cos\theta|}{|\mathbf{n}|}.$$

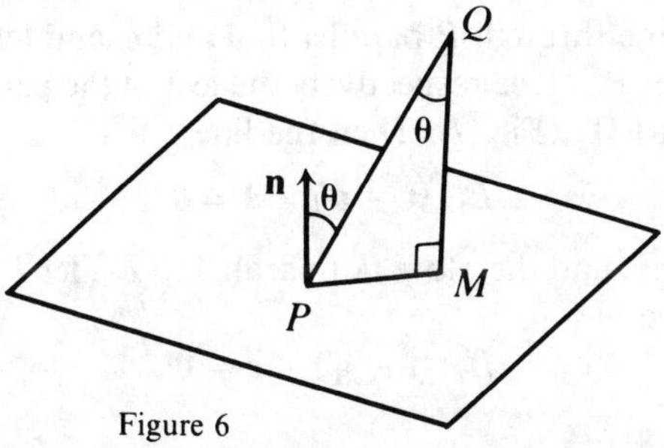

Figure 6

Therefore the distance of Q from the plane through P with normal $\mathbf{n}$ is

$$\frac{|(\mathbf{q} - \mathbf{p}) \cdot \mathbf{n}|}{|\mathbf{n}|} = |(\mathbf{q} - \mathbf{p}) \cdot \hat{\mathbf{n}}|.$$

Notice how similar this is to the expression for the distance of a point from a line (p. 204).

If Q is (x_1, y_1, z_1) and the plane is $ax + by + cz = k$ then, as in §13.1,

$$\mathbf{n} = \begin{bmatrix} a \\ b \\ c \end{bmatrix} \quad \text{and} \quad \mathbf{p} \cdot \mathbf{n} = k.$$

The distance of Q from the plane is therefore

$$\frac{|\mathbf{q} \cdot \mathbf{n} - k|}{|\mathbf{n}|} = \frac{|ax_1 + by_1 + cz_1 - k|}{\sqrt{(a^2 + b^2 + c^2)}}.$$

Q.5 What is the corresponding formula for the distance of the point (x_1, y_1) from the line $ax + by = k$ in two dimensions?

Finally, we consider the two lines

$$L_1 : (\mathbf{r} - \mathbf{p}) \times \mathbf{d} = \mathbf{0} \quad \text{and} \quad L_2 : (\mathbf{r} - \mathbf{q}) \times \mathbf{e} = \mathbf{0}.$$

Suppose that these two lines are *skew*, i.e. they do not intersect and are not parallel to each other.

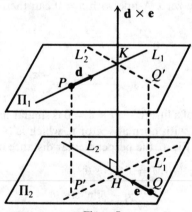

Figure 7

Let Π_1 be the plane through P parallel to $\mathbf{d}$ and $\mathbf{e}$, and let Π_2 be the parallel plane through Q. Let P', Q' be respectively the feet of the perpendiculars from P to Π_2 and from Q to Π_1 (Fig. 7). Then the line

$$L_1' : (\mathbf{r} - \mathbf{p}') \times \mathbf{d} = \mathbf{0}$$

is in Π_2 parallel to L_1, and therefore not parallel to L_2; let L_1' and L_2 meet at H. Similarly, let the line

$$L_2' : (\mathbf{r} - \mathbf{q}') \times \mathbf{e} = \mathbf{0}$$

meet L_1 at K. Then the transversal HK is perpendicular to both L_1 and L_2, and is the only such common perpendicular. The distance HK is the shortest distance between L_1 and L_2. This can be found easily, since it equals the distance from P to Π_2. Since $\mathbf{d}$ and $\mathbf{e}$ are parallel to Π_2, $\mathbf{d} \times \mathbf{e}$ is a normal vector.

Therefore the shortest distance between the skew lines L_1 and L_2 is

$$\frac{|(\mathbf{p} - \mathbf{q}) \cdot (\mathbf{d} \times \mathbf{e})|}{|\mathbf{d} \times \mathbf{e}|} = \frac{1}{|\mathbf{d} \times \mathbf{e}|} [\mathbf{p} - \mathbf{q}, \mathbf{d}, \mathbf{e}].$$

Notice that this is the length of the projection of an arbitrary transversal PQ on to a line perpendicular to both the skew lines. As an immediate consequence we see that the lines L_1 and L_2 intersect if and only if the least distance between them is zero, i.e.

L_1 and L_2 intersect $\Leftrightarrow (\mathbf{p} - \mathbf{q}) \cdot (\mathbf{d} \times \mathbf{e}) = 0$ and $\mathbf{d} \times \mathbf{e} \neq \mathbf{0}$.

Q.6   Obtain this condition again by noting that L_1 and L_2 intersect if and only if $\mathbf{p} - \mathbf{q}$, $\mathbf{d}$, $\mathbf{e}$ are coplanar and $\mathbf{d} \times \mathbf{e} \neq \mathbf{0}$.

Q.7   What happens if $\mathbf{d} \times \mathbf{e} = \mathbf{0}$?

Q.8   Write down $\mathbf{p}$, $\mathbf{q}$, $\mathbf{d}$, $\mathbf{e}$ for the lines of Exercise 13A, question 8. Hence check that these lines meet (without finding the point of intersection).

Example 5
A cuboid has edges given in magnitude and direction by $\mathbf{i}, 2\mathbf{j}, \mathbf{k}$. Find the shortest distance between a diagonal and an edge $\mathbf{k}$ which it does not meet.

Solution

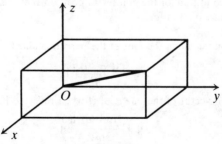

Figure 8

With the cuboid placed as in Fig. 8 we can take

$$\mathbf{p} = \begin{bmatrix} 0 \\ 0 \\ 0 \end{bmatrix}, \qquad \mathbf{d} = \begin{bmatrix} 1 \\ 2 \\ 1 \end{bmatrix}$$

$$\mathbf{q} = \begin{bmatrix} 1 \\ 0 \\ 0 \end{bmatrix}, \qquad \mathbf{e} = \begin{bmatrix} 0 \\ 0 \\ 1 \end{bmatrix}.$$

Then

$$\mathbf{p} - \mathbf{q} = \begin{bmatrix} -1 \\ 0 \\ 0 \end{bmatrix}, \quad \mathbf{d} \times \mathbf{e} = \begin{bmatrix} 2 \\ -1 \\ 0 \end{bmatrix}, \quad |\mathbf{d} \times \mathbf{e}| = \sqrt{5},$$

$$(\mathbf{p} - \mathbf{q}).(\mathbf{d} \times \mathbf{e}) = -2.$$

The required distance is $2/\sqrt{5} \approx 0.89$.

Exercise 13B

1 Five of the vertices of a cuboid are O, $A(2, 0, 0)$, $B(0, 5, 0)$, $C(0, 0, 3)$, $D(2, 5, 3)$. Calculate the following distances:

(a) from A to OD, (b) from C to BD, (c) from B to plane ACD, (d) from D to plane ABC, (e) between OD and AB, (f) between AC and BD.

2 The vertices of a regular octahedron are at $(\pm 1, 0, 0)$, $(0, \pm 1, 0)$, $(0, 0, \pm 1)$. Write down normal vectors for the faces which meet at the edge $x + y = 1$, $z = 0$. Hence find the angle between these two faces.

3 For the octahedron of question 2, find the shortest distance between two skew edges.

4 Find the shortest distance between the line joining $(0, 5, 2)$ and $(7, 9, -13)$ and the line joining $(6, 2, 4)$ and $(10, 12, 7)$.

5 For the skew lines $x + 1 = y - 4 = z$ and $x/2 = y + 1 = (z - 3)/3$ find

(a) the shortest distance between them;

(b) the equation of the common perpendicular transversal;

(c) the coordinates of the points where this transversal meets the lines.

6 The point Q has position vector $\mathbf{q}$, and the plane Π has equation $(\mathbf{r} - \mathbf{p}).\mathbf{n} = 0$. Write down the condition for the point with position vector $\mathbf{q} + \lambda\mathbf{n}$ to lie on Π, and solve the resulting equation for λ.

Deduce that

(a) the position vector of the foot of the perpendicular from Q to Π is

$$\mathbf{q} + \frac{(\mathbf{p} - \mathbf{q}).\mathbf{n}}{n^2}\,\mathbf{n};$$

(b) the position vector of the image of Q when reflected in Π is

$$\mathbf{q} + \frac{2(\mathbf{p} - \mathbf{q}).\mathbf{n}}{n^2}\,\mathbf{n}.$$

7 The equation of the plane Π is $2x - 3y + z = 4$. Find

(a) the foot of the perpendicular from $(4, 5, 1)$ to Π,

(b) the image of $(4, 5, 1)$ when reflected in Π.

8 Using a result from question 7, find the equation of the reflection of the line $\dfrac{x - 4}{1} = \dfrac{y - 5}{2} = \dfrac{z - 1}{-1}$ in the plane $2x - 3y + z = 4$.

9 Find the equation of the reflection of the line $\dfrac{x - 6}{5} = \dfrac{y - 7}{10} = \dfrac{z + 4}{-2}$ in the plane $3x + y - 5z = 10$.

10   Show that the equation of the plane passing through three points whose position vectors are **a**, **b**, **c** can be written in the form

$$\mathbf{r} \cdot \mathbf{n} = [\mathbf{a}, \mathbf{b}, \mathbf{c}]$$

and find **n** as a symmetric expression in terms of **a**, **b**, **c**.

11   Show that the equation of the plane containing the point with position vector **a** and parallel to the vectors **b** and **c** can be written in the form

$$[\mathbf{r}, \mathbf{b}, \mathbf{c}] = [\mathbf{a}, \mathbf{b}, \mathbf{c}].$$

Find in a similar form the equation of the plane containing the points with position vectors **a** and **b** and parallel to the vector **c**.

12   The planes $P_1: 2x + y = 1$ and $P_2: 2x + y + \frac{1}{4}z = 1$ meet in the line L. Show that the point A $(0, 1, 0)$ lies on L, and find an equation for L in the form $\mathbf{x} = \mathbf{a} + t\mathbf{b} \times \mathbf{c}$ (where, for example, **a** is the position vector of the point A). The point D lies in P_1 and is such that AD is perpendicular to L: write $\mathbf{d} - \mathbf{a}$ as a vector product. If the distance of D from P_2 is 1, show that D is $(0, 1, \pm 9)$.   [SMP]

14

Systems of particles

14.1 LINEAR MOTION OF A SYSTEM OF PARTICLES

We have already used the idea of a rigid body as a collection of particles, leading, for example, to methods of finding moments of inertia by integration. Before going further with the dynamics of a rigid body we shall investigate the mechanical behaviour of a system of particles. With one important exception (in §14.5) the work in this chapter does not use the rigidity condition (that the distance between any two particles remains fixed), so the results can be applied to all systems of particles, including, for example, the particles of a exploding firework, a pole-vaulter or the whole solar system, which are certainly not rigid bodies.

The general idea is to use Newton's laws for individual particles, and then by summing deduce results which apply to the system as a whole.

We start with the linear motion of the system. This may already be familiar (Note 14.1); it is repeated here both for completeness and to introduce some notation which may seem complicated at first.

Consider a system of n particles, with the ith particle having mass m_i and position vector $\mathbf{r}_i$ with respect to a fixed origin O. There may be forces of interaction between these particles, for example due to rigid or elastic connections or magnetic or gravitational attraction. Let $\mathbf{F}_{ij}$ be the force on the ith particle due to the jth particle; this is called an *internal* force of the system. There may also be an *external* force on the ith particle, not caused by any other particle of the system. Since the ith particle cannot exert a force on itself (Note 14.2), $\mathbf{F}_{ii}$ has not been used for an internal force, and it is convenient to let $\mathbf{F}_{ii}$ denote the external force on the ith particle.

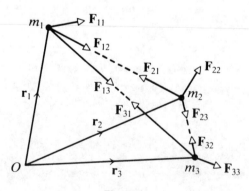

Figure 1

210

Fig. 1 shows these internal and external forces for a system of three particles. In general there are n^2 internal or external forces to be taken into account, though in a particular case some of these may be zero.

The total force acting on the ith particle is

$$\mathbf{F}_{i1} + \mathbf{F}_{i2} + \cdots + \mathbf{F}_{in} = \sum_j \mathbf{F}_{ij},$$

so the motions of the particles are governed by the n equations of motion

$$\sum_j \mathbf{F}_{ij} = m_i \ddot{\mathbf{r}}_i \qquad (i = 1, 2, 3, \ldots, n).$$

Q.1   Write out these equations fully for the case $n = 3$.

Although we need all these equations to see what happens to the individual particles, we can get useful information about the overall motion of the system by summing them. This gives

$$\sum_i \sum_j \mathbf{F}_{ij} = \sum_i m_i \ddot{\mathbf{r}}_i \tag{1}$$

Considerable simplification of (1) is possible. Firstly, on the left-hand side we have the sum of all internal and external forces. But by Newton's third law we know that for the internal forces $\mathbf{F}_{ij} = -\mathbf{F}_{ji}$, so that $\mathbf{F}_{ij} + \mathbf{F}_{ji} = \mathbf{0}$. All the internal forces therefore cancel in pairs and we are left with the sum of the external forces $\mathbf{F}_{ii}$:

$$\sum_i \sum_j \mathbf{F}_{ij} = \sum_i \mathbf{F}_{ii} = \mathbf{F} \quad \text{say,}$$

where $\mathbf{F}$ is the *total external force*.

Secondly, we know (Note 14.3) that the centre of mass of the system has position vector $\bar{\mathbf{r}}$ given by

$$M\bar{\mathbf{r}} = \sum_i m_i \mathbf{r}_i, \tag{2}$$

where $M = \sum_i m_i$, the total mass. The position of the centre of mass is independent of the origin chosen for the position vectors; see Exercise 14A, question 7.

Differentiating (2) with respect to t gives

$$M\dot{\bar{\mathbf{r}}} = \sum_i m_i \dot{\mathbf{r}}_i \quad \text{and} \quad M\ddot{\bar{\mathbf{r}}} = \sum_i m_i \ddot{\mathbf{r}}_i.$$

Therefore the right-hand side of (1) equals $M\ddot{\bar{\mathbf{r}}}$, and equation (1) simplifies to

$$\mathbf{F} = M\ddot{\bar{\mathbf{r}}}$$

total external force = total mass × acceleration of mass centre.

The centre of mass G is thus of fundamental importance, since its motion is

(a) independent of any internal forces;

(b) typical of the system as a whole, in the sense that if every particle had the same motion it would be the motion of G;

(c) the same as if all the particles were concentrated at G with all the external forces acting together there.

It is property (c) which justifies the common practice of treating a large body as if it were a particle, at least as a first approximation.

Example 1

Discuss the motion of two particles A and B of masses 2 and 3, initially at the points $(0, 0, 5)$ and $(0, 5, 0)$ and subjected to external forces of $\begin{bmatrix} 3 \\ 0 \\ -4 \end{bmatrix}$ and $\begin{bmatrix} -3 \\ 0 \\ -6 \end{bmatrix}$.

Solution

The initial position of G is given by

$$5\bar{\mathbf{r}}_0 = 2\begin{bmatrix} 0 \\ 0 \\ 5 \end{bmatrix} + 3\begin{bmatrix} 0 \\ 5 \\ 0 \end{bmatrix} \Rightarrow \bar{\mathbf{r}}_0 = \begin{bmatrix} 0 \\ 3 \\ 2 \end{bmatrix}.$$

From the ratio theorem, G always divides AB in the ratio 3:2. For the motion of G,

$$5\ddot{\bar{\mathbf{r}}} = \begin{bmatrix} 3 \\ 0 \\ -4 \end{bmatrix} + \begin{bmatrix} -3 \\ 0 \\ -6 \end{bmatrix} = \begin{bmatrix} 0 \\ 0 \\ -10 \end{bmatrix} \Rightarrow \ddot{\bar{\mathbf{r}}} = \begin{bmatrix} 0 \\ 0 \\ -2 \end{bmatrix}.$$

So G has constant acceleration parallel to $\mathbf{k}$. Its path will be a parabola or a straight line, depending on whether or not it has any initial velocity other than in the $\mathbf{k}$-direction.

Fig. 2 shows one possibility, when the initial velocity of G is in the plane $x = 0$. The motion of the particles themselves need not be in this plane, though G will always be 3/5 of the way from A to B.   □

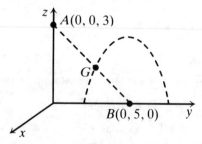

Figure 2

The *linear momentum* $\mathbf{P}_i$ of the ith particle of the system is defined by $\mathbf{P}_i = m_i\dot{\mathbf{r}}_i$, and the total linear momentum of the system is $\mathbf{P} = \sum_i \mathbf{P}_i$. The linear momentum of the total mass concentrated G is

$$\bar{\mathbf{P}} = M\dot{\bar{\mathbf{r}}} = \mathbf{P}, \quad \text{since } M\dot{\bar{\mathbf{r}}} = \sum_i m_i\dot{\mathbf{r}}_i.$$

Differentiating with respect to t gives

$$\mathbf{F} = \dot{\bar{\mathbf{P}}} = \dot{\mathbf{P}}$$

total external force = rate of change of total linear momentum.

This shows how Newton's second law applies to a system as well as to an individual particle.

In particular, if $\mathbf{F} = \mathbf{0}$ then $\mathbf{P}$ is constant, which gives the *principle of the conservation of linear momentum*:

If no external forces act on a system then its total linear momentum remains constant.

We may also take resolved parts in any fixed direction. If $\hat{\mathbf{e}}$ is a fixed unit vector then

$$\mathbf{F}.\hat{\mathbf{e}} = \dot{\mathbf{P}}.\hat{\mathbf{e}} = \frac{d}{dt}(\mathbf{P}.\hat{\mathbf{e}}).$$

In particular if $\mathbf{F}.\hat{\mathbf{e}} = 0$ then $\mathbf{P}.\hat{\mathbf{e}}$ is constant, and so of course is $\bar{\mathbf{P}}.\hat{\mathbf{e}}$. So if the total external force has zero resolved part in a particular direction then the resolved part in that direction of the velocity of G is constant.

Example 2
Discuss the motion of a man standing on smooth ice who loses his balance.

Solution
The only external forces on the man are his weight W and the contact force N from the ice, which is vertical since the ice is smooth (Fig. 3). The total external force has zero horizontal resolved part, so the horizontal velocity of the centre of mass G remains zero. Hence as he falls his centre of mass moves vertically.

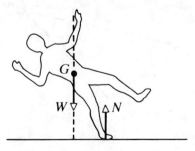

Figure 3

At first G accelerates downwards, so N is less than W (N may even be zero if both feet leave the ice). When he lands, G is rapidly brought to rest, so for a short time N is considerably larger than W!   □

Exercise 14A

1   Particles A, B, C of masses 1, 1, 2 are initially at rest at $(2, 0)$, $(0, 4)$, $(5, 2)$. Forces $\begin{bmatrix} 2 \\ 0 \end{bmatrix}$, $\begin{bmatrix} -1 \\ 2 \end{bmatrix}$, $\begin{bmatrix} 3 \\ 2 \end{bmatrix}$ act on A, B, C respectively.
Find the subsequent positions of A, B, C and the centre of mass G in terms of the time t. Plot these positions on a diagram for $t = 0, 1, 2$.

2   The particles A, B of Example 1 have initial velocities $\begin{bmatrix} -3 \\ -1 \\ 5 \end{bmatrix}$, $\begin{bmatrix} 2 \\ 4 \\ 0 \end{bmatrix}$. Find the initial velocity of G.
   Find the position vectors of A, B and G when $t = 2$, and check that $AG:GB = 3:2$ then.

3   Three identical ink-pots fly through the air. Their mass centre lands in the wastepaper basket and one of them is observed to land a few feet away. Is it possible to say from this where the others landed? Would it make any difference if (a) the masses were not equal, (b) they were rigidly joined together?

4   A space-ship blasts off, powered only by an adjustable rocket which is kept pointing vertically downwards. How do the rates of lift of the mass centre compare when the rocket is located (a) centrally, (b) off-centre? How do the rates of lift of the tip of the nose compare?

5   Discuss how it is possible for the mass centre of a pole-vaulter to pass under a bar which he clears.

6   A bicycle is lightly held stationary with the pedal crank arms vertical. A backward horizontal force is applied to the lower pedal. Which way does the bicycle move?

*7   The position vector of the ith particle of a system with respect to a point C is $\mathbf{s}_i$, and $OC = \mathbf{c}$ (Fig. 4). If $\bar{\mathbf{s}} = \dfrac{1}{M} \sum_i m_i \mathbf{s}_i$, prove that $\bar{\mathbf{r}} = \mathbf{c} + \bar{\mathbf{s}}$.
   Deduce that the position of the mass centre is independent of the origin chosen for position vectors.

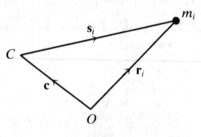

Figure 4

*8   Let the position vector of the ith particle relative to the mass centre be $\boldsymbol{\rho}_i$, so that $\mathbf{r}_i = \bar{\mathbf{r}} + \boldsymbol{\rho}_i$. ($\rho$ is the Greek letter rho.) Prove that
$$\sum_i m_i \boldsymbol{\rho}_i = \sum_i m_i \dot{\boldsymbol{\rho}}_i = \sum_i m_i \ddot{\boldsymbol{\rho}}_i = \mathbf{0}.$$

14.2 ROTATIONAL MOTION OF A SYSTEM OF PARTICLES

The *moment of momentum*, also called *angular momentum*, of the system about O is

$$\mathbf{H}_O = \sum_i \mathbf{r}_i \times \mathbf{P}_i = \sum_i \mathbf{r}_i \times m_i \dot{\mathbf{r}}_i.$$

Differentiating with respect to t,

$$\dot{\mathbf{H}}_O = \sum_i \frac{d}{dt} (\mathbf{r}_i \times m_i \dot{\mathbf{r}}_i)$$

$$= \sum_i (\dot{\mathbf{r}}_i \times m_i \dot{\mathbf{r}}_i + \mathbf{r}_i \times m_i \ddot{\mathbf{r}}_i)$$

$$= \sum_i \mathbf{r}_i \times m_i \ddot{\mathbf{r}}_i,$$

since $\dot{\mathbf{r}}_i \times m_i \dot{\mathbf{r}}_i = \mathbf{0}$ (vector product of parallel vectors).

But we know that $m_i \ddot{\mathbf{r}}_i = \sum_j \mathbf{F}_{ij}$, so

$$\dot{\mathbf{H}}_O = \sum_i \left(\mathbf{r}_i \times \sum_j \mathbf{F}_{ij} \right), \tag{1}$$

a sum with n^2 terms.

Q.2 Write out this equation fully for the case $n = 3$.

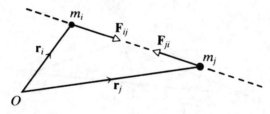

Figure 5

As before, Newton's third law leads to great simplification. Since $\mathbf{F}_{ij}$ and $\mathbf{F}_{ji}$ act along the same line (Fig. 5),

$$\mathbf{r}_i \times \mathbf{F}_{ij} = \mathbf{r}_j \times \mathbf{F}_{ij} = -\mathbf{r}_j \times \mathbf{F}_{ji},$$

so

$$\mathbf{r}_i \times \mathbf{F}_{ij} + \mathbf{r}_j \times \mathbf{F}_{ji} = \mathbf{0}.$$

So when the sum in (1) is evaluated all the terms involving moments of internal forces cancel in pairs, and we are left with

$$\dot{\mathbf{H}}_O = \sum_i \mathbf{r}_i \times \mathbf{F}_{ii}.$$

The right-hand side here is the total moment about O of the external forces, which we denote by $\mathbf{L}_O$. Therefore

$$\mathbf{L}_O = \dot{\mathbf{H}}_O$$

moment about O of external forces = rate of change of moment of momentum about O.

In particular if $\mathbf{L}_O = 0$ then $\mathbf{H}_O$ is constant, which gives the *principle of conservation of moment of momentum*:

If the external forces on a system have zero moment about a fixed point then its moment of momentum about that point remains constant.

Also, if $\hat{\mathbf{e}}$ is a fixed unit vector, $\mathbf{L}_O . \hat{\mathbf{e}} = \dot{\mathbf{H}}_O . \hat{\mathbf{e}} = \dfrac{d}{dt}(\mathbf{H}_O . \hat{\mathbf{e}})$, so the moment of the external forces about a fixed axis equals the rate of change of moment of momentum about that axis. In particular if the moment of the external forces about an axis is zero then the moment of momentum about that axis remains constant.

A clear example of this is given by a skater spinning on smooth ice. All the external forces are vertical, so the moment of momentum about the vertical axis of her spin is constant. If she starts with her arms outstretched sideways and then moves them above her head, she decreases her moment of inertia, and so her angular velocity must increase, giving a spectacular end to the spin.

When applying these results it may be difficult to calculate $\mathbf{H}_O$ directly, and it is often easier to work relative to the mass centre G. Let the ith particle have position vector $\boldsymbol{\rho}_i$ relative to G, so that

$$\mathbf{r}_i = \bar{\mathbf{r}} + \boldsymbol{\rho}_i \qquad \text{(Fig. 6)}.$$

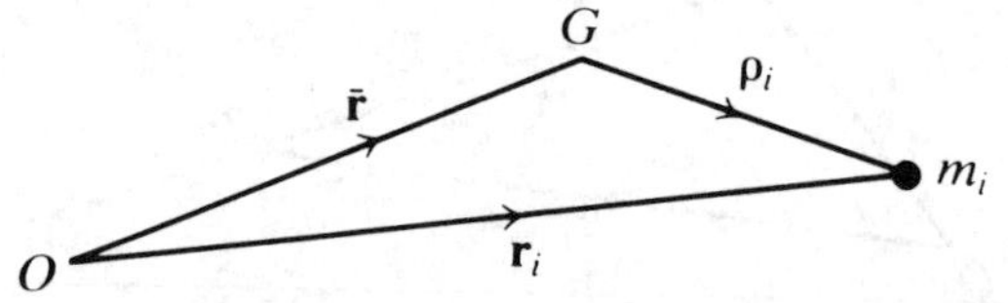

Figure 6

Then
$$\mathbf{H}_O = \sum_i \mathbf{r}_i \times m_i \dot{\mathbf{r}}_i$$

$$= \sum_i (\bar{\mathbf{r}} + \boldsymbol{\rho}_i) \times m_i \dot{\mathbf{r}}_i$$

$$= \sum_i \bar{\mathbf{r}} \times m_i \dot{\mathbf{r}}_i + \sum_i \boldsymbol{\rho}_i \times m_i \dot{\mathbf{r}}_i$$

$$= \bar{\mathbf{r}} \times \sum_i m_i \dot{\mathbf{r}}_i + \sum_i \boldsymbol{\rho}_i \times m_i \dot{\mathbf{r}}_i$$

$$= \bar{\mathbf{r}} \times M\dot{\bar{\mathbf{r}}} + \mathbf{H}_G$$

where $\mathbf{H}_G = \sum_i \boldsymbol{\rho}_i \times m_i \dot{\mathbf{r}}_i$ is the moment of momentum of the system about G.

Moreover,

$$\mathbf{H}_G = \sum_i \boldsymbol{\rho}_i \times m_i(\dot{\bar{\mathbf{r}}} + \dot{\boldsymbol{\rho}}_i)$$

$$= \sum_i \boldsymbol{\rho}_i \times m_i\dot{\bar{\mathbf{r}}}_i + \sum_i \boldsymbol{\rho}_i \times m_i\dot{\boldsymbol{\rho}}_i$$

$$= \left(\sum_i m_i\boldsymbol{\rho}_i\right) \times \dot{\bar{\mathbf{r}}} + \sum_i \boldsymbol{\rho}_i \times m_i\dot{\boldsymbol{\rho}}_i$$

$$= \sum_i \boldsymbol{\rho}_i \times m_i\dot{\boldsymbol{\rho}}_i, \quad \text{since} \sum_i m_i\boldsymbol{\rho}_i = 0 \quad \text{(Exercise 14A, question 8)}.$$

This means that when calculating $\mathbf{H}_G$ we can use the velocities $\dot{\boldsymbol{\rho}}_i$ relative to G instead of the velocities $\dot{\mathbf{r}}_i$ relative to O; this is often a great simplification.

Therefore $\qquad\qquad\qquad \mathbf{H}_O = \bar{\mathbf{H}}_O + \mathbf{H}_G$

where

$\bar{\mathbf{H}}_O = \bar{\mathbf{r}} \times M\dot{\bar{\mathbf{r}}}$, the moment of momentum about O of the whole mass concentrated at G,

and

$H_G = \sum_i \boldsymbol{\rho}_i \times m_i\dot{\mathbf{r}}_i = \sum_i \boldsymbol{\rho}_i \times m_i\dot{\boldsymbol{\rho}}_i$, the moment of momentum about G of the

system.

Example 3
The unit vectors $\mathbf{i}, \mathbf{j}$ are horizontal, and $\mathbf{k}$ is vertical. Attached to a light circular hoop of radius 0.5 are four particles, each of mass 3, which are equally spaced around the hoop. The hoop rolls without slipping along Oy away from O. At a certain instant its centre has speed 1.2 and one of the particles is at the point of contact $(0, 2, 0)$. Find the moment of momentum about O then, (a) by direct summation, (b) using $\mathbf{H}_O = \bar{\mathbf{H}}_O + \mathbf{H}_G$.

Solution
(a)

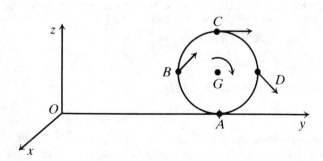

Figure 7

With the notation of Fig. 7, the position vectors of A, B, C, D are

$$\begin{bmatrix} 0 \\ 2 \\ 0 \end{bmatrix}, \begin{bmatrix} 0 \\ 1.5 \\ 0.5 \end{bmatrix}, \begin{bmatrix} 0 \\ 2 \\ 1 \end{bmatrix}, \begin{bmatrix} 0 \\ 2.5 \\ 0.5 \end{bmatrix}.$$

The velocity of each particle is the vector sum of the velocity of the centre G, $\begin{bmatrix} 0 \\ 1.2 \\ 0 \end{bmatrix}$, and a velocity of magnitude 1.2 along the tangent in the clockwise sense.

Thus the velocities of A, B, C, D are

$$\begin{bmatrix} 0 \\ 0 \\ 0 \end{bmatrix}, \begin{bmatrix} 0 \\ 1.2 \\ 1.2 \end{bmatrix}, \begin{bmatrix} 0 \\ 2.4 \\ 0 \end{bmatrix}, \begin{bmatrix} 0 \\ 1.2 \\ -1.2 \end{bmatrix}$$

respectively.

Therefore

$$\mathbf{H}_O = \begin{bmatrix} 0 \\ 2 \\ 0 \end{bmatrix} \times 3 \begin{bmatrix} 0 \\ 0 \\ 0 \end{bmatrix} + \begin{bmatrix} 0 \\ 1.5 \\ 0.5 \end{bmatrix} \times 3 \begin{bmatrix} 0 \\ 1.2 \\ 1.2 \end{bmatrix} + \begin{bmatrix} 0 \\ 2 \\ 1 \end{bmatrix} \times 3 \begin{bmatrix} 0 \\ 2.4 \\ 0 \end{bmatrix} + \begin{bmatrix} 0 \\ 2.5 \\ 0.5 \end{bmatrix} \times 3 \begin{bmatrix} 0 \\ 1.2 \\ -1.2 \end{bmatrix}$$

$$= \begin{bmatrix} 0 \\ 0 \\ 0 \end{bmatrix} + \begin{bmatrix} 3.6 \\ 0 \\ 0 \end{bmatrix} + \begin{bmatrix} -7.2 \\ 0 \\ 0 \end{bmatrix} + \begin{bmatrix} -10.8 \\ 0 \\ 0 \end{bmatrix} = \begin{bmatrix} -14.4 \\ 0 \\ 0 \end{bmatrix}.$$

(b) Since $\bar{\mathbf{r}} = \begin{bmatrix} 0 \\ 2 \\ 0.5 \end{bmatrix}$ and $\dot{\bar{\mathbf{r}}} = \begin{bmatrix} 0 \\ 1.2 \\ 0 \end{bmatrix}$,

$$\bar{\mathbf{H}}_O = \begin{bmatrix} 0 \\ 2 \\ 0.5 \end{bmatrix} \times 12 \begin{bmatrix} 0 \\ 1.2 \\ 0 \end{bmatrix} = \begin{bmatrix} -7.2 \\ 0 \\ 0 \end{bmatrix}.$$

The speed of each particle relative to G is 1.2, so

$$|\mathbf{H}_G| = 0.5 \times 12 \times 1.2 = 7.2.$$

For each particle the direction and sense of $\boldsymbol{\rho}_i \times m_i \dot{\boldsymbol{\rho}}_i$ are those of $-\mathbf{i}$. Therefore

$$\mathbf{H}_G = \begin{bmatrix} -7.2 \\ 0 \\ 0 \end{bmatrix} \text{ and so } \mathbf{H}_O = \bar{\mathbf{H}}_O + \mathbf{H}_G = \begin{bmatrix} -14.4 \\ 0 \\ 0 \end{bmatrix}. \qquad \square$$

By differentiating the previous result, $\dot{\mathbf{H}}_O = \dot{\bar{\mathbf{H}}}_O + \dot{\mathbf{H}}_G$ and so

$$\mathbf{L}_O = \dot{\bar{\mathbf{H}}}_O + \dot{\mathbf{H}}_G. \tag{2}$$

But for a moving system there may be no obvious fixed point O about which to take moments, and a beautifully simple result follows if we take moments about the mass centre G.

For
$$L_O = \sum_i \mathbf{r}_i \times \mathbf{F}_{ii}$$

$$= \sum_i (\bar{\mathbf{r}} + \boldsymbol{\rho}_i) \times \mathbf{F}_{ii}$$

$$= \sum_i \bar{\mathbf{r}} \times \mathbf{F}_{ii} + \sum_i \boldsymbol{\rho}_i \times \mathbf{F}_{ii}$$

$$= \bar{\mathbf{r}} \times \mathbf{F} + \sum_i \boldsymbol{\rho}_i \times \mathbf{F}_{ii}$$

$$= \bar{\mathbf{r}} \times M\ddot{\bar{\mathbf{r}}} + \mathbf{L}_G,$$

where $\mathbf{L}_G$ is the total moment of the external forces about G.

But
$$\bar{\mathbf{H}}_O = \bar{\mathbf{r}} \times M\dot{\bar{\mathbf{r}}}$$

$$\Rightarrow \dot{\bar{\mathbf{H}}}_O = \dot{\bar{\mathbf{r}}} \times M\dot{\bar{\mathbf{r}}} + \bar{\mathbf{r}} \times M\ddot{\bar{\mathbf{r}}}$$

$$= \bar{\mathbf{r}} \times M\ddot{\bar{\mathbf{r}}}, \quad \text{since } \dot{\bar{\mathbf{r}}} \text{ and } M\dot{\bar{\mathbf{r}}} \text{ are parallel.}$$

Therefore
$$\mathbf{L}_O = \dot{\bar{\mathbf{H}}}_O + \mathbf{L}_G. \tag{3}$$

Comparing (2) and (3) gives

$$\mathbf{L}_G = \dot{\mathbf{H}}_G$$

moment of external forces about G = rate of change of moment
of momentum about G.

The two results $\mathbf{F} = M\ddot{\bar{\mathbf{r}}}$ and $\mathbf{L}_G = \dot{\mathbf{H}}_G$ enable us to treat the motion of the system as the linear motion of G together with the rotational motion about G. This will be used frequently in Chapter 16.

Exercise 14B

1 Particles A, B, C have masses 1, 2, 3, position vectors $\begin{bmatrix} 4 \\ 2 \\ 6 \end{bmatrix}$, $\begin{bmatrix} 1 \\ 5 \\ 3 \end{bmatrix}$, $\begin{bmatrix} -4 \\ 0 \\ 2 \end{bmatrix}$, and velocities $\begin{bmatrix} 0 \\ 3 \\ -7 \end{bmatrix}$, $\begin{bmatrix} 6 \\ 3 \\ -1 \end{bmatrix}$, $\begin{bmatrix} -4 \\ 1 \\ -1 \end{bmatrix}$ respectively.

(a) Calculate $\mathbf{H}_O$ by direct summation.
(b) Find $\bar{\mathbf{r}}$ and $\dot{\bar{\mathbf{r}}}$.
(c) Calculate $\mathbf{H}_O$ again, using $\mathbf{H}_O = \bar{\mathbf{H}}_O + \mathbf{H}_G$.

2 A space station consisting essentially of four masses of 1000 kg at the corners of a square of diagonal length 20 m is initially stationary in space. It is to be made to rotate at 1 rad s^{-1} about the axis of symmetry perpendicular to the square. This is to be done in 10 s by firing small rockets attached to the masses.

(a) If two rockets are used, where should they be placed and in which direction should they face? What is the least thrust required from each rocket?
(b) Repeat (a) if four rockets are used.
(c) What happens if only one rocket is used?
(d) The four-rocket method of (b) is used, but one rocket fails to fire. Describe the motion of the space station after 10 s.

3   A small model plane of mass M flies at speed v in a horizontal circle of radius a at a height h above the operator. Determine the force between (a) the string and the plane, (b) the string and the operator.

4   In a square dance, four dancers hold hands so that they rotate in a ring at 1 rad s^{-1}. If their masses are 60 kg each and they are symmetrically 1.8 m apart, determine the tension in their arms (ignore the horizontal reactions between their feet and the ground). State the assumptions you have made. Still rotating freely with arms straight, two dancers move to the centre while the other two move further apart. What is now their angular speed and the tension in their arms?

5   A conker on the end of a string of length $2l$ is travelling in a horizontal circle when the middle of the string hits a circular lamp post of circumference c. By what factor has the speed of the conker increased when the string has wrapped itself once round the lamp post?

6   A transverse force of magnitude F acts on a particle of mass m whose position has polar coordinates (r, θ) (Fig. 8). What is the acceleration of the particle? Write down L_O and H_O, and deduce that the transverse acceleration can be written as $\dfrac{1}{r}\dfrac{d}{dt}(r^2\dot\theta)$. (See Exercise 2D, question 7.)

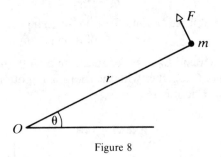

Figure 8

7   A boy has masss 70 kg and his body has moment of inertia 1 kg m^2 about the vertical axis through his mass centre. His arms add an additional 0.2 kg m^2 when at his sides and 2 kg m^2 when extended horizontally. He grasps a dumbbell of mass 3 kg in each hand. With his arms outstretched, so that the dumbbells are 1.5 m apart he spins at $\frac{1}{2}$ rev s^{-1} on a freely turning platform. He now lowers his arms to his sides, so that the dumbbells are 0.5 m apart. What is his new angular velocity?

*8   We know that $\mathbf{L}_O = \dot{\mathbf{H}}_O$ and $\mathbf{L}_G = \dot{\mathbf{H}}_G$; are there any other points C for which $\mathbf{L}_C = \dot{\mathbf{H}}_C$? Let C have position vector $\mathbf{c}$ with respect to a fixed origin O, and let $\mathbf{r}_i = \mathbf{c} + \mathbf{s}_i$. We define

$$\mathbf{L}_C = \sum_i \mathbf{s}_i \times \mathbf{F}_{ii} \quad \text{and} \quad \mathbf{H}_C = \sum_i \mathbf{s}_i \times m_i\dot{\mathbf{r}}_i.$$

Prove that $\mathbf{L}_C = \mathbf{L}_O - \mathbf{c} \times M\ddot{\mathbf{r}}$

and $\dot{\mathbf{H}}_C = \dot{\mathbf{H}}_O - \dot{\mathbf{c}} \times M\dot{\mathbf{r}} - \mathbf{c} \times M\ddot{\mathbf{r}}.$

Deduce that $\mathbf{L}_C = \dot{\mathbf{H}}_C \Leftrightarrow \dot{\mathbf{c}} \times M\dot{\mathbf{r}} = 0$

                $\Leftrightarrow C$ is stationary or has velocity parallel to that of G.

14.3 IMPULSE–MOMENTUM EQUATIONS

If we integrate the equation $\mathbf{F} = \dot{\mathbf{P}}$ of §14.1 with respect to t from t_1 to t_2 we obtain

$$\int_{t_1}^{t_2} \mathbf{F}\, dt = [\mathbf{P}]_{t_1}^{t_2}.$$

Now
$$\int_{t_1}^{t_2} \mathbf{F}\, dt = \int_{t_1}^{t_2} \left(\sum_i \mathbf{F}_{ii} \right) dt = \sum_i \int_{t_2}^{t_2} \mathbf{F}_{ii}\, dt$$

$$= \sum_i \mathbf{J}_i,$$

where $\mathbf{J}_i$ is the impulse of the external force acting on the ith particle (Note 14.4). (Note that the impulses of the internal forces cancel in pairs by Newton's third law.) Therefore

$$\sum_i \mathbf{J}_i = [\mathbf{P}]_{t_1}^{t_2}$$

sum of external impulses = change of linear momentum.

Similarly we can integrate the equation $\mathbf{L}_O = \dot{\mathbf{H}}_O$ of §14.2 to obtain

$$\int_{t_1}^{t_2} \mathbf{L}_O\, dt = [\mathbf{H}_O]_{t_1}^{t_2}.$$

The interpretation of the left-hand side needs some care.

$$\int_{t_1}^{t_2} \mathbf{L}_O\, dt = \int_{t_1}^{t_2} \left(\sum_i \mathbf{r}_i \times \mathbf{F}_{ii} \right) dt = \sum_i \int_{t_1}^{t_2} \mathbf{r}_i \times \mathbf{F}_{ii}\, dt.$$

Now during the interval from t_1 to t_2 both $\mathbf{r}_i$ and $\mathbf{F}_{ii}$ may change, and so this sum cannot be simplified. But if $\mathbf{F}_{ii}$ is a very large force acting for a very short time (for example, due to a hammer blow or a kick) the change in $\mathbf{r}_i$ during this time is negligible, so that $\mathbf{r}_i$ may be taken as constant. The impulse of such a force is called a *jerk*.

For jerks,
$$\int_{t_1}^{t_2} \mathbf{r}_i \times \mathbf{F}_{ii}\, dt = \mathbf{r}_i \times \int_{t_1}^{t_2} \mathbf{F}_{ii}\, dt = \mathbf{r}_i \times \mathbf{J}_i,$$

and so
$$\sum_i \mathbf{r}_i \times \mathbf{J}_i = [\mathbf{H}_O]_{t_1}^{t_2}$$

sum of moments of jerks = change of moment of momentum.

Example 4
Three particles A, B, C, each of mass m, are connected by equal taut strings AB and BC of length l; A, B, C lie at the corners of an equilaterial triangle on a smooth horizontal table. A jerk $\mathbf{J}$ is applied to B along the bisector of ABC away from A and C.
  (a) What is the initial impulse in the strings?
  (b) Describe the subsequent motion of the system.

Solution

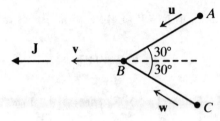

Figure 9

Let the initial velocities of A, B, C be **u**, **v**, **w**; A and C must start to move along the lines of their strings (Fig. 9). By symmetry **v** is in the direction of **J** and

$$|\mathbf{u}| = |\mathbf{w}| = u \quad \text{say.}$$

The linear impulse–momentum equation is

$$\mathbf{J} = m\mathbf{u} + m\mathbf{v} + m\mathbf{w}. \tag{1}$$

Resolving this in the direction of **J**,

$$J = 2mu \cos 30° + mv. \tag{2}$$

Also, because the string is taut,

speed of A in direction AB = speed of B in direction AB

$$\Rightarrow u = v \cos 30°. \tag{3}$$

From equations (2) and (3)

$$v = \frac{2J}{5m} \quad \text{and} \quad u = \frac{\sqrt{3}J}{5m}.$$

Hence the initial impulses $m\mathbf{u}$ and $m\mathbf{w}$ in the strings each have magnitude

$$\frac{\sqrt{3}J}{5}.$$

In the subsequent motion no external force acts upon the system, so the mass centre has constant velocity, which from (1) is $\mathbf{J}/3m$. The moment of momentum about the mass centre is also constant ($=\mathbf{0}$), but this is of little help. The fact that AB and BC are taut means that A and C must move in circles relative to B, and with constant angular speeds ω and $-\omega$ since no force (there are tensions in the strings) has any moment about B.

Velocity of A relative to $B = \mathbf{u} - \mathbf{v}$

$$= \begin{bmatrix} u - v \cos 30° \\ -v \sin 30° \end{bmatrix} \quad \begin{array}{l} \text{along } AB \\ \text{perpendicular to } AB \end{array}$$

$$= \begin{bmatrix} 0 \\ -\tfrac{1}{2}v \end{bmatrix}.$$

The constant angular speeds of AB and BC are thus $v/2l = J/5ml$ towards each other. When A and C collide all particles will be moving forward with the same speed. If the collision is perfectly elastic then the angular velocities will be reversed in direction and A and C will swing around, colliding next in front of B. The process of collision will continue fore and aft of B, each collision occurring after $\pi/(J/5ml)$ seconds. If the coefficient of restitution is e, then the angular velocity will be reduced by a factor e and the time between each collision will increase by a factor $1/e$, but the centre of mass will continue at its constant rate.

$\square$

Q.3 Describe in general terms how the motion would differ if the same impulse had been applied but during a far greater length of time.

Exercise 14C

1 Assuming perfectly elastic collisions for the particles of Example 4, calculate the speed of B when A, B, C are collinear (in that order) with A and B travelling (a) in the same sense, (b) in opposite senses.

2 Three equal particles A, B, C lie in order on a straight line on a smooth table. They are connected by strings of length l, and $AB = BC = l$. A jerk gives B a velocity $\mathbf{v}$ perpendicular to ABC. Determine the initial velocities of A and C, and describe the subsequent motion of the system on the assumption that the collisions are perfectly elastic.

3 Repeat question 3 for the case in which the connecting strings are of length $5l/4$ (but initially $AB = BC = l$ still).

4 Two particles A and B are connected by a light string of length l, and rest on a smooth table. If the string is just taut when A is struck with an impulse J at right angles to AB, describe the subsequent motion (a) if the particles are of equal mass, (b) if A has mass m and B has mass $2m$.

5 Two particles A and B of masses m and M respectively are connected by a light rigid rod. They lie on a smooth horizontal table and the particle B is given an impulse $\mathbf{I}$ which sets both particles in motion. If $\mathbf{w}$ and $\mathbf{W}$ are the initial velocities of A and B respectively, and $\mathbf{n}$ is a unit vector in the direction from A to B, explain why

$$(\mathbf{W} \cdot \mathbf{n})\mathbf{n} = \mathbf{w}.$$

Show that
$$\mathbf{w} = \frac{(\mathbf{I} \cdot \mathbf{n})\mathbf{n}}{m + M},$$

and find the corresponding result for $\mathbf{W}$.   [MEI]

6 Four similar particles, each of mass m, lie at the corners of a rhombus $ABCD$ with the longer diagonal being AC. The particles are joined by four light inextensible strings along the sides of the rhombus and are at rest on a frictionless horizontal plane surface. An impulse I is applied to the mass at A in the direction C to A.
If the angle $BAD = 2\alpha$, find the initial velocities of each of the four particles.
[MEI]

14.4 VARIABLE MASS APPLICATIONS

The linear impulse–momentum equation obtained in §14.3 can be used to investigate the motion of a body whose mass changes as it moves, such as a raindrop which accumulates mass as it falls through a cloud, or a rocket whose mass decreases as it uses fuel. In such cases it is best to think of the whole system (raindrop and cloud droplets or rocket and fuel) and use the fact that the change in the *total* linear momentum in an interval of small duration δt equals the impulse of the *external* forces acting on the *whole* system. By taking limits as $\delta t \to 0$ we derive a differential equation which, in some cases, we can then solve. The masses of the particles forming the system do not in fact vary, but during the motion particles are re-distributed from one part of the system to another.

Consider first a raindrop growing as it falls freely under gravity through a stationary cloud, so that at time t its mass is m and its speed v. The system here consists of the raindrop and the droplets, of mass δm, which condense onto it during the subsequent interval δt.

Since the droplets are initially at rest the initial momentum of the system is mv; the final momentum is $(m + \delta m)(v + \delta v)$. The external force acting on the whole system during this interval is the total weight $(m + \delta m)g$. Therefore

$$(m + \delta m)g\, \delta t = (m + \delta m)(v + \delta v) - mv$$

$$\Rightarrow mg + \delta m\, g = m\frac{\delta v}{\delta t} + \frac{\delta m}{\delta t} v + \delta m\frac{\delta v}{\delta t}.$$

Taking limits as $\delta t \to 0$ gives

$$mg = m\frac{dv}{dt} + \frac{dm}{dt} v$$

which can also be written as

$$mg = \frac{d}{dt}(mv). \tag{1}$$

Q.4 Show that if the cloud is moving downward with constant speed $u(<v)$ then the equation corresponding to (1) is

$$mg = \frac{d}{dt}(mv) - u\frac{dm}{dt}.$$

Example 5
As a spherical raindrop falls from rest through a stationary cloud its mass increases at a rate proportional to its surface area. Investigate its motion.

Solution
Let the density be ρ and the initial radius r_0. If the radius at time t is r then

$$m = \tfrac{4}{3}\pi r^3 \rho$$

and

$$\frac{dm}{dt} = 4\pi r^2 \rho \frac{dr}{dt}.$$

But we are given that $dm/dt \propto 4\pi r^2$ (the surface area). Therefore dr/dt is constant, k say, and so $r = r_0 + kt$.

Since the cloud is stationary we may use (1):

$$\frac{d}{dt} \left(\tfrac{4}{3}\pi(r_0 + kt)^3 \rho v \right) = \tfrac{4}{3}\pi(r_0 + kt)^3 \rho g.$$

Integrating and using $v = 0$ when $t = 0$ gives

$$(r_0 + kt)^3 v = \frac{g}{4k}\left[(r_0 + kt)^4 - r_0^4\right]$$

$$\Leftrightarrow v = \frac{g}{4k}\left[r_0 + kt - \frac{r_0^4}{(r_0 + kt)^3}\right].$$

This can be integrated to give the distance fallen, s, or differentiated to give the acceleration, a:

$$s = \frac{g}{4k}\left[r_0 t + \tfrac{1}{2}kt^2 + \frac{r_0^4}{2k(r_0 + kt)^2} - \frac{r_0^2}{2k}\right];$$

$$a = \frac{g}{4}\left[1 + \frac{3r_0^4}{(r_0 + kt)^4}\right].$$

(Check the details for yourself.)

Notice that the acceleration is initially g, but approaches $g/4$ as t becomes large.   □

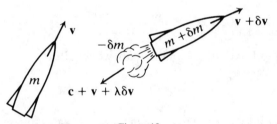

Figure 10

In the case of a rocket of mass m which is burning fuel and moving subject to an external force $\mathbf{F}$, let the velocity of the rocket relative to a fixed origin be $\mathbf{v}$ at time t, and suppose that the gas produced by combustion of the fuel is ejected with constant velocity $\mathbf{c}$ relative to the rocket. Let the mass of the rocket after a further time δt be $m + \delta m$; since the rocket is burning fuel, δm is negative, and the mass ejected is the positive quantity $-\delta m$. (See Fig. 10.) During the interval the velocity of the fuel particles varies from $\mathbf{c} + \mathbf{v}$ to $\mathbf{c} + \mathbf{v} + \delta\mathbf{v}$, so we may take the average velocity of these particles as $\mathbf{c} + \mathbf{v} + \lambda\,\delta\mathbf{v}$, where $0 < \lambda < 1$. Then

initial momentum $= m\mathbf{v}$

final momentum $= (m + \delta m)(\mathbf{v} + \delta\mathbf{v}) + (-\delta m)(\mathbf{c} + \mathbf{v} + \lambda\,\delta\mathbf{v})$

external impulse $= \mathbf{F}\,\delta t,$

so that

$$\mathbf{F}\,\delta t = (m + \delta m)(\mathbf{v} + \delta \mathbf{v}) + (-\delta m)(\mathbf{c} + \mathbf{v} + \lambda\,\delta\mathbf{v}) - m\mathbf{v}$$

$$\Rightarrow \mathbf{F} = m\frac{\delta\mathbf{v}}{\delta t} - \frac{\delta m}{\delta t}\mathbf{c} + (1 - \lambda)\frac{\delta m}{\delta t}\,\delta\mathbf{v}.$$

Taking limits as $\delta t \to 0$ gives

$$\mathbf{F} = m\frac{d\mathbf{v}}{dt} - \frac{dm}{dt}\mathbf{c}. \tag{2}$$

Example 6
A rocket of initial total mass M propels itself by ejecting gas at a constant rate k per unit time with constant speed c relative to the rocket. The rocket is initially at rest on the ground pointing vertically upward. Investigate its motion, ignoring the variation of g with height.

Solution
Since $dm/dt = -k$ the mass after time t is $M - kt$. With $\mathbf{i}$ as the vertically upward unit vector,

$$\mathbf{F} = -(M - kt)g\mathbf{i}, \qquad \mathbf{v} = v\mathbf{i}, \qquad \mathbf{c} = -c\mathbf{i},$$

so from (2) $-(M - kt)g = (M - kt)\dfrac{dv}{dt} - (-k)(-c)$

$$\Leftrightarrow \frac{dv}{dt} = \frac{kc - (M - kt)g}{M - kt} \tag{3}$$

For the rocket to leave the ground initially we require

$$\frac{dv}{dt} > 0 \quad \text{when } t = 0, \text{ i.e. } kc > Mg.$$

If this condition does not hold there will be no lift-off until

$$kc - (M - kt)g > 0, \quad \text{i.e. } t > \frac{Mg - kc}{kg};$$

if M is too large or k or c too small the fuel may be exhausted before t reaches this value, and there will be no lift-off.

Assuming that $kc > Mg$, (3) gives the acceleration

$$\frac{dv}{dt} = \frac{kc}{M - kt} - g,$$

which increases as t increases, until the fuel is exhausted.

Integrating, $v = -c \ln (M - kt) - gt + A$

where, since $v = 0$ when $t = 0$, $0 = -c \ln M + A$.

Therefore $$v = -c \ln(1 - kt/M) - gt.$$

To find the height s reached in time t we integrate again (remembering that $\int \ln x \, dx = x \ln x - x + \text{constant}$):

$$s = c\left(\frac{M}{k} - t\right) \ln\left(1 - \frac{kt}{M}\right) + ct - \tfrac{1}{2}gt^2$$

(check the details for yourself).

These formulae apply until the fuel runs out; suppose this happens when $t = t_1$, $s = s_1$ and $v = v_1$. Then for $t > t_1$ the rocket continues as a free projectile, reaching the maximum height $s_1 + v_1^2/2g$. $\qquad\qquad\square$

Finally, although it is strictly beyond the scope of this book, it is worth mentioning that in 1905 Albert Einstein presented in his special theory of relativity an alternative mechanical model, in which the mass m of each particle does genuinely vary with its speed v according to the formula

$$m = m_0/\sqrt{(1 - v^2/c^2)},$$

where c is the speed of light ($\approx 3 \times 10^8$ m s^{-1}) and m_0 is called the *rest-mass*. In Einstein's model the equation of motion is

$$F = \frac{d}{dt}(mv)$$

i.e. $\qquad\qquad$ force = rate of change of momentum

which is in fact the form in which Newton originally stated his second law of motion. The justification for using this equation of motion is the excellent match between theoretical predictions based on it and experimental observations. A few of the simplest deductions are given in Exercise 14D, question 11 (Note 14.5).

Exercise 14D

1 As a spherical hailstone falls freely under gravity in still air its radius r increases according to the law $dr/dt = kr$, where k is constant. Show that the mass m at time t is given by $m = m_0 e^{3kt}$, where m_0 is the initial mass, and that the velocity has the limiting value $g/3k$.

2 (a) Show that equation (1) of §14.4 can be written in the form

$$mg = mv\frac{dv}{ds} + \frac{dm}{ds}v^2.$$

(b) A raindrop starts from rest and falls through a stationary cloud. Its mass m varies according to the law $dm/ds = km$, where s is the distance fallen and k is constant.

Show that $v^2 = \dfrac{g}{k}(1 - e^{-2ks})$, and find the acceleration.

3   Show that as $k \to 0$ the results of §14.4 Example 5 and Exercise 14D, question 2, give the usual results for free fall without condensation.

4   A small particle is projected from the origin of a coordinate system with speed V at an angle of elevation of θ. The mass of the particle is initially m_0 and increases at a rate k due to the condensation of moisture from a stationary cloud.
    Find the coordinates of the particle as a function of time and the maximum height attained during its trajectory.   [MEI]

5   A rocket in space of mass M (including fuel) is moving directly ahead with speed U free from all external forces. The motor is fired so that a mass αM ($0 < \alpha < 1$) of fuel is ejected backwards with speed c relative to the rocket. Prove that the increase in the rocket's speed is $-c \ln (1 - \alpha)$. (Notice that this does not depend on the rate at which fuel is consumed.)

6   If the rocket in question 5 is initially at rest, what values of α maximises its final kinetic energy?

7   A two-stage rocket consists of a first stage of mass M_1, when fuelled, a second stage of mass M_2, when fuelled, and a payload of mass m. The mass of fuel in each stage is αM_1 and αM_2 respectively where $0 < \alpha < 1$. Each has a rocket motor which burns fuel at a mass rate k and ejects it with exhaust speed c relative to the rocket.
    If the circumstances of firing are such that gravity may be neglected and $M_1 + M_2 = M$ find the optimum ratio of M_2 to M to produce the maximum final speed of the payload.
    Determine this maximum speed as a multiple of c if $\alpha = 0.8$ and $m/M = 0.01$.
                                                                                [MEI]

8   A spherical asteroid of radius a and mass M_0 is travelling with constant velocity V when it enters a cloud of cosmic dust. The dust particles are at rest and are distributed throughout the cloud with uniform density ρ.
    If all the particles with which the asteroid collides adhere to its surface, find the mass of the asteroid as a function of its depth of penetration into the cloud. Assume that the dimensions of the asteroid do not change.
    Derive the equation of motion of the asteroid and hence find its speed and depth of penetration as functions of the time after it entered the cloud.   [MEI]

9   A meteor of mass M and radius a is travelling in a straight line with constant speed V when it enters the edge of the atmosphere. The meteor then experiences a resisting force of $\alpha A v^2$, where α is a constant, A the cross-sectional area and v the speed of the meteor.
    Friction causes the meteor to burn up so that its radius is decreasing at a rate βv, where β is another constant. Mass stripped off may be assumed to be instantaneously brought to rest.
    If it is assumed that gravitational forces may be neglected, find the radius of the meteor and its distance of penetration into the atmosphere as functions of time and hence the time it takes the meteor to burn up and its distance of penetration at this time.   [MEI]

10 A Catharine wheel firework consists of a spiral tube of fuel wound round a circular central core of radius a and the same density, so that the whole wheel is initially of radius b and mass M.
    The wheel is pinned at its centre, and is free to rotate. As the fuel burns at a constant rate it is expelled tangentially with speed c relative to the wheel. After time t the mass of the wheel is $M(1 - kt)$; find the radius and the moment of inertia about

the pin then. Neglecting gravity, find the angular velocity of the wheel when the fuel is fully burnt.

11 This question deals with the motion of a particle moving from rest under the action of a constant force F in Einstein's model, in which $m = \dfrac{m_0}{\sqrt{(1 - v^2/c^2)}}$ and $F = \dfrac{d}{dt}(mv)$, where c is the speed of light.

(a) Prove that $\dfrac{v^2}{c^2} = 1 - \dfrac{1}{1 + k^2 t^2}$, where $k = \dfrac{F}{m_0 c}$. Deduce that the speed approaches but never exceeds the speed of light.

(b) Prove that $s = \dfrac{c}{k}[\sqrt{(1 + k^2 t^2)} - 1]$. Deduce that

(i) if t is large, $s \approx ct$,

(ii) if k and t are small the value of s given by Einstein's model is about $ck^3 t^4/8$ less than the value of s given by Newton's model.

(c) By eliminating t from the results in (a) and (b) prove that

$$\frac{v^2}{c^2} = 1 - \left(\frac{c}{c + ks}\right)^2.$$

Deduce that the increase in mass, $m - m_0$, is proportional to s, and find the constant of proportionality.

14.5 WORK–ENERGY EQUATIONS

Finally we use the equations of motion of §14.1 to obtain an equation of energy of the system. The equation of motion for the ith particle is

$$\sum_j \mathbf{F}_{ij} = m_i \ddot{\mathbf{r}}_i.$$

We take the scalar product of both sides with $\dot{\mathbf{r}}_i$, and then sum for all the particles.

$$\sum_i \sum_j \mathbf{F}_{ij} \cdot \dot{\mathbf{r}}_i = \sum_i m_i \ddot{\mathbf{r}}_i \cdot \dot{\mathbf{r}}_i \tag{1}$$

Q.5 Write this out fully for the case $n = 3$.

Now $\ddot{\mathbf{r}}_i \cdot \dot{\mathbf{r}}_i = \tfrac{1}{2}\dfrac{d}{dt}(\dot{\mathbf{r}}_i^2) = \tfrac{1}{2}\dfrac{d}{dt}(v_i^2)$, where v_i is the speed of the ith particle.

The right-hand side of (1) is therefore $\dfrac{d}{dt}\left(\sum_i \tfrac{1}{2}m_i v_i^2\right) = \dfrac{dT}{dt}$, where $T = \sum_i \tfrac{1}{2}m_i v_i^2$ is the kinetic energy of the system.

Also $\mathbf{F}_{ij} \cdot \dot{\mathbf{r}}_i$ is the rate of working of the force $\mathbf{F}_{ij}$ (Note 14.6), so (1) states that

the total rate of working of the internal and external forces on the system equals the rate of change of its kinetic energy

or, equivalently,

the total work done by the internal and external forces on the system equals the change of its kinetic energy.

Now we look at the contribution of the work done by the internal forces. We know that the sum of the internal forces, the sum of their moments about O, the sum of their impulses, and the sum of the moments of their impulses are all zero. It would be convenient if the same were true of the total work done by the internal forces.

The pair of forces $\mathbf{F}_{ij}$ and $\mathbf{F}_{ji}$ contribute

$$\mathbf{F}_{ij}.\dot{\mathbf{r}}_i + \mathbf{F}_{ji}.\dot{\mathbf{r}}_j$$

to the left-hand side of (1). Since $\mathbf{F}_{ji} = -\mathbf{F}_{ij}$, this contribution is

$$\mathbf{F}_{ij}.\dot{\mathbf{r}}_i - \mathbf{F}_{ij}.\dot{\mathbf{r}}_j = \mathbf{F}_{ij}.(\dot{\mathbf{r}}_i - \dot{\mathbf{r}}_j).$$

In the general case there is no reason why this should be zero, so we may not ignore the work done by the internal forces. But *if the body is rigid* then the distance between the ith and jth particles is constant, so that

$$(\mathbf{r}_i - \mathbf{r}_j)^2 = \text{constant}$$

$$\Rightarrow \quad \frac{d}{dt}[(\mathbf{r}_i - \mathbf{r}_j)^2] = 0$$

$$\Rightarrow (\mathbf{r}_i - \mathbf{r}_j).(\dot{\mathbf{r}}_i - \dot{\mathbf{r}}_j) = 0$$

$$\Rightarrow \quad \mathbf{F}_{ij}.(\dot{\mathbf{r}}_i - \dot{\mathbf{r}}_j) = 0, \quad \text{since } \mathbf{F}_{ij} \text{ is parallel to } \mathbf{r}_i - \mathbf{r}_j.$$

Therefore *for a rigid body* the internal forces contribute nothing to the left-hand side of (1), and so

$$\sum_i \mathbf{F}_{ii}.\dot{\mathbf{r}}_i = \frac{dT}{dt}$$

or   total work done by external forces
        acting on a rigid body = change of kinetic energy

To calculate the kinetic energy T it is often more convenient to work relative to the centre of mass G, as in §14.2. Then

$$T = \sum_i \tfrac{1}{2}m_i\dot{\mathbf{r}}_i^2$$

$$= \sum_i \tfrac{1}{2}m_i(\dot{\bar{\mathbf{r}}} + \dot{\boldsymbol{\rho}}_i)^2$$

$$= \sum_i \tfrac{1}{2}m_i(\dot{\bar{\mathbf{r}}}^2 + 2\dot{\bar{\mathbf{r}}}.\dot{\boldsymbol{\rho}}_i + \dot{\boldsymbol{\rho}}_i^2)$$

$$= \tfrac{1}{2}M\dot{\bar{\mathbf{r}}}^2 + \dot{\bar{\mathbf{r}}}.\sum_i m_i\dot{\boldsymbol{\rho}}_i + \sum_i \tfrac{1}{2}m_i\dot{\boldsymbol{\rho}}_i^2$$

$$= \tfrac{1}{2}M\dot{\bar{\mathbf{r}}}^2 + \sum_i \tfrac{1}{2}m_i\dot{\boldsymbol{\rho}}_i^2, \quad \text{since } \sum_i m_i\dot{\boldsymbol{\rho}}_i = \mathbf{0}.$$

Thus $$T = \bar{T} + T_G$$

where $\bar{T} = \tfrac{1}{2}M\dot{\bar{\mathbf{r}}}^2$, the KE of the whole mass concentrated at G

and $T_G = \sum_i \tfrac{1}{2}m_i\dot{\boldsymbol{\rho}}_i^2$, the KE using velocities relative to G.

Exercise 14E

1   Particles of masses 1, 2, 3, 4 are moving with velocities $\begin{bmatrix} -3 \\ 0 \\ 2 \end{bmatrix}$, $\begin{bmatrix} 5 \\ 1 \\ -3 \end{bmatrix}$, $\begin{bmatrix} 2 \\ 6 \\ 0 \end{bmatrix}$, $\begin{bmatrix} 3 \\ -4 \\ 1 \end{bmatrix}$

respectively. Calculate T, $\bar{T}$ and T_G directly, and check that $T = \bar{T} + T_G$.

2   Find the kinetic energy of the hoop in Example 3.

3   Find the work done by the boy of Exercise 14B, question 7 in lowering his arms. (Neglect the work done by gravity on his arms.)

4   Find the work done by the dancers of Exercise 14B, question 4 in performing their manoeuvre.

5   Prove that, for two particles of masses m_1, m_2 moving along a straight line with relative velocity u,

$$T_G = \frac{m_1 m_2}{2(m_1 + m_2)} u^2.$$

If these two particles collide, prove that the loss of energy is

$$\frac{m_1 m_2}{2(m_1 + m_2)} u^2(1 - e^2),$$

where e is the coefficient of restitution.

6   A shell of mass M kg is travelling at V m s^{-1} when there is an internal explosion and the shell splits into two parts. One part, of mass m kg, moves off at v m s^{-1} at an angle θ to the original line of travel.
   (a) Show that the direction of motion of the other part makes an angle ϕ with the original direction of travel, where

$$\tan \phi = \frac{mv \sin \theta}{MV - mv \cos \theta},$$

and determine the magnitude of its velocity.
   (b) Determine in terms of M, m, V, v and θ the overall change in kinetic energy. Show that your expression has the same sign whatever the numerical values, and hence state whether the change is a gain or a loss.

7   A small ring is free to slide along a smooth horizontal rail. A particle of equal mass is attached to the ring by a string of length a. The particle is initially held in contact with the rail, with the string taut, and is then released. When the string makes an angle θ with the rail the speed of the ring is u, and the speed of the particle *relative to the ring* is v. Prove that

$$u^2 = \frac{ga \sin^3 \theta}{1 + \cos^2 \theta} \quad \text{and} \quad v^2 = \frac{4ga \sin \theta}{1 + \cos^2 \theta}.$$

Find the speed of the particle in terms of g, a, θ.

8   Two stars, of masses m_1 and m_2, deemed to be unaffected by all other objects in the universe, are initially at a great distance apart and moving with velocities $\mathbf{u}_1, \mathbf{u}_2$. They come close enough to influence each other's motion and then separate to a great distance, their velocities then being $\mathbf{v}_1, \mathbf{v}_2$. Show on a single diagram the initial and final momenta of both stars, the impulse $\mathbf{I}$ of the force which m_1 exerts on m_2, and the total momentum $\mathbf{Q}$ of the system.

Explain why one would expect the initial and final kinetic energies of the system to be the same. On this assumption, prove that

$$\mathbf{I}.(\mathbf{u} + \mathbf{v}) = 0,$$

where $\mathbf{u}$, $\mathbf{v}$ are the velocities of m_2 relative to m_1 at the beginning and end of the period of effective interaction.   [SMP]

9 (a) Prove the identity

$$\left(\sum_i m_i\right)\left(\sum_i m_i v_i^2\right) = \sum_{i<j} m_i m_j (\mathbf{v}_i - \mathbf{v}_j)^2 + \left(\sum_i m_i \mathbf{v}_i\right)^2,$$

where $\sum\limits_{i<j}$ means that the sum is to be taken over the $\frac{1}{2}n(n-1)$ pairs (i,j) for which $i < j$ (for example, when $n = 4$, the 6 pairs $(1, 2)$, $(1, 3)$, $(1, 4)$, $(2, 3)$, $(2, 4)$, $(3, 4)$).

$$\text{Deduce that } T = \bar{T} + \frac{1}{2M} \sum_{i<j} m_i m_j v_{ij}^2,$$

where v_{ij} is the relative speed of m_i and m_j and $M = \sum\limits_i m_i$. (This expression for kinetic energy is due to J. L. Lagrange (1736–1813); it generalises the first result of question 5.)

(b) A shell of mass M explodes in flight into n pieces with masses $m_1, m_2, \ldots, m_n$. Show that the gain in kinetic energy due to the explosion is

$$\frac{1}{2M} \sum_{i<j} m_i m_j v_{ij}^2.$$

15

Rigid body kinematics

15.1 ANGULAR VELOCITY AS A VECTOR

In §11.1 we found that the moment of a force about a point is a vector quantity, although in two dimensions its vector nature appears only in the distinction between clockwise and anticlockwise turning effects. Much the same is true of angular velocity, and this leads to a further application of the vector product.

First we consider a rigid body rotating about a fixed axis. Let O be a point on the axis, R a point of the body, and N the foot of the perpendicular from R to the axis (Fig. 1).

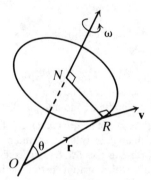

Figure 1

If the rate of rotation of NR is ω (the same for all points of the body, as in §9.1), then the *vector angular velocity* $\boldsymbol{\omega}$ is defined to be the vector with magnitude ω in the direction of the axis and with the sense in which a right-hand corkscrew rotating with the body would move.

The velocity $\mathbf{v}$ of the point R has magnitude $|\boldsymbol{\omega}|RN = |\boldsymbol{\omega}|\,|\mathbf{r}|\sin\theta$, is perpendicular to both $\boldsymbol{\omega}$ and $\mathbf{r}$, and has the sense in which a right-hand corkscrew turning from $\boldsymbol{\omega}$ to $\mathbf{r}$ would move. Therefore

$$\mathbf{v} = \boldsymbol{\omega} \times \mathbf{r}.$$

Example 1
A space platform is spinning with angular speed 4 rad s^{-1} about an axis with direction $\begin{bmatrix} 0 \\ 2 \\ 1 \end{bmatrix}$ passing through the point $(1, 3, -2)$ (coordinates relative to some fixed point in space). Find the velocity of the point on the space platform with coordinates $(4, -2, 1)$.

Solution

The unit vector in the direction and sense of $\begin{bmatrix} 0 \\ 2 \\ 1 \end{bmatrix}$ is $\dfrac{1}{\sqrt{5}} \begin{bmatrix} 0 \\ 2 \\ 1 \end{bmatrix}$, so $\boldsymbol{\omega} = \dfrac{4}{\sqrt{5}} \begin{bmatrix} 0 \\ 2 \\ 1 \end{bmatrix}$.

The position vector **r** of the point with respect to the fixed point $(1, 3, -2)$ on

the axis is $\begin{bmatrix} 4 \\ -2 \\ 1 \end{bmatrix} - \begin{bmatrix} 1 \\ 3 \\ -2 \end{bmatrix} = \begin{bmatrix} 3 \\ -5 \\ 3 \end{bmatrix}$.

So the velocity $\mathbf{v} = \boldsymbol{\omega} \times \mathbf{r} = \dfrac{4}{\sqrt{5}} \begin{bmatrix} 0 \\ 2 \\ 1 \end{bmatrix} \times \begin{bmatrix} 3 \\ -5 \\ 3 \end{bmatrix} = \dfrac{4}{\sqrt{5}} \begin{bmatrix} 11 \\ 3 \\ -6 \end{bmatrix}$.   □

Q.1   Find the coordinates of another point on the axis, and check that using this point gives the same velocity.

Exercise 15A

1   A rigid body is spinning with angular speed 6 rad s^{-1} about an axis through the origin parallel to $2\mathbf{i} + \mathbf{j} - 2\mathbf{k}$.
   (*a*) Find its angular velocity.
   (*b*) Find the velocity of the point of the body with coordinates $(5, 3, -2)$.
   (*c*) Find which points of the body are moving parallel to the plane $x = 0$.
   (*d*) Find which points of the body are moving parallel to the z-axis.

2   Fig. 2 shows a cuboid with edges of lengths a, $2a$, $2a$. The cuboid is rotating about the diagonal through O with angular velocity $\boldsymbol{\omega}$, and at a particular instant three of its edges coincide with coordinate axes Ox, Oy, Oz fixed in space. Find the velocities of the corners of the cuboid which at that instant lie in the plane $z = 0$. Give the magnitudes of these velocities, and describe their directions in terms of angles made with the specified lines in the specified planes.   [SMP]

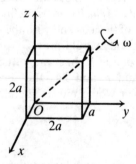

Figure 2

3   A rigid body has angular velocity $3\mathbf{i} - 2\mathbf{j} + \mathbf{k}$ about an axis passing through the point $(6, 9, 1)$. Find
   (*a*) the angular speed of the body,
   (*b*) the speed of the point of the body at $(2, 7, 5)$.

4   A rigid body moves so that the velocities of its points at $(1, 0, 0)$ and $(0, 1, 0)$ are $\begin{bmatrix} 0 \\ 3 \\ 2 \end{bmatrix}$
and $\begin{bmatrix} -3 \\ 0 \\ 5 \end{bmatrix}$ respectively. Show that this is consistent with rotation about an axis through the origin, and find the angular velocity.

5   Cog wheel A, with radius 3 and centre at origin, has angular velocity $2\mathbf{k}$. Cog wheel B has centre at $(0, 4, 2)$ and is such that the two wheels mesh at $(0, 3, 0)$. Find the angular velocity and angular speed of B. Find also the relative velocity of the points on the two wheels which are diametrically opposite $(0, 3, 0)$.

6   Show that if a body is rotating with angular velocity $\boldsymbol{\omega}$ and the velocity of a point A of it is $\mathbf{V}$ then the velocity of any other point B of the body is $\mathbf{V} + \boldsymbol{\omega} \times \mathbf{AB}$.

7   A solid is rotated through an angle α in a clockwise sense about an axis through the origin; $\mathbf{i}$ is a unit vector in the direction of the axis. The points whose position vectors relative to O are $\mathbf{r}, \mathbf{r}'$ are transformed to those whose position vectors are $\mathbf{R}, \mathbf{R}'$. Prove that
(a) $\mathbf{r} - \mathbf{r}' = t\mathbf{i} \Rightarrow \mathbf{R} - \mathbf{R}' = t\mathbf{i}$ for scalar t,
(b) $\mathbf{r} \cdot \mathbf{i} = 0 \Rightarrow \mathbf{R} = \mathbf{r} \cos \alpha + \mathbf{i} \times \mathbf{r} \sin \alpha$.
By splitting $\mathbf{r}$ into the two vectors, parallel and perpendicular to $\mathbf{i}$, deduce that in general
$$\mathbf{R} = \mathbf{i}(\mathbf{i} \cdot \mathbf{r}) + \mathbf{i} \times \mathbf{r} \sin \alpha - \mathbf{i} \times (\mathbf{i} \times \mathbf{r}) \cos \alpha. \qquad \text{[SMP]}$$

*8   A rigid body moves with a constant angular velocity $\boldsymbol{\omega}$. Prove that the acceleration of the point with position vector $\mathbf{r}$ is $\boldsymbol{\omega} \times (\boldsymbol{\omega} \times \mathbf{r})$.

15.2   GENERAL MOTION OF A RIGID BODY

Next we remove the restriction that the body is turning about a fixed axis, and require only that one point O of the body be fixed. With O as origin, let $\mathbf{i}, \mathbf{j}, \mathbf{k}$ be the usual mutually perpendicular unit vectors fixed in space, and let $\mathbf{I}, \mathbf{J}, \mathbf{K}$ be a right-handed triple of mutually perpendicular unit vectors embedded in the body. As the body moves $\mathbf{I}, \mathbf{J}, \mathbf{K}$ vary, but since they are unit vectors

$$\mathbf{I} \cdot \mathbf{I} = \mathbf{J} \cdot \mathbf{J} = \mathbf{K} \cdot \mathbf{K} = 1,$$

and since they are mutually perpendicular

$$\mathbf{J} \cdot \mathbf{K} = \mathbf{K} \cdot \mathbf{I} = \mathbf{I} \cdot \mathbf{J} = 0.$$

Differentiating these relations with respect to time gives

$$\mathbf{I} \cdot \dot{\mathbf{I}} = \mathbf{J} \cdot \dot{\mathbf{J}} = \mathbf{K} \cdot \dot{\mathbf{K}} = 0 \qquad (1)$$

and $$\mathbf{J} \cdot \dot{\mathbf{K}} + \dot{\mathbf{J}} \cdot \mathbf{K} = \mathbf{K} \cdot \dot{\mathbf{I}} + \dot{\mathbf{K}} \cdot \mathbf{I} = \mathbf{I} \cdot \dot{\mathbf{J}} + \dot{\mathbf{I}} \cdot \mathbf{J} = 0. \qquad (2)$$

From (1) $\dot{\mathbf{I}}$ is perpendicular to $\mathbf{I}$, and so $\dot{\mathbf{I}}$ is coplanar with $\mathbf{J}$ and $\mathbf{K}$. Therefore $\dot{\mathbf{I}} = a_1\mathbf{J} + a_2\mathbf{K}$, where a_1, a_2 are scalars (varying with t). Similarly $\dot{\mathbf{J}} = b_1\mathbf{K} + b_2\mathbf{I}$ and $\dot{\mathbf{K}} = c_1\mathbf{I} + c_2\mathbf{J}$.

From (2), $I \cdot \dot{J} + \dot{I} \cdot J = 0 \Rightarrow I \cdot (b_1 K + b_2 I) + (a_1 J + a_2 K) \cdot J = 0$

$$\Rightarrow b_2 + a_1 = 0$$

$$\Rightarrow a_1 = -b_2 = \omega_3 \text{ (say)}.$$

Similarly $b_1 = -c_2 = \omega_1$ (say)   and $c_1 = -a_2 = \omega_2$ (say),

so that $\dot{I} = \omega_3 J - \omega_2 K,$ $\dot{J} = \omega_1 K - \omega_3 I,$ $\dot{K} = \omega_2 I - \omega_1 J.$

We can write these more simply by introducing the vector

$$\boldsymbol{\omega} = \omega_1 I + \omega_2 J + \omega_3 K.$$

Then $\boldsymbol{\omega} \times I = \omega_2 J \times I + \omega_3 K \times I = \omega_2(-K) + \omega_3 J = \dot{I}$

and similarly $\dot{J} = \boldsymbol{\omega} \times J$ and $\dot{K} = \boldsymbol{\omega} \times K.$

Now consider the motion of the particle P with position vector

$$\mathbf{r} = x\mathbf{i} + y\mathbf{j} + z\mathbf{k} = X\mathbf{I} + Y\mathbf{J} + Z\mathbf{K}.$$

In this motion x, y, z vary, but X, Y, Z remain fixed, since I, J, K move with the body. Therefore

$$\dot{\mathbf{r}} = X\dot{I} + Y\dot{J} + Z\dot{K}$$

$$= X\boldsymbol{\omega} \times I + Y\boldsymbol{\omega} \times J + Z\boldsymbol{\omega} \times K$$

$$= \boldsymbol{\omega} \times (X\mathbf{I} + Y\mathbf{J} + Z\mathbf{K})$$

i.e. $\mathbf{v} = \boldsymbol{\omega} \times \mathbf{r}.$

Comparing this with the main result of the previous section shows that the motion of the body at this instant is the same as if it were turning with angular speed $|\boldsymbol{\omega}|$ about an axis through O in the direction of $\boldsymbol{\omega}$. (This explains the use of the letter ω in what we have just done.) This axis is called the *instantaneous axis of rotation*. Since, in general, $\omega_1, \omega_2, \omega_3$ vary with t, the direction of the instantaneous axis is not fixed (either in space or in the body).

Finally, if the body is in general motion, with O moving with velocity $\mathbf{V}$, then the velocity of P equals the velocity of O plus the velocity of P relative to O, i.e.

$$\mathbf{v} = \mathbf{V} + \boldsymbol{\omega} \times \mathbf{r}. \tag{3}$$

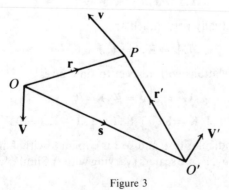

Figure 3

Moreover, if O' is another point of the body, with $\mathbf{OO'} = \mathbf{s}$ and $\mathbf{O'P} = \mathbf{r'}$ (Fig. 3), then the velocity of P is

$$\begin{aligned} \mathbf{v} &= \mathbf{V} + \boldsymbol{\omega} \times \mathbf{r} \\ &= \mathbf{V} + \boldsymbol{\omega} \times (\mathbf{s} + \mathbf{r'}) \\ &= \mathbf{V} + \boldsymbol{\omega} \times \mathbf{s} + \boldsymbol{\omega} \times \mathbf{r'} \\ &= \mathbf{V'} + \boldsymbol{\omega} \times \mathbf{r'}, \quad \text{where } \mathbf{V'} \text{ is the velocity of } O'. \end{aligned}$$

This is in the same form as (3), with the same $\boldsymbol{\omega}$, so the instantaneous angular velocity is a property of the body as a whole, and is independent of the particular point O.

Exercise 15B

1   As a lamina moves in its plane the velocity of a point C of the lamina is $\begin{bmatrix} u \\ v \end{bmatrix}$, referred to axes fixed in the plane of the motion. Prove that the velocity of the point P for which $\mathbf{CP} = \begin{bmatrix} \xi \\ \eta \end{bmatrix}$ is $\begin{bmatrix} u - \eta\omega \\ v + \xi\omega \end{bmatrix}$, where ω is the angular velocity.

Deduce that the point I for which $\mathbf{CI} = \begin{bmatrix} -v/\omega \\ u/\omega \end{bmatrix}$ has zero velocity; I is called the *instantaneous centre of rotation*. What happens if $\omega = 0$?

(It may happen that I is outside the boundary of a finite lamina; if so, we take I to be rigidly attached to the lamina.)

2   With the notation of question 1, show that P moves with a speed ωPI at right angles to PI.

3   Find the position of the instantaneous centre of rotation in each of the following cases:

(a) A ladder slipping in a vertical plane while in contact with the horizontal ground and a vertical wall.

(b) A wheel rolling along horizontal ground without slipping.

(c) A wheel of radius a skidding along horizontal ground so that its centre and lowest point have speeds u and v respectively, in the same sense with $u > v$.

(d) A set square moving so that the edges forming the $60°$ angle are in contact with two fixed pins.

4   Find the locus in the fixed plane of the instantaneous centre for each part of question 3.

5   A straight rod is constrained so that it passes through a fixed point and one end moves along a fixed straight line. Taking $(a, 0)$ as the fixed point and the y-axis as the fixed line, find the equation of the locus of the instantaneous centre, and sketch this locus.

6   The motion of a rigid body is given by the velocity $\mathbf{V}$ of a point O together with an angular velocity $\boldsymbol{\omega}$ ($\neq\mathbf{0}$). Show that there is a point of the body instantaneously at rest if and only if $\mathbf{V}$ is perpendicular to $\boldsymbol{\omega}$, and that in this case there is a line of points which are all instantaneously at rest.

7   The point $(4, 1, 2)$ of a rigid body is moving with velocity $\begin{bmatrix} 2 \\ 3 \\ -1 \end{bmatrix}$, and the angular

velocity is $\begin{bmatrix} 1 \\ 1 \\ 5 \end{bmatrix}$. Find the line of points which are instantaneously at rest.

8   Three point-elements A, B, C of a lamina moving in its own plane are such that their position vectors are given, as functions of time t, by

$$r_A = R(t)$$
$$r_B = R(t) + aS(t)$$
$$r_C = R(t) + bS'(t)$$

where $S(t)$ is a *unit* vector, $S'(t)$ is its derivative with respect to time, and a, b are constants.
   Prove that
   (a) the angle subtended by BC at A is a right-angle;
   (b) the magnitude of the body's angular velocity is constant.   [SMP]

9   A rigid body rotates about a fixed body point O with angular velocity ω. The moment of momentum about O is H_O, and the kinetic energy is T. Prove that $\omega . H_O = 2T$.

10   A point P is said to describe an 'epicyclic' path if it moves in a plane, round a circle centre Q whilst Q itself moves with constant speed round a circle with fixed centre O. Assuming OQ and QP rotate in the same direction with angular velocities in the ratio 1:4 sketch the epicyclic path of P.
   Fixed rectangular axes Oxy are taken in a plane, together with two concentric circles centre O and radii r, s respectively, $r > s$. A point A (x_A, y_A) moves round the outer circle at constant speed u, and a point B moves round the inner circle at constant speed v. Initially, at the time $t = 0$, $(x_A, y_A) = (r, 0)$ and $(x_B, y_B) = (s, 0)$. Show that the path of the point with coordinates $(x_A - x_B, y_A - y_B)$ is epicyclic.
   'Planets appear to observers on earth to stop and reverse their motions at regular intervals.' Comment.   [SMP]

11   The motion of a rigid body is given as in question 6. Prove that the point A for which $OA = a$ moves with velocity parallel to ω if and only if

$$\omega \times (V + \omega \times a) = 0.$$

Use Exercise 12C, question 13 to transform this equation, and hence to show that its solutions are

$$a = \frac{\omega \times V}{\omega^2} + \lambda\omega, \quad \text{where } \lambda \text{ is arbitrary.}$$

This shows that there is a line of points moving parallel to ω. The instantaneous motion of the body is therefore equivalent to a *screw motion* about this line. (Compare Exercise 11C, question 15.)

15.3   COMBINING ANGULAR VELOCITIES

Sometimes the motion of a rigid body is due to the combination of two or more simultaneous angular velocities.

For example, a system of rings (called gimbals) is often used to keep a ship's compass horizontal despite the motion of the ship. The compass is pivoted at A and B to the inner ring, which is itself pivoted at C and D to the outer ring fixed to the ship. Then as the ship moves the motion of the compass point relative to the ship is due to the simultaneous angular velocities about the compass spindle, the axis AB, and the axis CD (Fig. 4).

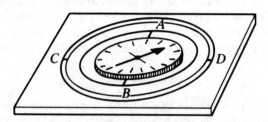

Figure 4

To deal with this sort of motion we first consider successive small rotations of a rigid body about a fixed point O. Suppose that the body turns first through a small angle $\delta\alpha$ about an axis defined by the unit vector $\hat{\mathbf{e}}$, and then through a small angle $\delta\beta$ about an axis $\hat{\mathbf{f}}$. Let the position vectors of the point R of the body be $\mathbf{r}$ initially, $\mathbf{r}_1$ after the first rotation, and $\mathbf{r}_2$ after the second rotation. The change of position during the first rotation is approximately $\delta\alpha|\mathbf{r}|\sin\theta$ in the direction perpendicular to both $\hat{\mathbf{e}}$ and $\mathbf{r}$ (Fig. 5; compare §15.1).

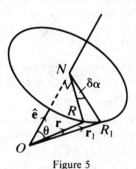

Figure 5

Therefore $\qquad\qquad\qquad \mathbf{r}_1 \approx \mathbf{r} + \delta\alpha\hat{\mathbf{e}} \times \mathbf{r}$.

Similarly $\qquad \mathbf{r}_2 \approx \mathbf{r}_1 + \delta\beta\hat{\mathbf{f}} \times \mathbf{r}_1$

$$= \mathbf{r} + \delta\alpha\hat{\mathbf{e}} \times \mathbf{r} + \delta\beta\hat{\mathbf{f}} \times (\mathbf{r} + \delta\alpha\hat{\mathbf{e}} \times \mathbf{r})$$

$$= \mathbf{r} + \delta\alpha\hat{\mathbf{e}} \times \mathbf{r} + \delta\beta\hat{\mathbf{f}} \times \mathbf{r} + \delta\beta\delta\alpha\hat{\mathbf{f}} \times (\hat{\mathbf{e}} \times \mathbf{r}).$$

Now suppose that these two rotations occur during a small time interval δt. Then

$$\frac{\mathbf{r}_2 - \mathbf{r}}{\delta t} = \left(\frac{\delta\alpha}{\delta t}\hat{\mathbf{e}} + \frac{\delta\beta}{\delta t}\hat{\mathbf{f}}\right) \times \mathbf{r} + \frac{\delta\alpha}{\delta t}\delta\beta\hat{\mathbf{f}} \times (\hat{\mathbf{e}} \times \mathbf{r}).$$

As $\delta t \to 0$ the final term vanishes and we have

$$\dot{\mathbf{r}} = (\boldsymbol{\omega}_1 + \boldsymbol{\omega}_2) \times \mathbf{r},$$

where $\qquad \boldsymbol{\omega}_1 = \dfrac{d\alpha}{dt}\hat{\mathbf{e}}$ and $\boldsymbol{\omega}_2 = \dfrac{d\beta}{dt}\hat{\mathbf{f}}$.

This shows that the effect of simultaneous angular velocities $\boldsymbol{\omega}_1$ and $\boldsymbol{\omega}_2$ is equivalent to the single angular velocity $\boldsymbol{\omega}_1 + \boldsymbol{\omega}_2$; in other words, angular velocities are added by normal vector addition. (But angular displacements may *not* be combined by vector addition; see Exercise 15C, question 1.)

Exercise 15C

1 The base vectors **i, j, k** are due south, due east, and vertically up respectively. A cube is placed with its centre at the origin O and its edges parallel to the base vectors. The face which faces south is marked *.
   (a) The cube is rotated about O
       (i) through 90° anticlockwise about **k**,
   then (ii) through 180° about **i**.
   Which direction does * now face?
   (b) Repeat (a), but with (ii) before (i).
   (c) Deduce that combination of successive rotations is not commutative, and so may not be represented by vector addition.

2 A rigid body has simultaneous angular velocities $\boldsymbol{\omega}_1 = \omega_1\hat{\mathbf{e}}$ and $\boldsymbol{\omega}_2 = \omega_2\hat{\mathbf{e}}$ about parallel axes through the points with position vectors $\mathbf{s}_1$ and $\mathbf{s}_2$. Prove that the velocity of the point with position vector $\mathbf{r}$ is

$$(\boldsymbol{\omega}_1 + \boldsymbol{\omega}_2) \times \left(\mathbf{r} - \frac{\omega_1\mathbf{s}_1 + \omega_2\mathbf{s}_2}{\omega_1 + \omega_2}\right).$$

Deduce that the motion is equivalent to an angular velocity $\boldsymbol{\omega}_1 + \boldsymbol{\omega}_2$ about a parallel axis, and describe the position of this axis in relation to $\mathbf{s}_1$ and $\mathbf{s}_2$. (Compare §8.5.)

3 What happens in question 2 if $\omega_1 + \omega_2 = 0$?

4 A rigid body is given simultaneous angular velocities $k\mathbf{AB}$, $k\mathbf{BC}$, $k\mathbf{CA}$, where ABC is any triangle. Prove that all points of the body have the same velocity.

5 A rigid cube is given simultaneous angular velocities of equal magnitude about all its twelve edges, those about parallel edges being in the same sense. Prove that the cube rotates about a diagonal.

6 To each point R of a rigid body there corresponds a point R^* whose *position* vector relative to a fixed origin equals the *velocity* vector of R. Prove that all the points R^* are coplanar.

15.4 ROTATING AXES

One of the basic assumptions of Newtonian mechanics is the existence of an *inertial frame of reference* with respect to which Newton's second law holds. A frame of reference with origin at the Sun and directions referred to the so-called fixed stars serves as a very good approximation to an inertial frame, at least as far as the solar system is concerned. But in many terrestrial applications the frame of reference moves with the earth, which is of course rotating relative to the fixed stars. To see the effect of this rotation we now extend the work of §15.2.

Let **i, j, k** be fixed base vectors of an inertial frame of reference $\mathscr{F}_0$, and let **I, J, K** be base vectors in a frame of reference $\mathscr{F}_1$ which has the same origin as $\mathscr{F}_0$ but rotates with constant angular velocity $\boldsymbol{\omega}$.

Consider the particle P with position vector

$$\mathbf{r} = x\mathbf{i} + y\mathbf{j} + z\mathbf{k} = X\mathbf{I} + Y\mathbf{J} + Z\mathbf{K};$$

this particle is not necessarily stationary in either frame of reference.

The velocity of P is

$$\dot{\mathbf{r}} = \dot{x}\mathbf{i} + \dot{y}\mathbf{j} + \dot{z}\mathbf{k}$$

$$= \dot{X}\mathbf{I} + \dot{Y}\mathbf{J} + \dot{Z}\mathbf{K} + X\dot{\mathbf{I}} + Y\dot{\mathbf{J}} + Z\dot{\mathbf{K}}$$

$$= \dot{\mathbf{R}} + \boldsymbol{\omega} \times \mathbf{r},$$

where $\dot{\mathbf{R}} = \dot{X}\mathbf{I} + \dot{Y}\mathbf{J} + \dot{Z}\mathbf{K}$ is the velocity of P *as seen by an observer moving* with $\mathscr{F}_1$. This means that the velocity of P is the sum of its velocity relative to $\mathscr{F}_1$ and the velocity of the point fixed in $\mathscr{F}_1$ which instantaneously coincides with P.

To find the corresponding result for the acceleration of P we differentiate again:

$$\ddot{\mathbf{r}} = (\ddot{X}\mathbf{I} + \ddot{Y}\mathbf{J} + \ddot{Z}\mathbf{K}) + 2(\dot{X}\dot{\mathbf{I}} + \dot{Y}\dot{\mathbf{J}} + \dot{Z}\dot{\mathbf{K}}) + (X\ddot{\mathbf{I}} + Y\ddot{\mathbf{J}} + Z\ddot{\mathbf{K}}).$$

Each of the three bracketed expressions can be simplified.

(a) $\ddot{X}\mathbf{I} + \ddot{Y}\mathbf{J} + \ddot{Z}\mathbf{K} = \ddot{\mathbf{R}}$, the acceleration of P as seen by an observer moving with $\mathscr{F}_1$.

(b) $2(\dot{X}\dot{\mathbf{I}} + \dot{Y}\dot{\mathbf{J}} + \dot{Z}\dot{\mathbf{K}}) = 2(\dot{X}\boldsymbol{\omega} \times \mathbf{I} + \dot{Y}\boldsymbol{\omega} \times \mathbf{J} + \dot{Z}\boldsymbol{\omega} \times \mathbf{K})$

$$= 2\boldsymbol{\omega} \times \dot{\mathbf{R}},$$

which is called the *Coriolis acceleration* after its discoverer G. Coriolis (1792–1843); this is proportional to the speed and at right angles to the direction of motion as seen by an observer moving with $\mathscr{F}_1$.

(c) $\dot{\mathbf{I}} = \boldsymbol{\omega} \times \mathbf{I} \Rightarrow \ddot{\mathbf{I}} = \boldsymbol{\omega} \times \dot{\mathbf{I}}$ (since $\boldsymbol{\omega}$ is constant)

$$= \boldsymbol{\omega} \times (\boldsymbol{\omega} \times \mathbf{I})$$

$$\Rightarrow X\ddot{\mathbf{I}} + Y\ddot{\mathbf{J}} + Z\ddot{\mathbf{K}} = \boldsymbol{\omega} \times (\boldsymbol{\omega} \times \mathbf{R}) = \boldsymbol{\omega} \times (\boldsymbol{\omega} \times \mathbf{r}),$$

which is the acceleration of the point fixed in $\mathscr{F}_1$ which instantaneously coincides with P (Exercise 15A, question 8).

Therefore $\qquad\qquad \ddot{\mathbf{r}} = \ddot{\mathbf{R}} + 2\boldsymbol{\omega} \times \dot{\mathbf{R}} + \boldsymbol{\omega} \times (\boldsymbol{\omega} \times \mathbf{r}).$

If the particle has mass m and is acted on by a force $\mathbf{F}$ then

$$\mathbf{F} = m\ddot{\mathbf{r}} = m\ddot{\mathbf{R}} + 2m\boldsymbol{\omega} \times \dot{\mathbf{R}} + m\boldsymbol{\omega} \times (\boldsymbol{\omega} \times \mathbf{r})$$

or $\qquad\qquad \mathbf{F} - 2m\boldsymbol{\omega} \times \dot{\mathbf{R}} - m\boldsymbol{\omega} \times (\boldsymbol{\omega} \times \mathbf{r}) = m\ddot{\mathbf{R}}.$

This means that an observer in the rotating frame $\mathscr{F}_1$ can work as if he were in an inertial frame provided that he adds to the force $\mathbf{F}$ the *Coriolis force* $-2m\boldsymbol{\omega} \times \dot{\mathbf{R}}$ and the *centrifugal force* $-m\boldsymbol{\omega} \times (\boldsymbol{\omega} \times \mathbf{r})$.

For the rotation of the Earth $\omega = \dfrac{2\pi}{24 \times 36\,000} \approx 7.27 \times 10^{-5}$ rad s^{-1} so for local applications in which r is not large the centrifugal force is negligible. The Coriolis force is also usually small, but it is important in the movement of the atmosphere. It is found that for a particle of air with horizontal velocity $\mathbf{v}$ the Coriolis acceleration $2\boldsymbol{\omega} \times \mathbf{v}$ is the most important term in the acceleration. The dominant force is the pressure force $\mathbf{F}$ directed from high pressure to low. So a first approximation for the equation of motion is

$$\mathbf{F} \approx 2m\boldsymbol{\omega} \times \mathbf{v}.$$

From this it follows that $\mathbf{v}$ is perpendicular to $\mathbf{F}$, so that the wind blows *along* the isobars (lines of equal pressure) and not from high pressure to low pressure as might have been expected (Fig. 6).

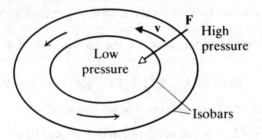

Figure 6

Q.2   By considering the direction of $\boldsymbol{\omega}$ show that winds blow anticlockwise round centres of low pressure in the northern hemisphere, but clockwise in the southern hemisphere.

Exercise 15D

1   A pendulum bob hangs at rest relative to the Earth at a point on the Earth's surface with latitude 50 °N. Find the angle between the pendulum string and the true vertical.

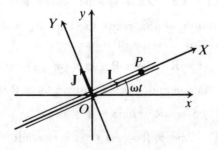

Figure 7

2 Coordinate axes OXY are rotating in a vertical plane about a horizontal axis through O with constant angular velocity ω (Fig. 7). Show that if

$$\mathbf{I} = \begin{bmatrix} \cos \omega t \\ \sin \omega t \end{bmatrix}, \qquad \mathbf{J} = \begin{bmatrix} -\sin \omega t \\ \cos \omega t \end{bmatrix}$$

are unit vectors rotating with these axes then

$$\frac{d\mathbf{I}}{dt} = \omega \mathbf{J}, \qquad \frac{d\mathbf{J}}{dt} = -\omega \mathbf{I}.$$

A particle P of mass m is free to move without friction along the axis OX inside a thin hollow tube rotating with OX. Show that when P has position vector $\mathbf{r} = X\mathbf{I}$, its velocity and acceleration are

$$\dot{\mathbf{r}} = \dot{X}\mathbf{I} + \omega X\mathbf{J}, \qquad \ddot{\mathbf{r}} = (\ddot{X} - \omega^2 X)\mathbf{I} + 2\omega \dot{X}\mathbf{J}.$$

Assuming that the only forces acting on P are a normal reaction $N\mathbf{J}$ from the tube, and a gravitational force mg acting vertically downwards, deduce that the motion of P satisfies the equation

$$\ddot{X} - \omega^2 X = -g \sin \omega t.$$

Find a particular solution of this equation which represents a simple harmonic motion of P.   [SMP]

3 A particle is free to move in a smooth straight tube. The tube is inclined at an acute angle α to the upward vertical, and rotates with angular velocity ω about a vertical axis through its lower end O.
(a) Find the distance from O of the point A of the tube at which the particle could remain at rest relative to the tube.
(b) Show that the motion of the particle relative to the tube is the same as if the tube were stationary and the particle were repelled from A by a force proportional to its distance from A.

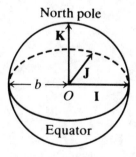

Figure 8

4 Consider the motion of a mass m of air near a point P on the Equator, given that the Earth rotates at angular velocity $\mathbf{\Omega} = \Omega \mathbf{k}$ along the line joining the poles. Take the centre of the Earth O as origin, use unit vectors $\mathbf{I}$, $\mathbf{J}$, $\mathbf{K}$ as in Fig. 8, and let b be the radius of the Earth. Let the mass of air have position vector $(X + b)\mathbf{I} + Y\mathbf{J} + Z\mathbf{K}$ and let a total force $F\mathbf{J}$ act on it. Find equations for $\ddot{Y}$ and $\ddot{Z}$.

[SMP, part]

5   With the notation of question 4, suppose that a particle falls from rest from the point
$(h + b)\mathbf{I}$ above the equator. Obtain the equations

$$\ddot{X} - 2\Omega\dot{Y} - \Omega^2(X + b) = -g$$
$$\ddot{Y} + 2\Omega\dot{X} - \Omega^2 Y = 0$$
$$\ddot{Z} = 0.$$

In these equations $\Omega^2 X$ and $\Omega^2 Y$ are negligible, and so is $\Omega^2 b$ in comparison with g.
Obtain the solutions $X = h - \frac{1}{2}gt^2$, $Y = \frac{1}{3}\Omega gt^3$, $Z = 0$. Deduce that the point where
the particle reaches the Earth is about $\frac{1}{3}\Omega g\left(\dfrac{2h}{g}\right)^{3/2}$ due east of the point vertically
below its initial position. How far is this when $h = 100$ m?

16

Rigid body dynamics

16.1 THE EQUATIONS OF MOTION FOR A RIGID BODY

Since a rigid body is an important special case of a system of particles, the results of Chapter 14 can be used to solve a wide variety of problems involving the motion of rigid bodies. We shall deal only with two-dimensional motion, in which all parts of the body move parallel to a plane, since an adequate discussion of general three-dimensional motion is beyond the scope of this book. These applications rest on two basic results from Chapter 14:

(1) the equation of linear motion (§14.1)

$$\mathbf{F} = M\ddot{\mathbf{r}}$$

total external force = total mass × acceleration of mass centre G;

(2) the equation of rotational motion (§14.2)

$$\mathbf{L}_C = \dot{\mathbf{H}}_C$$

moment of external forces about C = rate of change of moment of momentum about C provided that C is

(a) a fixed point O

or (b) the mass centre G

or (c) a point whose velocity is parallel to that of G (Exercise 14B, question 8).

Here 'moment about C' means of course 'moment about the axis through C perpendicular to the plane of motion'. Cases (a) and (b) are really special examples of (c), but they are used so frequently that it is worth drawing attention to them.

For a rigid lamina rotating in its plane with angular velocity $\boldsymbol{\omega}$ about a fixed axis through O we have

$$\dot{\mathbf{r}}_i = \boldsymbol{\omega} \times \mathbf{r}_i \qquad \text{(Fig. 1)}.$$

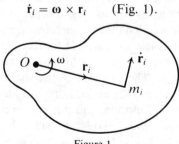

Figure 1

Therefore

$$\mathbf{H}_O = \sum \mathbf{r}_i \times m_i(\boldsymbol{\omega} \times \mathbf{r}_i)$$

$$= \sum m_i \mathbf{r}_i \times (\boldsymbol{\omega} \times \mathbf{r}_i)$$

$$= \sum m_i((\mathbf{r}_i \cdot \mathbf{r}_i)\boldsymbol{\omega} - (\mathbf{r}_i \cdot \boldsymbol{\omega})\mathbf{r}_i) \quad \text{using Exercise 12C, question 13}$$

$$= \sum m_i r_i^2 \boldsymbol{\omega} \quad \text{since } \mathbf{r}_i \text{ is perpendicular to } \boldsymbol{\omega}.$$

Thus
$$\mathbf{H}_O = I_O \boldsymbol{\omega},$$

where I_O is the MI of the lamina about the axis through O.

The same result applies for a rigid body rotating about a fixed axis, as can be shown by splitting the body into laminas perpendicular to the axis.

The equation of rotational motion now takes the form

$$\mathbf{L}_O = \dot{\mathbf{H}}_O = I_O \dot{\boldsymbol{\omega}}.$$

Since the vectors $\mathbf{L}_O$, $\boldsymbol{\omega}$ and $\dot{\boldsymbol{\omega}}$ are all in the fixed direction perpendicular to the plane of motion, the importance of this result lies in the scalar equation

$$L_O = I_O \dot{\omega}$$

which is familiar from §10.2.

If we take moments about the parallel axis through the mass centre G then, replacing $\mathbf{r}_i$ by $\boldsymbol{\rho}_i$ in the working given above, we obtain

$$\mathbf{H}_G = I_G \boldsymbol{\omega}$$

and hence
$$\mathbf{L}_G = I_G \dot{\boldsymbol{\omega}}.$$

The alternative form
$$\mathbf{H}_O = \bar{\mathbf{H}}_O + \mathbf{H}_G$$

can now be written as
$$\mathbf{H}_O = \bar{\mathbf{r}} \times M\dot{\bar{\mathbf{r}}} + I_G \boldsymbol{\omega},$$

from which
$$\dot{\mathbf{H}}_O = \frac{d}{dt}(\bar{\mathbf{r}} \times M\dot{\bar{\mathbf{r}}}) + I_G \dot{\boldsymbol{\omega}}$$

$$= \dot{\bar{\mathbf{r}}} \times M\dot{\bar{\mathbf{r}}} + \bar{\mathbf{r}} \times M\ddot{\bar{\mathbf{r}}} + I_G \dot{\boldsymbol{\omega}}.$$

Since
$$\dot{\bar{\mathbf{r}}} \times M\dot{\bar{\mathbf{r}}} = 0 \quad \text{and} \quad \mathbf{L}_O = \dot{\mathbf{H}}_O$$

this gives
$$\mathbf{L}_O = \bar{\mathbf{r}} \times M\ddot{\bar{\mathbf{r}}} + I_G \dot{\boldsymbol{\omega}}.$$

This equation, together with $\mathbf{F} = M\ddot{\bar{\mathbf{r}}}$, leads to a convenient way of dealing with rigid body problems. We consider two systems of vectors. One is the set of external forces. The other is called the *mass-acceleration* system (Note 16.1). This consists of the mass-acceleration vector $M\ddot{\bar{\mathbf{r}}}$ localised to act through the mass centre G, together with the *spin couple* formed of vectors which have zero resultant and moment $I_G \dot{\boldsymbol{\omega}}$. The moment of the spin couple $I_G \dot{\boldsymbol{\omega}}$ is the same about any point (as in §11.6, p. 182), and is not a localised vector; its direction is perpendicular to the plane of motion, and it is shown in diagrams as in Fig. 2.

These two systems have equal resultants, since $\mathbf{F} = M\ddot{\bar{\mathbf{r}}}$, and have equal moments about O, since $\mathbf{L}_O = \mathbf{r} \times M\ddot{\bar{\mathbf{r}}} + I_G \dot{\boldsymbol{\omega}}$. Therefore, as in §11.6, p. 181, the

Force:

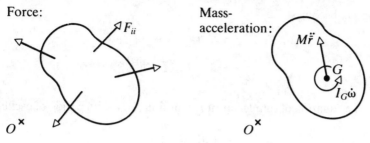

Mass-acceleration:

Figure 2

systems have equal moments about any point, and so:

| The external force system and the mass-acceleration system are equivalent. |

The equivalence of these comparatively simple systems gives a straightforward way of dealing with problems involving two-dimensional rigid body motion, as illustrated in Example 1 (which includes finding the reaction at a fixed axis) and Example 2 (where there is no fixed axis).

Example 1

A rigid body is free to swing about a fixed horizontal axis. Investigate the motion and the reaction at the axis.

Solution

The first step is to draw separate diagrams of the force and mass-acceleration systems (Fig. 3):

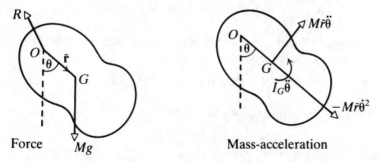

Force

Mass-acceleration

Figure 3

The forces are the weight Mg and the reaction $\mathbf{R}$ at the axis. The mass-acceleration $M\ddot{\bar{r}}$ is shown in radial and transverse components. Taking moments about O gives the angular acceleration directly (Note 16.2):

$$\bar{\mathbf{r}} \times M\mathbf{g} = I_0\ddot{\theta}\hat{\mathbf{e}}, \quad \text{where } \hat{\mathbf{e}} \text{ is perpendicular to the plane of motion,}$$

$$\Rightarrow -Mg\bar{r}\sin\theta = I_0\ddot{\theta}. \tag{1}$$

If θ remains small throughout the motion we can approximate $\sin\theta$ by θ; then equation (1) becomes

$$-Mg\bar{r}\theta = I_O\ddot{\theta}$$

or

$$\ddot{\theta} = \frac{-Mg\bar{r}\theta}{I_O},$$

which is the equation of simple harmonic motion (§1.4) with period of oscillation

$$2\pi\sqrt{\left(\frac{I_O}{Mgr}\right)}.$$

Whether or not θ is small we can replace $\ddot{\theta}$ by $\dot{\theta}\dfrac{d\dot{\theta}}{d\theta}$ in (1), and then integrate both sides with respect to θ to obtain

$$Mg\bar{r}\cos\theta = \tfrac{1}{2}I_O\dot{\theta}^2 + C.$$

The constant of integration, C, depends on the initial conditions. In particular, if $\theta = \alpha$ when $\dot{\theta} = 0$ then $C = Mg\bar{r}\cos\alpha$, and

$$\tfrac{1}{2}I_O\dot{\theta}^2 = Mg\bar{r}(\cos\theta - \cos\alpha).$$

(Note that this could have been obtained by using conservation of energy.)

To find the reaction $\mathbf{R}$ we use the equation of linear motion:

$$\mathbf{R} + M\mathbf{g} = M\ddot{\mathbf{r}} = M(-\bar{r}\dot{\theta}^2\hat{\mathbf{r}} + \bar{r}\ddot{\theta}\hat{\mathbf{u}}).$$

Using the expression for $\dot{\theta}^2$ and $\ddot{\theta}$ obtained above gives

$$\mathbf{R} = \frac{M^2g\bar{r}^2}{I_O}[-2(\cos\theta - \cos\alpha)\hat{\mathbf{r}} - \sin\theta\hat{\mathbf{u}}] - M\mathbf{g}.$$

From this we can find the component of $\mathbf{R}$ in any chosen direction. For example, the component of $\mathbf{R}$ perpendicular to OG is

$$\mathbf{R}_u = Mg\sin\theta(1 - M\bar{r}^2/I_O)\hat{\mathbf{u}}. \qquad \square$$

Q.1   Find the component of $\mathbf{R}$ along OG.

Example 2
A uniform circular disc of radius a and mass M rolls down a ramp of gradient $\tan\alpha$.

(*a*) If it does not slip, find the acceleration.

(*b*) If the coefficient of friction μ is less than the value needed to prevent slipping, find the linear and angular accelerations.

Solution
Let the normal contact force be $\mathbf{N}$ and the friction force $\mathbf{F}$, and let $\mathbf{R} = \mathbf{N} + \mathbf{F}$. Let P be the point of contact, with $\mathbf{GP} = \mathbf{a}$ (Fig. 4). There is no convenient fixed

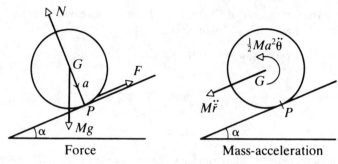

Force   Mass-acceleration

Figure 4

point to take as O, so we take moments about G. The equations of motion are

linear $\qquad\qquad$ $\mathbf{R} + M\mathbf{g} = M\ddot{\mathbf{r}}$

rotational $\qquad\qquad$ $\mathbf{a} \times \mathbf{R} = \tfrac{1}{2}Ma^2\ddot{\theta}\hat{\mathbf{e}}.$

Without further information we cannot solve for $\mathbf{R}$, $\ddot{\mathbf{r}}$ and θ since $\ddot{\mathbf{r}}$ and θ are independent for a body which is not pivoted.

(a) If there is no slipping then the point of the disc at P must be momentarily stationary. Therefore

$$\dot{r} - a\dot{\theta} = 0 \quad \text{(the rolling condition)},$$

and hence $\ddot{r} = a\ddot{\theta}$. Substituting for $\mathbf{R}$ and $a\ddot{\theta}$ in the rotational equation gives

$$\mathbf{a} \times (M\ddot{\mathbf{r}} - M\mathbf{g}) = \tfrac{1}{2}Ma\ddot{r}\hat{\mathbf{e}}$$

$$\Rightarrow -Ma\ddot{r} + Mga\sin\alpha = \tfrac{1}{2}Ma\ddot{r}$$

$$\Rightarrow \qquad\qquad \ddot{r} = \tfrac{2}{3}g\sin\alpha.$$

(b) If there is slipping with coefficient of friction μ then $F = \mu N$. Taking components of the linear equation perpendicular to and parallel to the slope gives

$$N - Mg\cos\alpha = 0$$

and $\qquad\qquad$ $-F + Mg\sin\alpha = M\ddot{r},$

so $\qquad\quad$ $F = \mu N \Rightarrow M\ddot{r} - Mg\sin\alpha = -\mu Mg\cos\alpha$

$$\Rightarrow \qquad\qquad \ddot{r} = g(\sin\alpha - \mu\cos\alpha).$$

The rotational equation gives

$$aF = \tfrac{1}{2}Ma^2\ddot{\theta}$$

$$\Rightarrow \ddot{\theta} = 2(-M\ddot{r} + Mg\sin\alpha)/Ma$$

$$= 2\mu g\cos\alpha/a.$$

The minimum coefficient of friction needed to prevent slipping is the one for which $a\ddot{\theta} = \ddot{r}$, which is $\tfrac{1}{3}\tan\alpha$. $\qquad\qquad\qquad\square$

Q.2   Show that the result of Example 2(a) can be obtained directly by taking moments about the point of contact P.

Q.3   Check that putting $\mu = 0$ in the results of Example 2(b) gives what you would expect.

Exercise 16A

1   Draw two diagrams in each of the following cases, one to show the external forces, the other to show the mass-accelerations.

   (a) A uniform hoop of radius r and mass M hangs over a horizontal knife edge, and is allowed to make small oscillations in a plane perpendicular to the knife edge.

   (b) A uniform square plate of side l and mass M, freely pivoted about the horizontal axis through one corner at right angles to the plane of the plate, is released from rest when an edge through the pivot is vertically down. Take the position at time t when the angle turned through is θ.

   (c) A uniform cylinder of radius a and mass m has a light string wrapped around its circumference with one end attached to the cylinder. The cylinder can turn freely about its axis, which is horizontal. A mass m is attached to the other end of the string, and is released from rest when the string is just taut.

   (d) A compound pendulum consists of a uniform disc of mass $4m$ and radius a and a uniform rod of mass m and length $4a$ attached to the circumference of the disc so that one end of the rod is $5a$ from the centre of the disc. The pendulum is pivoted about this end of the rod and swings freely in the plane of the disc. Take the angle turned through to be θ at time t from the equilibrium position.

2   Use the results of question 1 as follows:
   in (a) find the period of small oscillations;
   in (b) find the vertical component of the force on the pivot at the lowest part of the swing;
   in (c) find the acceleration of the mass and the reaction at the pivot;
   in (d) find the period of small oscillations, and the horizontal component of the reaction at the pivot when the pendulum is vertical.

3   At a fairground sideshow coins are rolled down an inclined track in an attempt to gain prizes. Take the coin to be a disc of mass m and radius a, and the track to have side walls of height $\frac{1}{4}a$, and to be inclined to the horizontal at angle α. The track is made of rough material which provides a frictional force at the rim of the coin sufficient to ensure rolling, and another frictional force which acts at the point A of Fig. 5 in a direction opposed to the local motion and with amount $\frac{1}{10}mg$ when

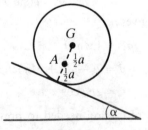

Figure 5

motion is taking place. The plane of the coin is vertical. Find equation(s) for the motion of the coin down the track and find the acceleration of the centre of the coin. What is the least angle of inclination at which motion will take place? [SMP]

4 The upper end A of a uniform rigid rod of length $2a$ and mass m is forced to move along the parabola

$$(x, y) = (2ap, ap^2)$$

in such a way that $\dot{p} = c$, a constant. The force required to give this motion acts at A, and has components F and G as shown; otherwise the rod swings freely under gravity. The angle between the rod and the vertical at time t is θ, as shown in Fig. 6. Show that the position of the centre of mass of the rod is given by the coordinates

$$(2ap + a \sin \theta, ap^2 - a \cos \theta).$$

Hence find three equations involving F, G, θ (and its derivatives) which could be used to determine the motion of the rod. [SMP]

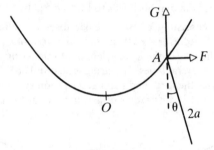

Figure 6

5 A cylinder rotating about its axis, which is horizontal, with angular velocity ω is lowered gently onto a flat rough table and immediately released. Its radius is r and its moment of inertia about the axis is I. As long as slipping persists at the line of contact, the force of friction is given by the expression μmg, where m is the mass of the cylinder and μ is constant. At a time t after the cylinder is placed on the table, but before slipping stops at the line of contact, find
(a) the velocity of the axis of the cylinder;
(b) the angular velocity of the cylinder;
(c) the velocity of the particles of the cylinder in contact with the table.
Hence show that, after a time $Ir\omega/\{\mu g(I + mr^2)\}$, slipping ceases. Describe the motion of the cylinder after this time, and draw a graph showing the velocity of the axis of the cylinder as a function of the time for $t > 0$. [SMP]

6 A vertical circular hoop of radius r and mass m is projected in its plane along a rough horizontal surface with velocity U. The coefficient of friction is μ. Find when slipping ceases and what the final velocity of the hoop is
(a) when the initial angular velocity is zero;
(b) when the hoop initially has 'back spin' of angular velocity Ω.
In (b) describe the motion in three cases (i) $U > r\Omega$, (ii) $U = r\Omega$, (iii) $U < r\Omega$.

7 A heavy dumbbell, of mass M and moment of inertia I about its axis of symmetry, consists of two heavy discs of radius a rigidly connected by an axle of radius b: it rests on a very rough horizontal floor. A rope is fixed on the axle and wound round it several times, leaving it from the underside and pulled with a steady horizontal force P. The force and mass-acceleration diagrams are illustrated in Fig. 7 (i) and (ii)

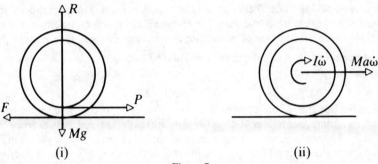

(i)   (ii)

Figure 7

respectively. By taking moments about a suitable axis, or otherwise, obtain an equation of the form $A\dot{\omega} = Pd$. Give A in terms of M, I and a, and give d in terms of a and b. State whether the dumbbell will roll to the right or to the left.   [SMP]

8   A yo-yo is a toy consisting of two circular discs of radius R fixed to a short cylindrical axle of radius r ($<R$) so that the resulting object has rotational symmetry about the axis of the axle. A length of thin string is attached to the axle and wound round it several times. The string is held still and the yo-yo released from rest: Fig. 8 illustrates the force and mass-acceleration systems, where m is the total mass of the yo-yo and k is its radius of gyration about the axis of symmetry.

Figure 8

Show that, if the string is initially vertical, then it remains so while unwinding. State a relationship between the linear acceleration a and the angular acceleration $\dot{\omega}$, and show that

$$\dot{\omega} = \frac{gr}{r^2 + k^2}.$$

In order to keep the yo-yo going it is customary to give the string an upward acceleration. Assuming that the string is given a constant upward acceleration f, find the angular and linear acceleration of the yo-yo and show that the tension in the string is

$$\frac{m(g + f)k^2}{r^2 + k^2}.$$ [SMP]

9   A uniform circular disc can spin freely in a vertical plane about a horizontal axis through a point on its circumference. Show that if the disc is to make complete revolutions then the supports of the axis must be able to bear at least 11/3 times the weight of the disc.

10   A train door has mass M, width $2k$ and moment of inertia I about its hinge. The hinge is on the leading edge of the door (assumed to be vertical), and the door is partly open when the train starts from rest with constant acceleration a. If the hinge is smooth, show that the acute angle θ between the door and the side of the train satisfies the equation

$$\ddot{\theta} = -\frac{Mka}{I}\sin\theta.$$

Using $\ddot{\theta} = \dot{\theta}\dfrac{d\dot{\theta}}{d\theta}$, find the angular velocity of the door when it shuts, in terms of M, k, a, I and θ_0 (the initial value of θ).

Suppose now that friction at the hinge can produce a maximum resisting couple of moment L. Show that the door will not begin to shut unless

$$a > \frac{L}{Mk\sin\theta_0}.$$

If this condition is satisfied, what is the initial angular acceleration of the door?

11   Fig. 9 shows the mass-acceleration of a particle of mass m_i at P in the form obtained by expressing the acceleration of P as the acceleration of the mass centre G plus the acceleration of P relative to G, given in radial and transverse components.

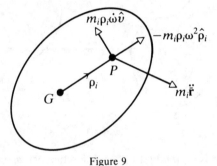

Figure 9

Explain why, when these mass-acceleration vectors are summed for the whole body,
(a) the $m_i\ddot{\mathbf{r}}$ vectors are equivalent to a vector $M\ddot{\mathbf{r}}$ localised through G,
(b) the $-m_i\rho_i\omega^2\hat{\boldsymbol{\rho}}_i$ vectors are in equilibrium,
(c) the $m_i\rho_i\dot{\omega}\hat{\boldsymbol{v}}$ vectors produce a spin couple of moment $I_G\dot{\omega}$.
(This gives a direct proof that the mass-acceleration system of §16.1 is equivalent to the system of mass-acceleration vectors of the particles which form the body.)

16.2 IMPULSE–MOMENTUM EQUATIONS FOR A RIGID BODY

We recall from §14.3 that a jerk is the impulse of a large force acting for a short time, during which the change of position of the point of application is negligible.

When a system is subject to external jerks $\mathbf{J}_i$

$$\sum \mathbf{J}_i = [\mathbf{P}]$$

sum of external jerks = change of linear momentum

and
$$\sum \mathbf{r}_i \times \mathbf{J}_i = [\mathbf{H}_O]$$

sum of moments of external jerks = change of moment of momentum about O.

For a rigid body we know that
$$\mathbf{P} = M\bar{\mathbf{v}}$$

and
$$\mathbf{H}_O = \bar{\mathbf{H}}_O + \mathbf{H}_G = \bar{\mathbf{r}} \times M\bar{\mathbf{v}} + I_G\boldsymbol{\omega}.$$

Therefore in solving problems we can use the idea of equivalent systems of vectors, as in §16.1. In this case one system is the set of external jerks. The other system consists of the momentum vector $M\bar{\mathbf{v}}$ localised to act through the mass centre of G, together with vectors which form the momentum-couple $I_G\boldsymbol{\omega}$, representing the moment of momentum about G; this is called the *momentum system* (Fig. 10).

Jerk: Momentum:

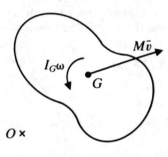

Figure 10

Then the jerk system is equivalent to the difference between the final and initial momentum systems.

Example 3

A uniform square plate of mass M and side $2a$ is at rest on a smooth horizontal table. It is struck at one corner A by a blow of impulse J in the direction of one of its edges. Find the velocity of A immediately after the blow.

Solution

Jerk:

Initial momentum: null
Final momentum:

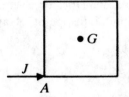
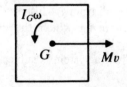

Figure 11

Since there was no motion before the blow, the jerk system is equivalent to the final momentum system (Fig. 11). Therefore the mass centre moves in the direction of the blow with velocity $\bar{\mathbf{v}}$, where

$$\mathbf{J} = M\bar{\mathbf{v}}, \quad \text{so that } \bar{\mathbf{v}} = \mathbf{J}/M.$$

Also $I_G = \frac{2}{3}Ma^2$ (Exercise 9C, question 1) so, taking moments about G,

$$aJ = \tfrac{2}{3}Ma^2\omega \Rightarrow \omega = 3J/2Ma.$$

After the blow A has velocity $\mathbf{U}$, the vector sum of the velocity of G and the velocity of A relative to G. The latter has magnitude

$$\sqrt{2}a\omega = \sqrt{2}a \cdot \frac{3J}{2Ma} = \sqrt{2} \cdot \tfrac{3}{2}\bar{v},$$

and is perpendicular to GA (Fig. 12), so its components parallel to and perpendicular to $\bar{\mathbf{v}}$ are each of magnitude $\frac{3}{2}\bar{v}$ (Fig. 13).

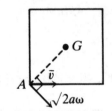

Figure 12

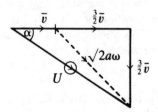

Figure 13

Therefore

$$U^2 = (\tfrac{5}{2}\bar{v})^2 + (\tfrac{3}{2}\bar{v})^2$$

$$U = \frac{\sqrt{34}}{2}\bar{v} = \frac{\sqrt{34}J}{2M},$$

and the direction of $\mathbf{U}$ makes an angle $\alpha = \tan^{-1} 0.6 \approx 31°$ with the side of the square.

(Note that A does *not* move in the direction of the blow.)   □

Example 4

A uniform rod AB, of mass M and length $2a$, rotates with angular velocity ω about the end A, which is fixed. It is brought to rest by colliding with an inelastic stop S at a distance $a + x$ from A. Find the impulses on the rod at S and A.

Solution
Let the impulses at S and A be **J** and **K** respectively as shown in Fig. 14.

Jerk:

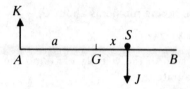

Initial momentum:

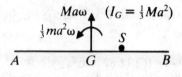

Final momentum: null

Figure 14

Taking moments about A (with anticlockwise sense positive):

$$- (a + x)J = 0 - (\tfrac{1}{3}Ma^2\omega + a.Ma\omega)$$

$$\Rightarrow J = \frac{4Ma^2\omega}{3(a + x)}.$$

Taking moments about S:

$$-(a + x)K = 0 - (\tfrac{1}{3}Ma^2\omega - x.Ma\omega)$$

$$\Rightarrow K = \frac{Ma\omega(a - 3x)}{3(a + x)}.$$

Notice that if $x = \tfrac{1}{3}a$ then $K = 0$; there is then no jar at the hinge A when the rod is stopped. In this case the position of S is called the *centre of percussion* (see Exercise 16B, question 3). This shows why a door stop should be fixed two-thirds of the way across the width of a door. □

Example 5
A uniform disc of radius a is rolling without slipping along a smooth horizontal plane with speed U when its highest point suddenly becomes fixed. Find the speed of its centre immediately after this.

Solution

Initial momentum: Final momentum:

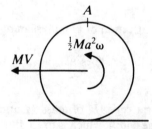

Figure 15

Since the plane is smooth the only jerk is at the highest point A. The moment of momentum about A is therefore unchanged by the jerk, so with the notation of Fig. 15

$$\tfrac{1}{2}Ma^2\omega_0 - aMU = \tfrac{1}{2}Ma^2\omega - aMV.$$

Since the disc is initially rolling,

$$a\omega_0 = U$$

Since A is at rest after the disc is seized,

$$a\omega = -V.$$

Hence
$$\tfrac{1}{2}MaU - aMU = -\tfrac{1}{2}MaV - aMV$$

$$\Rightarrow V = U/3. \qquad\qquad \square$$

Exercise 16B

1   A uniform rod AB of mass M and length $2a$, at rest on a smooth horizontal table, is set in motion by simultaneous horizontal jerks J, K applied at right angles to the rod in the same sense at A and B. Find the velocities with which A and B start to move.

2   Two equal uniform rods AB, BC, each of mass M and length $2a$, are freely jointed at B. Initially A, B, C are in a straight line and are at rest on a smooth horizontal table. A horizontal jerk J is applied at A perpendicular to AB. Find the velocity with which C begins to move.

3   A rigid lamina with mass centre G is free to rotate in its plane about a fixed point O. It is set in motion by an impulse of magnitude J acting at a point A on the line OG in the direction at right angles to OG. Let $OA = a$, $OG = h$, and let k be the radius of gyration about G.
   (i) Find the impulsive reaction at the support in terms of a, h, k, J.
   (ii) Show that this reaction is zero if $a = h + k^2/h$. In this case A is the *centre of percussion*.
   (iii) If A is the centre of percussion when the lamina is suspended from O, show that
      (*a*) a simple pendulum of length OA has the same period of free oscillation as the lamina;
      (*b*) O is the centre of percussion when the lamina is suspended from A.

4   A rod is at rest on a smooth table when it is struck by a horizontal blow at right angles to its length at a point P. Prove that the rod begins to turn about the centre of percussion corresponding to the point P.

5   A uniform horizontal rod AB of length $2a$ is falling without rotation. When it has speed U the end A is suddenly fixed. What is the speed of B immediately after this?

6   A rectangular lamina $ABCD$, as shown in Fig. 16, has mass m and is lying at rest on a smooth table when it is set in motion by an impulsive force J acting at A in a direction perpendicular to AC (as shown).

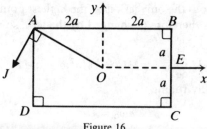

Figure 16

Show that the angular velocity of the lamina in its subsequent motion is

$$\omega = 3J/(ma\sqrt{5}).$$

Let Oxy be coordinate axes fixed in space and directed so that the sides of the lamina are initially parallel to them as shown. Find the components of the velocity of the centroid of the lamina. Hence, or otherwise, show that the x-coordinate of the point E of the lamina after a time t is

$$2a \cos \omega t - Jt/(m\sqrt{5}). \qquad \text{[SMP]}$$

7   A heavy metal ball of radius a is spinning with angular velocity ω about a horizontal axis when it is dropped vertically on to a horizontal plane surface. Assuming there is no slipping and no rebound, show that the ball rolls over the surface with speed $v = 2\omega a/7$.   [SMP]

8   A penny of mass m travelling with speed v slides along a smooth table and hits a square sheet of cardboard, mass M and side a, at one corner in the direction of one edge. Describe the subsequent motion of the cardboard on the assumption that $e = \frac{1}{2}$ (that is, assume the relative velocity of separation of the points of impact perpendicular to the surfaces which impact equals half the relative velocity of approach).

9   Two equal uniform rods AB, BC, each of mass M and length $2a$, are at rest on a smooth horizontal table, with AB at right angles to BC. A horizontal jerk J is applied at A in the direction of BC. Find the velocity with which C begins to move
   (i) if the rods are rigidly connected at B;
   (ii) if the rods are freely jointed at B.

10   A uniform rod of length l and mass m rests symmetrically on a pair of pegs A, B (which should be assumed to be rough and inelastic) a distance d apart at the same level. The end further from A is raised a small distance (so that the rod turns about A through a small angle) and is then released; just before the rod hits B again it is rotating about A with angular velocity ω. Write down an expression for the moment of momentum of the rod about B at this instant.

   Show that if l is considerably greater than d then immediately after the impact the rod will be rotating about B with angular velocity

$$\frac{l^2 - 3d^2}{l^2 + 3d^2}\,\omega.$$

Describe the subsequent motion of the rod in this case.

   Show that, on the other hand, if l is only slightly greater than d, there will be no further motion after the impact. Explain what happens to the moment of momentum about B at the impact in this case, and why. What is the critical value of l?

     [SMP]

16.3 WORK-ENERGY EQUATIONS FOR A RIGID BODY

In §14.5 we found that the equation

total work done by external forces = change of kinetic energy

holds for rigid bodies, but not necessarily for non-rigid systems. In order to make use of this we need to be able to find the kinetic energy T of a rigid body. We have already found in §9.1 that if the body is turning about a fixed axis through O with angular speed ω then $T = \frac{1}{2}I_O\omega^2$, where I_O is the moment of inertia about this axis. If there is no fixed axis we use

$$T = \bar{T} + T_G$$

where $\qquad \bar{T} = \frac{1}{2}M\dot{\bar{r}}^2 \quad$ and $\quad T_G = \sum \frac{1}{2}m_i\dot{\rho}_i^2$

(see §14.5).

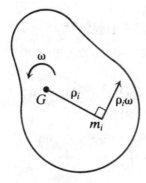

Figure 17

For a rigid body with angular speed ω, the speed of m_i relative to the mass centre G is $\rho_i\omega$ (Fig. 17), and so

$$T_G = \sum \tfrac{1}{2}m_i\rho_i^2\omega^2 = \tfrac{1}{2}I_G\omega^2.$$

Thus $\qquad\qquad\qquad T = \frac{1}{2}M\dot{\bar{r}}^2 + \frac{1}{2}I_G\omega^2$

If the only external forces which do work are the weights of the body's component particles, then, as in §10.1, the work done when the body moves equals the loss of potential energy Mgz. In this case

kinetic energy + potential energy = constant.

Example 6
Solve Example 2(*a*) again by considering energy.

Solution
The external forces acting on the disc are its weight Mg and the contact force $\mathbf{R}$ (Fig. 18). Since the disc is rolling without slipping the point of contact P is instantaneously at rest, and so $\mathbf{R}$, which acts at P, does no work.

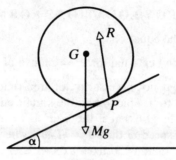

Figure 18

Let the speed of G be $\bar{v}$ when the disc has rolled a distance x down the slope from rest. The angular speed is then $\bar{v}/a$ (the rolling condition), and the kinetic energy gained is

$$\tfrac{1}{2}M\bar{v}^2 + \tfrac{1}{2}\cdot\tfrac{1}{2}Ma^2(\bar{v}/a)^2 = \tfrac{3}{4}M\bar{v}^2.$$

The centre of the disc changes height by $x \sin \alpha$, so the work done by the weight is $Mgx \sin \alpha$. Therefore

$$\tfrac{3}{4}M\bar{v}^2 = Mgx \sin \alpha.$$

Differentiating with respect to time,

$$\tfrac{3}{2}M\bar{v}\dot{\bar{v}} = Mg\bar{v} \sin \alpha, \quad \text{since } \dot{x} = \bar{v}.$$

Hence $\ddot{r} = \dot{\bar{v}} = \tfrac{2}{3}g \sin \alpha$, as before.   □

Example 7
A uniform solid cylinder of mass M and radius a rolls without slipping inside a hollow cylinder of radius $5a$ which is fixed with its axis horizontal. Find the period of small oscillations about the lowest position.

Solution

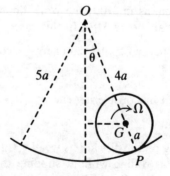

Figure 19

Fig. 19 shows a vertical cross-section of the cylinders. Let the lines of centres make angle θ with the vertical, and let the angular speed of the rolling cylinder be Ω. Then

$$\text{velocity of } P = \text{velocity of } G +$$
$$\text{velocity of } P \text{ relative to } G$$
$$= 4a\dot\theta - a\Omega.$$

But, since there is no slipping, P is instantaneously at rest.

Therefore $\qquad\qquad \Omega = 4\dot\theta.$

The kinetic energy is

$$\tfrac{1}{2}M(4a\dot\theta)^2 + \tfrac{1}{2}.\tfrac{1}{2}Ma^2\Omega^2 = 12Ma^2\dot\theta^2.$$

The contact force does no work in rolling motion, so the only external force doing work is the weight.

The potential energy is $\qquad Mg.4a(1 - \cos\theta),$

taking the lowest position of G as the zero level. Therefore

$$12Ma^2\dot\theta^2 + Mg.4a(1 - \cos\theta) = \text{constant}.$$

Differentiating with respect to time,

$$24Ma^2\dot\theta\ddot\theta + 4Mga\sin\theta\dot\theta = 0$$

$$\Rightarrow \ddot\theta + \frac{g}{6a}\sin\theta = 0$$

For small oscillations this is approximately simple harmonic motion with period

$$2\pi\sqrt{\left(\frac{6a}{g}\right)}. \qquad\qquad \square$$

Exercise 16C

1 Taking the sun as fixed, estimate the ratio $\bar{T}:T_G$ for the earth. (Mean distance of earth from sun $\approx 1.5 \times 10^{11}$ m, radius of earth $\approx 6.4 \times 10^6$ m.)

2 A solid uniform cylinder of radius a and mass m rolls down a slope of inclination α. Determine the ratio of its translational to its rotational energy. Compare the same situation for a hollow cylinder, radius a and mass m, of negligible thickness.

3 A wheel of radius a and radius of gyration k about the axis through its centre perpendicular to its plane is set rolling with angular speed ω up a rough slope of inclination α. How far up the slope will it go?

4 A uniform rod PQ of length l and mass m is attached at P to a small ring of negligible mass which is free to slide on a smooth horizontal wire. The rod is released from rest when the end Q is in contact with the wire. Find the angular velocity of the rod when it has turned through angle θ. Find the speed of Q then.

5 Repeat Example 7 when the radius of the fixed cylinder is b ($>a$) instead of $5a$.

6 Fig. 20 shows two uniform discs, each of mass M and radius a. These are joined by a uniform rod of mass m and length $2a$ which is freely attached to the centres of the discs. The whole configuration is in a vertical plane with one disc vertically above the other. With the lower disc held fixed, the upper disc is slightly displaced, and rolls round the fixed disc without slipping. Find the angular velocity of the rod as it passes through its lowest position.

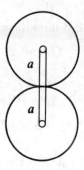

Figure 20

7 (i) A rough uniform sphere of radius a rests on the top of a fixed rough sphere of radius $4a$, and is then slightly displaced. Find the velocity of the centre of the moving sphere when the line of centres makes angle θ with the upward vertical (assuming that the spheres are still in contact). By considering the equation of linear motion, find the value of θ when the moving sphere leaves the fixed sphere.

   (ii) Repeat (i) when the spheres are smooth.

8 An oscillator consists of a uniform rod OA of length l and mass m, and a weight of mass $3m$ attached to the rod at A. The oscillator is free to rotate in a vertical plane about a fixed axis through O perpendicular to the rod. What is its moment of inertia I about this axis?

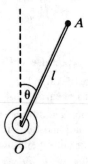

Figure 21

In equilibrium A is vertically above O; this equilibrium is maintained by a spring at O which produces a restoring couple $-4mgl\theta$ when OA makes an angle θ with the vertical (Fig. 21). Show that when the oscillator is in motion the angular velocity $\dot{\theta}$ satisfies the equation

$$\tfrac{1}{2}I(\dot{\theta}^2 - \Omega^2) = \tfrac{7}{2}mgl(1 - \cos\theta) - 2mgl\theta^2,$$

where Ω is the angular velocity when $\theta = 0$. Find the value of Ω required to achieve a maximum deflection of $\frac{1}{2}\pi$ from the vertical. Show also that for small oscillations the maximum deflection of the oscillator is

$$\alpha \approx \Omega \Bigg/ \left(\frac{20}{3} \frac{l}{g} \right).$$ [SMP]

16.4 FURTHER APPLICATIONS OF MOMENTUM AND ENERGY

Some problems are best tackled by using a combination of the methods given in the previous three sections.

Example 8
A uniform rod AB of length $2a$ and mass M is freely pivoted at A and is held with B vertically above A. It is then allowed to fall, and when B is vertically below A it strikes a small stationary particle, also of mass M, which sticks to the rod at B. The rod then turns through a further angle α before first coming to rest. Find α.

Solution
For the rod

$$I_A = \tfrac{1}{3}Ma^2 + Ma^2 = \tfrac{4}{3}Ma^2 \quad \text{(parallel axis rule)}.$$

The potential energy lost as the rod falls from vertically above A to vertically below A is $2Mga$. So if ω_0 is the angular velocity of the rod just before impact,

$$\tfrac{1}{2}.\tfrac{4}{3}Ma^2\omega_0^2 = 2Mga$$

$$\Rightarrow \omega_0 = \sqrt{(3g/a)}.$$

At impact there are internal impulses between the rod and the particle, and an external impulse at A, so the moment of momentum about A is conserved. Therefore, if the angular velocity after impact is ω, then

$$(\tfrac{4}{3}Ma^2 + M(2a)^2)\omega = \tfrac{4}{3}Ma^2\omega_0$$

$$\Rightarrow \omega = \omega_0/4.$$

The kinetic energy after impact is

$$\tfrac{1}{2}(\tfrac{4}{3}Ma^2 + M(2a)^2)\omega^2 = \tfrac{8}{3}Ma^2\omega^2$$

$$= \tfrac{1}{6}Ma^2\omega_0^2$$

$$= Mga/2.$$

This equals the gain in potential energy as the rod turns through the further angle α (Fig. 22), which is

$$Mg.a(1 - \cos \alpha) + Mg.2a(1 - \cos \alpha).$$

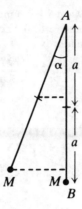

Figure 22

Therefore $\qquad\qquad 3Mga(1 - \cos \alpha) = Mga/2$

$$\Rightarrow \cos \alpha = \tfrac{5}{6}$$

$$\Rightarrow \qquad \alpha \approx 34°. \qquad\qquad \square$$

Example 9
A uniform circular disc of radius a and mass M rolls, without slipping, with speed U towards a step of height $a/4$. When the disc hits the step there is no slipping. Investigate the subsequent motion.

Solution

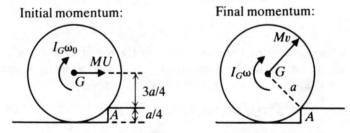

Figure 23

Let the velocity of the mass centre after the disc hits the step be v. Since the disc rolls initially and does not slip when it hits the step the angular velocities before and after impact are $\omega_0 = U/a$ and $\omega = v/a$. Also $I_G = \tfrac{1}{2}Ma^2$ (Fig. 23).

The only impulse acts at A, so the moment of momentum about A is conserved. Therefore

$$aMv + \tfrac{1}{2}Ma^2 \cdot \frac{v}{a} = \tfrac{3}{4}aMU + \tfrac{1}{2}Ma^2 \cdot \frac{U}{a}$$

$$\Rightarrow v = \tfrac{5}{6}U.$$

The disc starts to rotate about A, but if this is to continue it must remain in contact with the step. So we next find the condition for the normal reaction R at A not to become zero.

Force: Mass-acceleration:

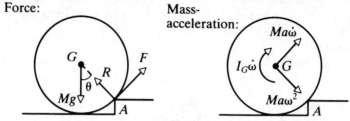

Figure 24

The force and mass-acceleration systems just after the disc hits the step are shown in Fig. 24. Considering the component of linear acceleration along GA,

$$Mg \cos \theta - R = Ma\omega^2$$

$$\Leftrightarrow R = Mg \cos \theta - Ma\omega^2.$$

But

$$\cos \theta = \tfrac{3}{4} \quad \text{and} \quad \omega = \frac{v}{a} = \frac{5U}{6a},$$

so

$$R \geqslant 0 \Leftrightarrow \tfrac{3}{4}Mg - Ma \cdot \frac{25U^2}{36a^2} \geqslant 0$$

$$\Leftrightarrow U^2 \leqslant \tfrac{27}{25}ga.$$

If this is the case the disc will turn about A; as it does so ω decreases (potential energy is gained, so kinetic energy is lost) and $\cos \theta$ increases (θ decreases), so R will remain non-zero. So if the disc does not leave A initially it will not do so subsequently. If the disc is to mount the step its kinetic energy at the bottom after impact must not be less than the potential energy the disc could gain in mounting the step, which is $\tfrac{1}{4}Mga$.

Thus the disc mounts the step if

$$\tfrac{1}{2}Mv^2 + \tfrac{1}{2} \cdot \tfrac{1}{2}Ma^2 \left(\frac{v}{a}\right)^2 \geqslant \tfrac{1}{4}Mga$$

$$\Leftrightarrow 3v^2 \geqslant ga$$

$$\Leftrightarrow U^2 \geqslant \tfrac{12}{25}ga.$$

In this case, if v' is the velocity of the centre of the disc when it rolls on the top of the step,

$$\tfrac{1}{2}Mv'^2 + \tfrac{1}{2} \cdot \tfrac{1}{2}Ma^2 \left(\frac{v'}{a}\right)^2 = \tfrac{1}{2}Mv^2 + \tfrac{1}{2} \cdot \tfrac{1}{2}Ma^2 \left(\frac{v}{a}\right)^2 - \tfrac{1}{4}Mga$$

$$\Leftrightarrow v'^2 = v^2 - \frac{ga}{3}$$

$$\Leftrightarrow v' = \sqrt{\left(\frac{25U^2}{36} - \frac{ga}{3}\right)}.$$

If $U^2 < \frac{12}{25}ga$ the disc will turn about A until its angular velocity is zero, and then fall back to the ground and roll away from the step. When it hits the ground the speed of G is again reduced by a factor $\frac{5}{6}$, since the momentum–impulse systems are symmetrical to those when it strikes the step, with the roles of the step and the ground interchanged. Thus the disc rolls away from the step with velocity $\frac{25}{36}U$.

To summarise:

If $U^2 < \frac{12}{25}ga$ the disc fails to mount the step, and rolls back with velocity $\frac{25}{36}U$.

If $\frac{12}{25}ga \leqslant U^2 \leqslant \frac{27}{25}ga$ the disc mounts the step and rolls along the top with velocity

$$\sqrt{\left(\frac{25U^2}{36} - \frac{ga}{3} \right)}.$$

If $U^2 > \frac{27}{25}ga$ the disc bounces off the step; its mass centre then describes the parabolic path of a projectile. □

Exercise 16D

1   Repeat Example 8 if the particle is moving with horizontal velocity $\sqrt{(ga)}$ towards the rod when it strikes and sticks to the rod at B.

2   In certain circumstances a person slipping over from a rigid vertical stance on an ice rink can be modelled by a uniform rod of length $2l$, disturbed from a vertical position while standing on a smooth floor. Diagrams representing the force and the mass-acceleration systems at a subsequent instant are given in Fig. 25 (a) and (b) respectively. (Here x represents the vertical distance fallen from rest by the centre of mass, G, of the rod.) Justify briefly the absence of a horizontal mass-acceleration term.

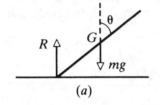
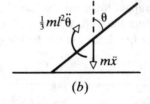

(a)   (b)

Figure 25

Use the principle of energy to obtain an equation relating $\dot{x}^2$, $\dot{\theta}^2$ and $\cos\theta$. By equating the force system to the mass-acceleration system, obtain an equation relating $\ddot{x}$, $\ddot{\theta}$ and θ, but excluding R.   [SMP]

3   Continuing question 2, show that $\dot{x} = l\sin\theta\,\dot{\theta}$. Hence obtain $\dot{\theta}^2$ in terms of θ. Use this to find $\ddot{\theta}$ in terms of θ. Use the equation of rotational acceleration to find R in terms of θ. Hence show that the rod never loses contact with the ground as it slips.

4   A rigid uniform hoop of radius a and mass m rolls in a vertical plane along a horizontal road until it comes to a step of height ka ($k < 1$) at right angles to its path. When the hoop comes into contact with the step at A, there is no slipping at A nor any subsequent loss of contact with A. If the hoop was rolling with angular velocity

ω immediately before striking the step, show that the hoop begins to mount the step with an angular velocity of $\omega(1 - \frac{1}{2}k)$. Find the condition that the hoop surmounts the step and begins to roll across it.

[SMP, adapted]

5   Show that it is impossible for a uniform disc of radius a to surmount a step of height $\frac{1}{2}a$. Investigate the possibility of a uniform hoop of radius a surmounting this step.

6   A uniform circular disc is rotating about its centre on a smooth horizontal table. If it is suddenly pinned to the table through a point on its edge, what fraction of the angular velocity is lost, and what fraction of the kinetic energy?

7   As part of a circus act, a clown of mass M drops vertically from a height h on to one end of a see-saw, at the other end of which is balanced a bag of flour of mass $\frac{1}{4}M$. The see-saw consists of a plank of length $2l$ and mass m balanced on a pivot at its centre, the pivot being at a height $l/3$ above the ground (Fig. 26).

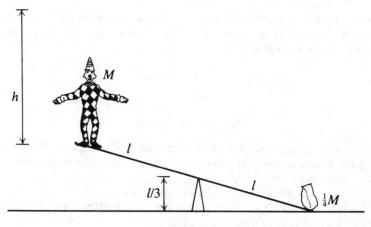

Figure 26

Assuming that the clown makes a successful landing on the see-saw, and that the bag of flour remains balanced, show that the angular velocity of the see-saw just after the clown lands is

$$\omega_0 = \frac{4Ml}{3I} \sqrt{(gh)}$$

where

$$I = (\tfrac{1}{3}m + \tfrac{5}{4}M)l^2.$$

Show also that the angular velocity of the see-saw just before the clown hits the ground is given by

$$\omega^2 = \omega_0^2 + \frac{Mgl}{I}.$$

[SMP]

8   A uniform solid cylinder of mass M and radius r is rolling towards the edge of a step with velocity v perpendicular to the edge of the step. Assuming that the cylinder does not slip at the edge, prove that it will leave horizontally if $v^2 \geqslant gr$, but that otherwise it will turn about the edge before dropping off.

9   A lamina of mass M is free to move in a horizontal plane. It is initially at rest with its mass centre at the origin of fixed coordinates Oxy in the plane. The point of the lamina at (a, b) is suddenly given the velocity $\begin{bmatrix} u \\ v \end{bmatrix}$. Prove the angular velocity ω which the lamina acquires is given by

$$\omega = \frac{av - bu}{a^2 + b^2 + k^2},$$

where k is the radius of gyration about the mass centre.

Suppose now that the lamina moves so that the point (a, b) still has velocity $\begin{bmatrix} u \\ v \end{bmatrix}$, but the angular velocity is ω'. Find an expression for the kinetic energy, and show that this is least when $\omega' = \omega$.

[This proves *Kelvin's Theorem*: when a point of a lamina is seized and moved with a prescribed velocity, the kinetic energy imparted to the lamina is as small as possible.]

10   When a rigid body is set in motion by external impulses the point of the body at which the impulse $\mathbf{J}_i$ acts is given velocity $\mathbf{v}_i$. Prove that the kinetic energy T acquired by the body is given by

$$T = \tfrac{1}{2} \Sigma \, \mathbf{J}_i . \mathbf{v}_i.$$

Project Exercise 16E

In this exercise the ideas of Chapters 14–16 are applied to some aspects of the motion of snooker balls. Experience and experiment suggest that the following assumptions are reasonable (Note 16.3).
(1) Each ball is a uniform sphere of radius a and mass M.
(2) When a ball slides on the table there is friction, with coefficient of friction μ; when a ball rolls on the table the friction is negligible.
(3) The collision between two balls is perfectly elastic, i.e. coefficient of restitution = 1 (Note 16.4); friction between the balls during impact is negligible.

Striking the cue ball
1   In a central blow the cue is horizontal and in line with the centre of mass G of the ball. The cue ball then starts to slide with initial velocity U and no initial rotation.
   Find the linear and angular accelerations, and hence show that (a) rolling occurs after time $2U/7\mu g$; (b) the linear and angular velocities are then $5U/7$ and $5U/7a$ respectively.
   Find the distance travelled before rolling commences.

2   For the average snooker table $\mu = 0.2$. For a cue ball hit as in question 1 find the duration of the sliding phase and the distance the ball travels before rolling (a) when $U = 3 \text{ m s}^{-1}$ (a strongly cued ball), (b) when $U = 1 \text{ m s}^{-1}$.

3   If the cue strikes the cue ball horizontally at height h above the table, giving G initial velocity U, find the initial angular velocity of the ball. Deduce that the ball rolls immediately if $h = 7a/5$. [This critical height is the height of the centre of percussion if the ball were pivoted at its point of contact; it is also the height of the cushions above the table.]
   Describe the initial motion of the ball (a) when $h > 7a/5$, (b) when $h < 7a/5$.

Direct impact of two balls

4   Prove that in a perfectly elastic direct collision between two particles of equal mass the velocities of the particles are interchanged.

5   Suppose that the cue ball, rolling so that its centre of mass G has velocity U, collides directly with a stationary object ball. Show that the object ball moves initially with velocity U and no rotation, and hence (from question 1) that it eventually rolls with velocity $5U/7$.

   Show also that immediately after the impact G is stationary but the cue ball eventually rolls after the object ball with velocity $2U/7$. Question 2 shows that these eventual velocities are reached quite quickly; show that an observer who takes these to be the velocities immediately after impact will think that the coefficient of restituion is $3/7$ (when it is actually 1).

6   Suppose that just before impact the cue ball is sliding (*a*) with top spin, (*b*) with bottom spin. Describe in each case its motion after impact.

   Explain how to achieve the 'stun shot', in which the cue ball stops and remains at rest after impact.

Swerving

7   A *snooker* occurs when there is a third ball directly between the cue ball and the object ball. The cue ball can be made to swerve round this obstruction by giving it spin to produce a friction force which has a sideways component.

   Suppose that the table top is the horizontal $z = 0$ plane, with the cue ball initially at rest at the origin, i.e. with G at $(0, 0, a)$. To produce a swerve the cue must be inclined downwards to hit the upper hemisphere of the ball off-centre.

   The downward component of the blow is cancelled by the impulsive reaction of the table, so G moves horizontally, with initial velocity $\begin{bmatrix} U \\ V \\ 0 \end{bmatrix}$, say. Let the initial spin be $\begin{bmatrix} \Omega_1 \\ \Omega_2 \\ \Omega_3 \end{bmatrix}$. Show that the initial velocity of the point of contact is $\begin{bmatrix} U - a\Omega_2 \\ V + a\Omega_1 \\ 0 \end{bmatrix}$, and hence that the initial friction force acting at the point of contact is $\begin{bmatrix} -F_1 \\ -F_2 \\ 0 \end{bmatrix}$, where $F_1:F_2:1 = U - a\Omega_2:V + a\Omega_1:1$ and $F_1^2 + F_2^2 = (\mu Mg)^2$.

8   To see what happens subsequently we need to use the equation of rotational motion $\mathbf{L}_G = \dot{\mathbf{H}}_G$ of §16.1. But in this case the motion is not two-dimensional, so we must go back to first principles to find $\dot{\mathbf{H}}_G$.

   (*a*) Starting with $\mathbf{H}_G = \sum m_i \boldsymbol{\rho}_i \times \dot{\boldsymbol{\rho}}_i$ (§14.2)

   show that $\mathbf{H}_G = \sum m_i \rho_i^2 \boldsymbol{\omega} - \sum m_i (\boldsymbol{\rho}_i . \boldsymbol{\omega}) \boldsymbol{\rho}_i$.

   (*b*) Taking $\boldsymbol{\rho}_i = \begin{bmatrix} \xi_i \\ \eta_i \\ \zeta_i \end{bmatrix}$ and $\boldsymbol{\omega} = \begin{bmatrix} \omega_1 \\ \omega_2 \\ \omega_3 \end{bmatrix}$ show that the x-component of $\mathbf{H}_G$ is

   $\sum m_i ((\eta_i^2 + \zeta_i^2)\omega_1 - \xi_i \eta_i \omega_2 - \xi_i \zeta_i \omega_3)$.

   (*c*) Explain why, for the snooker ball,

   $\sum m_i (\eta_i^2 + \zeta_i^2) = \tfrac{2}{5} M a^2$ and $\sum m_i \xi_i \eta_i = \sum m_i \xi_i \zeta_i = 0$.

   (*d*) Deduce that, for the snooker ball,

   $\mathbf{H}_G = \tfrac{2}{5} M a^2 \boldsymbol{\omega}$.

9   Show that as long as slipping occurs the subsequent motion of the ball is determined
by the equations

$$M\ddot{x} = -F_x, \qquad M\ddot{y} = -F_y$$

$$\tfrac{2}{5}Ma^2\dot{\omega}_1 = -aF_y, \qquad \tfrac{2}{5}Ma^2\dot{\omega}_2 = aF_x, \qquad \dot{\omega}_3 = 0$$

where $F_x:F_y:1 = \dot{x} - a\omega_2:\dot{y} + a\omega_1:1$ and $F_x^2 + F_y^2 = (\mu Mg)^2$.

10   From the equations of question 9 show that

$$\ddot{x} - a\dot{\omega}_2 = -7F_x/2M$$

and find $\ddot{y} + a\dot{\omega}_1$ similarly.

Deduce that $\qquad\qquad \dfrac{\ddot{x} - a\dot{\omega}_2}{\dot{x} - a\omega_2} = \dfrac{\ddot{y} + a\dot{\omega}_1}{\dot{y} + a\omega_1}$

11   By integrating the final equation of question 10 show that

$$\frac{\dot{x} - a\omega_2}{\dot{y} + a\omega_1} = \frac{U - a\Omega_2}{V + a\Omega_1}$$

12   By taking the y-axis in the direction of the initial motion of the point of contact we
have $U - a\Omega_2 = 0$, and so from question 11 $\dot{x} - a\omega_2 = 0$ always (i.e. there is never
any sliding in the x-direction). Deduce from question 9 that $F_x = 0$ and $F_y = \mu Mg$
always.

Hence show that while slipping occurs G moves along the parabola

$$x = Ut, \qquad y = Vt - \tfrac{1}{2}\mu gt^2, \qquad z = a.$$

13   Show that the duration of the sliding phase is $2(V + a\Omega_1)/7mg$.

14   After a rolling cue ball A has struck a stationary object ball B obliquely it is observed
that B moves along the line of centres while A moves initially at right angles to this
line but swerves towards the direction of motion of B (Fig. 27). Explain this.

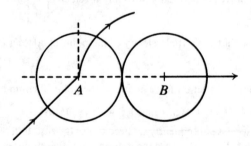

Figure 27

Miscellaneous exercise B

1   Two uniform rods AB and BC, each of weight per unit length w, have lengths $3a$ and $5a$ respectively, and are smoothly jointed together at B. The system is in equilibrium in the position shown in Fig. 1 with C resting on a rough horizontal floor at a distance $6a$ from a rough vertical wall, with which A is in contact. The rod AB is horizontal and the plane of the rods is perpendicular to the floor and the wall.

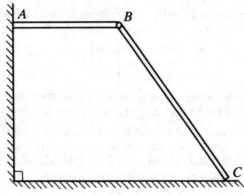

Figure 1

(a) Find the height of AB above the floor.

(b) Find the frictional force exerted by the wall at A.

(c) Find the horizontal and vertical components of the force exerted on BC at C.

(d) Show that the coefficient of friction at C must be at least $6/13$, and find the least possible value of the coefficient of friction at A.   [MEI]

2   A horizontal axle passes through the point O of a plane lamina, which swings freely in a vertical plane about this axle. The lamina has mass M, moment of inertia I

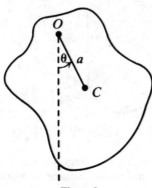

Figure 2

271

about the axle, and centre of mass C, where $OC = a$. The angle θ from the downward vertical to OC is shown in Fig. 2. Show that

$$\ddot{\theta} + (Mga/I) \sin \theta = 0.$$

Write down an expression for the period of small oscillations. If the position of O (and thus the value of a) can be varied, show that this period is least when

$$a = (I_c/M)^{\frac{1}{2}},$$

where I_c is the moment of inertia about C (assuming that such a position can be found).

3 The following forces act at $(1, 0, 1)$, $(-1, 0, 1)$ and $(1, 1, 1)$ respectively:

$$\begin{bmatrix} 2 \\ 1 \\ 1 \end{bmatrix}, \quad \begin{bmatrix} 1 \\ -1 \\ -1 \end{bmatrix} \quad \text{and} \quad \begin{bmatrix} -2 \\ -3 \\ 1 \end{bmatrix}.$$

An equivalent system comprises a force $\mathbf{F}$ acting at $(0, 0, 0)$ together with a couple $\mathbf{G}$. Find $\mathbf{F}$ and show that

$$\mathbf{G} = \begin{bmatrix} 4 \\ -2 \\ 1 \end{bmatrix}.$$

An alternative equivalent system comprises a force $\mathbf{F}^*$ acting at $(0, 0, 1)$ together with a couple $\mathbf{G}^*$. Find $\mathbf{F}^*$ and show that $\mathbf{G}^* = \lambda\mathbf{F}^*$. State the value of λ.

4 A light thread is wound round the circumference of the central section of a solid cylindrical block of wood, and the free end is held steady as shown in Fig. 3. If originally the straight part of the thread is vertical, explain why it remains vertical as the block falls, and calculate the acceleration of the block.

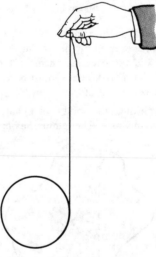

Figure 3

5 $\hat{\mathbf{i}}$ and $\hat{\mathbf{j}}$ are fixed perpendicular unit vectors, and $\mathbf{r}$ is the position vector of a variable point R of three-dimensional euclidean space such that

$$\mathbf{r} \times \hat{\mathbf{i}} = c\hat{\mathbf{j}},$$

where c is a constant number. Prove that R lies on a line l parallel to $\hat{\imath}$ at a distance c from the origin O, the plane containing O and l being perpendicular to $\hat{\jmath}$.

Hence write down an explicit expression for $\mathbf{r}$ in terms of c, $\hat{\imath}$, $\hat{\jmath}$ and a variable parameter λ.

6   A solid metal bobbin of mass M is made in the form of a double cone of length $2l$ and radius r which rotates about the axis joining the vertices. Calculate its moment of inertia about this axis.

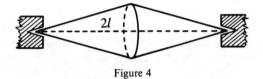

Figure 4

7   A framework is acted on by a force

$$\mathbf{F}_1 = 3\mathbf{i} - \mathbf{j} + \mathbf{k}$$

acting at the point A $(0, 1, 1)$, and by another force

$$\mathbf{F}_2 = \mathbf{i} + \mathbf{j} + 2\mathbf{k}$$

acting at the point B $(1, -1, 0)$. [The units are newtons and metres.] Show, by using a scalar triple product or otherwise, that the lines of action of $\mathbf{F}_1$ and $\mathbf{F}_2$ are not coplanar.

Calculate the moment of the couple and the force through O which will be in equilibrium with the two given forces.

8   Find the volume of a tetrahedron whose vertices are at the points A $(3, 0, -2)$, B $(5, 2, 4)$, C $(4, 3, 0)$ and D $(2, 5, 3)$.

9   Two lines L_1 and L_2 are given by

$$\mathbf{r}_1 = \begin{bmatrix} 2 \\ 3 \\ 1 \end{bmatrix} + \lambda \begin{bmatrix} 1 \\ 1 \\ 2 \end{bmatrix} \quad \text{and} \quad \mathbf{r}_2 = \begin{bmatrix} 4 \\ -2 \\ 5 \end{bmatrix} + \mu \begin{bmatrix} 2 \\ 1 \\ -1 \end{bmatrix}$$

respectively.

Write down a vector $\mathbf{p}$ whose direction is perpendicular to the directions of both L_1 and L_2. By comparing $\mathbf{r}_1 - \mathbf{r}_2$ and $\mathbf{p}$, or otherwise, find the mutually perpendicular transversal of L_1 and L_2.

10   A circular disk skims parallel to and just above the plane

$$x - 2y + 2z = 5$$

where the z-axis is vertically upwards. (All quantities are in SI units.) The disk has an angular velocity of magnitude 6. Show that the angular velocity vector of the disk is $2\mathbf{i} - 4\mathbf{j} + 4\mathbf{k}$.

At a certain instant the centre of the disk has a velocity vector with magnitude 5, no vertical component, and a positive x-component. Calculate this velocity vector, and also the velocity vector of a point on the disk with coordinates $(2, 3, 2)$ relative to the centre.

11   A pair of step ladders mass 20 kg consists of two equal uniform flights, each of length 3 m, freely hinged at the top and held together by a horizontal rope of length 1.5 m and negligible weight fitted midway up. A man of mass 100 kg stands on a step two thirds of the way up one side.

Given that friction between the ladders and the ground is neglected, find the tension in the rope. [MEI]

12 A charged particle has mass m and position vector $\mathbf{r}$, and it moves in a constant magnetic field $B\mathbf{k}$, the force on the particle being $c\dot{\mathbf{r}} \times B\mathbf{k}$ (where c is a constant and $\times$ denotes a vector product). Write down the equation of motion of the particle, and verify by differentiation that it is satisfied by

$$\dot{\mathbf{r}} = A\mathbf{r} \times \mathbf{k} + \mathbf{D}, \tag{1}$$

where A and $\mathbf{D}$ are constant, provided A has a particular value, which must be stated.

Plane polar coordinates (r, θ) are used in the plane perpendicular to the magnetic field and the position vector $\mathbf{r}$ is expressed as

$$\mathbf{r} = r\hat{\mathbf{r}} + z\mathbf{k},$$

where $\hat{\mathbf{r}}, \hat{\boldsymbol{\theta}}, \mathbf{k}$ are unit vectors defined in Fig. 5. Derive an expression for $\dot{\mathbf{r}}$ (you may state without proof a result for a derivative of $\hat{\mathbf{r}}$). Find the three components of the equation (1) above, when $\mathbf{D}$ is given as

$$D_1\hat{\mathbf{r}} + D_2\hat{\boldsymbol{\theta}} + D_3\mathbf{k}.$$

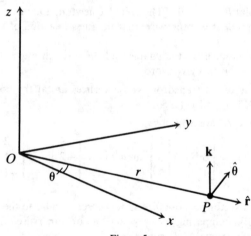

Figure 5

13 Let $\mathbf{a}, \mathbf{b}, \mathbf{c}$ be three linearly independent vectors. Explain why $\mathbf{a}.(\mathbf{b} \times \mathbf{c}) \neq 0$.
If

$$\mathbf{d} = x\mathbf{a} + y\mathbf{b} + z\mathbf{c}$$

show that

$$x = \{\mathbf{d}.(\mathbf{b} \times \mathbf{c})\}/\{\mathbf{a}.(\mathbf{b} \times \mathbf{c})\}.$$

Calculate x when $\mathbf{a} = \mathbf{i} + 2\mathbf{j} + \mathbf{k}$, $\mathbf{b} = \mathbf{i} - \mathbf{j} + 2\mathbf{k}$, $\mathbf{c} = \mathbf{i} + \mathbf{j} - \mathbf{k}$, $\mathbf{d} = \mathbf{i} + 4\mathbf{k}$.

14 Fixed points A, B lie in a plane and O is their midpoint; the variable point P also lies in the plane. The vectors $\mathbf{q}$, $\mathbf{s}$ are defined in Fig. 6 and $\mathbf{c} = \mathbf{AO} = \mathbf{OB}$.
Curves in the plane are defined by the equation

$$\alpha(\mathbf{q} \times \mathbf{s})^2 = 4c^2(\mathbf{q}.\mathbf{s} - 3c^2)$$

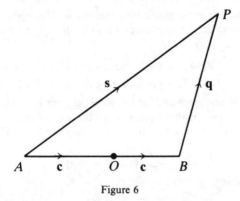

Figure 6

for differing values of the constant α (where $\times$ denotes a vector product, and $\mathbf{a}^2$ means $\mathbf{a} \cdot \mathbf{a}$). By taking axes at O, or otherwise, identify the curves for $\alpha > 1$.

What is the eccentricity of these curves?

15 A door of mass M is smoothly hinged along one edge and is prevented from opening too far by a door stop. Its centre of mass is situated at a distance a from the line of hinges, and I is its moment of inertia about an axis parallel with the line of hinges through the centre of mass. Fig. 7 (a) is a floor-level plan of the situation with the door against the door stop. O is vertically below the line of hinges, G is vertically below the centre of mass and S, which is a distance b from O, is the position of the door stop. Fig. 7 (b) shows the impulse system on the door at impact. If the door, rotating with angular velocity ω, hits the door stop and is brought to rest, obtain an equation of the form $K = C\omega$, and identify C.

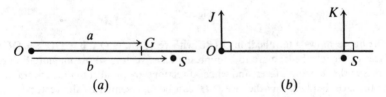

Figure 7

Find an expression for J, the impulse at the hinge, in terms of I, M, ω, a and b. Hence find an expression in terms of I, M and a for the distance, b, of the door stop from O that minimises $|J|$.

16 A roundabout in a children's playground is rotating with a constant angular velocity about a fixed vertical shaft offering negligible resistance to motion. A child is standing next to the roundabout and subsequently performs the following sequence of activities.

(a) He steps onto the edge of the roundabout and then sits still (relative to the roundabout).

(b) Then he crawls along a radius of the roundabout until he reaches the middle, when he stops crawling.

(c) Then he crawls along a radius to the edge of the roundabout where he again sits still (relative to the roundabout).

(d) Then he inadvertently falls off the roundabout.

State in qualitative terms, giving brief reasons, what happens to the magnitude of the angular velocity of the roundabout during each of the four activities of the child.

17 A body is acted on by forces

$$\begin{cases} \mathbf{F}_1 = 2\mathbf{i} + \mathbf{j} + \mathbf{k} & \text{acting at} \quad \mathbf{r}_1 = \mathbf{i} - \mathbf{j} + \mathbf{k} \\ \mathbf{F}_2 = 3\mathbf{i} + \mathbf{j} - \mathbf{k} & \text{acting at} \quad \mathbf{r}_2 = 2\mathbf{i} + \mathbf{j} - \mathbf{k} \end{cases}$$

where the units are newtons and metres. Find the force $\mathbf{F}$ at O and the moment $\mathbf{G}$ of the couple which are together equivalent to the given forces.

Evaluate $\mathbf{F} \times \mathbf{G}$ and show that the total moment of $\mathbf{F}$ and $\mathbf{G}$ about any point of the line

$$\mathbf{r} = \lambda \mathbf{F} + (\mathbf{F} \times \mathbf{G})/|\mathbf{F}|^2$$

is a vector parallel to $\mathbf{F}$.

18

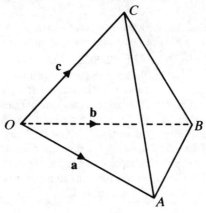

Figure 8

The figure shows a tetrahedron $OABC$ with vectors $\mathbf{a} = \mathbf{OA}, \mathbf{b} = \mathbf{OB}, \mathbf{c} = \mathbf{OC}$. The faces of the tetrahedron are to be represented as vectors whose magnitudes are the areas of the respective faces, and whose directions are parallel to the *outward* normal to the face. Explain why the face OAB can be represented by the vector

$$\tfrac{1}{2}\mathbf{b} \times \mathbf{a},$$

and find expressions for the other three faces in terms of $\mathbf{a}, \mathbf{b}, \mathbf{c}$. Show that the sum of the vectors representing all four faces is zero.

Given that the volume of the tetrahedron is

$$V = \tfrac{1}{6}\mathbf{a} \cdot (\mathbf{b} \times \mathbf{c}),$$

calculate V when A, B, C have coordinates $(2, -1, -1), (3, -1, 2), (1, -2, 1)$ respectively.

19 Let L_1 and L_2 be the lines given by

$$\mathbf{r}_1 = \mathbf{a} + \lambda \mathbf{s}, \qquad \mathbf{r}_2 = \mathbf{b} + \mu \mathbf{t}$$

respectively, where $\mathbf{s}$ and $\mathbf{t}$ are linearly independent. Explain why the vectors

$$\mathbf{s}, \mathbf{t}, \mathbf{s} \times \mathbf{t}$$

are linearly independent, and deduce that there exist unique values of λ, μ, ν such that

$$\mathbf{r}_2 - \mathbf{r}_1 = \nu(\mathbf{s} \times \mathbf{t}).$$

Show that

$$v = (\mathbf{b} - \mathbf{a}).(\mathbf{s} \times \mathbf{t})/|\mathbf{s} \times \mathbf{t}|^2.$$

Hence deduce that the shortest distance between the lines L_1 and L_2 is

$$d = |(\mathbf{b} - \mathbf{a}).(\mathbf{s} \times \mathbf{t})|/|\mathbf{s} \times \mathbf{t}|.$$

20

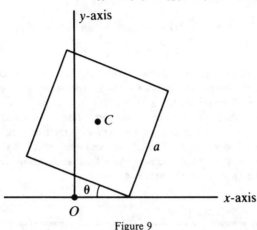

Figure 9

A pioneer in the development of the wheel-barrow experimented with a 'square-wheeled' version. Show that when such a 'wheel' of side a has turned through an angle θ (without any slipping), the coordinates of the centre C relative to the axes given in the diagram are, for $0 \leqslant \theta \leqslant \tfrac{1}{2}\pi$, if C is at $(0, \tfrac{1}{2}a)$ when $\theta = 0$,

$$\begin{cases} x = \tfrac{1}{2}a - (a/\sqrt{2}) \cos (\theta + \tfrac{1}{4}\pi), \\ y = (a/\sqrt{2}) \sin (\theta + \tfrac{1}{4}\pi). \end{cases}$$

Sketch the path of C for $0 \leqslant \theta \leqslant 2\pi$. Given that the centre of the wheel moves forward (again without the wheel slipping) at a constant horizontal speed V, show that a horizontal axle through C has a vertical velocity, for $0 \leqslant \theta \leqslant \tfrac{1}{2}\pi$,

$$\dot{y} = V \cot (\theta + \tfrac{1}{4}\pi).$$

Calculate the impulse that would be imparted to a body of mass m mounted on the axle as the wheel passes through the position $\theta = \tfrac{1}{2}\pi$.

21 A triangular frame, ABC, is constructed from three similar uniform rods each of length $2a$ and mass m. The frame rests in a vertical plane with the side AB on a horizontal surface. A horizontal force F, acting parallel to AB, is applied to the vertex C.

If no slipping occurs, find the magnitude and direction of the total reaction on the frame at vertex B if it is on the point of rotating about the vertex B.

Find also F as a function of θ, the angle between AB and the horizontal, as the frame slowly rotates about B. [MEI]

22 A particle P of mass m and electric charge q is moving with velocity $\mathbf{v}$ in a constant magnetic field $\mathbf{B}$ and a constant electric field $\mathbf{E}$, so that it is acted on by a force

$$\mathbf{F} = q(\mathbf{E} + \mathbf{v} \times \mathbf{B}).$$

Write down the equation of motion for P and show that it can be written

$$\frac{d}{dt}(m\dot{\mathbf{r}} - q\mathbf{r} \times \mathbf{B}) = q\mathbf{E}.$$

Given that $\mathbf{r} = \mathbf{0}$ and $\dot{\mathbf{r}} = \mathbf{0}$ at time $t = 0$, deduce that at time t

$$\dot{\mathbf{r}} - \frac{q}{m}\mathbf{r} \times \mathbf{B} = \frac{q}{m}\mathbf{E}t.$$

If $\mathbf{E} = E\mathbf{i}$ and $\mathbf{B} = B\mathbf{k}$, where $\mathbf{i}, \mathbf{j}, \mathbf{k}$ have the usual meanings, verify that a solution of this equation consistent with the initial conditions is

$$\mathbf{r} = \frac{E}{\omega B}[(1 - \cos \omega t)\mathbf{i} + (\sin \omega t - \omega t)\mathbf{j}],$$

where $\omega = qB/m$. Sketch the path of P for $0 \leqslant t \leqslant 4\pi/\omega$.

23 A simple balance consists of a semicircular metal arc of mass $2m$ and radius $3a$, which is joined to a metal strip of mass $\frac{3}{2}m$ which forms the diameter of the arc. This D-shaped piece of metal lies in a vertical plane and is freely pivoted about a horizontal axle A through the centre of the semicircle and normal to its plane. Two circular discs of radius a and mass m are fixed with their centres at the ends of the diameter. Their planes contain the diameter and are normal to the semicircle. The balance is completed by a light pointer and a fixed scale. Show that the moment of inertia of the balance about the axle is $41ma^2$.

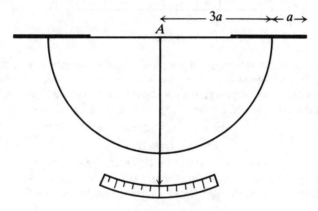

Figure 10

Displacement of the balance from its equilibrium position is measured by the angle θ between the pointer and the downward vertical. Show that the differential equation for small oscillations of the balance is

$$\ddot{\theta} + \frac{12g}{41\pi a}\theta = 0.$$

(You may assume that the centre of mass of a semicircular arc is at a distance $2/\pi$ times the radius from the centre.)

State the period T of this oscillation in terms of g and a.

The balance is started impulsively at $\theta = t = 0$ with angular velocity Ω. Show that the maximum deflection of the pointer in the subsequent motion is $\Omega T/(2\pi)$. What impulsive moment is needed to start the balance from rest with this angular velocity?

24 (a) A uniform disc of mass M and radius a rolls (without slipping) up a line of greatest slope of a plane which is inclined at angle ψ to the horizontal. By taking moments about a suitable point, obtain the equation

$$3\dot{V} = -2g \sin \psi,$$

where V is the velocity of the centre of the disc. Show that this is the same equation as would be obtained for the frictionless sliding of a particle of mass M, but whose weight is taken to be $\frac{2}{3}Mg$, up the same slope.

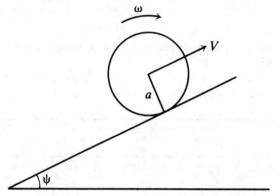

Figure 11

(b) A bicycle free-wheels over a hump-backed bridge. This situation is modelled (in view of the result described in (a) above) in the following way. A particle of mass m and weight αmg, where $\alpha < 1$, slides without friction on the portion of the parabola

$$y = c - x^2/(k^2 c)$$

between $(-kc, 0)$ and $(kc, 0)$; it starts at $x = -kc$ with speed U. Show from energy considerations that the speed v at $(0, c)$ is given by

$$v^2 = U^2 - 2\alpha g c.$$

Write down an equation for the upward force N exerted on the particle by the parabola at $(0, c)$, and show that it vanishes if

$$k^2 = 2[U^2/(\alpha g c) - 2].$$

25 A uniform rectangular block of mass M with height $2a$ and square cross-section of side a stands vertically on rough ground. Calculate the moment of inertia of the block about the horizontal edge AE (see Fig. 12).

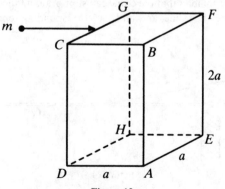

Figure 12

The block is struck at the midpoint of the edge CG by a steel ball of mass m moving horizontally with speed V at right angles to the face $CDHG$. After impact the ball rebounds with speed $\frac{1}{2}V$ along the same line. Assuming that the block tips about the edge AE without slipping, show that the angular velocity of the block immediately after the impact is

$$\Omega = \frac{9mV}{5Ma}.$$

By using the energy equation, or otherwise, find the minimum value of V required to cause the block to tip over.

26 A crane on a building site consists of a vertical tower upon which is mounted a uniform horizontal frame of mass m as shown in Fig. 13.

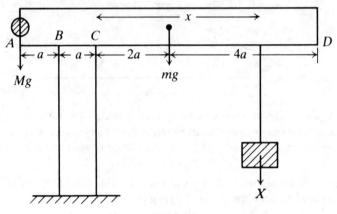

Figure 13

A counterweight of mass M is fitted to the back of the frame at A and the load X is supported by a hook hanging from a light trolley which can travel along the frame from the point C to the point D.

The supporting tower can withstand a maximum compressive force F and a maximum tensile force T at the points of support B and C. When unladen, the crane is designed to be just on these limiting values.

Find the maximum load that the crane can support as a function of x, the distance the trolley is along the frame, and find the corresponding forces at B and C.

[MEI]

27

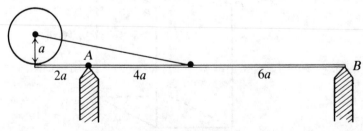

Figure 14

A car park barrier consists of a uniform thin pole of length $12a$ and mass m with a uniform circular disc of radius a and mass $4m/3$ welded tangentially at one end. A light tie joins the centre of the disc to the centre of the pole (for added strength).

Show that the centre of mass of the barrier lies on this tie at distance $4a/7$ to the right of the smooth axle A which supports the barrier (as shown in Fig. 14), and $4a/7$ above the horizontal line AB. Find the moment of inertia of the barrier about A.

The barrier is designed so that it pivots about A in a vertical plane, and has an equilibrium position in which it is partly open. Find the angle between the barrier and AB in this equilibrium position. The pole is slightly disturbed from this equilibrium position, and falls towards the horizontal. Show that the angular velocity ω of the pole is given by

$$53a\omega^2 = 4\sqrt{2g}\{1 - \sin(\theta + \tfrac{1}{4}\pi)\}$$

where θ is the angle between the pole and the horizontal.

What vertical impulsive force is then needed at B to stop the barrier?

28 An electron of mass m and charge q is moving in the x, y plane under the influence of a constant magnetic field $\mathbf{B} = B\mathbf{k}$ perpendicular to this plane. The velocity of the electron is $\mathbf{v}$. If z denotes the complex number $x + jy$, explain why the force $q\mathbf{v} \times \mathbf{B}$ exerted on the electron can be written as a complex number $-qB\dot{z}j$. Write down the vector equation of motion for the electron, and deduce that this equation can be written

$$\ddot{z} + \frac{qB}{m}j\dot{z} = 0.$$

Verify that for an electron projected from the origin in the x-direction with velocity V the solution of the equation is

$$z = \frac{mV}{qB}j\left[\exp\left(-\frac{qB}{m}jt\right) - 1\right].$$

Write down expressions for x and y at time t. Show that the path of the electron is a circle and that it returns to the origin at times with a period

$$\frac{2\pi m}{qB}.$$

29 The motion of a tray sliding across a table is under discussion, and the following two problems arise.

(*a*) A uniform circular lamina of radius a and mass m is set in motion at time $t = 0$ on a rough horizontal table by being given an angular velocity Ω about a vertical axis through its centre, which remains at rest. The frictional force on each element of the lamina is assumed to be of magnitude μ times the weight of the element, acting against the velocity of the element. Show that the total frictional force on the lamina is zero, and find the total moment of the frictional forces about the axis of rotation. Hence show that the lamina stops after a time $3a\Omega/(4\mu g)$, and find the total angle turned through.

(*b*) A general lamina is in motion on a horizontal plane. Its mass centre C has velocity $\mathbf{V}$ at some instant, and the angular velocity is then $\boldsymbol{\omega}$. Write down the velocity $\mathbf{v}_P$ of a point P of the lamina which has position $\mathbf{r}^*$ from C. Show that, provided $\boldsymbol{\omega} \neq \mathbf{0}$, the equation $\mathbf{v}_P = \mathbf{0}$ has a solution $\mathbf{r}^* = \mathbf{s}$, corresponding to a point S. (S need not be a point of the lamina.) Show that, for a general point P, $\mathbf{v}_P = \boldsymbol{\omega} \times \mathbf{SP}$.

30 A hollow cylinder of uniform density has mass M, external radius a and internal radius b. Show that the moment of inertia of the cylinder about its central axis is

$$I = \tfrac{1}{2}M(a^2 + b^2).$$

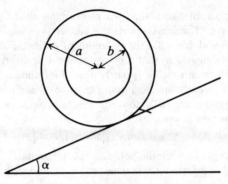

Figure 15

The cylinder rolls from rest without slipping (and with its axis horizontal) down a rough plane which is inclined at an angle α to the horizontal. Show that the angular acceleration of the cylinder is

$$\dot{\omega} = \frac{2ga \sin \alpha}{3a^2 + b^2}.$$

Hence, or otherwise, show that the velocity of the cylinder after it has descended a vertical height h is

$$V = 2\sqrt{\left(\frac{gh}{3 + b^2/a^2}\right)}.$$

In a demonstration of these principles, a variety of cylinders of the same external radius but varying internal radii are rolled down the plane (starting from rest). The coefficient of friction of the plane is μ, so that slipping occurs when the frictional force is μ times the normal reaction. Show that, for slipping to be avoided in all possible cases, the angle α must be set so that $\tan \alpha \leqslant 2\mu$.

Notes

1.1   A fuller presentation of these ideas is found in, for example, *RAM* Chapter 7.

1.2   The result is $x^4 + y^4 + 2x^2y^2 - 9x^2 - 9y^2 + 4x + 12 = 0$. If you want to prove this, start by showing that $x^2 + y^2 = 5 + 4\cos t$.

1.3   See *RAM* Chapter 13.

1.4   It is difficult to be precise about this. For example, the curve $y = x^2$ has a tangent ($y = 0$) at $(0, 0)$. The 'obvious' parametric equations $x = p$, $y = p^2$ give this when $p = 0$ with no trouble, but if we put $p = q^3$ we get 'bad' parametric equations $x = q^3$, $y = q^6$ for the same curve, for which $\dfrac{dx}{dq} = \dfrac{dy}{dq} = 0$ when $q = 0$.

1.5   See *RAM* Chapter 12, §5.

1.6   See *RAM* Chapter 34, §2.

1.7   See *RAM* Chapter 36, §3.

1.8   See *RAM* Chapter 36, §4.

1.9   See §7.6 of *An Introduction to Mechanics and Modelling* by D. G. Medley (Heinemann 1982).

2.1   In Fig. 8 and the following working we take $\delta\theta > 0$. If $\delta\theta < 0$ there are some obvious sign changes in the proof, but the main result is the same.

2.2   Here we use the fact that $(\sin x)/x \to 1$ as $x \to 0$, taking $x = \delta\theta/2$. See *RAM* Chapter 6, §3 and Chapter 28, §2.5.

2.3   See *RAM* Chapter 13.

2.4   See *RAM* Chapter 16.

3.1   An alternative method, using coordinates, is given in *RAM* Project Exercise 4, p. 1107.

4.1   See *RAM* Chapter 24.

4.2   See *RAM* Chapter 36.

5.1   'Mean distance' here means the semi major axis of the ellipse; see §5.4.

5.2   See *RAM* Chapter 25, §3.

5.3   See Arthur Koestler, *The Sleepwalkers* (Pelican), Part IV, Chapter 6.

5.4   In fact the only solution.

5.5   Compare *RAM* Chapter 26.

6.1   See *RAM* Chapter 22, §4.2, and Chapter 30, §5.2.

8.1   See *RAM* Chapter 12.

8.2   Further details and examples of both methods are given in *RAM* Chapters 7 and 12.

8.3   See *RAM* Chapter 14, §3.2.

8.4   See *RAM* Chapter 14, §3, where the equivalence is seen by putting $\lambda = \dfrac{p}{p + q}$, $\mu = \dfrac{q}{p + q}$.

8.5   As we shall see in §11.1, moment is really a vector quantity, but in this two-dimensional work we need only the magnitude of the moment together with the appropriate sign to show the sense of turning.

8.6 The components can be taken in non-perpendicular directions, but this is rarely needed in practice.

8.7 See *RAM* Chapter 24.

9.1 See *RAM* Chapter 36.

9.2 See *RAM* Chapter 31.

9.3 See *RAM* Chapter 9, §3.2.

9.4 See *RAM* Chapter 24, §3.

9.5 There is a close analogy between the radius of gyration and the standard deviation σ of a variable x distributed with frequency f, since $k^2 = \dfrac{\sum mr^2}{\sum m}$ and $\sigma^2 = \dfrac{\sum fd^2}{\sum f}$, where $d = x - \bar{x}$.
See *RAM* Chapter 11, §§5 and 7.

10.1 See *RAM* Chapter 36.

10.2 See *RAM* Chapter 10, §7.

10.3 This is the two-dimensional version of a more general three-dimensional vector equation which will be met in §16.1.

10.4 See *RAM* Chapter 34.

11.1 Because $\mathbf{a} \times \mathbf{a}$ is always zero we can (and shall) use $\mathbf{a}^2$ to mean $\mathbf{a}.\mathbf{a}$ without ambiguity.

11.2 For simplicity we omit the ranges of summation $i = 1, \ldots, m$ and $j = 1, \ldots, n$ since they are clear from the context.

12.1 See *RAM* Chapter 18, §1.

12.2 An alternative way of finding the expansion of the determinant, using properties of transformations, is given in *RAM* Chapter 40, §2.

13.1 See *RAM* Chapter 21.

14.1 For example, from *RAM* Chapter 24, §3.

14.2 This is one of the assumptions of the Newtonian model, which does not hold, for example, in quantum electrodynamics.

14.3 See *RAM* Chapter 24, §3.

14.4 See *RAM* Chapter 34, §4.

14.5 For further details see for example *An Introduction to Relativity* by L. Marder (Longman 1968).

14.6 See *RAM* Chapter 36, §§2 and 4.

16.1 Some writers use the term *kineton* for mass-acceleration.

16.2 The moment about O of the mass-acceleration system is $\bar{\mathbf{r}} \times Mr\ddot{\theta}\hat{\mathbf{u}} + I_G\ddot{\theta}\hat{\mathbf{e}} = M\bar{r}^2\ddot{\theta}\hat{\mathbf{e}} + I_G\ddot{\theta}\hat{\mathbf{e}} = I_O\ddot{\theta}\hat{\mathbf{e}}$, by the parallel axis rule. But it is easier to use $I_O\ddot{\theta}\hat{\mathbf{e}}$ directly.

16.3 See *The Physics of Ball Games* by C. G. Daish (English Universities Press 1972), Chapters 8, 14 and *An Introduction to Mechanics and Modelling* by D. G. Medley (Heinemann Educational Books 1982), §9.4.

16.4 See *RAM* Chapter 34, §5.

Solutions to questions in the text

Chapter 1

Q.1 Size of ball, spin of ball, air resistance, wind, slope of ground.

Q.2

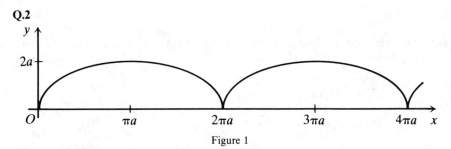

Figure 1

Q.3 $A = x_0$, $B = v_0/\omega$.

Q.4 Acceleration of $Q = -\omega^2 a \begin{bmatrix} \cos(\omega t + \alpha) \\ \sin(\omega t + \alpha) \end{bmatrix}$;

i-component of this $= -\omega^2 a \cos(\omega t + \alpha) = -\omega^2 x$.

Q.5 $T = 2\pi\sqrt{(l/g)} \Rightarrow T^2 = 4\pi^2 l/g \Rightarrow l = gT^2/4\pi^2$.

Q.6 $v = 0 \Rightarrow t = \dfrac{m}{k} \ln\left(1 + \dfrac{ku}{mg}\right) \Rightarrow 1 - e^{-kt/m} = 1 - \dfrac{mg}{mg + ku} = \dfrac{ku}{mg + ku}$.

Substitute this in the expression for y:

$$y_{max} = \frac{m}{k}\left(\frac{mg + ku}{k}\right)\frac{ku}{mg + ku} - \frac{m^2 g}{k^2}\ln\left(1 + \frac{ku}{mg}\right)$$

$$= \frac{mu}{k} - \frac{m^2 g}{k^2}\ln\left(1 + \frac{ku}{mg}\right).$$

Q.7 Forces for $v > 0$ (particle rising) are weight mg downwards, resistance kv^2 downwards.

Forces for $v < 0$ (particle falling) are weight mg downwards, resistance kv^2 upwards.

Q.8 Separate the variables

$$\int \frac{d\dot{x}}{\dot{x}} = \int\left(-\frac{k}{m}\right)dt \Rightarrow \ln \dot{x} = -kt/m + \ln u_1 \quad \text{(since } \dot{x} = u_1 \text{ when } t = 0\text{)}$$

$$\Rightarrow \quad \dot{x} = u_1 e^{-kt/m}.$$

Integrate: $x = \dfrac{mu_1}{k}(1 - e^{-kt/m})$ (since $x = 0$ when $t = 0$).

Q.9   From Q.8, $x \to mu_1/k$ as $t \to \infty$; the trajectory has a vertical asymptote $x = mu_1/k$.

Chapter 2

Q.1   Turning $\hat{\mathbf{u}}$ through $+\dfrac{\pi}{2}$ gives $-\hat{\mathbf{r}}$; multiply by θ and the result follows.

Alternatively, $\dot{\hat{\mathbf{u}}} = \begin{bmatrix} -\cos\theta\dot{\theta} \\ -\sin\theta\dot{\theta} \end{bmatrix} = -\dot{\theta}\begin{bmatrix} \cos\theta \\ \sin\theta \end{bmatrix} = -\dot{\theta}\hat{\mathbf{r}}.$

Chapter 3

Q.1 $(0, \pm b)$.

Q.2   The latus rectum through S meets the ellipse at $(ae, \pm l)$. Substituting these coordinates in equation (1) of §3.4,

$$\frac{a^2 e^2}{a^2} + \frac{l^2}{a^2(1 - e^2)} = 1$$

$\Rightarrow \qquad\qquad \dfrac{l^2}{a^2(1 - e^2)} = 1 - e^2$

$\Rightarrow \qquad\qquad l^2 = a^2(1 - e^2)^2 \qquad\qquad\qquad (2)$

$\Rightarrow \qquad\qquad l = a(1 - e^2)$ since $l > 0, a > 0, 0 < e < 1$.

Hence $\qquad\qquad a = \dfrac{l}{1 - e^2},$

Since $b^2 = a^2(1 - e^2)$, (2) gives $l^2 = b^2(1 - e^2)$, and hence $b^2 = \dfrac{l^2}{1 - e^2}$.

Q.3   By arguments similar to those of Q.2, $a = \dfrac{l^2}{e^2 - 1}, b^2 = \dfrac{l^2}{e^2 - 1}$.

Q.4   Draw the normal at P (Fig. 2). We have proved that $\phi = \psi$. But these are the complements of i and r, so $i = r$. Therefore the ray SP will be reflected along PX, which is parallel to the axis. Similarly an incoming ray parallel to the axis will be reflected through S.

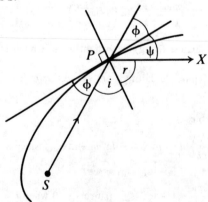

Figure 2

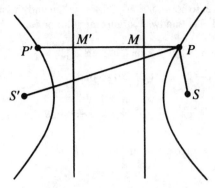

Figure 3

Q.6
$$SP = ePM, \qquad S'P = ePM'$$
$$\Rightarrow S'P - SP = eM'M$$
$$= e \cdot \frac{2a}{e}$$
$$= 2a.$$

Similarly $SP' - S'P' = 2a$.

Q.7 For the hyperbola $SP - S'P$ is constant, so that as P moves on the hyperbola the rate of increase of SP equals the rate of increase of $S'P$. The velocity of P has equal resolved parts in the direction of **SP** and **S'P**, so the tangent at P is equally inclined to SP and $S'P$.

Q.8 On the asymptote, $x = a \sec \theta \Rightarrow y = b \sec \theta$. The required distance is
$$b \sec \theta - b \tan \theta = b \frac{1 - \sin \theta}{\cos \theta}.$$

Let $\phi = \dfrac{\pi}{2} - \theta$, so that $\phi \to 0$ as $\theta \to \dfrac{\pi}{2}$.

Then $\dfrac{1 - \sin \theta}{\cos \theta} = \dfrac{1 - \cos \phi}{\sin \phi} \approx \dfrac{1 - (1 - \frac{1}{2}\phi^2)}{\phi}$ when ϕ is small.
$$= \tfrac{1}{2}\phi$$
$$\to 0 \quad \text{as} \quad \phi \to 0.$$

Q.9 (a) Plane perpendicular to axis of symmetry.

(b) Plane through vertex.

Chapter 4

Q.1 $r^2\dot{\theta}$ and r are both constant, so $\dot{\theta}$ is constant. Hence the particle moves round the circle with constant speed.

Q.2 $m^2 s^{-1}$.

Q.3 δr is then negative, so $\frac{1}{2}(r + \delta r)^2 \, \delta\theta < \delta A < \frac{1}{2}r^2 \, \delta\theta$ and the subsequent inequalities are also reversed. The sandwich argument still applies.

Q.4 Area from $\pi/2$ to $\pi = [\frac{9}{4}\theta + 2 \sin \theta + \frac{1}{8} \sin 2\theta]_{\pi/2}^{\pi} = \frac{9}{8}\pi - 2$.

Time taken is $(\frac{9}{8}\pi - 2) \div \frac{15}{2}$ (≈ 0.20) seconds.

Q.5
$$\dot{x} = \dot{r} \cos \theta - r \sin \theta \dot{\theta}, \qquad \dot{y} = \dot{r} \sin \theta + r \cos \theta \dot{\theta}$$
$$x\dot{y} - y\dot{x} = r\dot{r} \sin \theta \cos \theta + r^2 \cos^2 \theta \dot{\theta} - r\dot{r} \cos \theta \sin \theta + r^2 \sin^2 \theta \dot{\theta}$$
$$= r^2(\cos^2 \theta + \sin^2 \theta)\dot{\theta} = r^2\dot{\theta}.$$

Q.6 $2 \times 2 = 8 \times \frac{1}{2} = 4$.

Chapter 5

Q.1 Circle centre O.

Q.2 (a) $C = -3.5$, $e = 0.75$; (b) $C = -1.5$, $e = 0.5$; (c) $C = -0.155$, $e = 0.9375$.

Chapter 7

Q.1

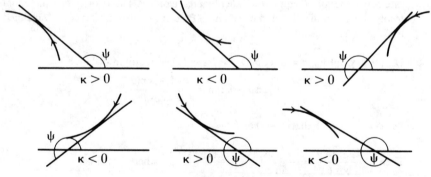

Figure 4

Q.2

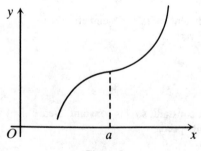

Figure 5

Q.3 $\dfrac{1}{c}$, at P_0.

Q.4 ψ decreases as S increases. Greatest $|\kappa|$ is $\frac{1}{10}$, at $t = 0$ (i.e. at the vertex).

Q.5
$$\cot \psi = \frac{\dot{x}}{\dot{y}} \Rightarrow -\operatorname{cosec}^2 \psi \dot{\psi} = \frac{\ddot{y}\dot{x} - \dot{x}\ddot{y}}{\dot{y}^2}$$

$$\Rightarrow -\left(1 + \frac{\dot{x}^2}{\dot{y}^2}\right)\dot{\psi} = \frac{\ddot{y}\dot{x} - \dot{x}\ddot{y}}{\dot{y}^2}$$

$$\Rightarrow \dot{\psi} = \frac{\dot{x}\ddot{y} - \dot{y}\ddot{x}}{\dot{x}^2 + \dot{y}^2}$$

$$\Rightarrow \kappa = \frac{\dot{\psi}}{\dot{s}} = \frac{\dot{x}\ddot{y} - \dot{y}\ddot{x}}{(\dot{x}^2 + \dot{y}^2)^{3/2}}$$

Q.6
$$\kappa = \frac{x'y'' - y'x''}{(x'^2 + y'^2)^{3/2}},$$

where the dash denotes differentiation with respect to p.

Q.7
$$\kappa = \frac{(-a \sin \theta)(-a \sin \theta) - (a \cos \theta)(-a \cos \theta)}{((-a \sin \theta)^2 + (a \cos \theta)^2)^{3/2}}$$

$$= \frac{a^2(\sin^2 \theta + \cos^2 \theta)}{a^3(\sin^2 \theta + \cos^2 \theta)^{3/2}} = \frac{a^2}{a^3} = \frac{1}{a}.$$

Q.8
$$\kappa = \frac{\dfrac{d^2x}{dy^2}}{\left(\left(\dfrac{dx}{dy}\right)^2 + 1\right)^{3/2}}$$

Q.9 Rotating $\hat{\mathbf{t}}$ through $+\pi/2$ gives $\hat{\mathbf{n}}$; rotating $\hat{\mathbf{n}}$ through $+\pi/2$ gives $-\hat{\mathbf{t}}$. Each of these vectors has rate of turning $\dot{\psi}$. The results follow as in §2.3.

Q.10

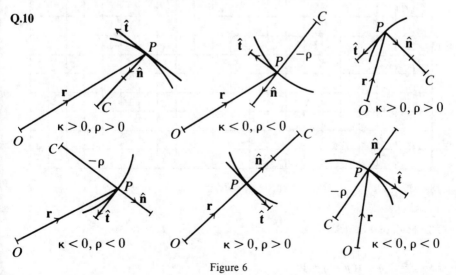

Figure 6

Chapter 8

Q.1   See Fig. 7.

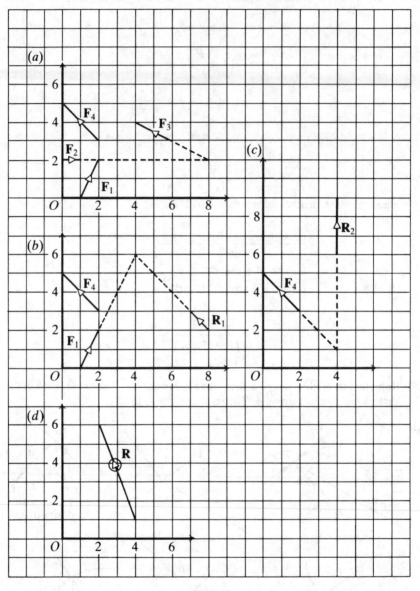

Figure 7

Q.2   Midpoint of *AB*.

Q.3 $p = 2, q = 1; p = q = 1.$

Q.4

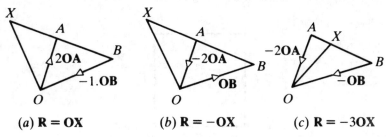

(a) **R = OX**   (b) **R = −OX**   (c) **R = −3OX**

Figure 8

Q.5 For example, take $p = 1, q = -1$. The resultant of **OA** and −**OB** is **OC**, where **OC** is parallel to **BA**. So this resultant is not a multiple of **OX** for any point X on AB.

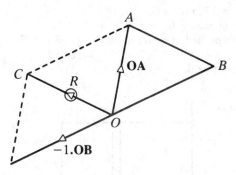

Figure 9

Q.6 Resultant of 30 N at B and 60 N at C is 90 N at F, where
$BF:FC = 60:30 \Rightarrow BF = \frac{2}{3}BC = \frac{4}{3}$ m $\Rightarrow AF = 5\frac{1}{3}$ m.
Resultant of 10 N at A and 90 N at F is 100 N at G, where
$AG:GF = 90:10 \Rightarrow AG = \frac{9}{10}AF = 4.8$ m, as before.

Q.7 (a) 2.4 m from A,   (b) 1.5 m from A,   (c) 1 m from A.

Q.8 (a) 48 N,   (b) 240 N.

Q.9 40 N, 3 m from A (at the other end of the rod). No upper limit.

Q.10 Sum of moments = $-20 \times 3 + 80 \times 1.5 - 60 \times 1 = 0$.

Q.11 If there were a non-zero resultant it would be perpendicular to **i**, since $\sum X_r = 0$. Since **AB** is not perpendicular to **i**, A and B could not both lie on the line of action of the resultant, and so the moments about A and B could not both be zero. Hence the resultant is zero. The system does not form a couple, since the moment about A is zero. Hence the system is in equilibrium.

Q.12 For example, equal forces acting along the edge of a square.

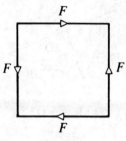

Figure 10

Chapter 9

Q.1   Centre of mass is 0.7 m from O.
Speed of centre of mass $= 0.7 \times 5 = 3.5 \text{ m s}^{-1}$.
KE of 6 kg concentrated at centre of mass $= \frac{1}{2} \times 6 \times 3.5^2$
$$= 36.75 \text{ J.}$$
The KE would not be the same.

Q.2

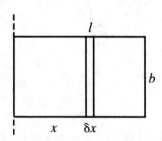

Figure 11

Mass of strip $= \dfrac{M}{lb} \times b\,\delta x = \dfrac{M}{l}\,\delta x$

$$\text{MI} = \lim_{\delta x \to 0} \sum_{x=0}^{x=l} \frac{M}{l}\,\delta x \times x^2$$

$$= \int_0^l \frac{M}{l} x^2\,dx = \left[\frac{M}{l} \frac{x^3}{3} \right]_0^l = \tfrac{1}{3}Ml^2.$$

Q.3   Cylindrical shell with open ends. Ma^2.

Q.4   Cylinder $=$ stretched disc $\Rightarrow$ MI $= \tfrac{1}{2}Ma^2$.

Q.5 G is at the centre of the rod, and $h = l/2$. $I = \tfrac{1}{3}Ml^2$, $I_G = \tfrac{1}{12}Ml^2$, $Mh^2 = \tfrac{1}{4}Ml^2$ and $\tfrac{1}{3}Ml^2 = \tfrac{1}{12}Ml^2 + \tfrac{1}{4}Ml^2$, as required.

Q.6 Mh^2 cannot be negative, and is zero only when $h = 0$, so $I \geqslant I_G$, with equality only when the axis passes through G.

Q.7 Multiply throughout by M, and the results follow.

Chapter 10

Q.1 With the notation of Fig. 12
$$L = Mga \cos \phi,$$
so the work done by the weight is
$$\int_{\theta_0}^{\theta} Mga \cos \phi \, d\phi = [Mga \sin \phi]_{\theta_0}^{\theta}$$
$$= Mga \sin \theta - Mga \sin \theta_0$$
$$= Mgz_G - Mgz'_G$$
since $a \sin \phi = GN =$ height of G above the horizontal plane through O.

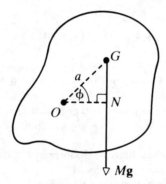

Figure 12

Q.2 In Fig. 13 the left-hand part of the string exerts tension T downwards on the pulley and tension T upwards on the heavier mass. As this mass descends by δx these tensions do work $T \delta x$ and $-T \delta x$ respectively, so the total work done by these tensions is zero, as it is similarly for the tensions in the right-hand part.

The temptation of saying merely that the tensions are internal forces and therefore do no work should be resisted; see §14.5.

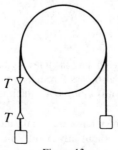

Figure 13

Q.3   Substituting for $\dot{\omega}$ in (2) gives $T_2 = mg\left(\dfrac{4mr^2 + I}{3mr^2 + I}\right)$.

Q.4   (a) $I_A\omega$,   (b) $I_A\omega\left(\dfrac{b^2 I_A - abI_B}{b^2 I_A + a^2 I_B}\right)$.

Moments not taken about a common axis.

Chapter 11

Q.1   Towards.

Q.2   If $h > 0$ both sides have magnitude $h|\mathbf{a} \times \mathbf{b}|$ and the same direction as $\mathbf{a} \times \mathbf{b}$.
If $h = 0$ both sides are zero.
If $h < 0$ both sides have magnitude $-h|\mathbf{a} \times \mathbf{b}|$ and the opposite direction to $\mathbf{a} \times \mathbf{b}$.
$(h\mathbf{a}) \times (k\mathbf{b}) = h(\mathbf{a} \times (k\mathbf{b})) = -h((k\mathbf{b}) \times \mathbf{a}) = -hk(\mathbf{b} \times \mathbf{a}) = hk(\mathbf{a} \times \mathbf{b})$.

Q.3   **0**.

Q.4 $\mathbf{i} \times \mathbf{j} = -\mathbf{j} \times \mathbf{i} = \mathbf{k}$, $\mathbf{j} \times \mathbf{k} = -\mathbf{k} \times \mathbf{j} = \mathbf{i}$, $\mathbf{k} \times \mathbf{i} = -\mathbf{i} \times \mathbf{k} = \mathbf{j}$,
$\mathbf{i} \times \mathbf{i} = \mathbf{j} \times \mathbf{j} = \mathbf{k} \times \mathbf{k} = \mathbf{0}$.

Q.5   No. $\mathbf{i} \times (\mathbf{i} \times \mathbf{j}) = \mathbf{i} \times \mathbf{k} = -\mathbf{j}$, $(\mathbf{i} \times \mathbf{i}) \times \mathbf{j} = \mathbf{0} \times \mathbf{j} = \mathbf{0}$. Not associative.

Q.6 $\mathbf{a} \times \mathbf{b} = \mathbf{0} \Leftrightarrow |\mathbf{a}||\mathbf{b}| \sin \theta = 0 \Leftrightarrow |\mathbf{a}| = 0$ or $|\mathbf{b}| = 0$ or $\sin \theta = 0 \Leftrightarrow \mathbf{a} = \mathbf{0}$ or $\mathbf{b} = \mathbf{0}$ or
$\theta = 0$ or $\pi \Leftrightarrow \mathbf{a} = \mathbf{0}$ or $\mathbf{b} = \mathbf{0}$ or $\mathbf{a}$ is parallel to $\mathbf{b}$.

Q.7 $(h\mathbf{r}) \times (k\mathbf{F}) = hk\mathbf{r} \times \mathbf{F}$: multiplying the force by k and moving its point of application to $h\mathbf{r}$ multiplies the moment by hk.
$\mathbf{r} \times \mathbf{F} = \mathbf{0} \Leftrightarrow \mathbf{r} = \mathbf{0}$ (force applied at O) or $\mathbf{F} = \mathbf{0}$ (no force)
or $\mathbf{r}$ is parallel to $\mathbf{F}$ (line of action passes through O).

Q.8 $(\mathbf{a} + \mathbf{b}) \times \mathbf{c} = -\mathbf{c} \times (\mathbf{a} + \mathbf{b}) = -(\mathbf{c} \times \mathbf{a} + \mathbf{c} \times \mathbf{b}) = -(-\mathbf{a} \times \mathbf{c} - \mathbf{b} \times \mathbf{c})$
$\quad\quad\quad\quad\quad\;\; = \mathbf{a} \times \mathbf{c} + \mathbf{b} \times \mathbf{c}$.

Q.9 $(\mathbf{a} + \mathbf{b}) \times (\mathbf{a} - \mathbf{b}) = \mathbf{a} \times \mathbf{a} - \mathbf{a} \times \mathbf{b} + \mathbf{b} \times \mathbf{a} - \mathbf{b} \times \mathbf{b}$;
the middle two terms do not cancel, since $\mathbf{a} \times \mathbf{b} \neq \mathbf{b} \times \mathbf{a}$.

Q.11 $\mathbf{r} = 3\mathbf{i} + 4\mathbf{j} + 6\mathbf{k}$, $\mathbf{F} = 8\mathbf{k}$
$\quad\quad\;\; \mathbf{r} \times \mathbf{F} = (4 \times 8 - 6 \times 10)\mathbf{i} + (6 \times 0 - 3 \times 8)\mathbf{j} + (3 \times 0 - 4 \times 0)\mathbf{k}$
$\quad\quad\quad\quad\; = 32\mathbf{i} - 24\mathbf{j}$

Q.12   The lines of action of the weight and the tensions all pass through A. The reaction of the ground must therefore also pass through A, since the total moment about A is zero. Therefore the reaction is along OA, which is vertical.

Q.13   The vector sums of the two systems are equal, since each sum is zero. The systems have equal total moments about any point, since they form equal couples. The systems therefore meet the requirements for equivalence on p. 181.

Chapter 12

Q.1 Distributivity of vector or scalar product over vector subtraction.

Chapter 13

Q.1 $2 \times 2 + 0 - 2 = 2, 2 \times 2 + (-1) - 1 = 2.$

Q.2 The general point of the first line is $(1 - s, 5 + 2s, s)$; this lies in the plane since $(1 - s) + (5 + 2s) - s = 6.$

Q.3 The general point of the line is $(1, -1 + t, 2t)$; this lies in the planes since $3 \times 1 + 2(-1 + t) - 2t = 1$ and $1 - 4(-1 + t) + 2 \times 2t = 5.$

Q.4 (*a*) Take $x = 1$. Then

$$\left. \begin{array}{c} 3 + 2y - z = 1 \\ 1 - 4y + 2z = 5 \end{array} \right\} \Leftrightarrow 2y - z = -2 \Leftrightarrow y = p, z = p + 2,$$

giving the line in the form

$$\begin{bmatrix} x \\ y \\ z \end{bmatrix} = \begin{bmatrix} 1 \\ 0 \\ 2 \end{bmatrix} + p \begin{bmatrix} 0 \\ 1 \\ 2 \end{bmatrix}.$$

(*b*) Take $x = \alpha$. Then

$$\begin{array}{ccc} 3\alpha + 2y - z = 1 & & 2y - z = 1 - 3\alpha \\ & \Leftrightarrow & \\ \alpha - 4y + 2z = 5 & & 2y - z = \dfrac{\alpha - 5}{2} \end{array}$$

Unless $1 - 3\alpha = \dfrac{\alpha - 5}{2}$ (i.e. $\alpha = 1$, as in (*a*)) these equations are inconsistent, and have no solution.

Q.5 $\dfrac{|ax_1 + by_1 - k|}{\sqrt{(a^2 + b^2)}}.$

Q.6 $\mathbf{p} - \mathbf{q}, \mathbf{d}, \mathbf{e}$ are coplanar $\Leftrightarrow$ volume of parallelepiped with these edges is zero
$$\Leftrightarrow (\mathbf{p} - \mathbf{q}).(\mathbf{d} \times \mathbf{e}) = 0.$$

Q.7 The lines are parallel.

Q.8 $\mathbf{p} = \begin{bmatrix} -15 \\ 2 \\ 8 \end{bmatrix}, \mathbf{q} = \begin{bmatrix} 1 \\ -6 \\ -2 \end{bmatrix}, \mathbf{d} = \begin{bmatrix} -8 \\ 4 \\ 5 \end{bmatrix}, \mathbf{e} = \begin{bmatrix} -2 \\ 1 \\ 4 \end{bmatrix},$

$$\mathbf{p} - \mathbf{q} = \begin{bmatrix} -16 \\ 8 \\ 10 \end{bmatrix}$$

$$(\mathbf{p} - \mathbf{q}).(\mathbf{d} \times \mathbf{e}) = \begin{vmatrix} -16 & -8 & -2 \\ 8 & 4 & 1 \\ 10 & 5 & 4 \end{vmatrix} = 0,$$

since row 1 = $-2 \times$ row 2.

Chapter 14

Q.1 $F_{11} + F_{12} + F_{13} = m_1\ddot{r}_1$
$F_{21} + F_{22} + F_{23} = m_2\ddot{r}_2$
$F_{31} + F_{32} + F_{33} = m_3\ddot{r}_3.$

Q.2 $\dot{H}_O = r_1 \times F_{11} + r_1 \times F_{12} + r_1 \times F_{13} + r_2 \times F_{21} + r_2 \times F_{22} + r_2 \times F_{23}$
$+ r_3 \times F_{31} + r_3 \times F_{32} + r_3 \times F_{33}.$

Q.3 Motion of centre of mass ultimately the same. *A* and *C* still move in circles relative to *B* with collisions fore and aft, but their angular velocities relative to *B* now increase over the period of duration of the impulse, and the greatest angular velocity reached is less than in the case of the jerk.

Q.4 The droplets have initial momentum δmu, so
$$(m + \delta m)g\,\delta t = (m + \delta m)(v + \delta v) - mv - \delta mu.$$
Then proceed as before.

Q.5 $F_{11}\cdot\dot{r}_1 + F_{12}\cdot\dot{r}_1 + F_{13}\cdot\dot{r}_1 + F_{21}\cdot\dot{r}_2 + F_{22}\cdot\dot{r}_2 + F_{23}\cdot\dot{r}_2 + F_{31}\cdot\dot{r}_3 + F_{32}\cdot\dot{r}_3 +$
$F_{33}\cdot\dot{r}_3 = m_1\ddot{r}_1\cdot\dot{r}_1 + m_2\ddot{r}_2\cdot\dot{r}_2 + m_3\ddot{r}_3\cdot\dot{r}_3.$

Chapter 15

Q.1 General point on axis $(1, 3 + 2t, -2 + t)$. Position vector of $(4, -2, 1)$ relative to this point is $\begin{bmatrix} 3 \\ -5 - 2t \\ 3 - t \end{bmatrix}$.

$$v = \frac{4}{\sqrt{5}}\begin{bmatrix} 0 \\ 2 \\ 1 \end{bmatrix} \times \begin{bmatrix} 3 \\ -5 - 5t \\ 3 - t \end{bmatrix} = \frac{4}{\sqrt{5}}\begin{bmatrix} 11 \\ 3 \\ -6 \end{bmatrix}, \text{ as before.}$$

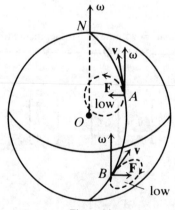

Figure 14

Q.2 The earth rotates from west to east, so ω is in the direction **ON**. Consider air particles *A* and *B* in the northern and southern hemispheres respectively, each moving due north with velocity $\mathbf{v}$ (Fig. 14). The direction of $\mathbf{F}$ towards the centre of low pressure is the same as the direction of $\boldsymbol{\omega} \times \mathbf{v}$, which is due west at A and due east at B. So the air moves anticlockwise in the northern hemisphere, and clockwise in the southern hemisphere.

Chapter 16

Q.1 $\dfrac{2M^2 g\bar{r}^2}{I_0} \cos \alpha - Mg \cos \theta \left(1 + \dfrac{2M\bar{r}^2}{I_0} \right),$

since $M\mathbf{g} = Mg \cos \theta \hat{\mathbf{r}} - Mg \sin \theta \hat{\mathbf{u}}$.

Q.2 Taking moments about P gives

$$Mga \sin \theta = Ma\ddot{\bar{r}} + \tfrac{1}{2}Ma^2\ddot{\theta}$$
$$= \tfrac{3}{2}Ma\ddot{\bar{r}} \quad \text{since} \quad \ddot{\bar{r}} = a\ddot{\theta}.$$

So $\qquad\qquad\qquad \ddot{\bar{r}} = \tfrac{2}{3}g \sin \theta.$

Q.3 $\mu = 0 \Rightarrow \ddot{\bar{r}} = g \sin \alpha$ and $\ddot{\theta} = 0$; the disc slips down the slope without rotating, with the same acceleration as a particle sliding down a smooth slope.

Answers

1

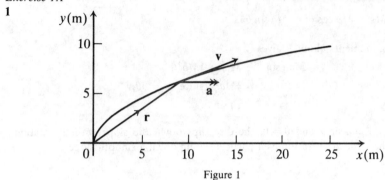

Figure 1

$\mathbf{r} = 9\mathbf{i} + 6\mathbf{j}$

$\mathbf{v} = 6\mathbf{i} + 2\mathbf{j}$

$\mathbf{a} = 2\mathbf{i}$

2 (a) $\dot{\mathbf{r}} = 10\mathbf{i} + (17 - 9.8t)\mathbf{j}$, $\mathbf{r} = (2 + 10t)\mathbf{i} + (1 + 17t - 4.9t^2)\mathbf{j}$.
(b) $\sqrt{(10^2 + 7.2^2)} \approx 12 \text{ m s}^{-1}$.   (c) $\sqrt{(22^2 + 15.4^2)} \approx 27$ m.
(d) $\tan^{-1}(-12.4/10) \approx -51°$, i.e. $51°$ below horizontal.

3

t	-1	0	1	2	3	4	5	6	7
$\mathbf{r}$	$\begin{bmatrix} 7 \\ -21 \end{bmatrix}$	$\begin{bmatrix} 0 \\ 0 \end{bmatrix}$	$\begin{bmatrix} 5 \\ 15 \end{bmatrix}$	$\begin{bmatrix} 16 \\ 24 \end{bmatrix}$	$\begin{bmatrix} 27 \\ 27 \end{bmatrix}$	$\begin{bmatrix} 32 \\ 24 \end{bmatrix}$	$\begin{bmatrix} 25 \\ 15 \end{bmatrix}$	$\begin{bmatrix} 0 \\ 0 \end{bmatrix}$	$\begin{bmatrix} -49 \\ -21 \end{bmatrix}$

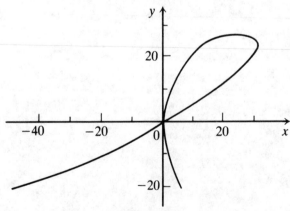

Figure 2

$$\mathbf{v} = \begin{bmatrix} 12t - 3t^2 \\ 18 - 6t \end{bmatrix}, \quad \mathbf{a} = \begin{bmatrix} 12 - 6t \\ -6 \end{bmatrix}$$

$|\mathbf{a}|^2 = (12 - 6t)^2 + (-6)^2 \geqslant 36,$
so $|\mathbf{a}|$ is at least 6.

$|\mathbf{a}| = 6 \Leftrightarrow 12 - 6t = 0 \Leftrightarrow t = 2 \Leftrightarrow \mathbf{r} = \begin{bmatrix} 16 \\ 24 \end{bmatrix}.$

4 Circle, radius 5, centre $(0, 5)$; acceleration towards centre.

5 Ellipse, semi-axes 4 and 3; frequency 20; $314°$.
Greatest speed 0.4π when $t = 5(2n + 1)$.
Acceleration parallel to $\mathbf{i}$ when $t = 10n$.

6 $\left.\begin{array}{l} x = 3 + 4\sin^2 t \\ y = 1 + 2\cos^2 t \end{array}\right\} \Rightarrow x + 2y = 9$ since $\sin^2 t + \cos^2 t = 1$ and $3 \leqslant x \leqslant 7$ since
$0 \leqslant \sin^2 t \leqslant 1.$

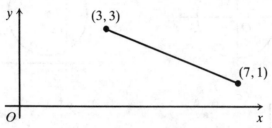

Figure 3

Period $= \pi$.
When acceleration is zero particle is at $(5, 2)$ with speed $2\sqrt{5}$.

7 $\dfrac{d}{dt}(\mathbf{v} \cdot \mathbf{v}) = \mathbf{v} \cdot \dot{\mathbf{v}} + \dot{\mathbf{v}} \cdot \mathbf{v}$ (product rule)

$\qquad = 2\mathbf{v} \cdot \dot{\mathbf{v}} = 2\mathbf{v} \cdot \mathbf{a}.$

But $\mathbf{v} \cdot \mathbf{v} = |\mathbf{v}|^2$, so

speed constant $\Rightarrow \mathbf{v} \cdot \mathbf{v} = \text{constant} \Rightarrow \dfrac{d}{dt}(\mathbf{v} \cdot \mathbf{v}) = 0 \Rightarrow \mathbf{v} \cdot \mathbf{a} = 0 \Rightarrow \mathbf{v} \perp \mathbf{a}.$

Exercise 1B

1

(i)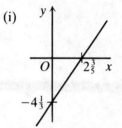

(ii)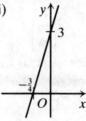

(iii)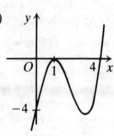

(iv)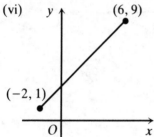

(v)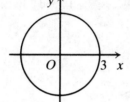

(vi)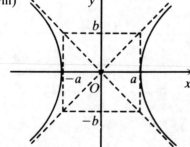

(vii)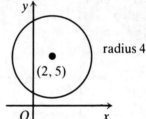

(viii)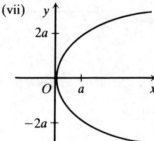

Figure 4

2 (i) $5x - 3y - 13 = 0$; (ii) $y = 4x + 3$; (iii) $y = (x - 1)^3 - 3(x - 1)^2$;
(iv) $x^2 + y^2 = 9$; (v) $(x - 2)^2 + (y - 5)^2 = 16$; (vi) $y = x + 3$, $-2 \le x \le 6$;
(vii) $y^2 = 4ax$; (viii) $\dfrac{x^2}{a^2} - \dfrac{y^2}{b^2} = 1$. (i), (ii), (iii), (vi) are functions.

3 (i) No points;   (ii) no points;   (iii) parallel to **i** at $(1, 0)$ and $(3, 4)$;   (iv) parallel to **i** at $(0, \pm 3)$, parallel to **j** at $(\pm 3, 0)$;   (v) parallel to **i** at $(2, 1)$ and $(2, 9)$, parallel to **j** at $(-2, 5)$ and $(6, 5)$;   (vi) no points;   (vii) parallel to **j** at $(0, 0)$;   (viii) parallel to **j** at $(\pm a, 0)$.

4 (i)

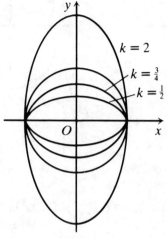

Figure 5

(iii) $\begin{bmatrix} b/a & 0 \\ 0 & 1 \end{bmatrix}$

6 Quadrant of ellipse $\dfrac{x^2}{a^2} + \dfrac{y^2}{b^2} = 1$. Locus of head is a congruent elliptical quadrant, translated vertically.

7

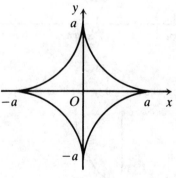

Figure 6

$x^{2/3} + y^{2/3} = a^{2/3}$;

$\dfrac{d\mathbf{r}}{dp} = \begin{bmatrix} -3a \sin p \cos^2 p \\ 3a \sin^2 p \cos p \end{bmatrix}$;

cusps at $(\pm a, 0)$, $(0, \pm a)$.

8 (*c*)

(i)

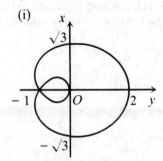

(ii)

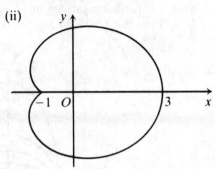

Figure 7

9 $\dfrac{d\mathbf{r}}{d\theta} = \begin{bmatrix} a - a\cos\theta \\ a\sin\theta \end{bmatrix}$, $\mathbf{PN} = \begin{bmatrix} a\sin\theta \\ a\cos\theta - a \end{bmatrix}$.

The wheel is instantaneously turning about N, which is at rest on the ground (see questions 1, 2, 3 of Exercise 15B).

10 $\mathbf{OC} = \begin{bmatrix} 2a\theta \\ 2a \end{bmatrix}$, $\mathbf{CL} = \begin{bmatrix} -a\sin\theta \\ -a\cos\theta \end{bmatrix}$, $\mathbf{CM} = \begin{bmatrix} -3a\sin\theta \\ -3a\cos\theta \end{bmatrix}$.

$L: x = a(2\theta - \sin\theta)$, $y = a(2 - \cos\theta)$
$M: x = a(2\theta - 3\sin\theta)$, $y = a(2 - 3\cos\theta)$.

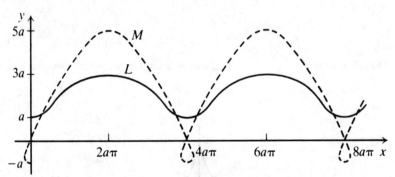

Figure 8

11 $x = m^2$, $y = m^3$. Cusps when $m = 0$. $y = x^{3/2}$ is the upper half of this curve.

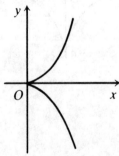

Figure 9

12   (a) $m \neq -1$.

(b)

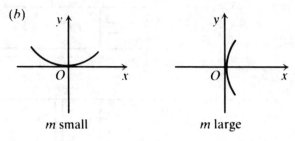

m small m large

(d)

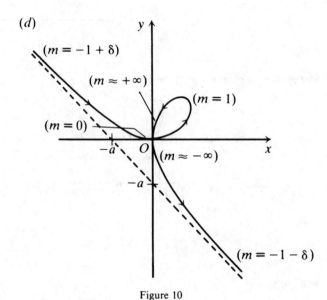

Figure 10

Exercise 1C

1 8 m s^{-2}.

3 6 m s^{-1}.

4   Let $\angle QPN = \psi$ = angle between normal and v-axis.

  = angle between tangent and x-axis,

so $\tan \psi = \dfrac{dv}{dx}$.

$QN = PQ \tan \psi = v \dfrac{dv}{dx}$ = acceleration.

5   Acceleration $= v \dfrac{dv}{dx} > 0$. But $v = 0$, so $\dfrac{dv}{dx}$ is infinite.

7 11.2 km s^{-1}.

8   Initial $P \times xA = P_0 \times aA$
    position $\Rightarrow P = P_0 a/x.$

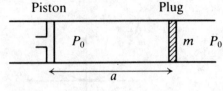

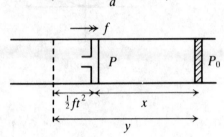

Figure 11

Position $y = \frac{1}{2} ft^2 + x$
at time t $\Rightarrow \ddot{y} = f + \ddot{x}$

Equation of motion of plug: $m\ddot{y} = A(P - P_0)$.

So $mf + m\ddot{x} = AP_0\left(\dfrac{a}{x} - 1\right)$

or $\dot{x}\dfrac{d\dot{x}}{dx} = \dfrac{AP_0 a}{mx} - \dfrac{AP_0}{m} - f$

$$t = \int \frac{1}{\sqrt{2}}\left[\frac{AP_0 a}{m}\ln\frac{x}{a} - \left(\frac{AP_0}{m} + f\right)(x - a)\right]^{-1/2} dx.$$

Exercise 1D

1   $2\pi/5 \approx 1.26$ s, 0.5 m.

2   1.70 s.

3   0.106 m, 37.7 m s^{-2}, 0.0276 m.

5   6.37 a.m.

7   (a) -0.60 m, 1.68 s;   (b) -0.85 m, 2.00 s.

8   $\dfrac{na}{2} - \dfrac{nh^2}{2a} + h.$

9   No energy is lost, so the particle rises to its original height. Therefore
$$\tfrac{3}{4}l + \tfrac{1}{4}l \cos \beta = l \cos \alpha.$$
Using $\cos \theta \approx 1 - \tfrac{1}{2}\theta^2$ in this gives $\beta = 2\alpha$, so distance travelled $= 3l\alpha$. Length of equivalent pendulum $= \tfrac{9}{16}l$.

10   $\dfrac{k(a + b)}{h + k}; \; 2\pi\sqrt{\left(\dfrac{m}{h + k}\right)}.$

11

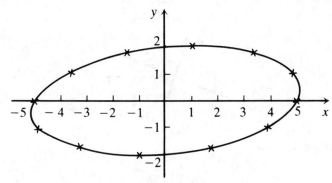

Figure 12

12 (d) 23°.

Exercise 1E

1 2.45 m s^{-1}, 0.58 s, 0.86 m.

3 $\dfrac{dv}{dx} = \dfrac{-2D}{m} \cdot \dfrac{x^2}{a^2 + x^2}$ (where x = distance travelled since touchdown); $D = \dfrac{2mV}{a(4 - \pi)}$.

4 $mv\dfrac{dv}{dx} = -P - Qv^2$; $\lambda = \dfrac{m}{2Q}$, $\mu = \dfrac{Q}{P}$; 512 m.

5 Use $\ln(1 + x) \approx x - \dfrac{x^2}{2} + \cdots$, $\tan^{-1} x \approx x - \dfrac{x^3}{3} + \cdots$

6 Use $v\dfrac{dv}{dx}$ to show that $U^2 = 100 + 2400\, e^{-10g}$ (where U is the speed just before landing) and hence that $U \approx 10 + 120\, e^{-10g}$. Then use $\dfrac{dv}{dt}$ to show that he reaches the ground in 48.9 s.

7 $v = \dfrac{3000\,(e^{33gt/1000} - 1)}{6e^{33gt/1000} + 5}$; 3.22 s.

10 Use $e^x \approx 1 + x + \dfrac{x^2}{2} + \cdots$.

11 $x = \dfrac{UV \cos \alpha}{g}(1 - e^{-gt/V})$, $y = \dfrac{V}{g}(V + U \sin \alpha)(1 - e^{-gt/V}) - Vt$;

$y = \left(\dfrac{V}{U \cos \alpha} + \tan \alpha\right)x + \dfrac{V^2}{g}\ln\left(1 - \dfrac{gx}{UV \cos \alpha}\right)$.

Exercise 2A

1

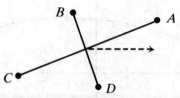

Figure 13

$ABCD$ is a rhombus.

2

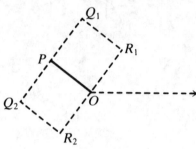

Figure 14

$$Q_1\left(3\sqrt{2},\frac{7\pi}{12}\right), R_1\left(3,\frac{\pi}{3}\right);$$

$$Q_2\left(3\sqrt{2},\frac{13\pi}{12}\right), R_2\left(3,\frac{4\pi}{3}\right).$$

3 (a) Circle, centre O, radius 3.   (b) Interior of circle,
   centre O, radius 3.

   (c) Annulus between circles   (d) Half-line $y = x$ in first
   radii 3 and 4.   quadrant.

   (e) Points in the third
   quadrant.

   (f)   (g)

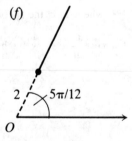 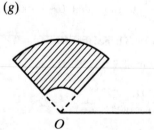

Figure 15

4 (a) $(-4, 0)$; (b) $(2.12, -2.12)$; (c) $(0, -5)$ (d) $(-6.93, 4)$
   (e) $(-4.58, -5.30)$.

5 (a) $(3, \pi)$; (b) $\left(2, \frac{\pi}{6}\right)$; (c) $\left(6, \frac{7\pi}{4}\right)$; (d) $(13, 4.32)$; (e) $(7.21, 2.85)$.

6 Conditions similar to 3 (g).

Exercise 2B

1 $r \le 0$ for $\pi \le \theta \le 2\pi$; curve repeated. Circle, centre $\left(5, \dfrac{\pi}{2}\right)$, radius 5.
$x^2 + y^2 - 10y = 0$.

2 k large: approximates to circle centre O, radius k.
k small: approximates to circle centre $(2\frac{1}{2}, \pi/2)$, radius $2\frac{1}{2}$, repeated.

3

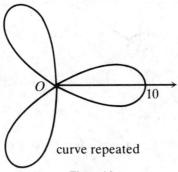

curve repeated

Figure 16

5 $x = a, y = a$.

7 $x^2 + y^2 - 2a \cos \alpha\, x - 2a \sin \alpha\, y + a^2 - b^2 = 0$.

8 $r(1 + \cos \theta) = 4$; $y^2 = 16 - 8x$.

Exercise 2C

1 (a) Velocities 0.737 m s^{-1} and 0.523 m s^{-1}; accelerations 1.49 m s^{-2} and 1.39 m s^{-2}.

(b) $0, \dfrac{\pi}{2}, \pi, \ldots$ s; acceleration towards O.

3 (a) Radial components -1.8 m s^{-2} and -16.2 m s^{-2}; transverse component 0.6 m s^{-2}.
(b) After 2.35 s.

5 9.2 m s^{-2} at $12.5°$ with downward vertical; 15.8 m s^{-1}.

6 (a) Speed zero; (b) speed constant.

Exercise 2D

1 $\mathbf{v} = \cos t\hat{\mathbf{r}} + (20 + 2 \sin t)\hat{\mathbf{u}}$, $\mathbf{a} = -(40 + 5 \sin t)\hat{\mathbf{r}} + 4 \cos t\hat{\mathbf{u}}$.

$t = \pi/3$: $\mathbf{v} = 0.5\hat{\mathbf{r}} + 21.7\hat{\mathbf{u}}$, $\mathbf{a} = -44.3\hat{\mathbf{r}} + 2\hat{\mathbf{u}}$

$t = 2\pi/3$: $\mathbf{v} = -0.5\hat{\mathbf{r}} + 21.7\hat{\mathbf{u}}$, $\mathbf{a} = -44.3\hat{\mathbf{r}} - 2\hat{\mathbf{u}}$.

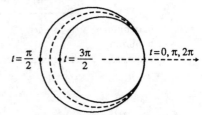

Figure 17

2 3.49 rad s^{-1}; $r = 0.86\theta$ (with r in cm); 42.0 cm s^{-1} at $86°$ to radius.

3 $\omega\sqrt{(r^2\omega^2 + 4u^2)}$ at α to radius as shown, where

$$\tan \alpha = \frac{2u}{r\omega}.$$

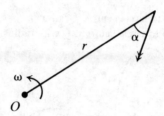

Figure 18

6 Data $\Rightarrow \dot{r} = r^2$ (1) and $r\dot\theta = \theta^2$ (2).

Separating variables in (1) $\Rightarrow \displaystyle\int \frac{dr}{r^2} = \int dt \Rightarrow r = (1-t)^{-1}$.

Separating variables in (2) and substituting for $r \Rightarrow \displaystyle\int \frac{d\theta}{\theta^2} = \int (1-t)\,dt$

$\Rightarrow \theta = 2/(2 - 2t + t^2)$.

8 Transverse acceleration $= 0 \Rightarrow r^2\dot\theta = k$, constant, by question 7,

$\Rightarrow r\dot\theta^2 = r\left(\dfrac{k}{r^2}\right)^2 = \dfrac{k^2}{r^3}$.

Also $r = \dfrac{a}{\theta} \Rightarrow \dot{r} = \dfrac{-a}{\theta^2}\dot\theta = \dfrac{-r^2\dot\theta}{a} = \dfrac{-k}{a} \Rightarrow \ddot{r} = 0$.

So acceleration $=$ radial acceleration $= \ddot{r} - r\dot\theta = \dfrac{-k^2}{r^3}$.

9 $\mathbf{r} = b\hat{\mathbf{u}} - b\theta\hat{\mathbf{n}}$, $\mathbf{v} = b\theta\dot\theta\hat{\mathbf{u}}$, $\mathbf{a} = b(\dot\theta^2 + \theta\ddot\theta)\hat{\mathbf{u}} + b\theta\dot\theta^2\hat{\mathbf{n}}$. Tension is parallel to $\hat{\mathbf{n}}$, so $\hat{\mathbf{u}}$-component of acceleration is zero. $\dot\theta^2 + \theta\ddot\theta = 0 \Rightarrow \dfrac{d}{dt}(\theta\dot\theta) = 0 \Rightarrow \theta\dot\theta = k$

$\Rightarrow \displaystyle\int \theta\, d\theta = \int k\, dt$, etc.

10

	$|\mathbf{r}|$	$|\dot{\mathbf{r}}|$	$|\ddot{\mathbf{r}}|$
maximum	a	$3\omega a$	$10\omega^2 a$
minimum	0	ωa	$6\omega^2 a$

Exercise 3A

2 $\dfrac{12}{1+e}, \dfrac{12}{1-e}$.

3 $\dfrac{24e}{1 - e^2}$.

4 $\dfrac{12}{1 + e} \to 6, \dfrac{12}{1 - e} \to \infty, \dfrac{24e}{1 - e^2} \to \infty$.

5 When $p < 0$, L_p is to the right of L_0.

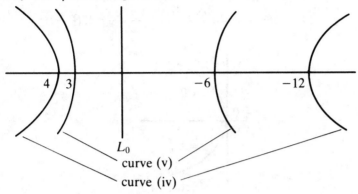

Figure 19

Exercise 3B

1 $\dfrac{4}{r} = 1 + \tfrac{1}{3}\cos\theta, \dfrac{6}{r} = 1 + \tfrac{1}{2}\cos\theta, \dfrac{12}{r} = 1 + \cos\theta, \dfrac{24}{r} = 1 + 2\cos\theta, \dfrac{36}{r} = 1 + 3\cos\theta.$

2 (a) $3, \tfrac{1}{2}$; (b) $3, 1$; (c) $3, \tfrac{3}{2}$.

3 $r = l\sec\theta/e$.

4 (a) Circle, centre S, radius l;
   (b) empty if $e < 1$, initial line if $e = 1$, line pair through S making angles $\pm\cos^{-1}(1/e)$ with initial line if $e > 1$.

5 If P has polar coordinates (p, α) then Q is $(q, \alpha + \pi)$. Substitute in polar equation of conic and add.

6 With notation of question 5, show that $p + q = 2l/(1 - e^2\cos^2\alpha)$, and similarly $h + k = 2l/(1 - e^2\sin\alpha)$. Take reciprocals and add.

8 Start as in question 5.

9 Let tangents TH, TK be $l/r = \cos(\theta - \alpha) + e\cos\theta$ and $l/r = \cos(\theta - \beta) + e\cos\theta$.
   These meet where $\cos(\theta - \alpha) = \cos(\theta - \beta)$, i.e. $\theta = \dfrac{\alpha + \beta}{2}$, so ST bisects angle HSK.

Exercise 3C

2 $y^2 + 12x - 10y - 59 = 0$.

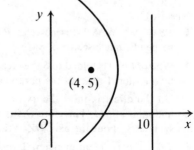

Figure 20

3 0.6.

4 $\frac{2}{3} \times$ area of circle $= 6\pi$.

5 $\sqrt{7}/4 \approx 0.66$.

7 $\dfrac{(x-5)^2}{4} - \dfrac{(y-3)^2}{12} = 1$; $(5, 3)$.

8 $8x^2 + 9y^2 - 24x + 36y + 36 = 0$; $\dfrac{(x - \frac{3}{2})^2}{\frac{9}{4}} + \dfrac{(y+2)^2}{2} = 1$; $(\frac{3}{2}, -2)$.

9

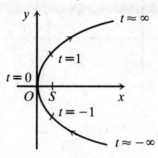

Figure 21

12 $\begin{bmatrix} a/b & 0 \\ 0 & 1 \end{bmatrix}$; πab.

14

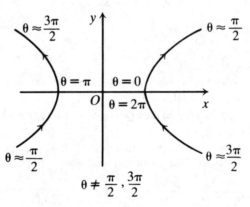

Figure 22

Exercise 3D

1 $PS = PM$, so $\triangle SPM$ is isosceles. PZ bisects $\angle SPM$ (reflector property) so PZ is the perpendicular bisector of SM.

2 When M on l is folded to S the crease is the perpendicular bisector PZ of SM, which by question 1 touches the parabola with focus S, directrix l.

3 Let the directrix meet the axis at A. Then O is the midpoint of SA and Z is the midpoint of SM. Therefore OZ is parallel to AM, i.e. perpendicular to SA. So, by symmetry about the axis, OZ is the tangent at O.

4 Taking m as OZ in question 3, the arms of the right angle lie along SZ and ZP.

5 19.5 m.

7 Let the centre of the circle be C. Length of focal chord $= h + k$, so radius of circle $= \frac{1}{2}(h + k) = CD$. Result follows.

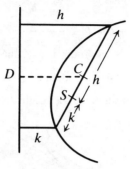

Figure 23

8 (a) When $u = v$ the parallelogram of velocities is a rhombus, so the tangent to the path (in direction of resultant velocity) bisects $\angle BPC$. By the converse of the reflector property, path is part of a parabola with focus B.

(Supplementary question: how long does the swimmer take to cross the river?)

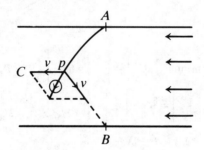

(b)

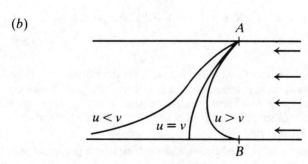

Figure 24

9 $(0, 4, 4)$; $x = 0$, $y = 4$.

10 PH is the reflection of PS in the tangent (reflector property).
$S'H = S'P + PH = S'P + PS = 2a$.

11 S and the centre of the circle.

12 O is midpoint of SS', Q is midpoint of SH, so $OQ = \frac{1}{2}S'H$ (midpoint theorem) $= a$.

14 Locus of Q is the circle with diameter the transverse axis AA'. Procedure of question 13 gives a hyperbola when S is outside the circle.

15 Tangent at $P(a \sec \theta, b \tan \theta)$ is $\dfrac{x \sec \theta}{a} - \dfrac{y \tan \theta}{b} = 1$. This meets the asymptotes

$\dfrac{x^2}{a^2} - \dfrac{y^2}{b^2} = 0$, where $\dfrac{x^2}{a^2} - \cot^2 \theta \left(1 - \dfrac{x \sec \theta}{a}\right)^2 = 0$, which simplifies to

$x^2 - 2ax \sec \theta + a^2 = 0$. This has roots x_1, x_2, the x-coordinates of U, V, with

$x_1 + x_2 = 2a \sec \theta$ and $x_1 x_2 = a^2$. Midpoint of UV has x-coordinate $\dfrac{x_1 + x_2}{2}$,

$\triangle OUV$ has area $\frac{1}{2} x_1 x_2 \sec^2 \alpha \sin 2\alpha$, so the results follow.

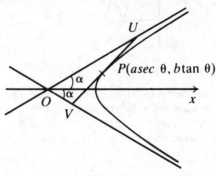

Figure 25

17 Under rotation through $\dfrac{\pi}{4}$, $\begin{bmatrix} x \\ y \end{bmatrix} \to \begin{bmatrix} X \\ Y \end{bmatrix}$ where $\begin{bmatrix} X \\ Y \end{bmatrix} = \mathbf{R}_{\pi/4} \begin{bmatrix} x \\ y \end{bmatrix}$ or

$$\begin{bmatrix} x \\ y \end{bmatrix} = \mathbf{R}_{-\pi/4} \begin{bmatrix} X \\ Y \end{bmatrix} = \begin{bmatrix} 1/\sqrt{2} & 1/\sqrt{2} \\ -1/\sqrt{2} & 1/\sqrt{2} \end{bmatrix} \begin{bmatrix} X \\ Y \end{bmatrix},$$

i.e. $x = \dfrac{1}{\sqrt{2}}(X + Y)$, $y = \dfrac{1}{\sqrt{2}}(X - Y)$. So

$$x^2 - y^2 = a^2 \Rightarrow \tfrac{1}{2}(X + Y)^2 - \tfrac{1}{2}(X - Y)^2 = a^2 \Rightarrow XY = c^2,$$

where $c^2 = a^2/2$.

18 $x + t_1^2 y = 2ct_1$.

19 Let the triangle have vertices $P_i(ct_i, c/t_i)$, $i = 1, 2, 3$. Let the altitude from P_1 to $P_2 P_3$ meet the hyperbola again at $P_4(ct_4, c/t_4)$. The gradients of $P_1 P_4$, $P_2 P_3$ are $-1/t_1 t_4$, $-1/t_2 t_3$ respectively, and since these lines are perpendicular $t_1 t_2 t_3 t_4 = -1$. This is symmetrical, so the other altitudes pass through P_4. (Note also that P_1 is the orthocentre of $\triangle P_2 P_3 P_4$, etc.)

20 The foci are the centres of the fixed circles. Use the focal length properties of §3.5(3). If C_1, C_2 intersect, the locus is a hyperbola.

21 $p = \frac{1}{2}(1 + \alpha)$, $q = \frac{1}{2}(1 - \alpha)$; $e = \sqrt{\left(\dfrac{2\alpha}{1 + \alpha}\right)}$ in both cases; (i) ellipse, (ii) hyperbola.

Project Exercise 3E

1 Tangents to the sphere from P.

9 No other sphere if $\alpha = \beta$. Otherwise one other sphere, touching Π at the other focus.

The second sphere is below Π, in the same half of the double cone if $\alpha < \beta$, in the other half if $\alpha > \beta$.

10 For ellipse, $SP + S'P = PQ + PQ' = QQ'$, which is constant since the circles of contact of the two spheres are parallel. (Dashes refer to the second sphere). Similarly for hyperbola.

11 By symmetry the locus is in the plane through AA' perpendicular to the plane of the ellipse. The light rays entering the eye form a circular cone, which contains a Dandelin sphere touching the plane of the ellipse at a focus. As the sphere varies

$$EA' - EA = (k' + z) - (k + z) = k' - k = \text{constant},$$

so E moves on a hyperbola with foci A, A'. As the sphere shrinks E approaches S, so the hyperbola has transverse axis SS'.

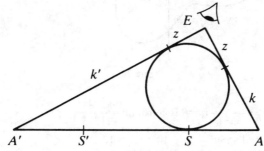

Figure 26

Exercise 4A

1 1 hour 35 minutes; 8360 N.

2 27 100 km h^{-1}, 6570 N.

3 mv^2/r.

4 27 400 km h^{-1}.

5 $V = \dfrac{2\pi r}{t} \Rightarrow F = \dfrac{mV^2}{r} = \dfrac{4\pi^2 mr^2}{rt^2} = \dfrac{4\pi^2 m}{kr^2}$ since $t^2 = kr^3$.

Exercise 4B

1 $h = 20$; 1.14 s.

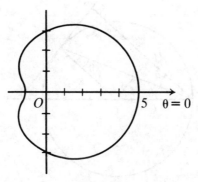

Figure 27

2   3.27 s.

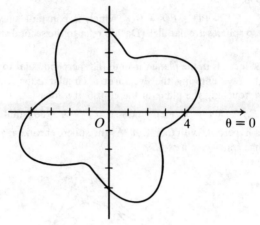

Figure 28

3 $v = \hat{r} - \dfrac{6\pi}{t}\,\hat{u}, \; a = \dfrac{-36\pi^2}{t^3}\,\hat{r}; \; r^2\dot{\theta}$ is constant; $\dfrac{9\pi^2}{2}, \dfrac{4\pi^2}{3}$.

4 $r^2\dot{\theta} = 2k = h$; areal speed $= \frac{1}{2}h = 10$, so $k = 10$.

5 $e^{4\pi k}$.

6 $T = \dfrac{k\pi}{2V}$; $\theta \approx 0.415 \approx 23.8°$.

Exercise 4C

1   Apsidal distances 5 and 1; apsidal speeds 4 and 20.

2   Apsidal distances 10/9 and 10; ratio 9:1.

3   5:3.

4   8000 km, 7000 km; $r(15 + \cos\theta) = 112\,000$.

5 $OH = k\cos 2\theta$, $HK = k$. Result follows.

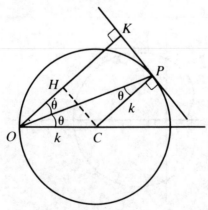

Figure 29

6 (a) $5\,\mathrm{m}^2\,\mathrm{s}^{-1}$, (b) $-675\,\mathrm{m}^2\,\mathrm{s}^{-1}$; h not constant, so not a central force.

7 $\dot{x} = 4\sin\left(\dfrac{10}{t}\right) - \dfrac{40}{t}\cos\left(\dfrac{10}{t}\right)$, $\dot{y} = 6\cos\left(\dfrac{10}{t}\right) + \dfrac{60}{t}\sin\left(\dfrac{10}{t}\right) \Rightarrow h = x\dot{y} - y\dot{x} = 240$; central force with centre O.

Exercise 4D

1 (a) 2; (b) 16; (c) $18, \frac{1}{3}$.

2 $\sqrt{6}$, $8/\sqrt{6}$.

3 1.53.

4 (c) The equation of (b) is a quadratic in r^2, with roots α, β, where $\alpha + \beta = c/k^2 > 0$ (since $c = v^2 + k^2 r^2$) and $\alpha\beta = h^2/k^2 \geqslant 0$. If $h \neq 0$ then α, β are both positive and $r = \pm\sqrt{\alpha}$ or $\pm\sqrt{\beta}$. If $h = 0$ the roots are $r = 0$, $\pm\sqrt{(c/k^2)}$, so there is one positive root. In this case the particle moves with simple harmonic motion centred at O along a straight line through O.

5 $v = \dfrac{2V}{1 + \cos 2\theta} = \dfrac{2V}{2\cos^2\theta} = \dfrac{4k^2 V}{r^2}$ since $r = 2k\cos\theta$.

6 (a) $\tan\phi = \dfrac{1 + \cos\theta}{-\sin\theta} = -\dfrac{2\cos^2(\theta/2)}{2\sin(\theta/2)\cos(\theta/2)} = -\cot(\theta/2)$

$\Rightarrow \phi = \pi - (\pi/2 - \theta/2) = \pi/2 + \theta/2$.

(b) $p = r\cos(\theta/2)$ and $r \propto \cos^2(\theta/2)$.

Exercise 5A

1 Jupiter $T = 11.885$, Saturn $a = 9.538$.

2 (a) $l = 1.25$, $e = \frac{3}{4}$, $\alpha = 0$.

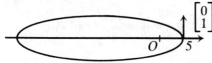

(b) $l = 5$, $e = \frac{1}{2}$, $\alpha = -90°$.

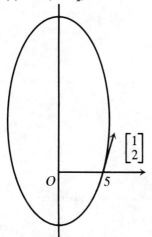

(c) $l = 7.8125$, $e = 0.9375$, $\alpha = -53.1°$.

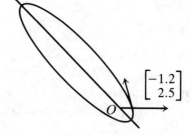

Figure 30

3 17.947 a.u.; $e = 0.967$; 35.307 a.u.

4 Equation of orbit $\Rightarrow \dfrac{-h^2/\mu}{r^2} \dot{r} = -e \sin \theta \dot{\theta} = \dfrac{-eh \sin \theta}{r^2}$, since

$$\dot{\theta} = \frac{h}{r^2} \Rightarrow \dot{r} = \frac{e\mu}{h} \sin \theta \Rightarrow \ddot{r} = \frac{e\mu}{h} \cos \theta \dot{\theta} = \frac{\mu}{h} \left(\frac{h^2/\mu}{r} - 1 \right) \frac{h}{r^2}$$

$$= \frac{h^2}{r^3} - \frac{\mu}{r^2} = r \left(\frac{h}{r^2} \right)^2 - \frac{\mu}{r^2} = r\dot{\theta}^2 - \frac{\mu}{r^2}.$$

5 $ez \cos \beta = eCD$

$\qquad = e(CS + SD)$

$\qquad = ae^2 + er \cos \theta = ae^2 + (l - r) = ae^2 + a(1 - e^2) - r$

$\qquad = a - r.$

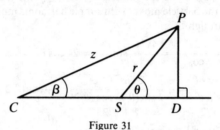

Figure 31

8 Given conditions $\Rightarrow C = \frac{4}{3}, A = \frac{1}{2}, B = 0.$

Exercise 5B

1 Distance to perigee $= \dfrac{l}{1 + \frac{1}{2}} = \dfrac{l_1}{1 + e_1}$ and $l_1 = \dfrac{h_1^2}{\mu} = \dfrac{1.21h^2}{\mu} = 1.21l$

$\qquad\qquad\qquad \Rightarrow e_1 = 0.815.$

$\quad e_1 < 1 \Rightarrow l_1 < \frac{4}{3}l \Rightarrow h_1 < \sqrt{(\frac{4}{3})}h \Rightarrow$ increase $< 15.5\%.$

2 Speed must be doubled.

3 $\theta = \pm 2\pi/3$; ultimate speed $= 5/\sqrt{3} \approx 2.89$ unit s^{-1}.

4 $\dfrac{1.563 \times 10^7}{r} = 1 + 1.084 \cos \theta$; hyperbolic orbit.

5 Three readings; $\dfrac{2.67}{r} = 1 + 0.33 \cos \theta.$

6 $C = \dfrac{\mu}{2a}.$

8 (a) 2.39 a.u./year; (b) 11 400 m s^{-1}.

9 30 400 m s^{-1}.

10 $a(1 - e), a(1 + e).$

11 (a) Orbit is circular; (b) orbit is parabolic; (c) orbit is hyperbolic.

12 $\dot{r}^2 = V^2 - \dfrac{2nq^2}{mr} - \dfrac{3n^2q^4}{m^2V^2r^2}.$

Exercise 5C

1 5.97×10^{24} kg.

2 3.83×10^8 m.

3 $3\sqrt{(\gamma M/l)}$.

4 (*a*) $\ddot{\mathbf{p}} = \dfrac{-\gamma M}{r^3}\,\mathbf{r}$.

7 Integrate from $u = a - r$ to $u = a + r$.

Exercise 6A

1 (*a*) $5\sqrt{17}$;   (*b*) 3π.

2 $\dfrac{\pi}{4}$.

3 16.7.

4 $S = 3(p^4 + p^2)$.

5 (*a*) $\mathbf{r} = 10^4\mathbf{i} + 10^4\mathbf{j}$, $\mathbf{v} = 200\mathbf{i} + 300\mathbf{j}$, $\mathbf{a} = 2\mathbf{i} + 6\mathbf{j}$;
   (*b*) 14 140 m;   (*c*) 14 400 m.

6 $\dfrac{3a}{2}$, $6a$; $\displaystyle\int_0^{2\pi} \dfrac{3a}{2} \sin 2p \, dp = 0$; $\sin 2p$ is negative when $\pi/2 < p < \pi$ or $3\pi/2 < p < 2\pi$.

7 $-4 \cos \dfrac{\theta}{2}$; 16.

8 1018 m (but might be 1019 since upper limit is 1018.52).

9 28.4.

10 2.35.

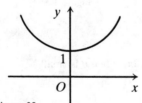

Figure 32

12 (*a*)

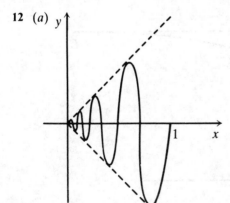

Figure 33

(*b*)

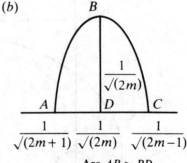

Arc $AB > BD$
Arc $BC > BD$

So Arc $ABC > 2BD = \dfrac{2}{\sqrt{(2m)}}$.

Exercise 6B

1 2α;

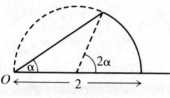

Figure 34

2 $5 \tan \alpha$;

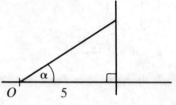

Figure 35

3 $\dfrac{a}{2\pi} \displaystyle\int_0^{2n\pi} \sqrt{(1 + \theta^2)}\,d\theta.$

4 (*a*) *D* and *Q* coincide initially. Arc $DX =$ arc QX since there is no slipping. So
$$\angle DBX = \angle QAX.$$

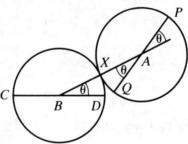

Figure 36

(*d*) 16.

5 $\sqrt{2}/2$.

6 $y = r \sin \theta = 2\pi a \dfrac{\sin \theta}{\theta} \approx 2\pi a$ when θ is small.

$$\int_{1/2}^{4/5} \frac{2\pi a}{t^2(1 - t^2)}\,dt.$$

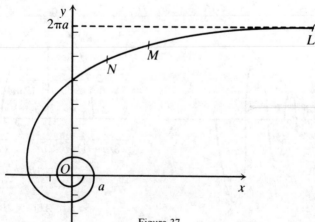

Figure 37

7 (a)

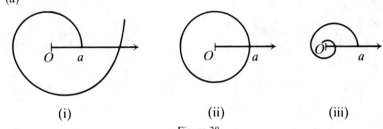

(i)   (ii)   (iii)

Figure 38

(b) $\dfrac{a\sqrt{(1+k^2)}}{k}(e^{k\beta}-e^{k\alpha})$.

(c) (i) Spirals in towards O, (ii) tends to $a\sqrt{(1+k^2)}e^{k\beta}/k$.

Project Exercise 6C

3 $S=\displaystyle\int_{p_1}^{p_2}2\pi y\,\dfrac{ds}{dp}\,dp$.

4 $\dfrac{8\pi a^2}{3}(5^{3/2}-2^{3/2})\approx 70a^2$.

6 (a) $4\pi a^2$;   (b) 2.11×10^7 km^2.

11 $4\pi^2 ab$.

12 On axis of symmetry $2a/\pi$ from diameter.

13 $(\pi a, 4a/3)$.

15 $4\pi c(h+k)$; $2\pi chk$.

16 $2\pi^2 a^2 b$.

17 On axis of symmetry $4a/3\pi$ from diameter.

18 (a) $4\pi a^2\sin\alpha$.

Exercise 7A

1 $\dfrac{8}{(1+64x^2)^{3/2}}$.   2 $\dfrac{-1}{6t(1+t^2)^{3/2}}$.   3 $\dfrac{-\sin x}{(1+\cos^2 x)^{3/2}}$.

4 $\dfrac{-2}{3a\sin 2p}$.   5 $\dfrac{3}{4a}\sec\dfrac{\theta}{2}$.   6 $\dfrac{1}{\sqrt{8e^\theta}}$.

7 0.0754.   8 $-1/2a$.   9 $2^{3/2}ab(a^2+b^2)^{-3/2}$.

13 $(\cot\alpha)/c$.   14 $s=4a\sin\psi$.

16 (a) $x'=\cos\psi\Rightarrow x''=-\sin\psi\,\dfrac{d\psi}{ds}=-y'\kappa$.

$$\Rightarrow \kappa=\dfrac{-x''}{y'},\text{ etc.}$$

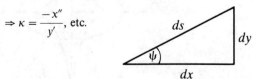

(b) $x'=\dfrac{y''}{\kappa}$, $y'=\dfrac{-x''}{\kappa}$ from (a), and $x'^2+y'^2=\left(\dfrac{ds}{ds}\right)^2=1$, etc.

Exercise 7B

1 (10, 10).

2 $\begin{bmatrix} 0 \\ 1 \end{bmatrix}, \dfrac{1}{\sqrt{5}} \begin{bmatrix} -2 \\ 1 \end{bmatrix}; -1, 0.$

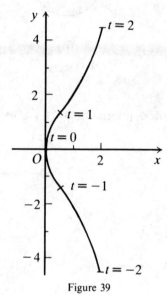

Figure 39

3 $\left(\dfrac{a}{2} (3 \cos p - \cos 3p), \dfrac{a}{2} (3 \sin p - \sin 3p) \right)$

The manipulations in this question are made much easier by using trigonometric expansion and factor formulae

$(\cos A \cdot \cos B = \frac{1}{2}(\cos (A + B) + \cos (A - B))$, etc.,

$\cos P + \cos Q = 2 \cos \dfrac{P + Q}{2} \cos \dfrac{P - Q}{2}$, etc.)

4 (a) $-6p(1 + p^2)^{3/2}$; $(6p + 8p^3, -3p^2 - 6p^4)$.

5 $\frac{1}{2}(4 \sin^2 \theta + \cos^2 \theta)^{3/2}$;

$\begin{bmatrix} 3/2 \\ 0 \end{bmatrix}, \begin{bmatrix} 96/125 \\ -81/125 \end{bmatrix}, \begin{bmatrix} 0 \\ -3 \end{bmatrix}.$

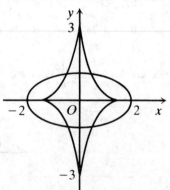

Figure 40

6

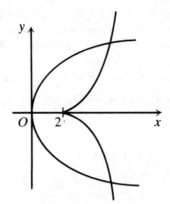

Figure 41

7 (a) $\rho \sin \psi = \dfrac{ds}{d\psi} \times \dfrac{dy}{ds} = \dfrac{dy}{d\psi}$, etc.

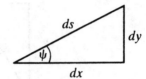

(b) $\psi = \theta$; $(\cos \theta, \sin \theta)$; circle centre O, radius a.

8 $s = e^\theta - 1$; $\mathbf{r} = \dfrac{s-1}{\sqrt 2} (\cos \ln (1 + s)\mathbf{i} + \sin \ln (1 + s)\mathbf{j})$.

$\hat{\mathbf{n}} = \dfrac{1}{\sqrt 2} (-(p + q)\mathbf{i} + (p - q)\mathbf{j})$.

11 14.

12

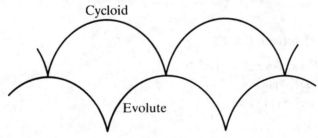

Figure 42

The equiangular spiral $r = ae^{k\theta}$ is its own evolute provided that k is chosen so that every normal touches the curve elsewhere. To find these values of k (there is an infinite sequence of them) use the fact that $\cot \phi = k$. See Example 3 of Chapter 4, p. 69).

Exercise 7C

1 110.6 m s^{-2} normal to the curve.

2 $\dot\psi = k \Rightarrow \rho = \dfrac{\dot s}{\dot\psi} = \dfrac{\dot s}{k} = \dfrac{v}{k} \Rightarrow$ normal acceleration $= \dfrac{v^2}{v/k} = kv.$

3   Along the straight $\kappa = 0$; on $y = x^2/9$, $\kappa = \frac{2}{9}$ at O; on $y = x^3/27$, $\kappa = 0$ at O. So with $y = x^2/9$ there is a sudden change in normal acceleration at O, and passengers feel a sideways jolt there. On $y = x^3/27$ the normal acceleration increases smoothly as the curve starts.

4   Most rapid cornering $\Rightarrow$ maximum normal force (fixed) $\Rightarrow$ normal acceleration is constant $\Rightarrow \dfrac{v^2}{\rho} \Rightarrow$ is constant $v \propto \sqrt{\rho}$.

5   $S = A\sqrt{\psi}$.

6   $\rho = r$ $\qquad\qquad \dfrac{v^2}{r} = \dot{v}\tan\alpha.$ $\qquad\qquad\qquad\qquad\qquad$ (1)

$$\dot{v} = \frac{dv}{dt} = \frac{dv}{ds}\times\frac{ds}{dt} = v\frac{ds}{ds};$$

substitute in (1), separate the variables, and integrate to obtain the final speed.

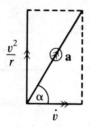

Figure 43

Separate the variables in (1) directly and integrate to find the time taken to round the bend,

$$\frac{r\tan\alpha}{v_0}\,(1 - e^{-(1/2)\pi\cot\alpha})$$

8   $a(1 - e^2)$; between C and S.

9   $\ddot{x} = \frac{1}{2}ak^2\sec^2\theta(\sec^2\theta + 2\tan^2\theta)$,

$\ddot{y} = ak^2\sec^2\theta\tan\theta$;

$\rho = 2a\sec^3\theta$; $(6a, -2a)$.

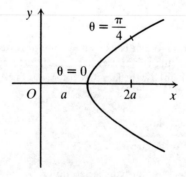

Figure 44

Miscellaneous exercise A

1 $\mathbf{a} = \begin{bmatrix} -10\sin(t^2) - 20t^2\cos(t^2) \\ 10\cos(t^2) - 20t^2\sin(t^2) \end{bmatrix}$; radial: $-20t^2$, transverse: 10;

(a) $-20t^2$, (b) 2k, (c) 10.

2 $(2, 2\pi/3), (2, 4\pi/3)$.

3 $c = a, \delta = \pi/2, e = \sqrt{3}/2$; least $OP = a$.

5 $y = 0, x = 0$; astroid (Exercise 1B, question 7).

6 $\mathbf{r} = \begin{bmatrix} cp - c\sin p \\ c - c\cos p \end{bmatrix}$; perpendicular to TK, where T is where the circle touches the line.

7 $\mathbf{v} = -a\omega\cos\theta\,\hat{\mathbf{r}} + a\omega(2 - \sin\theta)\hat{\mathbf{u}}$

$\mathbf{a} = \mathbf{0}$ when $\theta = \dfrac{\pi}{2}$.

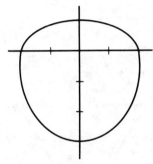

Figure 45

8 $y = g(kt + e^{-kt} - 1)/k^2$.

9 0.2375.

10 $2e^{2\theta}\hat{\mathbf{r}} + e^{2\theta}\hat{\mathbf{u}}$; $\sqrt{5}(e^{4\pi} - 1)/2 \approx 3.2 \times 10^5$.

12 $\pi/3; \pi/2$.

13 $d\mathbf{r}/d\theta \| \mathbf{TP}$.

14 $2; V\sqrt{3}$.

15 $\dfrac{3}{4}a\sin^2\dfrac{\theta}{3}$.

16 $\dfrac{g}{k}(1 - e^{-k\pi/\omega}) - \dfrac{E\omega}{k^2 + \omega^2}(e^{-k\pi/\omega} + 1)$.

17 $\dot{\mathbf{p}} = a\dot{\theta}\mathbf{m} + (-b\cos\phi\,\dot{\theta}\mathbf{e} - b\sin\phi\,\dot{\phi}\mathbf{m} + b\cos\phi\,\dot{\phi}\mathbf{k})$.

18 $\mathbf{F} = \begin{bmatrix} -4ma\omega^2\cos 2\omega t \\ -mu\omega\sin\omega t \end{bmatrix}$; $2\pi/\omega$.

19 $\dfrac{dv_1^2}{\mu} - 1$.

21

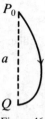

Figure 46

22 (c)

Parabola

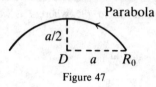

Figure 47

23 $AB: -\pi \leqslant \theta < -2\pi/3$
$CDE: -2\pi/3 < \theta < 2\pi/3.$
$FA: \dfrac{2\pi}{3} < \theta \leqslant \pi.$

$k = 100;$ time $= \displaystyle\int_{-\pi/2}^{\pi/2} \frac{1}{10} (1 + 2\cos\theta)^{-2}\, d\theta.$

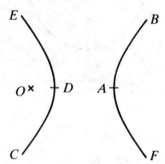

Figure 48

24 (b) $\displaystyle\int_0^\theta \frac{l^2/2}{(1 + e\cos\alpha)^2}\, d\alpha = \int_0^\phi \frac{l^2/2}{(1 - e\cos\alpha)^2}\, d\alpha;$ (c) $\dfrac{d\phi}{d\theta} = \left(\dfrac{1 - e\cos\phi}{1 + e\cos\theta}\right)^2.$

25 $c = \begin{bmatrix} 4 + 6p^2 \\ -4p^3 \end{bmatrix}.$

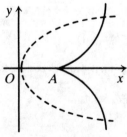

Figure 49

26 $z = \dfrac{ju^2}{4g}(1 - e^{2jgt/u}) + \tfrac{1}{2}ut.$

27   Radial $\dot{r}$, transverse $r\dot{\theta}$; major axis perpendicular to wind, eccentricity $= u/v$, ellipse if $u < v$.

29 $r \to 0$ as $\theta \to \infty$.

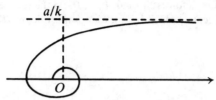

Figure 50

$$\mathbf{F} = \dfrac{-mh^2(1 + k^2)}{r^3}\,\hat{\mathbf{r}}.$$

30   861 km h^{-1}; $\alpha = 163°$.

Exercise 8A

1   26 N, 22.6°.

2 $0.4\mathbf{i} + 2.2\mathbf{j}$, 2.24 m s^{-2}, 79.7°.

3   11.8 N, 005.3°.

4   41.4 N at 268.3°.

5 $\sqrt{3}F$ at 180°.

6   (*a*) $W = 19.6$ N, $N = 17.0$ N, $F = 9.8$ N;   (*b*) $F = 11.0$ N.

7   30 N, 40.8 N.

8   53 500 N, 90 200 N.

9   (*a*) 58.7 N,   (*b*) 47.9 N,   (*c*) 45.0 N when **F** is perpendicular to the cable.

10   336 N, 448 N.

11

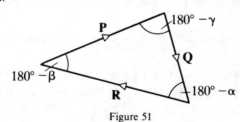

Figure 51

Exercise 8B

1   54.4 N at 74° to AD at the point on AD 1.43 m from A.

2 $5\mathbf{i} + \mathbf{j}$, $5y = x + 7$.

3 $\begin{bmatrix} 3 \\ 4 \end{bmatrix}$, $3y = 4x - 20$.

4   The forces have no resultants but are not in equilibrium; they have a turning effect but no shifting effect, and are said to form a *couple* (see Exercise 8C, question 9).

6 9RS where R is the point of trisection of AB nearer B and S is the point of trisection of BC nearer C.

7 The forces form a couple.

9 Since $AP = AS$ (tangents from A to the circle), the resultant of **AP** and **AS** passes through A and bisects $\angle PAS$, and so passes through the centre of the circle. Similarly for the pairs of forces through B, C, D. So the resultant of all eight forces passes through the centre, which by question 8 must lie on HK.

Exercise 8C

1 1.3 m.

2 30**j** acting along $x = 6$.

3 2.3 m.

5 Let T be the set of values of n for which the statement is true.
  (*a*) $1 \in T$ (trivially) and $2 \in T$, $3 \in T$ (by question 4).
  (*b*) $k \in T \Rightarrow$ resultant of $k + 1$ weights is resultant of force $w_1 + \cdots + w_k$ acting
  through G, where $OG = \dfrac{w_1 x_1 + \cdots + w_k x_k}{w_1 + \cdots + w_k}$, and force w_{k+1} acting through A,
  where $OA = x_{k+1} \Rightarrow$ resultant of $k + 1$ weights acts through G', where
  $GG':G'A = w_{k+1}:w_1 + \cdots + w_k$

$$\Rightarrow OG' = \frac{(w_1 + \cdots + w_k)OG + w_{k+1}OA}{(w_1 + \cdots + w_k) + w_{k+1}} = \frac{w_1 x_1 + \cdots + w_{k+1} x_{k+1}}{w_1 + \cdots + w_{k+1}}$$

$$\Rightarrow k + 1 \in T.$$

  From (*a*) and (*b*), by induction, $T = \mathbb{N}$.

7 (*a*) 225 N, 1 m from A and 0.5 m from B.
  (*b*) 75 N, 3 m from A and 1.5 m from B.

8 5**j** acting along $x = -3$.

10 (iii) All other permutations give couples.

Exercise 8D

1 $\sqrt{2}W$. **2** 26.0 N. **3** (*a*) 8.7 N, (*b*) 7.5 N, (*c*) 9.8 N.

4 1 m. **5** 1150 N, 739 N.

7

	A (up)	B (down)	C (up)
$0 \leqslant x \leqslant 2a$	$Mg\left(1 - \dfrac{x}{2a}\right)$	0	$mg + \dfrac{Mgx}{2a}$
$2a \leqslant x \leqslant 4a$	0	$Mg\left(\dfrac{x}{a} - 2\right)$	$mg + Mg\left(\dfrac{x}{a} - 1\right)$.

Greatest $M = 5m/2$.

8 Moment about $A = F(x + d) - Fx = Fd$

Moment about $B = F(d - y) + Fy = Fd$

Moment about $C = -Fz + F(z + d) = Fd$.

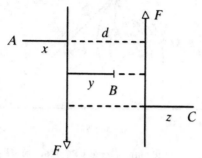

Figure 52

9 Total moment $= \sum_{r=1}^{n} [Y_r a_r - X_r b_r] - p \sum_{r=1}^{n} Y_r + q \sum_{r=1}^{n} X_r$, which is independent of p and q if, and only if, the coefficients of p and q are zero.

10 286 N.

11 240 N m, 2.8 m.

12 (b) These forces form a couple with moment of magnitude $2k \times$ area of polygon.

13 10.8 N, 56.3° to AB and 33.7° to AD, 10 N m, $\frac{5}{3}$ m from A on DA produced.

Exercise 8E

1 $\frac{5}{24} \approx 0.208$; equilibrium impossible.

2 (a) 118, (b) 9.4 N at A, 5.36 N at B.

3 267 N at upper hinge, 333 N at lower hinge.

4 56.3°, 208 N, 347 N.

5 300 N, 264 N at 18.4° to horizontal.

6 15°.

8 0.756 of the way up.

9 (a).

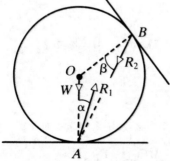 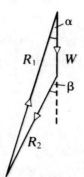

Figure 53

The three forces acting on the cylinder (weight W, reactions R_1, R_2 at A, B) concur at A. From the triangle of forces $\alpha < \beta$, so if either of these angles equals λ it must be β.

(b)

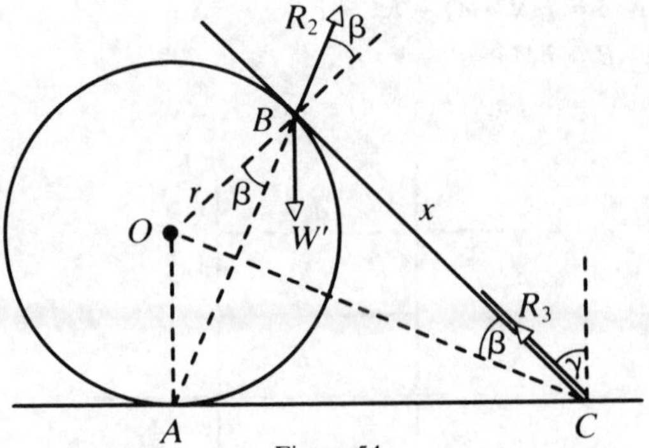

Figure 54

The three forces acting on the plank (weight W', reactions R_2, R_3 at B, C) concur at B, so R_3 acts along CB. From the angles at C

$$2\beta + \gamma = 90°.$$

Slipping at B and C simultaneously $\Rightarrow \beta = \gamma = \lambda \Rightarrow 3\lambda = 90° \Rightarrow \lambda = 30°$

$$\Rightarrow \mu = \tan 30° = \frac{1}{\sqrt{3}} \text{ and } \frac{r}{x} = \tan 30° = \frac{1}{\sqrt{3}}.$$

(c) Slipping at $B \Rightarrow \beta = \lambda$ and $\gamma < \lambda$

$$\Rightarrow 90° = 2\beta + \gamma < 3\lambda$$

$$\Rightarrow \lambda > 30° \Rightarrow \frac{r}{x} = \tan \beta = \tan \lambda > \frac{1}{\sqrt{3}} \text{ and } \mu = \tan \lambda > \frac{1}{\sqrt{3}}.$$

Slipping at $C \Rightarrow \beta < \lambda$ and $\gamma = \lambda$

$$\Rightarrow 90° = 2\beta + \gamma < 3\lambda$$

$$\Rightarrow \gamma = \lambda > 30°$$

$$\Rightarrow \beta = \tfrac{1}{2}(90° - \gamma) < 30°$$

$$\Rightarrow \frac{r}{x} = \tan \beta < \frac{1}{\sqrt{3}} \text{ and } \mu = \tan \lambda > \frac{1}{\sqrt{3}}.$$

In both cases $\mu > \dfrac{1}{\sqrt{3}}$.

Exercise 9A

1 (a) 3.96 kg m^2, (b) 0.66 kg m^2.

2 (a) 3.5 kg m^2, (b) 1.5 kg m^2, (c) 7 kg m^2, (d) 3 kg m^2.

3 0.24 kg m^2.

4 1.0 J.

5 3.02 kg m^2.

6 $\text{MI} = \sum_{i=1}^{n} \frac{M}{n}\left(\frac{il}{n}\right)^2 = \frac{Ml^2}{n^3} \sum_{i=1}^{n} i^2 = \frac{Ml^2}{n^3} \times \frac{1}{6} n(n+1)(2n+1)$

$= \frac{Ml^2}{6} \times \frac{n}{n}\left(\frac{n+1}{n}\right)\left(\frac{2n+1}{n}\right) = \frac{Ml^2}{6}\left(1 + \frac{1}{n}\right)\left(2 + \frac{1}{n}\right).$

As $n \to \infty$, $1 + \frac{1}{n} \to 1$ and $2 + \frac{1}{n} \to 2$; result follows.

7 Mass of element $= \dfrac{M\delta x}{l}$, so

$$\text{MI} = \lim_{\delta x \to 0} \sum_{x=0}^{x=l} \frac{M\delta x}{l} x^2 = \int_0^l \frac{Mx^2}{l} dx = \left[\frac{Mx^3}{3l} \right]_0^l = \tfrac{1}{3} M l^2.$$

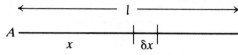

Figure 55

8 $\frac{1}{12} M l^2$.   **9** $M d^2$.   **10** $M a^2$.   **11** 5.55 kg m^2.

12 Mass $\propto$ volume $\propto$ (length)^3, so MI $\propto$ (length)^3 × (length)^2, i.e. MI $\propto$ (length)^5.

Exercise 9B

1 $\frac{5}{2} M a^2$.   **2** $\frac{1}{3} M l^2 \sin^2 \alpha$.   **3** $\frac{1}{4} M l^2$.   **4** 6 kg m^2.

5 (a) $\frac{1}{2} M l^2$; (b) $\frac{1}{3} M l^2$.

6 'Shearing' each part of the triangle onto the altitude produces a non-uniform rod as in 5(b). So MI $= \frac{1}{2} M h^2$.

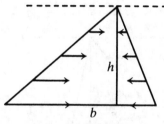

Figure 56

7 $\text{MI} = \lim_{\delta\theta \to 0} \sum_{\theta=0}^{\theta=\pi} \frac{M}{\pi a} (a\delta\theta)(a \sin \theta)^2$

$$= \int_0^\pi \frac{Ma^2}{\pi} \sin^2 \theta \, d\theta = \tfrac{1}{2} M a^2.$$

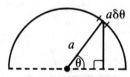

Figure 57

8 $I_x = \sum m(y^2 + z^2)$, $I_y = \sum m(x^2 + z^2)$; by symmetry $I_x = I_y = I_z$; result follows.

9 Mass of shell of radius r and thickness $\delta r = \dfrac{3M}{4\pi a^3} \times 4\pi r^2 \delta r$, so

$$\text{MI} = \int_0^a \frac{2}{3} \left(\frac{3Mr^2}{a^3} \right) r^2 dr = \int_0^a \frac{2M}{a^3} r^4 dr = \tfrac{2}{5} M a^2.$$

10 $2.6 \times 10^{29} \text{ J}$; less.

Exercise 9C

1   (a) $\frac{1}{12}M(a^2 + b^2)$,   (b) $\frac{1}{3}M(a^2 + b^2)$.

2   The centre of mass of each rod is $l/2$ from O, so $MI = 4(\frac{1}{12}Ml^2 + M(l/2)^2) = \frac{4}{3}Ml^2$.
    (Note as a check that this is the MI of the rod, length $2l$, mass $4M$, obtained when
    the rhombus collapses completely.)

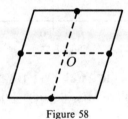

Figure 58

4   $a\sqrt{7}/\sqrt{5} \approx 1.18a$.

5   $r/\sqrt{3} \approx 0.58r$.

6   $I_A = I_G + M(\frac{2}{3}h)^2$
    $I_B = I_G + M(\frac{1}{3}h)^2$.
    Subtract: $I_A - I_B = \frac{1}{3}Mh^2 \Rightarrow I_B = \frac{1}{6}Mh^2$, since $I_A = \frac{1}{2}Mh^2$.

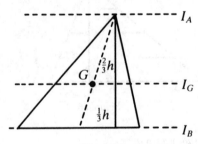

Figure 59

7   By the perpendicular axis rule
$$I_z = I_x + I_y = I_a + I_b.$$
But by symmetry $I_x = I_y$ and $I_a = I_b$. So $I_a = I_x = \frac{1}{12}Ml^2$.

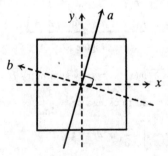

Figure 60

8 $\frac{1}{3}ml^2 + M(\frac{3}{2}a^2 + 2al + l^2)$.

9 (a) $\triangle AFE$ is similar to $\triangle ABC$, with half the linear dimensions.

(b) $AP = \frac{2}{3} \times \frac{1}{2}l$ and $AG = \frac{2}{3}l \Rightarrow PG = \frac{1}{3}l$, etc. Then use the parallel axis rule.

(c) $AB^2 + AC^2 = AD^2 + AD.CB + \frac{1}{4}CB^2 + AD^2 + AD.BC + \frac{1}{4}BC^2$

$= 2AD^2 + \frac{1}{2}CB^2$ since $AD.CB = -AD.BC$ and $CB^2 = BC^2$.

(d) Use (c) to obtain l^2, m^2, n^2 in terms of a^2, b^2, c^2, then substitute in (b).

Exercise 10A

1 (a) 5.4 rad s^{-1}, (b) 7.7 rad s^{-1}.

2 (a) 5.8 rad s^{-1}, (b) 8.2 rad s^{-1}.

3 9.9 rad s^{-1}, 0.025 m.

5 $\left[\dfrac{6gl(2M + m)}{3M + m} \right]^{\frac{1}{2}}$.

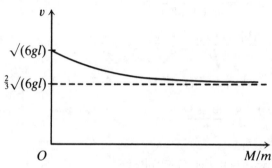

Figure 61

6 $\frac{2}{3}a^4\rho\delta$, $\sqrt{(3\sqrt{2g/a})}$.

7 0.011 kg m^2.

8 2.04×10^{-5} kg m^2, 2.21×10^3 rad s^{-1}.

9 0.383 kg m^2.

10 Let the frictional couple have moment L N m. Then work done by child in 2 revolutions = work done by friction in 3 revolutions, i.e.

$$150 \times \frac{1}{2} \times 4\pi = L \times 6\pi \Rightarrow L = 50.$$

While the child is pushing the resultant couple is $150 \times \frac{1}{2} - 50 = 25$ N m. The MI of the door is $\frac{1}{3}M \times 1^2 = \frac{1}{3}M$ kg m^2, where M kg is its mass. So

$$\frac{1}{2} \times \frac{1}{3}M \times 3^2 = 25 \times 4\pi \Rightarrow M = 209.$$

Exercise 10B

1 2400 rad s^{-1}.　　**2** $\dfrac{5(L - G)}{2Mr^2}$.　　**3** 4:1.

4 $\dfrac{2(T_1 - T_2)}{Mr}$　　**5** $2g/11r$.　　**6** 9:10.

7 10 rad s^{-1}; light gear wheels, no friction.

8 0.228 rad s^{-2}, 0.321 N.

9 92%.

10 $\dfrac{LT}{2I}$.

11 Ω rad s^{-1} (least), $\Omega + \dfrac{2L}{I}$ rad s^{-1} (greatest); $L/2$ N m, $\Omega \pm \dfrac{L}{4I}$ rad s^{-1}.

Exercise 10C

1 126 rad s^{-1} (by Simpson's rule).

2 (a) 24 rad s^{-1},   (b) 8.64 rad s^{-1}.

3 Frictional couple $= \mu mgR$.
For disc: $I\omega = I\omega_1 - \mu mgRt$
For ring: $mR^2\omega = -mR^2\omega_2 + \mu mgRt$.
Eliminating $\omega \Rightarrow t = \dfrac{IR(\omega_1 + \omega_2)}{\mu g(I + mR^2)}$.

4 $\dfrac{I_1\omega_1 + I_2\omega_2}{I_1 + I_2}, \dfrac{I_1 I_2|\omega_1 - \omega_2|}{L(I_1 + I_2)}$.

5 $\dfrac{mR^2 - mRv/\omega}{I + mR^2}$ where $I = \tfrac{8}{15}\rho\pi R^5$ and $\omega = 7.27 \times 10^{-5}$.

6 (a) $\dfrac{6m\sqrt{(2gh)}}{M + 3m}$,   (b) $\dfrac{M + 3m}{6m}$.

7 A is hollow: $0.87a$.

8 $\tfrac{7}{3}Ml^2; \dfrac{3m^2v^2x^2}{14Ml^2}; \left[\dfrac{14M^2l^3g(\sqrt{2} - 1)}{3m^2v^2}\right]^{\frac{1}{4}}$.

Exercise 11A

1 (a) $\begin{bmatrix} 0 \\ 7 \\ 0 \end{bmatrix}$,   (b) $\begin{bmatrix} 5 \\ 0 \\ 0 \end{bmatrix}$,   (c) $\begin{bmatrix} 9 \\ -9 \\ 9 \end{bmatrix}$.

2 8.31; 1.81.

3 2.6; perpendicular to $\begin{bmatrix} 4 \\ 12 \\ 3 \end{bmatrix}$.

4 (a) $\begin{bmatrix} 0 \\ 0 \\ 7 \end{bmatrix}$,   (b) $\begin{bmatrix} 0 \\ 0 \\ 0 \end{bmatrix}$,   (c) $\begin{bmatrix} 9 \\ -9 \\ 9 \end{bmatrix}$.

Exercise 11B

2 $\begin{bmatrix} -53 \\ 9 \\ 14 \end{bmatrix}$.

3 $\pm \dfrac{1}{\sqrt{3550}} \begin{bmatrix} 30 \\ -47 \\ -21 \end{bmatrix}$.

4 LHS $= |\mathbf{a}|^2 |\mathbf{b}|^2 \sin^2 \theta + |\mathbf{a}|^2 |\mathbf{b}|^2| \cos^2 \theta = |\mathbf{a}|^2 |\mathbf{b}|^2 (\sin^2 \theta + \cos^2 \theta) =$ RHS.

5 (a) $\begin{bmatrix} -1 \\ 1 \\ -2 \end{bmatrix}$; (b) $\begin{bmatrix} -26 \\ 38 \\ 15 \end{bmatrix}$.

6 $F_1 = \frac{1}{7},\ F_2 = -\frac{4}{7}$.

7 $\mathbf{a} + \mathbf{b} + \mathbf{c} = 0 \Rightarrow \mathbf{a} \times (\mathbf{a} + \mathbf{b} + \mathbf{c}) = 0$
$\phantom{\mathbf{a} + \mathbf{b} + \mathbf{c} = 0} \Rightarrow \mathbf{a} \times \mathbf{b} + \mathbf{a} \times \mathbf{c} = 0$, since $\mathbf{a} \times \mathbf{a} = 0$
$\phantom{\mathbf{a} + \mathbf{b} + \mathbf{c} = 0} \Rightarrow \mathbf{a} \times \mathbf{b} = \mathbf{c} \times \mathbf{a}$, since $\mathbf{c} \times \mathbf{a} = -\mathbf{a} \times \mathbf{c}$.
Similarly $\mathbf{a} \times \mathbf{b} = \mathbf{b} \times \mathbf{c}$.
Converse false; e.g. $\mathbf{a} = \mathbf{b} = \mathbf{c} = \mathbf{i}$.

8 (a) $\delta \boldsymbol{\omega} = (\mathbf{u} + \delta \mathbf{u}) \times (\mathbf{v} + \delta \mathbf{v}) - \mathbf{u} \times \mathbf{v}$; expand and simplify.

9 $\begin{bmatrix} 24t - 20t^3 \\ -8 - 5t^4 \\ 20t + 12t^3 \end{bmatrix}$

Exercise 11C

1 No.

2 (a) Couple $\begin{bmatrix} -2aF \\ -2aF \\ -2aF \end{bmatrix}$; (b) force $\begin{bmatrix} -2F \\ -2F \\ -2F \end{bmatrix}$ through O; (c) couple $\begin{bmatrix} 0 \\ -2aF \\ 0 \end{bmatrix}$.

3 45.5.

4 (a) 41.4; (b) 50.8.

5 Take moments about point of contact of rear wheel; $\frac{1}{4}Mg \sin \alpha$.

6 (a) If there were a resultant at least one of the three non-collinear points would not be on its line of action, and the total moment about this point would not be zero.
(b) Let the common total moment be **L**. Introducing a couple of moment $-\mathbf{L}$ reduces the system to equilibrium by (a), so the original system is equivalent to a couple of moment **L**.

7 (a) Force $\begin{bmatrix} 7 \\ -4 \\ 8 \end{bmatrix}$, couple $\begin{bmatrix} 45 \\ 15 \\ -3 \end{bmatrix}$; (b) force $\begin{bmatrix} 7 \\ -4 \\ 8 \end{bmatrix}$, couple $\begin{bmatrix} -19 \\ 13 \\ 52 \end{bmatrix}$.

8 $\mathbf{G} = \mathbf{L} - \mathbf{a} \times \mathbf{R}$.

9 Force $\begin{bmatrix} 2 \\ -2 \\ 2 \end{bmatrix}$ acting at $(0, 2, -\frac{1}{2})$.

10 Impossible, since **R** is not perpendicular to **L**.

11 Force $\sqrt{6}F\,\mathbf{i}$, couple $\sqrt{3}aF\,\mathbf{i}$, where $\mathbf{i} = \hat{\mathbf{AB}}$;
$\frac{3}{2}F$ perpendicular to AB and to CB.

12 Force $\begin{bmatrix} 1 \\ 0 \\ -1 \end{bmatrix}$ acting at $(1, -1, 0)$ and couple $\begin{bmatrix} 1 \\ 0 \\ -1 \end{bmatrix}$.

13 Force $\begin{bmatrix} 12 \\ 6 \\ 8 \end{bmatrix}$ acting at $\left(-\dfrac{11}{122}, \dfrac{3}{61}, \dfrac{6}{61} \right)$ and couple $\dfrac{1}{61} \begin{bmatrix} 12 \\ 6 \\ 8 \end{bmatrix}$.

14 Force $\begin{bmatrix} 1 \\ -3 \\ 1 \end{bmatrix}$ acting at $(1, 1, 2)$ and couple $\begin{bmatrix} 1 \\ -3 \\ 1 \end{bmatrix}$.

15 (b) $\mathbf{R}.\mathbf{L} = \mathbf{R}.(\mathbf{a} \times \mathbf{R}) + \lambda \mathbf{R}.\mathbf{R}$. Result follows since $\mathbf{R} \perp \mathbf{a} \times \mathbf{R}$.
   (c) $(\mathbf{a}_0 + t\mathbf{R}) \times \mathbf{R} = \mathbf{a}_0 \times \mathbf{R} + t\mathbf{R} \times \mathbf{R} = \mathbf{a}_0 \times \mathbf{R} = \mathbf{L} - \lambda \mathbf{R} \Rightarrow \mathbf{a}_0 + t\mathbf{R}$ is a solution. $\mathbf{a}_0$ and $\mathbf{a}$ both solutions $\Rightarrow \mathbf{a}_0 \times \mathbf{R} = \mathbf{a} \times \mathbf{R} \Rightarrow (\mathbf{a} - \mathbf{a}_0) \times \mathbf{R} = 0$
   $\Rightarrow \mathbf{a} - \mathbf{a}_0 \parallel \mathbf{R} \Rightarrow \mathbf{a} - \mathbf{a}_0 = t\mathbf{R} \Rightarrow \mathbf{a} = \mathbf{a}_0 + t\mathbf{R}$.
   (d) $\mathbf{a}_0 \perp \mathbf{R} \Rightarrow \mathbf{a}_0, \mathbf{R}, \mathbf{a}_0 \times \mathbf{R}$ are mutually perpendicular.
   $\mathbf{L}\ (=\mathbf{a}_0 \times \mathbf{R} + \lambda \mathbf{R})$ is in the plane containing $\mathbf{a}_0 \times \mathbf{R}$ and $\mathbf{R}$, so $\mathbf{R} \times \mathbf{L}$ is
   perpendicular to this plane, i.e. parallel to $\mathbf{a}_0$.
   (e) $(1) \Rightarrow \mu(\mathbf{R} \times \mathbf{L}) \times \mathbf{R} = \mathbf{L} - \dfrac{\mathbf{R}.\mathbf{L}}{\mathbf{R}.\mathbf{R}} \mathbf{R}$. Use the $\mathbf{i}$-component of each side to find μ.

Exercise 12A

1 -7.   2 -8; (a) $\pm(\sqrt{20}, -2\sqrt{20}, 0)$,   (b) $\pm(2\sqrt{20}, \sqrt{20}, 0)$.

3 $18\sqrt{3}$.   4 $\pm 20/\sqrt{6}$.   5 $\pm 142\frac{2}{3}$ N m.

6 The edges of the tetrahedron are diagonals of faces of a cube edge $3/\sqrt{2}$ m. The altitude
   from A is a space diagonal of this cube. This question is thus essentially the same as
   question 4. Moment $= \pm 6\sqrt{3}$ N m.

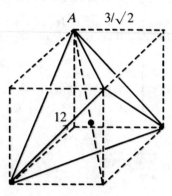

Figure 62

7 $\mathbf{PQ} = \begin{bmatrix} -x \\ 1-y \\ 1 \end{bmatrix}$, $|\mathbf{PQ}| = \sqrt{(x^2 + y^2 - 2y + 2)} = d$ say.

$\mathbf{F} = \dfrac{4}{d}\begin{bmatrix} -x \\ 1-y \\ 1 \end{bmatrix}$, $\mathbf{r} = \begin{bmatrix} 0 \\ 1 \\ 1 \end{bmatrix}$, $\hat{\mathbf{e}} = \begin{bmatrix} 0 \\ 0 \\ 1 \end{bmatrix}$ $\Rightarrow$ moment $= \dfrac{4x}{d} = 2$

$\Leftrightarrow 4x^2 = d^2$ and $x > 0 \Leftrightarrow 3x^2 - y^2 + 2y - 2 = 0$ and $x > 0$

$\Leftrightarrow 3x^2 - (y-1)^2 = 1$ and $x > 0$.

Locus is one branch of a hyperbola in the $z = 0$ plane, centre $(0, 1)$, asymptotes $y = \pm\sqrt{3}x + 1$.

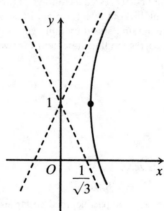

Figure 63

Exercise 12B

1    $\mathbf{a}.(\mathbf{b} \times \mathbf{c}) = (\mathbf{b} \times \mathbf{c}).\mathbf{a}$ (scalar product commutative)

                  $= (\mathbf{a} \times \mathbf{b}).\mathbf{c}$ (cyclic change)

2   0.

3   $\mathbf{e}.(\mathbf{r} \times \mathbf{F}) = 0 \Leftrightarrow \mathbf{e}, \mathbf{r}, \mathbf{F}$ coplanar,

   since $\mathbf{e}.(\mathbf{r} \times \mathbf{F}) = 0 \Leftrightarrow \mathbf{F}$ has zero moment about axis

                               $\Leftrightarrow$ line of action of $\mathbf{F}$ meets axis.

4   Volume $= \frac{1}{3} \times$ base area $\times$ height, base area $= \frac{1}{2} \times$ area of parallelogram with edges $\mathbf{b}, \mathbf{c}$; result follows. With the lettering of §12.2 Fig. 4, tetrahedra $OABC$, $AQPC$, $ABPC$, $PQRS$, $BSPC$, $QSPC$ have equal volumes, since for each pair one can find congruent bases with corresponding heights equal.

5   $[\mathbf{a}, \mathbf{c}, \mathbf{e}] + [\mathbf{a}, \mathbf{c}, \mathbf{f}] + [\mathbf{a}, \mathbf{d}, \mathbf{e}] + [\mathbf{a}, \mathbf{d}, \mathbf{f}] + [\mathbf{b}, \mathbf{c}, \mathbf{e}] + [\mathbf{b}, \mathbf{c}, \mathbf{f}] + [\mathbf{b}, \mathbf{d}, \mathbf{e}] + [\mathbf{b}, \mathbf{d}, \mathbf{f}]$.

6   $V_2 = [\mathbf{a} + \mathbf{b}, \mathbf{b} + \mathbf{c}, \mathbf{c} + \mathbf{a}]$; when this is 'expanded' as in question 5 six of the eight triple products are zero (as in question 2), so $V_2 = [\mathbf{a}, \mathbf{b}, \mathbf{c}] + [\mathbf{b}, \mathbf{c}, \mathbf{a}] = 2[\mathbf{a}, \mathbf{b}, \mathbf{c}]$ $= 2V_1$.

7   $y = \dfrac{[\mathbf{a}, \mathbf{d}, \mathbf{c}]}{[\mathbf{a}, \mathbf{b}, \mathbf{c}]}$, $z = \dfrac{[\mathbf{a}, \mathbf{b}, \mathbf{d}]}{[\mathbf{a}, \mathbf{b}, \mathbf{c}]}$.

8   $x = 4$, $y = 6$, $z = 7$.

9   Let the forces be $\mathbf{F}_i = F_i\hat{\mathbf{e}}_i$ $(i = 1, 2, 3, 4)$, where $\hat{\mathbf{e}}_i$ is the unit vector in the direction and sense of $\mathbf{F}_i$.

Equilibrium $\Rightarrow F_1\hat{\mathbf{e}}_1 + F_2\hat{\mathbf{e}}_2 + F_3\hat{\mathbf{e}}_3 + F_4\hat{\mathbf{e}}_4 = \mathbf{0}$

$\Rightarrow F_1\hat{\mathbf{e}}_1 \cdot (\hat{\mathbf{e}}_3 \times \hat{\mathbf{e}}_4) + F_2\hat{\mathbf{e}}_2 \cdot (\hat{\mathbf{e}}_3 \times \hat{\mathbf{e}}_4) + 0 + 0 = 0$

$$\Rightarrow \frac{F_1}{\hat{\mathbf{e}}_2 \cdot (\hat{\mathbf{e}}_3 \times \hat{\mathbf{e}}_4)} = \frac{F_2}{-\hat{\mathbf{e}}_1 \cdot (\hat{\mathbf{e}}_3 \times \hat{\mathbf{e}}_4)}$$

$\Rightarrow \dfrac{F_1}{V_1} = \dfrac{F_2}{V_2}$, where V_1 is the (positive) volume of the parallelepiped with edges $\hat{\mathbf{e}}_2, \hat{\mathbf{e}}_3,$ $\hat{\mathbf{e}}_4$, etc.

The complete result follows by similar arguments applied to other pairs. (Note that Lami's theorem could be expressed as follows: If three forces in two dimensions acting at a point are in equilibrium then the magnitude of each force is proportional to the area of the parallelogram defined by unit vectors in the direction of the other two forces. What is the corresponding statement for two forces in one dimension?)

Exercise 12C

1   (a) -3,   (b) 4,   (c) 0.

2   9.

3 $\frac{22}{3}$.

4   Volume of 'tetrahedron' is zero.

5 $(0, 0, 0)$, $(0, 0, 2)$, $(0, \frac{3}{2}, 0)$, $(2, -1, 0)$; 1.

6   (a) Reversal of handedness;   (b) parallelepiped collapses to a plane;
(c) one way stretch $\times \lambda$;   (d) shear.

8   Columns have factors 49, 16, 13 respectively; $2^5 \times 7^2 \times 13 \times 23$.

9   First step is wrong. $|\mathbf{a}\ \mathbf{b}\ \mathbf{c}| = |\mathbf{a} + \mathbf{b}\ \mathbf{b}\ \mathbf{c}| = |\mathbf{a} + \mathbf{b}\ \mathbf{b} + \mathbf{c}\ \mathbf{c}|$, but $\mathbf{c} - \mathbf{a}$ cannot be obtained in the last column since $\mathbf{a}$ is no longer a column.

10 $OP_1P_2P_3$ has base $P_1P_2P_3$ of area Δ and height 1.

11 P_1, P_2, P_3 are collinear.

12   (a) h^3, independent of $\mathbf{a}$;
(b) $\triangle ABC = \triangle BCD$ by (a), subtract common $\triangle BEC$ and the result follows.

13   (e) $(\mathbf{a} \times \mathbf{b}) \times \mathbf{c} = -\mathbf{c} \times (\mathbf{a} \times \mathbf{b}) = -[(\mathbf{c} \cdot \mathbf{b})\mathbf{a} - (\mathbf{c} \cdot \mathbf{a})\mathbf{b}] = (\mathbf{c} \cdot \mathbf{a})\mathbf{b} - (\mathbf{c} \cdot \mathbf{b})\mathbf{a}$.

15 $(\mathbf{a} \times \mathbf{b}) \cdot (\mathbf{c} \times \mathbf{d}) = (\mathbf{b} \times (\mathbf{c} \times \mathbf{d})) \cdot \mathbf{a}$ (cyclic change);
now use question 13.

16   (a) $\mathbf{v}_{n+2} = (\mathbf{v}_n \times \mathbf{b}) \times \mathbf{b} = (\mathbf{v}_n \cdot \mathbf{b})\mathbf{b} - (\mathbf{b} \cdot \mathbf{b})\mathbf{v}_n = -(\mathbf{b} \cdot \mathbf{b})\mathbf{v}_n$ since $\mathbf{v}_n \perp \mathbf{b}$.
(b) Interpreting the vectors as position vectors, let Π be the plane containing $\mathbf{a}$ and $\mathbf{b}$. Then

$$\mathbf{v}_1 \perp \Pi \quad \text{and} \quad \mathbf{v}_2 \perp \mathbf{v}_1 \Rightarrow \mathbf{v}_2 \text{ is in } \Pi,$$

and similarly successive $\mathbf{v}_n$ are alternately perpendicular to and in Π. Thus $\mathbf{v}_{2n} = \lambda_n\mathbf{a} + \mu_n\mathbf{b}$.

$$\mu_n = 0 \Rightarrow \mathbf{v}_{2n} = \lambda_n\mathbf{a} \Rightarrow \mathbf{v}_{2n+2} = k\lambda_n\mathbf{a} \text{ by } (a)$$
$$\Rightarrow \mu_{n+1} = 0, \text{ etc.}$$

Also $\mathbf{v}_{2n} \perp \mathbf{b} \Rightarrow (\lambda_n\mathbf{a}) \cdot \mathbf{b} = 0 \Rightarrow \mathbf{a} \cdot \mathbf{b} = 0$.

Exercise 13A

1   $17x - 2y + 5z = 18$.   2 No.   3 $29°$.

4   $12x - y - 21z = 23$.   5 $x + y - z = 3$.

6   (a) $7x - 4y - z = -20$;   (b) $x + 2y - z = -5$.

7   $\dfrac{x - 2}{p} = \dfrac{y + 1}{q} = \dfrac{z + 5}{3p + 2q}$ for $p, q \in \mathbb{R}$, not both zero.

8   $x + 2y = -11$.

9   $2x - 4y - 5z = -29$.

10 Parallel to $3\mathbf{i} + \mathbf{j} + 2\mathbf{k}$.

11 $a = 2, b = 1, c = -4, l = 2, m = -7, n = 8$, or equivalent.

12 $69.0°, 80.6°, 88.9°$.

13 $x - y + 2z = 6, x + y = 2$; $\begin{bmatrix} -6 \\ 6 \\ 6 \end{bmatrix}$; $\dfrac{x - 4}{-1} = y + 2 = z$ or equivalent.

Exercise 13B

1   (a) $\sqrt{(68/19)} \approx 1.89$, (b) $19/\sqrt{13} \approx 5.27$, (c) $60/19 \approx 3.16$,
    (d) $60/19 \approx 3.16$, (e) $30/\sqrt{661} \approx 1.17$, (f) 5.

2   $\begin{bmatrix} 1 \\ 1 \\ 1 \end{bmatrix}$, $\begin{bmatrix} 1 \\ 1 \\ -1 \end{bmatrix}$; $\cos^{-1}(-\tfrac{1}{3}) \approx 109.5°$.

3   $2/\sqrt{3} \approx 1.15$.

4   7.

5   (a) $4/\sqrt{6} \approx 1.63$;   (b) $\dfrac{x + 8}{2} = \dfrac{y + 5}{-1} = \dfrac{z + 9}{-1}$ (c) $(-\tfrac{28}{3}, -\tfrac{13}{3}, -\tfrac{25}{3})$,
    $(-8, -5, -9)$.

6   $(\mathbf{q} - \mathbf{p} + \lambda\mathbf{n}) . \mathbf{n} = 0, \lambda = \dfrac{(\mathbf{p} - \mathbf{q}) . \mathbf{n}}{n^2}$.

7   (a) $\left(\dfrac{38}{7}, \dfrac{20}{7}, \dfrac{12}{7} \right)$; (b) $\left(\dfrac{48}{7}, \dfrac{5}{7}, \dfrac{17}{7} \right)$.

8   $\dfrac{x - 2}{17} = \dfrac{y - 1}{-1} = \dfrac{z - 3}{-2}$.

9   $\dfrac{x - 1}{-1} = \dfrac{y + 3}{8} = \dfrac{z + 2}{8}$.

10 $\mathbf{b} \times \mathbf{c} + \mathbf{c} \times \mathbf{a} + \mathbf{a} \times \mathbf{b}$.

11 $[\mathbf{r}, \mathbf{b}, \mathbf{c}] + [\mathbf{a}, \mathbf{r}, \mathbf{c}] = [\mathbf{a}, \mathbf{b}, \mathbf{c}]$.

12 $\mathbf{x} = \begin{bmatrix} 0 \\ 1 \\ 0 \end{bmatrix} + t \begin{bmatrix} 2 \\ 1 \\ 0 \end{bmatrix} \times \begin{bmatrix} 2 \\ 1 \\ \frac{1}{4} \end{bmatrix}$; $\mathbf{d} - \mathbf{a} = \lambda \begin{bmatrix} 2 \\ 1 \\ 0 \end{bmatrix} \times \begin{bmatrix} 1 \\ -2 \\ 0 \end{bmatrix}$.

Exercise 14A

1 $\begin{bmatrix} 2 + t^2 \\ 0 \end{bmatrix}$, $\begin{bmatrix} -\frac{1}{2}t^2 \\ 4 + t^2 \end{bmatrix}$, $\begin{bmatrix} 5 + \frac{3}{4}t^2 \\ 2 + \frac{1}{2}t^2 \end{bmatrix}$, $\begin{bmatrix} 3 + \frac{1}{4}t^2 \\ 2 + \frac{1}{2}t^2 \end{bmatrix}$;

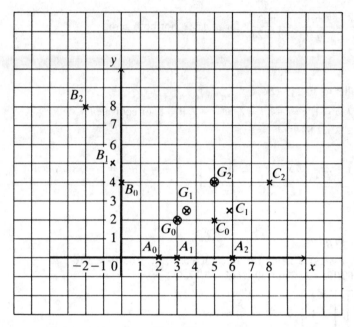

Figure 64

2 $\begin{bmatrix} 0 \\ 2 \\ 2 \end{bmatrix}$; $\begin{bmatrix} -3 \\ -2 \\ 11 \end{bmatrix}$, $\begin{bmatrix} 2 \\ 13 \\ -4 \end{bmatrix}$, $\begin{bmatrix} 0 \\ 7 \\ 2 \end{bmatrix}$.

3 No; (a) no, (b) yes, only two possible positions for each other ink-pot.

4 Mass-centre: same; nose: greater in (a) than in (b).

6 Backwards, since the total external force is backwards.

7 $\mathbf{r}_i = \mathbf{c} + \mathbf{s}_i \Rightarrow \sum m_i \mathbf{r}_i = \sum m_i \mathbf{c} + \sum m_i \mathbf{s}_i = M\mathbf{c} + \sum m_i \mathbf{s}_i$.
Divide by M; result follows.

8 Taking $\mathbf{c} = \bar{\mathbf{r}}$ in question 7 gives $\sum m_i \boldsymbol{\rho}_i = \mathbf{0}$. Differentiating twice gives the other results.

Exercise 14B

1 (a) $\begin{bmatrix} -66 \\ 30 \\ -54 \end{bmatrix}$; (b) $\begin{bmatrix} -1 \\ 2 \\ 3 \end{bmatrix}$, $\begin{bmatrix} 0 \\ 2 \\ -2 \end{bmatrix}$; (c) $\bar{\mathbf{H}}_O = \begin{bmatrix} -60 \\ -12 \\ -12 \end{bmatrix}$, $\mathbf{H}_G = \begin{bmatrix} -6 \\ 42 \\ -42 \end{bmatrix}$.

2 (a)   (b)

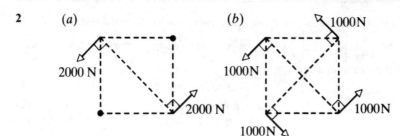

Figure 65

(c) Both translational and rotational motion is produced.

(d) Station rotates at $\frac{3}{4}$ rad s^{-1} and its centre of mass moves at 2.5 m s^{-1} in the direction opposite to that of the rocket which failed.

3 Equal and opposite forces of magnitude $Mv^2\sqrt{(a^2 + h^2)}/a^2$.

4 54 N, assuming each person's entire mass is concentrated at a point (so ignoring the mass of the arms and the size of the body); moment of momentum about the centre is conserved, so new angular speed $= \sqrt{2} \approx 1.41$ rad s^{-1}, new tension $= 108$ N.

5 $l/(l - c)$.

6 F/m; $L_O = rF$, $H_O = mr^2\dot{\theta}$.

7 2.02 rev s^{-1}.

8 $L_c = \sum (\mathbf{r}_i - \mathbf{c}) \times \mathbf{F}_{ii} = \sum \mathbf{r}_i \times \mathbf{F}_{ii} - \mathbf{c} \times \sum \mathbf{F}_{ii} = L_O - \mathbf{c} \times M\ddot{\bar{\mathbf{r}}}$

$H_c = \sum (\mathbf{r}_i - \mathbf{c}) \times m_i\dot{\mathbf{r}}_i = \sum \mathbf{r}_i \times m_i\dot{\mathbf{r}}_i - \mathbf{c} \times \sum m_i\dot{\mathbf{r}}_i = H_O - \mathbf{c} \times M\dot{\bar{\mathbf{r}}}$

$\Rightarrow \dot{H}_c = \dot{H}_o - \dot{\mathbf{c}} \times M\dot{\bar{\mathbf{r}}} - \mathbf{c} \times M\ddot{\bar{\mathbf{r}}}$ (differentiating the product $\mathbf{c} \times M\dot{\bar{\mathbf{r}}}$);

the results follow since $L_O = \dot{H}_O$.

Exercise 14C

1 (a) Speed of $B = U \Rightarrow$ speeds of A and C are each $U + J/5m$

(all moving in same direction and sense).

Speed of centre of mass $= J/3m$

$\Rightarrow 3m \times J/3m = mU + 2(mU + J/5) \Rightarrow U = J/5m$.

(b) $7J/15m$.

2 Initially, velocity of $A =$ velocity of $C = 0$. Mass centre continues to move with velocity $\frac{1}{3}v$. A and C rotate about B with angular velocity v/l.

3 Immediately after the strings tighten A and C move towards B with speed $\frac{15}{43}v$, and velocity of $B = \frac{25}{43}v$. Mass centre continues to move with velocity $\frac{1}{3}v$. A and C rotate about B with angular velocity $16v/43l$.

4 (a) Mass centre moves perpendicular to AB with speed $J/2m$; AB rotates with angular velocity J/lm.

(b) Mass centre moves perpendicular to AB with speed $J/3m$; AB rotates with angular velocity J/lm.

5 The impulse on A is due to the rod, and so along AB. Since the rod is rigid, $\mathbf{w} =$ component of $\mathbf{W}$ along $AB = (\mathbf{W}.\mathbf{n})\mathbf{n}$.

$$\mathbf{W} = \frac{M\mathbf{I} + m(\mathbf{I} - (\mathbf{I}.\mathbf{n})\mathbf{n})}{M(m + M)}.$$

6 Let the impulsive tensions be J and K as shown, and let the initial velocities of A, B, C, D be $\begin{bmatrix} u \\ 0 \end{bmatrix}$, $\begin{bmatrix} v \\ -w \end{bmatrix}$, $\begin{bmatrix} v \\ w \end{bmatrix}$, $\begin{bmatrix} z \\ 0 \end{bmatrix}$ respectively (using symmetry). The impulse–momentum equations are

for A:
$$I - 2J \cos \alpha = mu \tag{1}$$

for B:
$$\begin{cases} (J - K) \cos \alpha = mv & (2) \\ J + K \sin \alpha = mw & (3) \end{cases}$$

for C:
$$2K \cos \alpha = mz \tag{4}$$

The conditions for AB and BC to remain taut are

for AB:
$$u \cos \alpha = v \cos \alpha + w \sin \alpha \tag{5}$$

for BC:
$$z \cos \alpha = v \cos \alpha - w \sin \alpha \tag{6}$$

Solve (2) and (3) for J, K and substitute in (1) and (4). Then use (5) and (6) to obtain
$$u = I(1 + \sin^2 \alpha)/4m, \quad v = I/4m, \quad w = I \sin \alpha \cos \alpha/4m, \quad z = I(1 - \sin^2 \alpha)/4m.$$

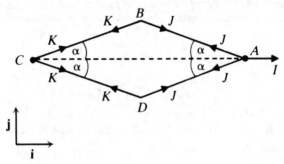

Figure 66

Exercise 14D

2 (a) ge^{-2ks}.

4 $x = \dfrac{m_0 V \cos \theta}{k} \ln\left(1 + \dfrac{kt}{m_0}\right)$,

$y = \left(\dfrac{m_0 V \sin \theta}{k} + \dfrac{m_0^2 g}{2k^2}\right) \ln\left(1 + \dfrac{kt}{m_0}\right) - \dfrac{m_0 gt}{2k} - \dfrac{gt^2}{4}$;

greatest height $= \dfrac{1}{2}\left(\dfrac{m_0 V \sin \theta}{k} + \dfrac{m_0^2 g}{2k^2}\right) \ln\left(1 + \dfrac{2kV \sin \theta}{m_0 g}\right) - \dfrac{m_0 V \sin \theta}{2k}$.

6 $1 - e^{-2} \approx 0.865$.

7 When the first stage's fuel has been used it separates from the rest.
Optimum ratio $= \sqrt{(m^2 + mM)} - m$: $M \cdot 2.55c$.

8 $M = M_0 + \pi a^2 \rho s$; $\dfrac{d}{dt}(Mv) = 0$;

$s = [\sqrt{(M_0^2 + 2\pi a^2 \rho M_0 Vt)} - M_0]/\pi a^2 \rho$;

$v = M_0 V/\sqrt{(M_0^2 + 2\pi a^2 \rho M_0 Vt)}$.

9 Distance penetrated $= \dfrac{a}{\beta}\left[1 - \left(1 - \dfrac{\beta CVt}{a}\right)^{1/C}\right]$,

radius $= a\left(1 - \dfrac{\beta CVt}{\alpha}\right)^{1/C}$, where $C = 4 - \dfrac{\pi\alpha a^3}{\beta M}$;

radius $= 0 \Rightarrow t = \dfrac{a}{\beta CV}$ and $s = \dfrac{a}{\beta}$.

10 $r = b\sqrt{(1 - kt)}$, $I = \frac{1}{2}Mb^2(1 - kt)^2$;
final angular velocity $= 4c(b - a)/b$.

11 (c) $m_0 k/c$.

Exercise 14E

1 153.5 J, 32.05 J, 121.45 J.

2 17.28.

3 Work done = new KE − old KE − PE lost by dumbbells = 66 J.

4 194 J.

5 Let the particles have velocities v_1, v_2; then $\dot{\bar{r}} = \dfrac{m_1 v_1 + m_2 v_2}{m_1 + m_2}$ and

$\dot{\rho}_1 = v_1 - \dfrac{m_1 v_1 + m_2 v_2}{m_1 + m_2} = \dfrac{m_2(v_1 - v_2)}{m_1 + m_2} = \dfrac{m_2 u}{m_1 + m_2}$, etc.

Relative velocity after impact $= -eu$, so T_G after impact $= \dfrac{m_1 m_2}{2(m_1 + m_2)} e^2 u^2$;

the result follows since $\bar{T}$ is unchanged by the impact.

6 (a) $[M^2 V^2 + m^2 v^2 - 2MmVv \cos\theta]^{\frac{1}{2}}/(M - m)$.

(b) $\frac{1}{2}mM((V - v\cos\theta)^2 + v^2 \sin^2\theta)/(M - m)$; always positive, so KE is gained.

7 $[ga \sin\theta(1 + 3\cos^2\theta)/(1 + \cos^2\theta)]^{\frac{1}{2}}$.

8

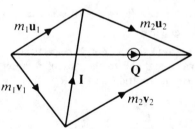

Figure 67

9 (a) LHS $= \displaystyle\sum_i m_i^2 v_i^2 + \sum_{i<j} m_i m_j v_i^2 + \sum_{i<j} m_i m_j v_j^2$

RHS $= \displaystyle\sum_{i<j} m_i m_j(v_i^2 - 2v_i v_j + v_j^2) + \sum_i m_i^2 v_i^2 + 2\sum_{i<j} m_i m_j v_i v_j$

$= \displaystyle\sum_{i<j} m_i m_j(v_i^2 + v_j^2) + \sum_i m_i^2 v_i^2 = $ LHS.

(Try writing out both sides in a particular case, $n = 4$ say.) Final result follows from dividing throughout by $2M$.

(b) The initial KE is $\bar{T}$ (treating the shell as a particle of mass M), which is unchanged by the explosion because of conservation of linear momentum. Result follows directly from (a).

Exercise 15A

1 (a) $4\mathbf{i} + 2\mathbf{j} - 4\mathbf{k}$; (b) $8\mathbf{i} - 12\mathbf{j} + 2\mathbf{k}$;
   (c) **i**-component of $\boldsymbol{\omega} \times \mathbf{r} = \mathbf{0} \Leftrightarrow 2y + z = 0$, so points in the plane $2y + z = 0$ move parallel to the plane $x = 0$.
   (d) **i**- and **j**-components of $\boldsymbol{\omega} \times \mathbf{r} = \mathbf{0} \Leftrightarrow 2y + z = 0$ and $x + z = 0$, so the required points lie in both these planes, i.e. on the line through O with direction vector $2\mathbf{i} + \mathbf{j} - 2\mathbf{k}$.

2

Point	$(a, 0, 0)$	$(a, 2a, 0)$	$(0, 2a, 0)$
has velocity	$\frac{2}{3}a\omega(\mathbf{j} - \mathbf{k})$	$\frac{2}{3}a\omega(-2\mathbf{i} + \mathbf{j})$	$\frac{2}{3}a\omega(-2\mathbf{i} + \mathbf{k})$
with magnitude	$2\sqrt{2}a\omega/3$	$2\sqrt{5}a\omega/3$	$2\sqrt{5}a\omega/3$
moving parallel to plane	$x = 0$	$z = 0$	$y = 0$
making these angles with the x-, y-, z-axes	$90°, 45°, 135°$	$153°, 63°, 90°$	$153°, 90°, 63°$

$(0, 0, 0)$ is stationary.

3 (a) $\sqrt{14} \approx 3.74$;   (b) $\sqrt{488} \approx 22.1$.

4 $\begin{bmatrix} 5 \\ -2 \\ 3 \end{bmatrix}$.

5 $\frac{6}{5}(2\mathbf{j} - \mathbf{k})$; $6/\sqrt{5} \approx 2.68$; 0.

6 Velocity of $B = \boldsymbol{\omega} \times \mathbf{b} = \boldsymbol{\omega} \times (\mathbf{a} + (\mathbf{b} - \mathbf{a})) = \boldsymbol{\omega} \times \mathbf{a} + \boldsymbol{\omega} \times (\mathbf{b} - \mathbf{a})$
   $= \mathbf{V} + \boldsymbol{\omega} \times \mathbf{AB}$.

7 Let A, A', B' have position vectors $\mathbf{r}$, $\mathbf{r}'$, $\mathbf{R}$ respectively.
   (a) $\mathbf{r} - \mathbf{r}' = t\mathbf{i} \Rightarrow \mathbf{AA}'$ is parallel to the axis of rotation and has length $|t|$; both properties survive the rotation, so $\mathbf{R} - \mathbf{R}' = t\mathbf{i}$.

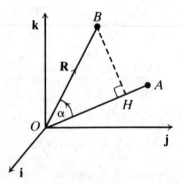

Figure 68

(b) $\mathbf{r} \cdot \mathbf{i} = 0 \Rightarrow A$ is in plane $x = 0 \Rightarrow B$ is in plane $x = 0$ too. Let H be the foot of the perpendicular from B to OA. Then $\mathbf{OH} = \mathbf{r} \cos \alpha$, since $|\mathbf{R}| = |\mathbf{r}|$. $\mathbf{HB}$ has magnitude $|\mathbf{r}| \sin \alpha$ and direction perpendicular to $\mathbf{i}$ and $\mathbf{r}$ and such that $\mathbf{i}, \mathbf{r}, \mathbf{HB}$ is right-handed. So $\mathbf{HB} = (\mathbf{i} \times \mathbf{r}) \sin \alpha$, since $|\mathbf{i} \times \mathbf{r}| = |\mathbf{r}|$. Thus $\mathbf{R} = \mathbf{OH} + \mathbf{HB} = \mathbf{r} \cos \alpha + (\mathbf{i} \times \mathbf{r}) \sin \alpha$. The components of $\mathbf{r}$ parallel and perpendicular to $\mathbf{i}$ are $\mathbf{i}(\mathbf{i} \cdot \mathbf{r})$ and $\mathbf{i} \times \mathbf{r}$; apply the results of (a) and (b) to these respectively.

8 $\dot{\mathbf{r}} = \boldsymbol{\omega} \times \mathbf{r} \Rightarrow \ddot{\mathbf{r}} = \boldsymbol{\omega} \times \dot{\mathbf{r}}$ (since $\boldsymbol{\omega}$ is constant)
$$= \boldsymbol{\omega} \times (\boldsymbol{\omega} \times \mathbf{r}).$$

Exercise 15B

1 In three dimensions $\mathbf{V} = \begin{bmatrix} u \\ v \\ 0 \end{bmatrix}, \boldsymbol{\omega} = \begin{bmatrix} 0 \\ 0 \\ \omega \end{bmatrix}, \mathbf{r} = \begin{bmatrix} \xi \\ \eta \\ 0 \end{bmatrix},$

and velocity of $P = \mathbf{V} + \boldsymbol{\omega} \times \mathbf{r}$; results follow. If $\omega = 0$ all points have the same velocity (translational motion); there is no instantaneous centre unless the lamina is stationary.

2 Velocity of $P = \mathbf{0} + \boldsymbol{\omega} \times \mathbf{IP}$ (since I is at rest). This is perpendicular to PI and has magnitude ωPI (since $\boldsymbol{\omega} \perp \mathbf{IP}$).

3 (a)

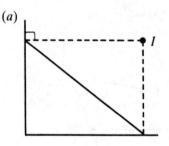

(b)

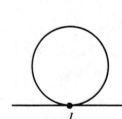

(c)

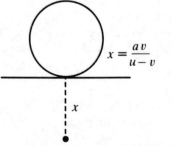

(d)

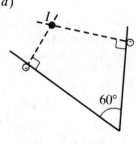

Figure 69

4 (*a*) Quadrant of circle centre *O*, radius = length of ladder.

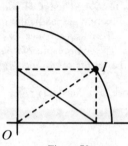

Figure 70

(*b*) The line on the ground along which the wheel rolls.

(*c*) The line at distance $av/(u - v)$ vertically below (*b*).

(*d*) The arc of the circle through the fixed pins such that the line joining the pins subtends 120° at a point of the arc.

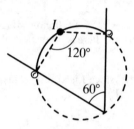

Figure 71

5 $y^2 = a(x - a)$.

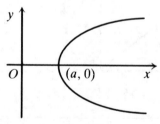

Figure 72

6 $\mathbf{v} = \mathbf{V} + \boldsymbol{\omega} \times \mathbf{r}$, so $\mathbf{v} = \mathbf{0} \Leftrightarrow \boldsymbol{\omega} \times \mathbf{r} = -\mathbf{V}$.

$\boldsymbol{\omega} \times \mathbf{r} \perp \boldsymbol{\omega}$, so no solution for $\mathbf{r}$ is possible unless $\mathbf{V} \perp \boldsymbol{\omega}$.

If $\mathbf{V} \perp \boldsymbol{\omega}$ the solution can be obtained as for Exercise 11C, question 15 with $\mathbf{V}, \boldsymbol{\omega}$ in place of $\mathbf{L}, \mathbf{R}$. Alternatively

$$\mathbf{v} = \mathbf{0} \Leftrightarrow \mathbf{r} \times \boldsymbol{\omega} = \mathbf{V}$$

$$\Rightarrow \boldsymbol{\omega} \times (\mathbf{r} \times \boldsymbol{\omega}) = \boldsymbol{\omega} \times \mathbf{V}$$

$$\Rightarrow \omega^2 \mathbf{r} - (\boldsymbol{\omega} . \mathbf{r})\boldsymbol{\omega} = \boldsymbol{\omega} \times \mathbf{V}$$

$$\Rightarrow \mathbf{r} = \frac{\boldsymbol{\omega} \times \mathbf{V}}{\omega^2} + \frac{\boldsymbol{\omega} . \mathbf{r}}{\omega^2}\boldsymbol{\omega} = \mathbf{a} + \lambda\boldsymbol{\omega} \text{ say,}$$

which gives a line of instantaneous centres.

7 $r = \begin{bmatrix} 2 \\ 0 \\ -5 \end{bmatrix} + \lambda \begin{bmatrix} 1 \\ 1 \\ 5 \end{bmatrix}.$

8 (a) $\mathbf{AB.AC} = ab\mathbf{S}(t).\mathbf{S}'(t) = 0$ since $\mathbf{S}'(t) \perp \mathbf{S}(t)$ as in §2.3.
(b) $|\mathbf{AC}|$ is constant, so $|\mathbf{S}'(t)| = \omega$ is constant too.

9 $\mathbf{H}_o = I_o\boldsymbol{\omega}$ (see §16.1) $\Rightarrow \boldsymbol{\omega}.\mathbf{H}_o = I_o\omega^2 = 2T.$

10

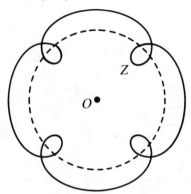

Figure 73

$\begin{bmatrix} x_A \\ y_A \end{bmatrix} = r\begin{bmatrix} \cos(ut/r) \\ \sin(ut/r) \end{bmatrix} = \mathbf{OQ}$ say; $\begin{bmatrix} x_B \\ y_B \end{bmatrix} = s\begin{bmatrix} \cos(vt/s) \\ \sin(vt/s) \end{bmatrix} = \mathbf{PQ}$ say.

OQ, QP each have constant length and rotate at constant rates.

$\begin{bmatrix} x_A - x_B \\ y_A - y_B \end{bmatrix} = \mathbf{OQ} + \mathbf{QP} = \mathbf{OP}$; P has epicyclic motion as before.

Taking A as a planet and B as the earth, reversal of motion relative to earth occurs at points such as Z.

Exercise 15C

1 (a) West; (b) east.

2 $\dot{\mathbf{r}} = \boldsymbol{\omega}_1 \times (\mathbf{r} - \mathbf{s}_1) + \boldsymbol{\omega}_2 \times (\mathbf{r} - \mathbf{s}_2)$
$= (\boldsymbol{\omega}_1 + \boldsymbol{\omega}_2) \times \mathbf{r} - \omega_1\mathbf{e} \times \mathbf{s}_1 - \omega_2\mathbf{e} \times \mathbf{s}_2$
$= (\boldsymbol{\omega}_1 + \boldsymbol{\omega}_1) \times \mathbf{r} - \mathbf{e} \times (\omega_1\mathbf{s}_1 + \omega_2\mathbf{s}_2)$
$= (\boldsymbol{\omega}_1 + \boldsymbol{\omega}_2) \times \mathbf{r} - \dfrac{\omega_1 + \omega_2}{\omega_1 + \omega_2} \times (\omega_1\mathbf{s}_1 + \omega_2\mathbf{s}_2)$
$= (\boldsymbol{\omega}_1 + \boldsymbol{\omega}_2) \times \left(\mathbf{r} - \dfrac{\omega_1\mathbf{s}_1 + \omega_2\mathbf{s}_2}{\omega_1 + \omega_2}\right).$

Parallel axis through point dividing S_1S_2 in the ratio $\omega_2:\omega_1$.

3 $\omega_1 + \omega_2 = 0 \Rightarrow \boldsymbol{\omega}_2 = -\boldsymbol{\omega}_1 \Rightarrow \dot{\mathbf{r}} = \boldsymbol{\omega}_1 \times (\mathbf{r} - \mathbf{s}_1) - \boldsymbol{\omega}_1 \times (\mathbf{r} - \mathbf{s}_2)$
$= \boldsymbol{\omega}_1 \times (\mathbf{s}_2 - \mathbf{s}_1)$

$\Rightarrow$ all points have the same velocity (translational motion).

4 $k\mathbf{AB} + k\mathbf{BC} = k\mathbf{AC}$; $k\mathbf{AC} + k\mathbf{CA} = \mathbf{0}$; result follows as in question 3.

5   Taking the edges of the cube as **i, j, k**, the resultant angular velocity is 4ω (**i** + **j** + **k**), which is in the direction of a diagonal.

6   **r*** = **v** = **V** + **ω** × **r**, so R^* is in the plane containing the point with position vector **V** and having normal vector **ω**.

Exercise 15D

1   Using $g = 9.812$
$$r = 6.37 \times 10^6$$
$$\omega = 7.27 \times 10^{-5}$$
gives $\alpha = 0.097°$.

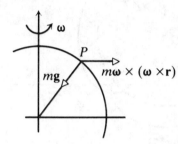 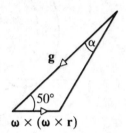

Figure 74

2 $X = g \sin \omega t / 2\omega^2$.

3 $\dot{\mathbf{R}} = \dot{X}\mathbf{I}$, so the Coriolis force $- 2m\boldsymbol{\omega} \times \dot{\mathbf{R}}$ is perpendicular to **I**.
$$|\boldsymbol{\omega} \times (\boldsymbol{\omega} \times \mathbf{r})| = \omega^2 X \sin \alpha.$$

Resolving along the tube:
$$m\ddot{X} = m\omega^2 X \sin^2 \alpha - mg \cos \alpha.$$

(*a*) $\ddot{X} = 0 \Rightarrow X = \dfrac{g \cos \alpha}{\omega^2 \sin^2 \alpha} = a$ say.

(*b*) $X = a + h \Rightarrow \ddot{h} = \omega^2(a + h) \sin^2 \alpha - g \cos \alpha$
$$= \omega^2 \sin^2 \alpha h \propto h.$$

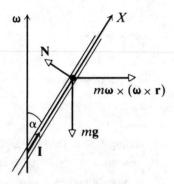

Figure 75

4 $\ddot{Y} = F/m - 2\Omega\dot{X} + \Omega^2 Y, \ddot{Z} = 0.$

5 Neglecting terms in Ω^2,

$$\ddot{X} - 2\Omega\dot{Y} = -g \tag{1}$$
$$\ddot{Y} + 2\Omega\dot{X} = 0 \tag{2}$$

Differentiate (2), substitute $\ddot{X}$ from (1) and neglect Ω^2 again:

$$\dddot{Y} = 2\Omega g.$$

Integrating three times gives $Y = \frac{1}{3}\Omega gt^3$, since when $t = 0$, $Y = \dot{Y} = \ddot{Y} = 0$ (the last following from (2)). Putting $\ddot{Y} = 2\Omega gt$ in (2) and integrating gives $X = h - \frac{1}{2}gt^2$.

$$X = 0 \Rightarrow t^2 = 2h/g \Rightarrow Y = \frac{1}{3}\Omega g\left(\frac{2h}{g}\right)^{3/2}. \ 0.022 \text{ m}.$$

Exercise 16A

1

(a)   (b)

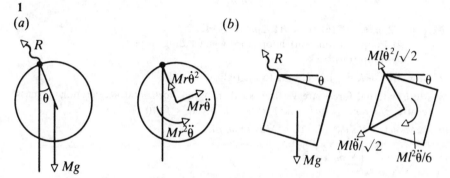

(c)   (d)

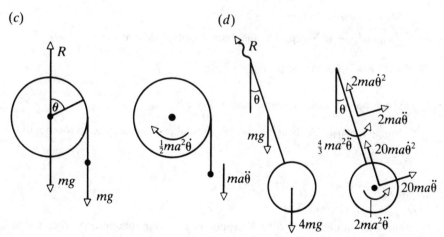

Figure 76

2 (a) $2\pi\sqrt{(2r/g)}$;   (b) $Mg\,(5/2 - 3\sqrt{2}/4)$;   (c) $2g/3$, $4mg/3$;
(d) $2\pi\sqrt{(161a/33g)}$, 0.

3 $\frac{2}{3}g(\sin \alpha - \frac{1}{20})$; $\sin^{-1}(1/20) \approx 2.9°$.

4 $F = ma(\cos \theta\, \ddot{\theta} - \sin \theta\, \dot{\theta}^2)$, $G = mg + ma(2c^2 + \sin \theta\, \ddot{\theta} + \cos \theta\, \dot{\theta}^2)$,
$F \cos \theta + G \sin \theta = -\frac{1}{3}ma\ddot{\theta}$.

5 (a) μgt; (b) $\omega - \mu mgrt/I$; (c) $\mu gt(1 + mr^2/I) - r\omega$.
After slipping ceases the cylinder rolls with constant velocity $Ir\omega/(I + mr^2)$.

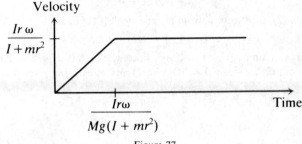

Figure 77

6 (a) $U/2\mu g$, $U/2$; (b) $(U + r\Omega)/2\mu g$, $(U - r\Omega)/2$;
     (i) hoop rolls on, (ii) hoop stops when sliding stops,
     (iii) hoop rolls back.

7 $A = Ma^2 + I$, $d = a - b$, rolls to the right.

8 Both external forces are vertical, so there is no horizontal acceleration of mass
centre; $a = r\dot\omega$; $a = (gr^2 - fk^2)/(r^2 + k^2)$, $\dot\omega = (g + f)r/(r^2 + k^2)$.

10 $[2Mka(1 - \cos\theta_0)/I]^{\frac{1}{2}}$; $(L - Mak\sin\theta_0)/I$.

11 (a) $\sum_i m_i\ddot{\mathbf{r}} = \left(\sum_i m_i\right)\ddot{\mathbf{r}} = M\ddot{\mathbf{r}}$.

    Moment about $G = \sum_i \boldsymbol{\rho}_i \times m_i\ddot{\mathbf{r}} = \left(\sum_i m_i\boldsymbol{\rho}_i\right) \times \ddot{\mathbf{r}} = \mathbf{0} \times \ddot{\mathbf{r}} = \mathbf{0}$, so the resultant
$M\ddot{\mathbf{r}}$ is localised through G.

    (b) $\sum_i m_i\rho_i\omega^2\hat{\boldsymbol{\rho}}_i = \omega^2\sum_i m_i\boldsymbol{\rho}_i = \mathbf{0}$, and these vectors concur at G.

    (c) $m_i\rho_i\dot\omega\hat{\mathbf{v}} = m_i\dot\omega\boldsymbol{\rho}_i$ turned through $+\dfrac{\pi}{2}$, so

    $\sum_i m_i\rho_i\dot\omega\hat{\mathbf{v}} = \sum m_i\dot\omega\boldsymbol{\rho}_i$ turned through $+\dfrac{\pi}{2} = \mathbf{0}$.

    Moment of $m_i\rho_i\dot\omega\hat{\mathbf{v}}$ about $G = m_i\rho_i^2\dot\omega$, so total moment of these vectors about G
$= \sum_i m_i\rho_i^2\dot\omega = I_G\dot\omega$.

Exercise 16B

1 $(4J - 2K)/M$, $(4K - 2J)/M$.

2 Let the internal impulse at B be K. Apply the results of question 1 to each rod in
turn. Velocity of $C = J/2M$.

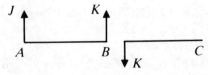

Figure 78

3 (i) $J\left(\dfrac{ah}{h^2 + k^2} - 1\right)$;

(iii) period of a simple pendulum of length l is $2\pi\sqrt{(l/g)}$, so from Example 1 the equivalent simple pendulum has length $I_0/Mh = M(h^2 + k^2)/Mh = h + k^2/h$;

(iv) $GA = a - h = k^2/h$, so the distance from A to the centre of percussion when the lamina is suspended from A is $k^2/h + \dfrac{k^2}{(k^2/h)} = OA$.

4 There would be no impulsive reaction at a pivot placed at the centre of percussion, so the introduction of such a pivot would not affect the initial motion.

5 $3u/2$.

6 $-\dfrac{J}{m\sqrt{5}}\begin{bmatrix}1\\2\end{bmatrix}$.

8 Velocity of mass centre $= \dfrac{3m}{5m + 2M}\mathbf{v}$, angular speed $= \dfrac{9mv}{(5m + 2M)a}$.

9 (i) $\dfrac{J}{20M}\begin{bmatrix}1\\-27\end{bmatrix}$; (ii) $\dfrac{J}{5M}\begin{bmatrix}-2\\0\end{bmatrix}$.

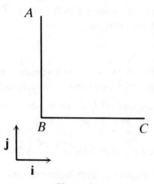

Figure 79

10 Moment of momentum about B before impact $= m\omega(l^2 - 3d^2)/12$. Subsequently the rod rocks about A, B alternately, with angular speeds in geometric sequence with common ratio $(l^2 - 3d^2)/(l^2 + 3d^2)$. If $l^2 < 3d^2$ the initial moment of momentum about B is negative and cannot be conserved; there is an impulse at A which destroys it. Critical $l = \sqrt{3}d$.

Exercise 16C

1 $10\,000:1$.   **2** $2:1;\ 1:1$.   **3** $(k^2 + a^2)\omega^2/2g \sin \alpha$.

4 $\left[\dfrac{12g \sin \theta}{l(1 + 3\cos^2 \theta)}\right]^{\frac{1}{2}}$; $[3gl \sin \theta]^{\frac{1}{2}}$.

5 $2\pi\sqrt{[3(b - a)/2g]}$.   **6** $\left[\dfrac{6g(2M + m)}{a(9M + 2m)}\right]^{\frac{1}{2}}$.

7 (i) $\sqrt{[50ga(1 - \cos \theta)/7]}$, $\cos^{-1}(10/17) \approx 54°$;

(ii) $\sqrt{[10ga(1 - \cos \theta)]}$, $\cos^{-1}(2/3) \approx 48°$.

8 $10ml^2/3$; $3(\pi^2 - 7)g/10l$.

Exercise 16D

1 $\alpha \approx 4°$.

2 No horizontal force; $3\dot{x}^2 + l^2\dot{\theta}^2 = 6gl(1 - \cos\theta)$;
   $3(g - \ddot{x})\sin\theta = l\ddot{\theta}$.

3 $\dot{\theta}^2 = \dfrac{6g(1 - c)}{l(1 + 3s^2)}$, where $c = \cos\theta$, $s = \sin\theta$;

   $\ddot{\theta} = \dfrac{3g}{l}\left[\dfrac{s + 3s^3 - 6sc + 6sc^2}{(1 + 3s^2)^2}\right]$

   $Rl\sin\theta = \frac{1}{3}ml^2\ddot{\theta} \Rightarrow R = mg\left[\dfrac{1 + 3s^2 - 6c + 6c^2}{(1 + 3s^2)^2}\right]$

   $\qquad\qquad = mg\left[\dfrac{1 + 3(c - 1)^2}{(1 + 3s^2)^2}\right] > 0$ for all θ.

4 $\omega^2 > \dfrac{4kg}{(2 - k)^2 a}$.

5 The conditions $\omega_0^2 \leqslant 9g/8a$ (to preserve contact) and $\omega_0^2 \geqslant 3g/2a$ (to mount the step) are incompatible. The corresponding conditions for the hoop are $\omega_0^2 \leqslant 8g/9a$ and $\omega_0^2 \geqslant 8g/9a$, which are satisfied if $\omega_0^2 = 8g/9a$.

6 2/3, 2/3.

8 Cylinder turns about edge $\Rightarrow$ mass centre has initial centripetal acceleration v^2/r vertically down.

   But the greatest downward force is Mg (when there is zero contact force at the edge), so for turning $Mv^2/r < Mg \Leftrightarrow v^2 < gr$.

9 The initial velocity of the mass centre is $\begin{bmatrix} u + \omega b \\ v - \omega a \end{bmatrix}$. The impulse is applied at (a, b), so the moment of momentum about (a, b) remains zero. Hence

   $$Mk^2\omega + M(u + \omega b)b - M(v - \omega a)a = 0 \tag{1}$$

   $$\Rightarrow \omega = \frac{av - bu}{a^2 + b^2 + k^2}.$$

   With angular velocity ω', $T = \frac{1}{2}Mk^2\omega'^2 + \frac{1}{2}M[(u + \omega'b)^2 + (v - \omega'a)^2]$

   $$\frac{dT}{d\omega'} = Mk^2\omega' + M(u + \omega'b)b - M(v - \omega'a)a;$$

   comparing with (1) shows that $\dfrac{dT}{d\omega'} = 0$ when $\omega' = \omega$. This gives the least T since T is quadratic in ω' with positive ω'^2 term.

10 Let the velocity of the mass centre and the angular velocity of the body be $\bar{\mathbf{v}}$, $\boldsymbol{\omega}$ respectively immediately after the impulses act.

   Then $M\bar{\mathbf{v}} = \sum \mathbf{J}_i$ and $I_G\boldsymbol{\omega} = \sum \boldsymbol{\rho}_i \times \mathbf{J}_i$.

   and $T = \frac{1}{2}M\bar{\mathbf{v}}^2 + \frac{1}{2}I_G\boldsymbol{\omega}^2 = \frac{1}{2}\bar{\mathbf{v}}\cdot M\bar{\mathbf{v}} + \frac{1}{2}\boldsymbol{\omega}\cdot I_G\boldsymbol{\omega}$

   $\qquad = \frac{1}{2}\sum(\bar{\mathbf{v}}\cdot\mathbf{J}_i + \boldsymbol{\omega}\cdot\boldsymbol{\rho}_i \times \mathbf{J}_i) = \frac{1}{2}\sum(\bar{\mathbf{v}}\cdot\mathbf{J}_i + \mathbf{J}_i\cdot\boldsymbol{\omega} \times \boldsymbol{\rho}_i)$

   $\qquad = \frac{1}{2}\sum \mathbf{J}_i\cdot(\bar{\mathbf{v}} + \boldsymbol{\omega} \times \boldsymbol{\rho}_i) = \frac{1}{2}\sum \mathbf{J}_i\cdot\mathbf{v}_i.$

Project Exercise 16E

1   $12U^2/49\mu g$.

2   (a) 0.44 s, 1.12 m;   (b) 0.15 s, 0.12 m.

3   $5U(h-a)/2a^2$; (a) moves with top spin; (b) moves with bottom spin.

6   (a) Cue ball rolls after object ball, faster than in question 5;
(b) cue ball rolls back away from object ball. Give the cue ball sufficient initial bottom spin so that on impact it is sliding with no rotation; a very strong central blow has almost the same effect.

8   (c) $\sum m_i(\eta_i^2 + \zeta_i^2)$ is the moment of inertia about the $\xi = 0$ axis; to each point of the sphere (ξ, η, ζ) there corresponds the point $(\xi, -\eta, -\zeta)$ by symmetry about $\xi = 0$, so in the sums $\sum m_i\xi_i\eta_i$ and $\sum m_i\xi_i\zeta_i$ all the terms cancel.

10   $-7F_y/2M$.

14   Linear motion: components of velocities along line of centres are exchanged (as in question 4), so after impact the cue ball's velocity has zero component along the line of centres, and so it moves at right angles to this line.
   The rotational motion of the cue ball is unchanged by the impact. Since its angular velocity is perpendicular to its direction of motion before impact there is a non-zero component of angular velocity perpendicular to the line of centres, which produces the sideways friction which causes the swerve.

Miscellaneous exercise B

1   (a) $4a$,   (b) $\frac{3}{2}aw$,   (c) $3aw$, $\frac{13}{2}aw$,   (d) $\frac{1}{2}$.

2   $2\pi\sqrt{(I/Mga)}$.

3   $F = \begin{bmatrix} 1 \\ -3 \\ 1 \end{bmatrix} = F^*, \lambda = 1.$

4   No horizontal force; $2g/3$.

5   $r = c(i \times j) + \lambda i.$

6   $\frac{3}{10}Mr^2$.

7   Couple $\begin{bmatrix} 0 \\ -1 \\ 1 \end{bmatrix}$, force $\begin{bmatrix} -4 \\ 0 \\ -3 \end{bmatrix}$.

8   22/3.

9   $\begin{bmatrix} -3 \\ 5 \\ -1 \end{bmatrix}$; $r = \begin{bmatrix} 3 \\ 4 \\ 3 \end{bmatrix} + v \begin{bmatrix} -3 \\ 5 \\ -1 \end{bmatrix}$.

10   $\begin{bmatrix} 2\sqrt{5} \\ \sqrt{5} \\ 0 \end{bmatrix}$, $\begin{bmatrix} 2\sqrt{5} - 20 \\ \sqrt{5} + 4 \\ 14 \end{bmatrix}$.

11   $\dfrac{230}{3\sqrt{3}} g \approx 434$ N.

12 $m\ddot{\mathbf{r}} = c\dot{\mathbf{r}} \times B\mathbf{k}$; $A = Bc/m$; $\dot{\mathbf{r}} = \dot{r}\hat{\mathbf{r}} + r\dot{\theta}\hat{\boldsymbol{\theta}} + \dot{z}\mathbf{k}$;
$\dot{r} = D_1$, $r\dot{\theta} = -Ar + D_2$, $\dot{z} = D_3$.

13 $x = 1$.   **14** Hyperbolas; $\sqrt{[\alpha/(\alpha - 1)]}$.

15 $C = (ma^2 + I)/b$; $J = (ma(b-a) - I)\frac{\omega}{b}$; $b = (ma^2 + I)/ma$.

16 (a) Suddenly decreases, (b) gradually increases, (c) gradually decreases, (d) suddenly increases.

17 $\mathbf{F} = \begin{bmatrix} 5 \\ 2 \\ 0 \end{bmatrix}$, $\mathbf{G} = \begin{bmatrix} -2 \\ 0 \\ 2 \end{bmatrix}$, $\mathbf{F} \times \mathbf{G} = \begin{bmatrix} 4 \\ -10 \\ 4 \end{bmatrix}$.

18 $OBC: \frac{1}{2}\mathbf{c} \times \mathbf{b}$, $OCA: \frac{1}{2}\mathbf{a} \times \mathbf{c}$, $ABC: \frac{1}{2}(\mathbf{a} \times \mathbf{b} + \mathbf{b} \times \mathbf{c} + \mathbf{c} \times \mathbf{a})$; $V = 2$.

20 Impulse $= 2mV$.

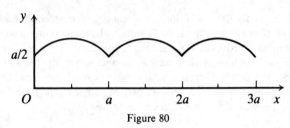

Figure 80

21 $2\sqrt{3}mg$ along BC; $F = \sqrt{3}mg \cos(\theta + \pi/6) \operatorname{cosec}(\theta + \pi/3)$.

22 $m\ddot{\mathbf{r}} = q(\mathbf{E} + \dot{\mathbf{r}} \times \mathbf{B})$.

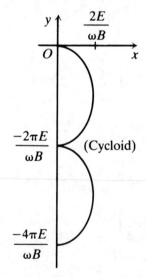

Figure 81

23 $T = 2\pi\sqrt{(41\pi a/12g)}$; $41ma^2\Omega$.

24 $N = \alpha mg\left(1 + \dfrac{4}{k^2}\right) - \dfrac{2mU^2}{k^2c}$.

25 $5Ma^2/3; \sqrt{[5(\sqrt{5}-2)M^2ga/27m^2]}$.

26 Maximum load $= (3M - 5m)ag/(x + a)$; compressive force F at C, tensile force $Mg - 3mg - X$ at B.

27 $106ma^2/3; \pi/4; \frac{2}{15}m\sqrt{[53ag(\sqrt{2}-1)]}$.

28 $x = \dfrac{mV}{qB}\sin\left(\dfrac{qBt}{m}\right), y = \dfrac{mV}{qB}\left(\cos\left(\dfrac{qBt}{m}\right) - 1\right)$.

29 $(a) -2\mu mga/3; 3\Omega^2 a/8\mu g;$ (b) $\mathbf{v}_P = \mathbf{V} + \boldsymbol{\omega} \times \mathbf{r}^*;$
$\mathbf{v}_P = \mathbf{0}$ when $\mathbf{r}^* = \dfrac{\boldsymbol{\omega} \times \mathbf{V}}{\omega^2}$.

Index